THE GOTHIC MISSAL

CORPVS CHRISTIANORVM
IN TRANSLATION

27

CORPVS CHRISTIANORVM
Series Latina
CLIX D

MISSALE GOTHICVM

E CODICE VATICANO REGINENSI LATINO 317
EDITUM

CURA ET STUDIO

Els ROSE

TURNHOUT
BREPOLS ✹ PUBLISHERS

THE GOTHIC MISSAL

Introduction, translation and notes by

ELS ROSE

BREPOLS

The English version of my Dutch translation of the prayers (Els Rose, *Communitas in commemoratione. Liturgisch Latijn en liturgische gedachtenis in het Missale Gothicum (Vat.reg.lat. 317)* [PhD Dissertation Utrecht University, 2001], p. 7–177) was made possible thanks to financial support from the following institutes and foundations: Department of Languages, Literature and Communication (TLC), Utrecht University; Institute for Cultural Inquiry (ICON), Utrecht University; M.A.O.C. Gravin van Bylandt Stichting; Stichting Fonds Legaat 'Ad Pias Causas'; Stichting Marguérite; Stichting Professor van Winter Fonds; Stichting Sormani Fonds; Stichting Zonneweelde; foundation that wishes to remain anonymous.

BX
2015
.A4
R67
2017

© 2017, Brepols Publishers n.v., Turnhout, Belgium

All rights reserved. No part of this publication may be reproduced, stored in a retrieval system, or transmitted, in any form or by any means, electronic, mechanical, photocopying, recording, or otherwise, without the prior permission of the publisher.

D/2017/0095/47
ISBN 978-2-503-53397-1
e-ISBN 978-2-503-56343-5
DOI 10.1484/M.CCT-EB.5.105912

Printed in the E.U. on acid-free paper.

In memoriam Elzemarieke

CONTENTS

CONTENTS

CONTENTS

PREFACE

To translate the prayers of the Gothic Missal is a perilous enterprise if we must believe the English liturgist Edmund Bishop (1846–1917), who claimed that 'the Gallican style' 'would not bear the test of translation into English'.[1] Decadent, vapid, barbarous – these are the labels that have clung to the liturgy of late Merovingian Gaul and its language ever since the early Carolingians stuck them on it – and such labels are difficult to remove. The effort of analysing the language of the Gothic Missal, which I undertook for the edition in Corpus Christianorum, series Latina 159D, and of translating the prayers into a language accessible to the modern reader perhaps unfamiliar with this kind of complex Latin, comes forth from a desire to approach this material in its own right. Negative labels must then yield to characterisations that are more proportionate, acknowledging the innovative nature of the language of this Mass book and the manner in which it nourished the later medieval tradition. The Gothic Missal is a unique reflection of the transition of the Latin language as it gradually developed into the plurality of the Romance languages. It is through such sources that we are able to grasp this historical process, and to catch a glimpse of the dynamic character of this language in its spoken and written forms.

When a project such as this approaches its completion, many thanks are due. First of all, it is my privilege to thank Stephen

---

[1] As quoted in PATRICK SIMS-WILLIAMS, *Religion and Literature in Western England, 600–800* (Cambridge: Cambridge University Press, 1990), p. 314.

Taylor, who took it upon him to translate my Dutch version of the prayers into English, in so doing making the texts available to a diverse audience. To work with him is and always has been a joyful pleasure. A number of private foundations have provided financial support, and I thank them all most cordially – without their assistance the project could not have been completed. I am grateful to Gerard Rouwhorst and Paul Bradshaw for their enduring and supportive trust. I am indebted to the colleagues at Corpus Christianorum in Translation, Loes Diercken and Bart Janssens, for their invaluable support and patience over a number of years. The anonymous reviewer for CCT is thanked for his or her constructive criticism and helpful suggestions, which have gone to improve the translation. I am grateful to Yitzhak Hen for his continual support and his perceptive observations on the introduction. All misinterpretations and errors are and remain mine.

My particular thanks go to the Institute for Advanced Study, Princeton, and its Historical School, for offering me the opportunity to work there on a project entitled *The Performance of Prayer in the Early Medieval West* during the first term of 2015–2016, when I wrote the introduction and notes to the translation. I thank the Institute, its director and staff for their hospitality and support, and the Herodotus Fund which generously facilitated my stay. Most of all I am grateful to Patrick Geary and the members of the Medieval Seminar, who were such inspiring and learned company during these fruitful months. My stay at the Institute would not have been so memorable without the cherished presence of my *carissimi* Jaap and Mattia.

The Gothic Missal has occupied me during an extensive period of my academic career. In these long years I have felt privileged through my friendship with Elzemarieke Veldhuijzen van Zanten (1960–2016). We shared a deep interest in medieval musical and liturgical traditions. It is to her that I dedicate this book, with gratitude and in memory of our lasting bond.

Utrecht, Eastertide 2016

INTRODUCTION

Vaticanus reginensis latinus 317: *Missale Gothicum*

The text that is known as *Missale Gothicum* is transmitted in a single manuscript (Vat. reg. lat. 317), preserved in the part of the Vatican Library's collection that once belonged to the bibliophile Queen Christina of Sweden (1626–1689), to whom the word *reginensis* in the siglum refers. *Missale Gothicum* is not the book's original title, but simply a reference to its content as it was understood by the fifteenth- or sixteenth-century scholar who added this title to the first folio of the manuscript in its then already incomplete state. The title was meant to tell that it was a book for Mass, although it is not a 'missal' as the term came to imply in the early Middle Ages, presenting around the twelfth century the full collection of prayers, chants, readings, rituals and other elements the priest needed in order to celebrate Mass.[1] The codex is better characterised by the term *sacramentarium*, the collection of prayers recited by the celebrant (priest or bishop) at Mass throughout the liturgical year, both Sundays and feast days.[2] The term 'Gothic' has little to do with the Gothic style of writing that developed in twelfth- and thirteenth-century palaeography. The

---

[1] Éric Palazzo, *Histoire des livres liturgiques. Le Moyen Âge. Des origines au XIIIe siècle* (Paris: Beauchesne, 1993), p. 124–127.

[2] Palazzo, *Histoire*, p. 47 and 53–58; Cyril Vogel, *Medieval Liturgy. An Introduction to the Sources* (Spoleto, 1983; transl. William G. Storey and Niels K. Rasmussen, Washington DC: Pastoral Press, 1986), p. 64.

writer of the caption presumably wished to indicate that the book was not written in the humanist style fashionable in the fifteenth century, but, to his mind, in a cruder letter that he associated with the pre-humanist period.[3] In fact the Gothic Missal is written in the imposing and archaic *littera uncialis*, used in the Merovingian and Carolingian periods for works with a distinctive authority.[4] We find the same type of script in the *de luxe* codices associated with the Carolingian rulers of the ninth century,[5] and the fact that the same letter was used in Vat. reg. lat. 317 is indicative of its prestigious character. This status relates not only to the book's possessor – most probably a bishop – but also to its content, since it contains the prayers for the most sacred core of Christian worship: the Eucharist.

Ever since the Gothic Missal was first edited in the seventeenth century, there has been much debate about its origin and destination.[6] The names of the saints that are included, as well as

---

[3] The term may also refer to the liturgy as it was celebrated in early medieval Spain in the time of the Visigothic kingdoms. Mabillon understood it as such and therefore located the book's origin in the South of France (Narbonne), which was under Visigothic rule in the seventh and eighth centuries; cf. HENRY M. BANNISTER (ed.), *Missale Gothicum: A Gallican Sacramentary* (London: Henry Bradshaw Society, 1917–1919), p. lxvi. Various scholars have suggested changing the title, but with little success; see LEO C. MOHLBERG (ed.), *Missale Gothicum (Vat. Reg. Lat. 317)*, Rerum ecclesiasticarum documenta, Series marior, Fontes 5 (Rome: Herder, 1961), p. xxvi–xxvii.

[4] ELIAS A. LOWE (ed.), *Codices latini antiquiores: A Palaeographical Guide to Latin Manuscripts prior to the Ninth Century* (Oxford: Clarendon Press, 1934–1971), 11 vols., vol. 1: *The Vatican City*, no. 106, p. 32.

[5] MS Vat. reg. lat. 317 has been on display in recent exhibitions of masterpieces of late antique and early medieval book culture, e.g. Paderborn 1999: CHRISTOPH STIEGEMANN and MATTHIAS WEMHOFF (eds), *799. Kunst und Kultur der Karolingerzeit. Karl der Große und Papst Leo III. in Paderborn. Band 2. Katalog der Ausstellung Paderborn 1999* (Mainz: Von Zabern, 1999), p. 782–784.

[6] The editions of the Gothic Missal comprise GIUSEPPE M. TOMASI (ed.), *Codices Sacramentorum nongentis annis uetustiores* (Rome: ex typographia Angeli Bernabò, 1680); HENRY M. BANNISTER (ed.), *Missale Gothicum: A Gallican Sacramentary* (London: Henry Bradshaw Society, 1917–1919); MOHLBERG (ed.), *Missale Gothicum* (1961); ELS ROSE (ed.), *Missale Gothicum e codice Vaticano Reginensi latino 317 editum*, CCSL 159D (Turnhout; Brepols, 2005). In addition, a facsimile edition was published by Mohlberg with a valuable and detailed introductory volume: LEO C. MOHLBERG (ed.), *Missale Gothicum. Das gallikanische Sakramentar*

the appeal to certain saints as *patronus noster* ('our patron'), have
guided the search for a specific community in which the book
was used. While some scholars have proposed, for example, that it
appertained to a centre where Gregory the Great was venerated,[7]
the hypothesis of a cathedral or monastery to which the cults of
the martyrs Symphorian and Leodegar of Autun can be related
has gained increasing support over the past decades. Autun itself
now seems to be the most likely place where the book was used,
not least in view of the Burgundian origin of the codex, the script
and decoration of which leave no doubt as to its production in
the scriptorium of Luxeuil, or one related to it.[8] While Morin's
hypothesis of its origins in Gregorienmünster would imply that
the book was used in a monastic community, the content of the
sacramentary, which includes an elaborate set of prayers for the
administration of Baptism, makes it more plausible that it was
used by a bishop in an urban, cathedral setting.

The date by which the manuscript was compiled is easier to
establish, given the inclusion of a Mass for Leodegar, in which
the dissemination of his relics through Gaul is mentioned. Leodegar was bishop of Autun from 663 and was killed in the fac-
tion fighting between the late Merovingian kings of Neustria and
Burgundy (Childeric II, Clothar III) and Ebroin, the Neustrian
mayor of the palace. Leodegar's death is dated 678 or 679 and his
relics were translated in 684 to the basilica of Autun.[9] The Gothic
Missal as a whole, therefore, cannot have been completed before
the second half of the 680s. On the other hand, the *terminus ante
quem* is usually based on palaeographic observations, particularly
the aforementioned relation of the manuscript with the tradition

*(Cod. Vatican. Regin. Lat. 317) des VII.-VIII. Jahrhunderts. Facsimile und Kom-
mentar* (Augsburg: Filser, 1929).

[7] Morin suggested Gregorienmünster, Alsace: GERMAIN MORIN, 'Sur la
provenance du "Missale Gothicum"', *Revue Bénédictine* 31 (1914), 326–332.

[8] LOWE, CLA I, p. 32; MOHLBERG (ed.), *Missale Gothicum*, p. xx; MOHLBERG,
Das gallikanische Sakramentar, p. 43–74.

[9] MOHLBERG, *Das gallikanische Sakramentar*, p. 98. See below, section The
liturgical year.

of the early eighth-century scriptorium of Luxeuil. This would imply that the manuscript was compiled between 690–710.

Under the somewhat confusing name *Missale Gothicum*, a collection of prayers is therefore preserved that yields insight into the liturgical practice of early medieval Gaul during the reign of the later Merovingian kings. Although the liturgy of the Eucharist is the main objective of a sacramentary, the Gothic Missal presents a much wider view of liturgy as a key social and cultural phenomenon of the period. The manuscript not only mirrors issues of faith and doctrine, but, through the prism of prayer and its rituals, gives insight into a large variety of cultural, social and linguistic developments. The broader framework of the liturgy of Merovingian Gaul will be sketched below, before we return to the more detailed perspective of the Gothic Missal.

Liturgy in late antique and Merovingian Gaul

The setting in which the Gothic Missal is situated according to its compilation and usage was the world of early medieval Gaul during the reign of the later Merovingian rulers (Clovis III and Childebert III, perhaps also Dagobert III and Chilperic II[10]). However, as a liturgical handbook (in the sense that it is a requisite of the priest or bishop in order to perform their liturgical and pastoral duties) the manuscript reflects a much longer period of developing liturgical customs and compositional creativity, going back at least to the late fourth century and perhaps even to the earliest phase of Christianity in the Roman province of Gaul. It is my aim here to sketch a portrait of the people involved in the composition of liturgical texts, as authors and as patrons.[11]

---

[10] For a genealogy of the Merovingian kings, see IAN WOOD, *The Merovingian Kingdoms, 450–751* (London-New York: Longman, 1994), p. 347–349.

[11] On royal patronage of liturgy in early medieval Gaul, see YITZHAK HEN, *The Royal Patronage of Liturgy in Frankish Gaul. To the Death of Charles the Bald (877)* (London: HBS, 2001).

The history of Christianity in Gaul is connected with a number of historical persons and legendary figures, whose influence is noticeable at several levels in the Gothic Missal, varying from textual content, for example the frequent references to the works of Irenaeus of Lyons in the prayers, to inclusion in the calendar of saints, for example missionary martyrs including Symphorian of Autun, Saturninus of Toulouse, Ferreolus and Ferrucio.[12] Élie Griffe began his analysis of the liturgy of the Roman province of Gaul with Justin Martyr and his *Apologia* (dated around 150).[13] Even if these ancient roots of the cultic and liturgical tradition that developed in late antique Gaul have unquestionably left their traces in the liturgical books that have come down to us, the Gothic Missal is not an immediate representative of this ancient layer. Irenaeus and Justin wrote in Greek and probably celebrated the liturgy in that language.[14]

The Gothic Missal comprises texts of various chronological and geographical origins. Some are based on non-Gallican liturgical sources. The collection of Mass orders transmitted in the seventh-century manuscript known as the *Sacramentarium Veronense* is a key source. Although this collection is traditionally considered a testimony to the liturgy of late antique Rome, its character and origin are less well-defined.[15] The book prescribes separate Mass orders (in many cases a number of alternatives for

---

[12] Cf. ROSE (ed.), *Missale Gothicum*, Introduction, p. 291 and, in the same Introduction, the separate sections on the saints mentioned.

[13] ÉLIE GRIFFE, 'Aux origines de la liturgie gallicane', *Bulletin de littérature ecclésiastique* 52 (1951), 17–33. See further below, section The prayers of Mass.

[14] MATTHIEU SMYTH, *La liturgie oubliée. La prière eucharistique en Gaule antique et dans l'Occident non romain* (Paris: Cerf, 2003), p. 14; on the transition from Greek to Latin as a liturgical language in the West, see CHRISTINE MOHRMANN, 'Les origines de la latinité chrétienne à Rome', in CHRISTINE MOHRMANN, *Études sur le latin des chrétiens*, vol. 3: *Latin chrétien et liturgique* (Rome: Edizioni di storia e letteratura, 1965), p. 67–126; THEODOR KLAUSER, 'Der Übergang der römischen Kirche von der griechischen zur lateinischen Liturgiesprache', in Leo C. MOHLBERG (ed.), *Miscellanea Giovanni Mercati*, vol. 1 (Città del Vaticano: Biblioteca apostolica vaticana, 1946), p. 467–482.

[15] VOGEL, *Medieval Liturgy*, p. 38–46; PHILIPPE BERNARD, *Transitions liturgiques en Gaule carolingienne. Une traduction commentée des deux 'lettres' faussement attribuées à l'évêque Germain de Paris* (Paris: Hora decima, 2008), p. 16.

one feast day) according to the monthly calendar from January
to December and must therefore be considered a (private?) collection of material rather than a service book in use at the altar. Many of the prayers in the Gothic Missal are also found in
other non-Roman sacramentaries, including the sources of the
early Milanese and Spanish rites, as well as in contemporary late
Merovingian sacramentaries. About half of the prayers are found
exclusively in the Gothic Missal, and for these we may assume
origins in Gaul between roughly the fourth and the late seventh
century.

Among the earliest known authors of Latin prayers are
fourth- and fifth-century bishops. A prominent figure among
them is Hilary of Poitiers (300–368), to whom Jerome attributed
the composition of a *liber hymnorum et mysteriorum*.[16] In other
sources Hilary is presented as an author of hymns, in the same
vein as Ambrose, hence his work was not confined to compilation but concerned the actual composition of liturgical texts.[17] In
the fifth century, southern Gaul, including the monastic island
of Lérins off the coast of Marseilles, remained an important area
of liturgical creativity.[18] Musaeus, a priest of Marseilles, is mentioned as the author of a lectionary, responsory and sacramentary. Claudianus Mamertus was responsible for the composition
of a lectionary, while his brother, Bishop Mamertus of Vienne,
introduced the new penitentiary custom of fasts and processions
on the days before Ascension (*Rogationes*), a usage that became
widely accepted in Gaul and beyond.[19] The latter information is
derived from the letter collection of Sidonius Apollinaris, who
became bishop of Clermont in 470 and composed a set of *con-*

---

[16] JEROME, *De viris illustribus* 100; HEN, *Royal Patronage*, p. 22.

[17] Fourth Council of Toledo (633), canon 13, ed. JOSÉ VIVES, *Concilios Visigóticos e Hispano-Romanos* (Barcelona-Madrid: Consejo Superior de Investigaciones
Científicas, 1963), p. 196–197; see further HEN, *Royal Patronage*, p. 22–23.

[18] ARCHDALE A. KING, *Liturgies of the Past* (London: Longman, Green, 1959),
p. 85.

[19] See SIDONIUS APOLLINARIS, *Epistula* 5.14.1–3, ed. ANDRÉ LOYEN, *Sidoine
Apollinaire*, vol. 2–3: *Lettres* (Paris: Belles Lettres, 1970), vol. 2, p. 196–197; see
HEN, *Royal Patronage*, p. 23–24. On the Rogation days, see below section The li-
turgical year.

testatiunculae[20] as well as a sacramentary.[21] Sixth-century bishops continued the liturgical production of their predecessors,[22] and they were joined by prominent persons outside the (episcopal) clergy, most conspicuously King Chilperic, to whom Gregory of Tours attributed the composition of *ymnus sive missas*.[23] It is unclear whether Gregory meant to say that the king composed entire Masses, or perhaps only *contestationes* as Sidonius did. In the seventh century, the centre of liturgical productivity seems to have shifted to the north and north-east of Gaul, where the influence of Irish monasticism was strong, through foundations such as Luxeuil.[24] The monastic scriptoria in Neustria and Burgundy produced the manuscripts to which we owe our foremost knowledge about the Gallican liturgy.[25] Paradoxically enough, we know little about the patrons who requested these service books. Were they bishops, like Venerius and Eustachius of Marseilles who ordered the service books made by Musaeus?[26] Or rather kings, who busied themselves increasingly with liturgical matters in the later Merovingian period?[27] The sources themselves give no decisive answer.

Scholarship of the past and more recent decades illustrates how difficult it is to study the liturgy of late antique and early

---

[20] On the term *contestatio* see below section The prayers of Mass.

[21] HEN, *Royal Patronage*, p. 24.

[22] Ibid., p. 25.

[23] GREGORY OF TOURS, *Historiae* VI.46, ed. MGH SRM I.1, p. 320; HEN, *Royal Patronage*, p. 25–26.

[24] On problems related to the study of Irish (Columbanian) monasticism and liturgical practices in Merovingian Gaul, see YANIV FOX, *Power and Religion in Merovingian Gaul: Columbanian Monasticism and the Frankish Elites*, Cambridge Studies in Medieval Life and Thought: Fourth Series 98 (Cambridge: Cambridge University Press, 2014), p. 233–234.

[25] HEN, *Royal Patronage*, p. 29–30; SMYTH, *Liturgie oubliée*, p. 71–85.

[26] See above and HUGHES O. OLD, *The Reading and Preaching of the Scriptures in the Worship of the Christian Church III: The Medieval Church* (Grand Rapids, MI-Cambridge: Eerdmans, 1999), p. 82.

[27] HEN, *Royal Patronage*, p. 56; ROSAMOND MCKITTERICK, 'Royal Patronage of Culture in the Frankish Kingdoms under the Carolingians: Motives and Consequences', in *Committenti e produzione artistico-letteraria nell'alto medioevo occidentale*, Settimane di studio 39 (Spoleto: La sede del centro, 1992), vol. 1, p. 93–129, at p. 99–103.

medieval Gaul in its own right. The validity of the texts transmitted in the Gothic Missal and other contemporary sources is questioned first by liturgists who tend to concentrate on Rome as the centre of the Latin liturgy, thus obfuscating a clear view of this particular liturgical tradition. A strong belief in the 'Romanisation' of the Frankish liturgy from the Carolingian period onwards has kept the liturgy of late antique and early medieval Gaul in the shadows.[28] A second obstacle is a tenacious tendency to judge late Merovingian evidence (which provides the main access to this liturgical tradition) in a negative manner as decay and decline, and the preserved manuscripts as witnesses to a period of 'vandalizing' (Pinell[29]), 'incompetence' and 'profound crisis' (Smyth[30]). In the last section of this introduction, we shall see that a similar harsh yet outdated judgment befalls the Merovingian sources because of their linguistic characteristics. Both criticisms have their own history, but are in the end of little help to those interested in the relevant liturgical sources, their content and context for their own sake. In the following section the Gothic Missal is at the centre. In the first subsection its festive cycle is reconstructed, whereas in the second, I will concentrate on the variety of prayers that constitute its Mass order.

[28] The most recent and convincing rejection of this Rome-centred approach is by BERNARD, *Transitions*, p. 20–22; see also SMYTH, *Liturgie oubliée*, p. 9–10; HEN, *Royal Patronage*, p. 57–64; 149–154; GISELA MUSCHIOL, 'Men, Women and Liturgical Practice in the Early Medieval West', in LESLIE BRUBAKER and JULIA M.H. SMITH (eds), *Gender in the Early Medieval World. East and West, 300–900* (Cambridge: Cambridge University Press, 2004), p. 198–216, at p. 198–199.

[29] JORDI PINELL, *Anamnesis y epiklesis en el antiquo rito galicano. Estudios y edición crítica de las formulas galicanas de la 'Post Sanctus' y 'Post Mysterium'* (Lisbon, 1974), p. 27, quoted in SMYTH, *Liturgie oubliée*, p. 11; see also JORDI PINELL, 'La Liturgia gallicana', in SALVATORE MARSILI (ed.), *Anàmnesis. Introduzione storico-teologica alla liturgia*, vol. 2: *La liturgia. Panorama storico generale* (Rome: Marietti, 1978), p. 62–67.

[30] SMYTH, *Liturgie oubliée*, p. 10–11. Smyth calls into question the applicability of the label 'Gallican liturgy' to the liturgy of the Merovingian period, distinguishing between the liturgy of Roman Gaul and Frankish Gaul, the latter qualified as 'fruit d'une hybridation croissante et de plus en plus maladroite' (p. 11). While this distinction between these two phases in the development of the Gallican liturgy is in itself helpful, one wonders why the second phase (*Regnum Francorum*) is continuously characterised with such negative qualifications.

The performance of prayer in the Gothic Missal

The liturgical year

The Gothic Missal is a sacramentary in the most restricted form possible, in the sense that it does not transmit anything but the prayers for the celebrant to recite. A calendar of the feasts celebrated in the community in which it was used is absent. What is more, the Gothic Missal, in contrast with contemporary sacramentaries and lectionaries outside Gaul, lacks any reference to dates in the Mass titles.[31] The calendar of the liturgical year as represented by the Gothic Missal can therefore only be reconstructed with the help of other sources, both liturgical books and other documents. A number of lists of feasts is known from early medieval Gaul, some more contemporary with the Gothic Missal than others. Among these is one real calendar, known as the *Calendar of Willibrord* (preserved in BnF lat. 10837), which presents each month on a separate folio. The document as such was compiled in the early eighth century, and owes its name to the notes inserted on f. 39v and traditionally attributed to Willibrord.[32] An earlier source which is generally indicated as a 'calendar' is the list of fasts and vigils as observed in Tours during the pontificate of Perpetuus (440–460). It is transmitted by Gregory of Tours in his *Historiae* and generally designated as the 'Calendar of Tours'.[33] In addition, much information is found in the *Martyrologium Hieronymianum*, a martyrology of Gallic origin which lists the

---

[31] Dating individual feasts seems to have been uncommon in early medieval Gaul, since service books for Mass (such as the *Missale Gallicanum Vetus*, Bobbio Missal, Irish Palimpsest Sacramentary, Lectionary of Luxeuil) generally lack dates.

[32] HENRY A. WILSON (ed.), *The Calendar of Willibrord*, HBS 55 (London: Henry Bradshaw Society, 1918), p. x–xi dates the notes around the year 728. Wilson's opinion is challenged by Yitzhak Hen on the basis of content as well as the palaeographical character of the note: YITZHAK HEN, 'Wilhelm Levison's Willibrord and Echternach', in MATTHIAS BECHER and YITZHAK HEN (eds), *Wilhelm Levison (1876–1947). Ein jüdisches Forscherleben zwischen wissenschaftlicher Anerkennung und politischem Exil*, Bonner historische Forschungen 63 (Siegburg: Franz Schmitt, 2010), p. 187–198, at p. 187–188.

[33] GREGORY OF TOURS, *Historiae* X.31, MGH SRM I.1, p. 529–530.

feasts of the martyrs. This document, whose attribution to Jerome is inspired by two fifth-century sources, is first transmitted in three eighth-century manuscripts, although the compilation is generally dated to the fifth or sixth century.[34] The source is certainly of great help in establishing dates for the feasts in the Gothic Missal, but can also be confusing, since it collects data from various traditions and therefore does not always give a decisive answer on ambiguous matters. Apart from these calendrical sources, narrative sources including sermons and the lives of saints can help us to reconstruct the cycle of feast days.

In the Gothic Missal, as in other service books of the Gallican rite, the temporal cycle (the feasts commemorating Christ's birth, passion and resurrection, i.e. from Christmas to Pentecost) and the sanctoral cycle (the feasts commemorating the deaths of saints and martyrs) are intertwined.[35] In addition to *proprium* Masses, providing special prayers for each unique feast, general Masses for one or several apostles, martyrs and confessors are included, as well as a series of Sunday Masses, and one daily Mass at the end (or possibly more: the manuscript is incomplete). In the following reconstruction, these non-proper[36] Masses will be omitted because they have no structural function in the calendar.[37]

The first matter to be kept in mind with regard to this reconstruction is the fact that the surviving codex is incomplete. There

[34] JACQUES DUBOIS, *Les martyrologes du Moyen Âge latin*, Typologie des sources du Moyen Âge occidental 26 (Turnhout: Brepols, 1978), p. 30–31; FELICE LIFSHITZ, *The Name of the Saint: The Martyrology of Jerome and Access to the Sacred in Francia, 627–827* (Notre Dame, IN: Notre Dame University Press, 2006), p. 13–29.

[35] This is the case in most early medieval service books for Mass, the Old Gelasian Sacramentary excepted, where the sanctoral cycle is given in a separate section; see VOGEL, *Medieval Liturgy*, p. 65.

[36] The word 'proper' indicates what is characteristic for a Sunday or feast, in contrast with 'ordinary' (standard) components.

[37] The Mass for one apostle-martyr following the *natale* of Peter and Paul is probably an exception, which celebrates the apostles as a group on 29 (*Sacramentarium Veronense*) or 30 June (*Sacramentarium Gelasianum Vetus*): see PHILIP HARNONCOURT and HANS-JÖRG AUF DER MAUR, *Feiern im Rhythmus der Zeit* II.1, Gottesdienst der Kirche, Handbuch der Liturgiewissenschaft VI.1 (Regensburg: Pustet, 1983), p. 117.

are lacunae of uncertain size both at the beginning and end of the book,[38] which makes any reconstruction hypothetical from the outset. What is more, the order of the Masses is not always similar to calendrical data of other sources. Most striking is the fact that five saints whose feasts occur in autumn (Cecilia, Clement, Saturninus, Andrew and Eulalia) are located in the Gothic Missal between the *natale* of Agnes (probably 21 January) and *Conversio Pauli* (25 January). The reason for this obvious misplacement remains unclear, although the change of scribes visible in the folios concerned may offer an explanation. Halfway through the Mass for Agnes a different hand took over, while the first hand recurs at the beginning of the Mass for Cecilia. A third hand then continued with work on *Conversio Pauli* after the group of autumn Masses was completed.[39] It is not inconceivable that the scribe who was interrupted or replaced in the middle of the Mass for Agnes became confused upon recommencing at the Mass for Cecilia.

The reconstruction given below of the liturgical year as observed by the community that used the Gothic Missal follows the manuscript as closely as possible, and therefore presents the Sanctorale and Temporale mixed from Christmas through to the feast day of Eulalia (10 December). The place of the latter feast is the most ambiguous. If the presence of one or more Advent Masses in the original form of the manuscript could be established with certainty, the feast of Eulalia would come first in a reconstructed calendar; in the present circumstances, however, it enters last.

Although the first feast included in the Gothic Missal is Christmas, we should assume that Advent Masses were celebrated in the community for which the sacramentary was compiled. Advent in the Gallican rite differed from the Roman tradition in choosing the feast of St Martin (11 November) as the point after which the preparatory season began. Consequently, there were

[38] The first four quires of the book are lost, and it is conceivable that four (Advent) Masses were included before the Christmas Vigil. The manuscript breaks off at the end after the first prayer of a daily 'Roman' Mass. The sacramentary would probably have included a full Roman Mass with the *canon missae*; a similar Mass ordo is found in the Bobbio Missal (but at the beginning, f. 10r–19v).

[39] Rose (ed.), *Missale Gothicum*, Introduction, p. 21.

six Sundays in Advent.[40] This practice, however, is not echoed in all related sources nor is it similar in all periods. Thus, the list of fasts of mid-fifth-century Tours prescribes fasts from St Martin to Christmas, whereas a century later the second Council of Tours (567) mentions normal fasting practice in the months of September, October and November, followed by a more demanding (daily) fasting pattern in December until Christmas Day, which suggests an Advent fast of four weeks rather than six.[41]

Christmas itself, though without date, will have taken place on 24 (Vigil) and 25 December as has been common in the West from the introduction of the feast in the fourth century. The feast is first mentioned in the Roman Calendar of 354, with the date spelt out as *VIII kal. ian. natus Christus in Betleem Iudeae*: 'Christ born in Bethlehem, Judea, on the eighth day before the Kalends of January' (25 December).[42] The week after Christmas, designated the Christmas Octave, is filled with saints' feasts. The custom to spread the celebration of a major feast over a full week has its origin in the celebration of Easter. The week following Easter Sunday, concluded by *Clausum Paschae* (Low Sunday), was filled with daily Masses, allowing the newly baptised to participate in a Eucharist every day, and also giving the bishop ample opportunity to initiate the new members, originally adults, in the secrets of the Christian rites, in occordance with the early Christian *disciplina arcani* (see below). The week following Christmas, echoing this Easter Octave, is filled with feasts of saints that are not only particularly close to Christ, but also typically represented in calendars originating from beyond the Western Church. The martyr Stephen, to begin with, is positioned on 26 December, the day on which relics of the saint were discovered in Caphar Gamala, near Jerusalem. The celebration of Stephen in the city where he suf-

---

[40] JEAN HILD, 'L'Avent', *La Maison-Dieu* 59 (1959) 10–24, at p. 14–16.

[41] *Calendar of Tours*, MGH SRM I.1, p. 529; Second Council of Tours (567), canon 18 (17), ed. JEAN GAUDEMET and BRIGITTE BASDEVANT, *Les canons des conciles mérovingiens (VIe–VIIe siècles)*, SChr 354.2 (Paris: Cerf, 1989), p. 362.

[42] The entry is found in the list of martyrs, part 12 of the Calendar: ed. HANS LIETZMANN, *Die drei ältesten Martyrologien* (Bonn: Marcus and Weber, 1911), p. 2–4, at p. 3.

fered martyrdom would seem to antedate the reinvention of his relics.[43] The insertion of James[44] and John, brothers and fishermen belonging to the closest circle of disciples and apostles, is found in most early Latin non-Roman traditions and follows several eastern calendars.[45] The commemoration of the sons of Zebedee in the Christmas Octave was widespread in the early medieval West, though the dates reveal discrepancies. Given the position of James and John between Stephen and the Holy Infants in the Gothic Missal, the date of 27 December seems to be certain. While Stephen is celebrated in the Christmas Octave as the *protomartyr*, and therefore close to Christ, the Holy Infants likewise occupy a prime position in the calendar as the first martyrs.[46] Evidence for a feast day commemorating the Infants on 28 December in the West is first found in the sixth-century Calendar of Carthage and in the sermons of Caesarius, bishop of Arles (502–542).[47] The Christmas Octave finds its biblically inspired closure in the com-

[43] S. VANDERLINDEN (ed.), 'Revelatio sancti Stephani (BHL 7850–6)', *Revue des études byzantines* 4 (1946), 178–217; EDWARD D. HUNT, *Holy Land Pilgrimage in the Later Roman Empire. AD 312–460* (Oxford: Clarendon Press, 1982), 214–218. The Jerusalem date for the feast in the Armenian Calendar is 27 December: ATHANASE RENOUX (ed.), *Le codex arménien. Introduction aux origines de la liturgie hiérosolymitaine. Lumières nouvelles*, in F. Graffin, Patrologia orientalis 35, vol. 1 (Turnhout: Brepols, 1969), p. 176, note 44; see also ROSE (ed.), *Missale Gothicum*, Introduction, p. 202.

[44] i.e. James the Greater as distinct from the other disciple/apostle James (the Less; cf. Matth. 10, 2–3; Marc. 3, 16–19; Luc. 6, 14–16; Act. 1, 13).

[45] A celebration of James and John together on 27 or 29 December (Jerusalem) is found in calendars (*Martyrologium Syriacum*, ed. LIETZMANN, *Die Martyrologien*, p. 8), sermons, e.g. GREGORY OF NISSA, *Eulogy for Stephen* and *Elegy on Basil* (PG 46, col. 721–736 and 787–790 resp.), and the *Armenian Lectionary* representing the liturgy of fifth-century Jerusalem (ed. RENOUX, *Le codex arménien*, vol. 2, p. 373 and vol. 1, p. 103–106); see ROSE (ed.), *Missale Gothicum*, Introduction, p. 206. On 27 December Rome celebrated only John the Evangelist; see ibid., p. 207.

[46] ...*prima Christi uictima*: PRUDENTIUS, *Hymnus epifaniae, Liber Cathemerinon* XII l. 129, ed. CUNNINGHAM, CCSL 126, p. 65–72, at p. 69.

[47] *Calendar of Carthage*, ed. LIETZMANN, *Die Martyrologien*, p. 4–6; CAESARIUS OF ARLES, *Sermo* 222, ed. MORIN, CCSL 104, p. 877. The *Armenian Lectionary* includes a feast day for the Infants on 18 May; RENOUX (ed.), *Le codex arménien*, vol. 2, p. 335 and comments in vol. 1, p. 70–73. Cf. ROSE (ed.), *Missale Gothicum*, Introduction, p. 214.

memoration of the Circumcision of the Lord. This feast is modelled on the Gospel, which recounts how Jesus, like all Jewish boys, was circumcised and given his name on the eighth day of his birth (Gen. 17, 12; Leu. 12, 3; Luc. 2, 21). The earliest sources date back to the sixth century and invariably discuss the Christian commemoration in relation to the Kalends of January, the ancient feast celebrating the New Year and the two-faced god Janus.[48] Both the biblical prescription to perform circumcision on the eighth day and the connection with the feasts of the Kalends of January place this commemoration firmly on 1 January.

The 'Calendar of Tours' gives two references to the importance of Epiphany in fifth-century Gaul, one explicit and the other implicit. The implicit one is in the list of fasts, where the beginning of renewed fasting after Christmas is appointed for St Hilary's day (13 January).[49] This would characterise the week after Epiphany (6 January) as an 'octave', in the sense that the celebration continues without being interrupted by fasting. The explicit reference is the observation of a vigil on the eve of the feast, coinciding with the Gothic Missal and other service books including the Lectionary of Luxeuil.[50] The observance of Epiphany in the West is first attested by the fourth-century historiographer Ammianus Marcellinus, who remarks on Emperor Julianus's (360–363) attempt to hide his rejection of the Christian cult by visiting a church 'on the day of the festival in January, which the Christians call Epiphany'.[51] Though initially a theological celebration of the manifestation[52] of God on earth, which had few parallels with Christmas both with

---

[48] Second Council of Tours (567), canon 18 (17), ed. GAUDEMET and BASDEVANT, SChr 354.2, p. 362; CAESARIUS OF ARLES, *Sermo* 191 and 192, ed. MORIN, CCSL 104, p. 778–782; cf. ROSE (ed.), *Missale Gothicum*, Introduction, p. 217.

[49] *Calendar of Tours*, MGH SRM I.1, p. 529.

[50] *Lectionary of Luxeuil*, ed. PIERRE SALMON, *Le lectionnaire de Luxeuil (Paris, ms. lat. 9427)* (Rome: 1944), p. 27–57.

[51] *... feriarum die, quem celebrantes mense Ianuario Christiani Epiphania dictitant.* AMMIANUS MARCELLINUS, *Rerum gestarum libri qui supersunt* 21.2.5, ed. WOLFGANG SEYFARTH (Stuttgart-Leipzig: Teubner, 1999), vol. 1, p. 219. The related event is dated 361.

[52] The Latin translation of the Greek ἐπιφάνεια is traditionally *manifestatio*; as such it occurs in the Gothic Missal, no. 76; cf. CAESARIUS OF ARLES, *Sermo* 195.1, ed. MORIN, CCSL 104, p. 789.

regard to place of origin and conceptualisation of the Incarnation, the feast of Epiphany was introduced in the Latin West later than Christmas, and therefore needed to acquire a profile of its own in relation to Christmas.[53] In fifth-century Gaul the feast could already be viewed as 'a solemn celebration coming forth from the nativity of our Lord'.[54] A general interpretation of Epiphany is the dissemination of the Christian faith throughout the world. The number twelve plays a significant role: Epiphany is not only the 'twelfth night' after Christmas, but it is also the number of the apostles who preached the Trinity to the four quarters of the world ($3 \times 4 = 12$).[55] Epiphany, in other words, is the manifestation of the Incarnation to the entire world.

In the Gallican liturgy the feast of Epiphany is characterised as the feast of the *tria miracula*, the miracles through which Christ manifested himself on earth. Although these would traditionally have been interpreted as the appearance of the star to the magi, Christ's Baptism in the river Jordan, and the miracle of the Wedding at Cana,[56] the Gallican rite includes the Feeding of the Five Thousand in this cluster of evangelical miracles, a tradition referred to in the Gothic Missal (91). Inspired by the theme of Christ's Baptism in the river Jordan, Epiphany was one of the most important dates in the year for the administration of Baptism,[57] as becomes clear from allusions in the prayers in the Gothic Missal (83, 86).

Four saints' feasts fill the period between Epiphany and Lent. The liturgical celebration of Mary expanded after the Council of

---

[53] JEAN LECLERCQ, 'Aux origines du cycle de Noël', *Ephemerides liturgicae* 60 (1946), 7–26.

[54] *Sollemnitatem quae de domini nostri nativitate processit*, as phrased in *Sermo Faustini episcopi in Epiphania domini aut ad missam de crastino in natale sancti Luciani martyris*, ed. MORIN, CCSL 104, p. 786–788, at p. 786. On the authorship of the sermons attributed to Faustus (of Riez, † 490–495) or Faustinus, see MORIN, CCSL 103, p. xxxii.

[55] CAESARIUS OF ARLES, *Sermo* 195.3, ed. MORIN, CCSL 104, p. 791.

[56] Baptism and the Wedding at Cana are the pericopes chosen in the Bobbio Missal, ed. LOWE, p. 34 (Matth. 3, 14–17 and Ioh. 2, 1–11, although the reading is entitled *Lictio sancti aeuangelii secundum Iohannem*). Similar readings are found in the Lectionary of Luxeuil, ed. SALMON, p. 59–60.

[57] HILD, 'L'Avent', p. 13.

Ephesus (431) phrased the doctrine of Mary mother of God (*theotokos*) in response to the Nestorian teaching that the two natures of Christ (his humanity and his divinity) were separable. By proclaiming Mary *theotokos* or God-bearer, her motherhood became a divine motherhood, not merely a human one.[58] The theme of Mary's motherhood is central to the only Marian feast in the Gothic Missal, which is positioned in January, as was common in early medieval Gaul. Gregory of Tours mentions the feast as the celebration of the translation of Mary into paradise, commemorating that she was a virgin before and after giving birth.[59] Gregory does not give an exact date ('in the middle of the month of January'), and the Gallican service books differ both with regard to the date (the Bobbio Missal gives two Masses for Mary after Peter's Chair) and to the title or main theme of the feast.[60] The positioning in the Gothic Missal gives no cause to think it differed from the Calendar of Willibrord and the *Martyrologium Hieronymianum* in choosing 18 January for this feast.

The virgin Agnes is the first of a series of Roman martyrs grouped together in the Gothic Missal. Though the feasts of Cecilia and Clement seem out of place, it is conceivable that they are included in the group because of their similar backgrounds. The feast of Agnes is among the oldest liturgical celebrations of martyrs and is included in the Roman Calendar of 354.[61] There it is dated 21 January, and the position in the Gothic Missal gives no reason to assume that the Roman date was not followed.

[58] Nestorius taught that Mary was mother of the human Christ, but not of the divine Christ: see STEPHEN BENKO, *The Virgin Goddess. Studies in the Pagan and Christian Roots of Mariology* (Leiden-New York-Cologne: Brill, 1993), p. 253–257.

[59] GREGORY OF TOURS, *In gloria martyrum* 8, MGH SRM I.2, p. 43. Gregory is the first witness of the liturgical feast, followed by the *Martyrologium Hieronymianum* (ed. DELEHAYE and QUENTIN, p. 45) and the *Calendar of Willibrord* (ed. WILSON, p. 3); cf. ROSE (ed.), *Missale Gothicum*, Introduction, p. 224. Gregory's account in his *Glory of the Martyrs* is close to – though less elaborate than – the apocryphal narratives on Mary's Assumption that circulated in early medieval Gaul; see the notes to prayers 94 and 98.

[60] See ROSE (ed.), *Missale Gothicum*, Introduction, p. 224.

[61] Ed. LIETZMANN, *Die Martyrologien*, p. 3; cf. ROSE (ed.), *Missale Gothicum*, Introduction, p. 272–273.

The feast of Paul's Conversion is an interesting phenomenon in the Christian calendar of saints. Although scholars have tried to read a Roman commemoration in it, mainly inspired by the entry *Romae translatio Pauli apostoli* in the *Martyrologium Hieronymianum*, the feast as such seems to be a Gallican institution celebrating the calling of the persecutor Saul rather than the relics of the martyr Paul.[62] The *Martyrologium Hieronymianum* and the Calendar of Willibrord again offer help in dating the feast, both giving 25 January (*VIII Kal. Feb.*).[63]

The dating of Peter's Chair is more complex, since two regular dates circulate in early medieval Gaul. Undoubtedly of Roman origin, as the Calendar of 354 testifies,[64] this feast disappeared from the Roman sources but is all the more manifest in the Gallican service books and calendars. The Calendar of Tours mentions a vigil for the feast, and Masses are given in the Bobbio Missal and the Lectionary of Luxeuil.[65] The *Martyrologium Hieronymianum* as well as the Calendar of Willibrord indicate both 22 February (the Roman date) and 18 January as possible dates, although they give the two commemorations of Peter's episcopacy different names (*in Roma*, *in Antiochia*). The question whether the duplication of the feast in the calendars indicates the existence of two separate feasts, or rather that an alternative date (18 January) is offered for those years in which 22 February fell in Lent, is as yet unsolved.[66] Yet with regard to the Gothic Missal the positioning leaves little doubt as to an intended celebration on 22 February.

---

[62] ROSE (ed.), *Missale Gothicum*, Introduction, p. 232–236.

[63] *Martyrologium Hieronymianum*, ed. HIPPOLYTE DELEHAYE, *Commentarius perpetuus in Martyrologium Hieronymianum ad recensionem H. Quentin*. AASS novembris II.2 (Paris: Palmé: 1931), p. 61 and the *Calendar of Willibrord*, ed. WILSON, p. 3; cf. ROSE (ed.), *Missale Gothicum*, Introduction, p. 232–233.

[64] Ed. LIETZMANN, *Die Martyrologien*, p. 3 dates the feast on 22 February. On the Calendar of 354, see MICHELE RENEE SALZMAN, *On Roman Time. The Codex-Calendar of 354 and the Rhythms of Urban Life in Late Antiquity*, The Transformation of the Classical Heritage 17 (Berkeley CA: University of California Press, 1990).

[65] *Calendar of Tours*, MGH SRM I.1, p. 530; *Bobbio Missal*, ed. LOWE, p. 35–37; *Lectionary of Luxeuil*, ed. SALMON, p. 66–68.

[66] ROSE (ed.), *Missale Gothicum*, Introduction, p. 236–244.

The Lenten season is introduced by a Mass *In inicium Qua-dragesimae*, after which five Lenten Sundays follow before Palm Sunday. Salmon suggests that Lent itself started on the Monday before the first Sunday of Lent.[67] Given the flexible date of Easter, which falls on the Sunday after the first full moon following the spring equinox, there is no fixed date for the beginning of Lent, dependent as it is on Easter.

After the six Masses for Lent, a Mass entitled *In symbuli traditione* is inserted. The title reflects the tradition to teach the Creed (*symbulum*) to the catechumens (*traditio symboli*) on the last Sunday before Easter,[68] so that they could learn it by heart and recite it from memory before their Baptism during the Easter Vigil (*redditio symboli*). The prayers in the Mass order include other themes apart from the instruction of the catechumens, primarily the Entry into Jerusalem (Ioh. 12, 12–19), where Jesus is portrayed as a meek rider on a humble donkey. Humility, triumph, death and renewed life are the main themes of the prayers, which lends the Mass a pivotal function in the transition from fasting to feasting (see no. 196). In addition, the death and resurrection of Lazarus (Ioh. 11) feature prominently in this Mass. His miraculous resurrection was originally celebrated on the Saturday preceding the last Sunday before Easter, but in the Mass in the Gothic Missal it seems to have merged with the themes of Palm Sunday.

The last Sunday before Easter is the beginning of Holy Week, indicated in the Lectionary of Luxeuil as *autentica ebdomada*.[69] Holy Week in the Gothic Missal is marked by two entries. The first is the Mass for Holy Thursday as the beginning of the Easter celebration and the commemoration of the pedilavium (Ioh. 13). The second is the series of prayers prescribed for *biduana*, the

[67] SALMON (ed.), *Le lectionnaire*, p. 75. On fasting and the Lenten season in Merovingian Gaul, see ELS ROSE, 'Fasting Flocks. Lenten Season in the Liturgical Communities of Early Medieval Gaul', in RICHARD CORRADINI et al. (eds), *Texts and Identities in the Early Middle Ages*, Forschungen zur Geschichte des Mittelalters 12 (Vienna: Verlag der Österreichischen Akademie der Wissenschaften, Philosophisch-historische Klasse, Denkschriften, 344, 2006), p. 289–301.
[68] BERNARD, *Transitions*, p. 406 and 426–465.
[69] *Lectionary of Luxeuil*, ed. SALMON, *Le lectionnaire*, p. 82s.

'two days' of Good Friday and Holy Saturday during which no full Eucharist was celebrated. The prayers for Good Friday focus on the chronology of the Passion and could be seen to follow the outline of a *via crucis*, which is at least suggested by the titles of the second and third prayers: 'for the sixth', 'for the ninth hour'.[70] These titles echo the synoptic accounts of Christ's Passion, the deepest agony of which is imagined as hours of complete and universal darkness, after which Christ gave up the spirit (Matth. 27, 45–50; Marc. 15, 33–37; Luc. 23, 44–46). The two texts for Holy Saturday, an exhortation to prayer and a collect, focus entirely on the *descensus ad inferos* and the liberation of those imprisoned in Hell.[71]

The eve of the great Easter celebration[72] is divided into four main episodes. The first, *Vespera paschae*,[73] is dedicated to the theme of light and the blessing of the paschal candle. The Gothic Missal is one of the oldest, if not the earliest manuscript that transmits the hymn in praise of the paschal candle, well known under the title of its incipit *Exultet*. It is a key text in the sacramentary, not only because it became the most important hymn in praise of the Easter light in the Latin liturgy,[74] but also because its style and composition relate to many other festive texts in the Gothic Missal, which together give us insight into the characteristics of

[70] However, the series is more complete in the *Missale Gallicanum Vetus*, where prayers are also entitled 'for the second' and 'for the third hour'; moreover, the prayers for Holy Saturday also bear titles referring to the canonical hours.

[71] On the theme of Christ's descent into Hell in Gallican prayers, see SMYTH, *Liturgie oubliée*, p. 392–396 with additional bibliography; on the origin of the theme in early Christianity, see RÉMI GOUNELLE, *La descente du Christ aux enfers. Institutionnalisation d'une croyance* (Paris: Cerf, 2000).

[72] The importance of the feast is reflected by the full-page illumination of the title on f. 169v.

[73] On the title, see no. 221.

[74] THOMAS F. KELLY, *The Exultet in Southern Italy* (New York-Oxford: Oxford University Press, 1996), confusingly refers to the Gallican *Exultet* as the 'Franco-Roman' or 'the Roman version' (p. 30, 43), even though he admits that the origin is not Rome and the style is 'not typical of Roman liturgical texts' (p. 31). Kelly fails to mention the stylistic relation between the *Exultet* and other texts transmitted in the Gallican sacramentaries and clearly traceable to liturgical authors from (late antique) Gaul. In addition, his remark on 'the Carolingian reform corrupted by Gallican obstinacy' (p. 30) raises questions.

prayer composition in Merovingian Gaul. This will be further discussed in the section on Style below, while matters of authorship, symbolic language and sources of inspiration are included in the footnotes to the translation of no. 225.[75]

The *Vespera* is followed by the elaborate intercession typical of the Easter liturgy, consisting of twelve 'Easter orations' with their collects.[76] These great intercessory prayers include all kinds of people both inside and outside the Church: exiles first; then clergy and those in holy orders, both male and female; those who give and receive alms; the sick, the penitents and travellers; kings and rulers and their efforts to maintain peace and unity; and, finally the deceased and the catechumens.

The third episode consists of the preparation and administration of Baptism. Baptism is one of the three main themes discussed in the second *Epistola de ordine sacrae oblationis*, as the *Expositio missae* formerly attributed to Germain of Paris is entitled in the manuscript tradition. Hence it is discussed elaborately in Bernard's commentary, where most relevant bibliography is included.[77] Rather than copying his findings and conclusions here, I have added comments to the order 'At Baptism', the prayers accompanying the blessing of the font, and the actual Baptism (252–265).

The fourth episode in the night before Easter Sunday is the Vigil Mass itself. This liturgy has the structure of a regular Mass, in which

---

[75] Unlike the famous South Italian Exultet rolls, the text in the Gothic Missal (and in other Merovingian sacramentaries, most importantly the *Missale Gallicanum Vetus* and the Bobbio Missal) is without clues to its performance, e.g. illustrations and musical notation as in the rolls. For a study of the performance of the Exultet based on the later South Italian copies, see ÉRIC PALAZZO, 'Performing the Liturgy', in THOMAS F.X. NOBLE and JULIA M.H. SMITH (eds), *The Cambridge History of Christianity vol. 3: Early Medieval Christianities, c. 600-c. 1100* (Cambridge: Cambridge University Press, 2008), p. 472–488, at p. 482–485; see also GIUSEPPE MICUNCO, *Exultet I di Bari: parole e immagini alle origine della litteratura di Puglia* (Bari: Stilo, 2011).

[76] The prayers occur in most Gallican service books and are studied comparatively by PAUL DE CLERCK, *La prière universelle dans les liturgies latines anciennes. Témoignages patristiques et textes liturgiques*, Liturgiewissenschaftliche Quellen und Forschungen 62 (Münster: Aschendorff, 1977), p. 231–268.

[77] BERNARD, *Transitions*, p. 396–425.

the *immolacio* is the most important text. The prayer has a direct
relation to the *Exultet* where both texts sing the praises of *haec nox*.
The *immolacio*, however, does so by linking in a remarkable manner one literal biblical quotation after the other, making it the text
with the highest density of biblical quotations in the Gothic Missal,
while the *Exultet*, conversely, quotes the Bible only once.[78]

The Mass for Easter Sunday is the very core of the sacramentary, a fact expressed by the elaborate illumination of its title, indeed
the only full-page illustration in the codex.[79] No less remarkable
is the choice of prayers in this festive liturgy. It corresponds to the
Mass for Christmas Day in its inclusion of collects after both the
Prophecy and the intercession. What is more, it is the only Mass in
the sacramentary that includes an *apologia sacerdotis*. The Mass for
Easter Day therefore contributes substantially to our knowledge
of the Gallican Mass ordo, further discussed in the next section.

As indicated in the *Exultet*, Easter is a multiform feast (*festa
paschalium*), of which Easter Day is both the peak and the com-
mencement of the festive season, which is roughly divided into
three periods before it is concluded by Pentecost, meaning 'fiftieth day'.[80] The first period is the Octave, the celebration of eight
days during which the newly baptised are further initiated by a
daily celebration of the Eucharist, probably accompanied by cat-
echetical sermons. The title of the series of six daily Masses for
Easter Week refers to this practice: 'Easter morning Mass for the
entire Easter Week, for the little children that are reborn'. The
word *pascha* in this phrase seems to refer to Easter 'Week' rather
than the fifty days of Eastertide. This is also suggested by the title
of the Mass for Low Sunday (*Missa clausum paschae*), concluding

[78] GUIDO FUCHS and HANS MARTIN WEIKMANN, *Das Exsultet. Geschichte,
Theologie und Gestaltung der österlichen Lichtdanksagung* (Regensburg: Pustet,
1992), p. 72.

[79] On style and provenance, see MOHLBERG, *Missale Gothicum. Das gallikanische Sakramentar*, p. 54–55 and 64; for a full-colour reproduction, see ROSE (ed.),
Missale Gothicum, Plate 3.

[80] Indicated as *die quinquagesimo* in the 'Calendar of Tours', MGH SRM I.1,
p. 530.

the Octave with an elaborate *immolacio* (316) in which several O-exclamations again call to mind the *Exultet* of the Easter Vigil.

The second period of Eastertide is one of festivities lasting forty days until the week of Ascension and including several saints' feast days. The first of these is the Mass for the Invention of the Holy Cross – not strictly a saint's day, although relics do play a key role. The legend of the 'True' Cross goes back to Helena, Constantine's mother. According to a legend of which the earliest testimonies circulated in the fifth century, she was urged in a vision to search for relics of the cross in Jerusalem.[81] The celebration of the relics that conquered the world, together with the various testimonies, led to the institution of a feast on 3 May, a date mentioned in the fifth-century legend.[82] Given the position of the Mass in the Gothic Missal, there is no reason to assume that another date was chosen. The dissemination of the relics of the True Cross, and their veneration in late antique Gaul, is linked once again to a woman. In this case it is Radegund (*c.* 520–587), the Merovingian queen who was married to Clothar I but left him to found the monastery of the Holy Cross at Poitiers. Here, she inspired the poet Venantius Fortunatus, not only as a close friend, but also through a mutual fascination for the Cross relics.[83]

The following Mass, in honour of John 'the apostle and evangelist', raises more questions, concerning both its content and calendar date. The Mass is simply entitled *Missa*, without further specification as to what aspect of John's life or death is celebrated. As the Christmas Octave already includes a Mass for the *natale* of John and his brother James (see above), a separate Mass *in natale* would be superfluous. What is more, the prayers in the

---

[81] Barbara Baert, *A Heritage of Holy Wood. The Legend of the True Cross in Text and Image*, Cultures, Beliefs and Traditions 22 (Leiden: Brill, 2004). Helena is first associated with relics of the cross by Ambrose in his funeral oration for Theodosius, who died in 395; ibid., p. 2.

[82] Baert, *Heritage*, p. 45; also 70–71 and footnote 67.

[83] Michael J. Roberts, *The Humblest Sparrow. The Poetry of Venantius Fortunatus* (Ann Arbor: University of Michigan Press, 2009), p. 283–313; cf. Venantius's hymns in honour of the cross *Vexilla regis* and *Pange lingua* in Guido Dreves (ed.), *Analecta Hymnica Medii Aevi*, vol. 50 (Leipzig: Reisland, 1907), p. 70–73 (*Pange lingua*) and 74–75 (*Vexilla regis*).

Mass do not refer in any way to John's death, either his peaceful
death according to the dominant tradition in the Latin West,[84] or
whichever kind of martyrdom. Conversely, the prominent use of
the word *natalicia*, referring by exception to an earthly birth, as is
the case most unambiguously in the Christmas Vigil (2) and the
Mass for John the Baptist on 21 June (373), seems to imply that the
Mass does indeed commemorate John's earthly birth. Although
this hypothesis may be most likely, it does not solve the matter of
the date. Despite near-parallels in various traditions,[85] it remains
impossible to pinpoint one of them as the most likely characteri-
sation of the Mass for John in the Gothic Missal. This makes it
equally difficult to link a date to the feast, which I provisionally
locate in the reconstructed calendar in 'early May'.

The third period of Eastertide is marked by three Masses for
Rogation Days and the subsequent intercession. At this point,
the mood of the prayers clearly changes. The festive season is interrupted by days of penance and fasting, instituted in Gaul by
Bishop Mamertus of Vienne around 470.[86] They included peni-

[84] ELS ROSE, 'The Cult of the Apostles in the Early Medieval West: From Eyewitnesses to Blood Witnesses', in KLAUS HERBERS and GORDON BLENNEMANN
(eds), *Vom Blutzeugen zum Glaubenszeugen? Formen und Vorstellungen des christlichen Martyriums im Wandel*, Beiträge zur Hagiographie 14 (Stuttgart: Franz
Steiner, 2014), p. 57–70.

[85] Various calendars in East and West prescribe a feast in honour of John in the
month of May. These include the commemoration of his peaceful death in Constantinople (8 May); of the miracle of the boiling oil in Rome (6 May: *Iohannes
ad portam latinam*); and the commemoration of John in the Georgian Lectionary
on 14 May, reflecting the liturgical practice of fifth-century Jerusalem. Moreover,
allowing for a misplacement of the Mass order in the Gothic Missal, the *Martyrologium Hieronymianum* and the Calendar of Willibrord have an entry for the
assumption of John on 24 June. For further details, see ROSE (ed.), *Missale Gothicum*, Introduction, p. 258–262.

[86] SIDONIUS APOLLINARIS, *Epistolae* 5.14.1–3; ed. LOYEN, vol. 2, p. 196–197
(see also footnote 19); ROB MEENS, *Penance in Medieval Europe 600–1200* (Cambridge: Cambridge University Press, 2014), p. 14 and 30–31; ROSE, 'Fasting Flocks',
p. 292–293; IAN WOOD, 'Liturgy in the Rhône Valley and the Bobbio Missal', in
YITZHAK HEN and ROB MEENS (eds), *The Bobbio Missal. Liturgy and Religious
Culture in Merovingian Gaul* (Cambridge: Cambridge University Press, 2004),
p. 206–218, at p. 207–208; id., 'Topographies of Holy Power in Sixth-Century
Gaul', in MAYKE DE JONG et al. (eds), *Topographies of Power in the Early Middle
Ages*, The Transformation of the Roman World 6 (Leiden-Boston-Cologne: Brill,

tential practice, fasting, and solemn processions accompanied by psalmody.[87] Masses were held every day, while the series of collects in the Gothic Missal (482–485) probably refer to litany-like intercessions, which apparently took place in the various churches along the processional route.[88]

Although we might speculate that the Rogation Days were intended as a turning point in the festive Eastertide, commemorating the ambivalent joy of Christ's departure from his disciples to ascend into heaven, references to Ascension Day are scarce in liturgical texts for the *Rogationes*. The Collect at the kiss of peace in the third Rogation Mass (340) refers to the promise of peace in Ioh. 14, 27 and links this farewell speech explicitly to Ascension: 'and grant to those who fast peace with their neighbour and with you, which, when you ascended to the Father, you left for us to follow'. The repeated references to the forty-day fast observed by Christ according to Matth. 4, 2 (322, 341) could be an implicit reference to Ascension as the fortieth day of Easter. The same applies to the sermon tradition, of which Caesarius of Arles is a telling example: his sermons for the Rogation Days do not mention the approaching celebration of Ascension, neither does his sermon for Ascension look back on the preceding days of fasting.[89]

2001), p. 137–154, at p. 150–153; JOYCE HILL, 'The *Litaniae maiores* and *minores* in Rome, Francia and Anglo-Saxon England: Terminology, Texts and Traditions', *Early Medieval Europe* 9 (2000), 211–246; ACHILLE M. TRIACCA, 'Teologia dell'anno liturgico nelle liturgie occidentale antiche non romane', *Anàmnesis* 6 (1988), 311–363, at p. 342.

[87] The latter perhaps referred to by the phrase 'praising your majesty by singing psalms' in the *contestacio* of the second Rogation Mass (336).

[88] JOHN BALDOVIN, *The Urban Character of Christian Worship. The Origins, Development, and Meaning of Stational Liturgy*, Orientalia christiana analecta 228 (Rome: Pontificium institutum studiorum orientalium, 1987), p. 159. The patrocinia of these respective churches are used frequently in attempts to localise the provenance of the Gothic Missal; see ROSE (ed.), *Missale Gothicum*, Introduction, p. 16–17.

[89] CAESARIUS OF ARLES, *Sermones* 148, 157, 160A, 207–209, ed. MORIN, CCSL 104, p. 605–608, 641–645, 658, 828–840. The strategies applied by Mamertus to position the new custom in the ecclesiastical year such that the innovation would be successful are described by WOOD, 'Topography', p. 151–152. See also BERNHARD JUSSEN, 'Liturgy and Legitimation, or How the Gallo-Romans Ended the Roman Empire', in BERNHARD JUSSEN (ed.), *Ordering Medieval So-*

The Mass for Ascension itself is brief and hardly specific, and the same must be said about that for Pentecost. The Gothic Missal does not refer in any way to the later development of the fiftieth day of Easter as a separate feast, provided with a vigil as at Easter itself, even though such a vigil was already included in the 'Calendar of Tours'.[90] The relation to Easter is indeed already indicated in the Gothic Missal, where the *immolacio* for Pentecost (362) speaks of the fiftieth day, but its phrasing and imagery is rather complex (see the footnotes to the translation).

The remaining datable Masses in the Gothic Missal are all in commemoration of one or more saints. Since the relation between hagiography and the liturgy of the saints is the main topic of the commentary accompanying my edition of the Gothic Missal, I shall only summarise the outlines of each feast here, while concentrating on material relevant to the reconstruction of the calendar.[91]

The order of the feasts that follow Ascension Day in the Gothic Missal corresponds with calendar dates in other sources. The date of the martyrdom of Ferreolus and Ferrucio, missionaries in the tradition of Irenaeus of Lyons, is 16 June, as appointed in the *Passio Ferreoli et Ferrucionis* (the existence of which is first attested to by Gregory of Tours: *sexto decimo Kalendas Iulii*).[92] The cult of these martyrs was primarily linked to Besançon,[93] and their passion is linked to the *passio* of Benignus of Dijon. However, relics of the saints spread to other regions of late antique Gaul, as the

---

ciety. Perspectives on Intellectual and Practical Modes of Shaping Social Relations, translated by Pamela Selwyn (Philadelphia: University of Pennsylvania Press, 2001), p. 147–199, at p. 171. According to Wood's account, Mamertus instituted the Rogation Days on the three days *following* Ascension Day, organising a first procession on the Friday (p. 151–152). How this planning could be realised without affecting the Sunday – as the Day of the Lord strictly free of fasting – remains unclear; Wood apparently reconsidered his reconstruction in the 2004 study (p. 207: 'three days before Ascension').

[90] MGH SRM I.1, p. 530.

[91] Relevant references to ROSE (ed.), *Missale Gothicum*, Introduction, p. 201–328 are given at the beginning of each saint's Mass in the translation.

[92] *Passio Ferreoli et Ferrucionis*, ed. *Acta Sanctorum Iunii IV*, vol. 24, p. 5–15, at p. 7.

[93] GREGORY OF TOURS, *In gloria martyrum* 70, MGH SRM I.2, p. 535.

translation by Mamertus in the context of the first Rogation Day exemplifies.[94]

Dating the nativity of John the Baptist is straightforward, given the biblical background that occasions the commemoration and the relation to Christmas as Christ's birth. As Luc. 1, 26 positions the conception of Christ in the sixth month of Elizabeth's pregnancy, John's birth naturally falls on 24 June.[95] In regions where it was customary to celebrate Christ's Incarnation at Epiphany, John's birth was commemorated in its shadow.[96]

The dual commemoration of Peter and Paul is found in the Roman Calendar of 354, where the *Depositio martyrum* includes them together on *III. Kal. Iulii*: 29 June. Oscar Cullmann proposed that the date was chosen because it was on this day that the foundation of Rome was commemorated, and that the institution of the new feast was a 'Christianisation' of this tradition, providing the city with new, Christian founders.[97] The feastday appears in the 'Calendar of Tours'.[98] The commemoration of the two apostles was later split into separate feasts, with Peter on 29 and Paul on 30 June.[99] A general commemoration of all the apostles was also appointed for 29 or 30 June.[100] The Mass 'for the feast of one apostle and martyr' may well refer to this practice.

The Mass commemorating the martyrdom of John the Baptist, as recounted in Matth. 14, 1–12, is much more complex than that for his birth. A liturgical commemoration of John's *passio* is first attested to in Gaul, where the Calendar of Tours inserts a vigil for the *passio Iohannis ad basilicam in baptisterio* between Pentecost

[94] Cf. WOOD, 'Topographies', p. 151, referring to SIDONIUS APOLLINARIS, *Epistulae* 7.1, ed. LOYEN, *Sidoine Apollinaire*, vol. 3: *Lettres*, p. 30–33.

[95] SUSAN ROLL, *Toward the Origins of Christmas* (Kampen: Kok, 1995), p. 87–106; THOMAS TALLEY, *The Origins of the Liturgical Year* (New York: Pueblo, 1986), p. 91–99.

[96] Cf. ROSE (ed.), *Missale Gothicum*, Introduction, p. 252.

[97] OSCAR CULLMANN, *Saint Pierre, disciple, apôtre, martyr: histoire et théologie* (Paris: Delachaux and Nestlié, 1952), p. 115–116.

[98] MGH SRM I.1, p. 530.

[99] SIBLE DE BLAAUW, *Cultus et decor. Liturgia e architettura nella Roma tardoantica e medievale* (Vatican City: Biblioteca Apostolica Vaticana, 1994), vol. 2, p. 600–601.

[100] HARNONCOURT and AUF DER MAUR, *Feiern*, p. 117; see footnote 37.

and the feast of Peter and Paul. The fact that the vigil was held in the baptistery, together with the absence of an actual martyrdom tradition for John the apostle, underpins the assumption that this feast celebrates the martyrdom of John the Baptist, even if its position in the sequence of feasts is puzzling.[101] The earliest evidence south of the Pyrenees points to a celebration on 24 September,[102] revealing a parallel with what is known as the Irish Palimpsest Sacramentary,[103] while the *Sacramentarium Gelasianum Vetus*, copied in mid-eighth-century Gaul, gives 29 August.[104] Given the subsequent commemorations in the Gothic Missal of Roman martyrs whose feast days fall in the first half of August, it cannot be assumed that this date was intended for the commemoration of John, unless the Mass is somehow out of place, for which there are no codicological or palaeographical indications.[105]

The subsequent feasts in honour of Sixtus, Lawrence and Hippolyte are interrelated: they commemorate the Roman bishop Sixtus, who found martyrdom together with his deacon Lawrence in the persecutions under Valerian in 258. In the Roman Calendar of 354 the two martyrs are commemorated on 6 and 10 August respectively, and the earliest Roman sacramentaries date their feasts accordingly.[106] Hippolyte's connection with Sixtus, and particularly with Lawrence, is first encountered in the fifth- or sixth-century cycle of *passiones*, where he is portrayed as Lawrence's custo-

---

[101] On this and related confusing entries found in the Calendar of Tours, see ROSE (ed.), *Missale Gothicum*, Introduction, p. 254–255 and 256.

[102] *Liber mozarabicus sacramentorum*, 947–955, ed. MARIUS FÉROTIN (Paris: Firmin-Didot, 1912, repr. by ANTHONY WARD and CUTHBERT JOHNSON [Rome: CLV Edizioni liturgiche, 1995]), col. 437–442); HARNONCOURT and AUF DER MAUR, *Feiern*, p. 201.

[103] *Irish Palimpsest Sacramentary*, ed. DOLD and EIZENHÖFER, *Das irische Palimpsestsakramentar*, p. 125–131.

[104] *Sacramentarium Gelasianum Vetus*, ed. LEO C. MOHLBERG, *Liber sacramentorum romanae ecclesiae ordinis anni circuli* (Rome: Herder, 1968), p. 156–157.

[105] Hand 'B' writes continuously from f. 208r–244r (apart from the Blessing in the Mass for John's nativity, 373 on f. 209r), where the Mass for John's passion is written on f. 213r–216r; see further ROSE (ed.), *Missale Gothicum*, Introduction, p. 13.

[106] LIETZMANN (ed.), *Die ältesten Martyrologien*, p. 3–4; ROSE (ed.), *Missale Gothicum*, Introduction, p. 282.

dian in prison. His martyrdom on 13 August is mentioned in the
Roman Calendar of 354.[107]

Two other pairs of Roman martyrs follow in the Gothic Missal. The first concerns Cornelius and Cyprian, of whom only the
North African Bishop Cyprian is mentioned in the Roman Calendar of 354.[108] Roman liturgical books later combined this feast
day with the commemoration of Cornelius, the Roman bishop
(251–253) with whom Cyprian was befriended, and who died in
exile in the year 253 when Cyprian suffered martyrdom. That
14 September was chosen to celebrate them together was perhaps
inspired by a translation of relics of Cornelius from Constantinople to Rome.[109]

The case of John and Paul is again more problematic. The two
are presented as 'brothers', not only according to blood kinship
but also 'in faith and suffering' (409). Although the *Liber pontificalis* mentions various Roman sanctuaries associated with their
names,[110] a specific calendar date is not given and cannot be established for the Gothic Missal.

Three saints of Gallic origin follow, all three martyrs though
in very different periods and circumstances. Symphorian is the
oldest of the three, though it is difficult to establish the exact period in which he fell victim to imperial persecutions, either under Aurelian (270–275) or Decius (mid-third century), or already
under Marcus Aurelius (161–180). The latter option would link
Symphorian to the group of martyrs around Irenaeus of Lyons
(† 177).[111] The first traces of a (liturgical) veneration are found in

[107] LIETZMANN (ed.), *Die ältesten Martyrologien*, p. 3–4. On the earlier tradition recorded by Prudentius and featuring Hippolyte as a Roman priest without connection to either Sixtus or Lawrence, nor the Valerian persecutions, see ROSE (ed.), *Missale Gothicum*, Introduction, p. 286.

[108] LIETZMANN (ed.), *Die ältesten Martyrologien*, p. 4.

[109] As suggested by PIERRE JOUNEL, 'L'été 258 dans le calendrier romain', *La Maison Dieu* 52 (1957), 44–58; cf. ROSE (ed.), *Missale Gothicum*, Introduction, p. 288.

[110] A *cameram* in St Peter's basilica dedicated by Leo I (440–461) and the embellishment of what appears to be a separate basilica with *grados post absidem* by Symmachus (498–514); LOUIS DUCHESNE (ed.), *Liber pontificalis* (Paris: De Boccard, 1955–1957), vol. I, p. 239 (apparatus of variants) and 262.

[111] ROSE (ed.), *Missale Gothicum*, Introduction, p. 297.

the *Passio* written by Euphronius of Autun, the bishop who also built a basilica for Symphorian in the mid-fifth century.[112]

Maurice is commemorated together with his companions, a large number of soldiers who were massacred in the mountain pass near Agaune in the early-third century. The *Passio Acaunensium* was written by Eucherius of Lyons around 450.[113] Eucherius himself gives the date of the passion: 22 September.[114]

Leodegar, finally, is nearest to the compilation of the Gothic Missal, both in time and probably in place. As bishop of Autun from 663, he became entangled in a political web of competition between the Merovingian kings and the *maior domus* of the Neustrian court, Ebroin. Choosing sides in this conflict, he lost his head to his opponent Ebroin in 678 or 679.[115] The day of his martyrdom is found in the *Passio* composed shortly after his death: 3 October.[116]

An elaborate series of Masses for one or more martyrs and *confessores* conclude with a Mass in honour of Martin of Tours. This first *confessor* on the Latin calendar is celebrated as a martyr of the missed opportunity: had times been different, Martin would willingly have given his life for the faith. As it is, he died in peaceful circumstances at an advanced age in a village near Tours (Candes), where he had settled a dispute among the clergy. After his death on 8 November 397, he was brought back to Tours by his disciples and deterred there on 11 November. This has been the main feast day for Martin ever since,[117] although the commemoration on 4 July of the translation of his relics during the episcopacy of Perpetuus of Tours (440–460) remained equally popular.

---

[112] ÉLIE GRIFFE, *La Gaule chrétienne à l'époque romaine*, 3 vols. (Paris: Letouzey and Ané, 1964–1966), vol. 1, p. 152; JOSEPH VAN DER STRAETEN, 'Les actes des martyrs d'Aurélien en Bourgogne', *Analecta Bollandiana* 79 (1961), 115–144, at p. 125. The passion links no date to Symphorian's martyrdom, *Passio Symphoriani*, ed. THIERRY RUINART, *Acta primorum martyrum sincera et selecta* (Amsterdam, 1713²), p. 79–83.

[113] *Passio Acaunensium*, ed. BRUNO KRUSCH, MGH SRM III (Hanover: Hahn, 1896), p. 23–41.

[114] *Passio Acaunensium* 19, ed. KRUSCH, p. 39.

[115] WOOD, *Merovingian Kingdoms*, p. 225–228.

[116] *Passio Leudegarii I* 44–45, ed. BRUNO KRUSCH and WILHELM LEVISON, MGH SRM V (Hanover-Leipzig: Hahn, 1910), p. 282–322, at p. 322.

[117] ROSE (ed.), *Missale Gothicum*, Introduction, p. 316–324.

Only the group of saints 'misplaced' between Agnes and Cathedra Petri now remains, who all have their feast day in November and early December. Cecilia and Clement are noteworthy Roman martyrs, although they are not mentioned in the Calendar of 354. Cecilia's martyrdom is legendary and is not mentioned by fourth-century authors such as Damasus, Ambrose or Prudentius.[118] Her *passio* was written towards the end of the fifth century, probably in relation to the church in Trastevere dedicated to her in the same period.[119] There Cecilia's feast day was celebrated on 22 November from the sixth century onwards.[120] The absence of Clement in the Calendar of 354 is perhaps more surprising, given his episcopacy of the city of Rome at the end of the first century. A date for the feast of this martyr, proclaimed in the legendary and apocryphal literature as the successor of Peter,[121] is first mentioned in the *Martyrologium Hieronymianum*[122] and the Calendar of Carthage:[123] 23 November.

Saturninus of Toulouse belongs to the group of missionaries who were martyred under the Emperors Decius and Gratus in the mid-third century. The dissemination of relics made Saturninus's veneration, initially localised in Toulouse, widespread, not only in Gaul but also south of the Pyrenees, where his death was commemorated on 29 November.[124] The next day in the calendar is dedicated to Andrew, whose feast day on 30 November is mentioned by the author of the Latin revision of the Greek Acts of this apostle, probably Gregory of Tours.[125] Finally, in the reconstructed

---

[118] ROSE (ed.), *Missale Gothicum*, Introduction, p. 277.

[119] *Passio Caeciliae*, ed. HIPPOLYTE DELEHAYE, *Étude sur le légendier romain. Les saints de novembre et de décembre*, Subsidia hagiographica 23 (Brussels: Société des Bollandistes, 1936), p. 194–220.

[120] DUCHESNE (ed.), *Liber pontificalis*, vol. 1, p. 297.

[121] *Passio Clementis*, I.1, ed. FRANCISCUS XAVERIUS FUNK and FRANCISCUS DIEKAMP, *Patres apostolici*, vol. 2 (Tübingen: Laupp, 1913), p. 50–91, at p. 50; *Recognitiones*, transl. PIERRE GEOLTRAIN and JEAN-DANIEL KAESTLI (eds). *Écrits apocryphes chrétiens*, vol. 2 (Paris: Gallimard, 2005), 1175–2003.

[122] Ed. DELEHAYE, p. 615.

[123] LIETZMANN (ed.), *Die ältesten Martyrologien*, p. 6.

[124] ROSE (ed.), *Missale Gothicum*, Introduction, p. 293.

[125] ELS ROSE, '*Virtutes apostolorum*: Origin, Aim, and Use', *Traditio* 68 (2013), 57–96, at p. 65–68.

calendar the martyr Eulalia is placed in the month of December, since a comparison of the prayers in the Gothic Missal with hagiographic material on the two Spanish martyrs of this name, Eulalia of Barcelona and Eulalia of Mérida, proves that Eulalia of Mérida is the subject here, whose feast day is on 10 December.[126]

In the following table the calendar of the Gothic Missal is reconstructed according to the mixed sequence of temporale and sanctorale feasts that the sacramentary contains:

FEAST	DATE
Advent?	flexible
Eulalia	10 December
Christmas Vigil	24 December
Christmas Day	25 December
Stephen	26 December
James and John	27 December
Holy Infants	28 December
Circumcision	1 January
Epiphany Vigil	5 January
Epiphany	6 January
Assumption of Mary	18 January
Agnes	21 January
Conversion of Paul	25 January
Peter's Chair	22 February
Beginning of Lent	flexible
Six Sundays of Lent	flexible
Palm Sunday	flexible
Holy Thursday	flexible
Biduana (Good Friday and Holy Saturday)	flexible
Easter Vigil	flexible
Easter Sunday	flexible, between 22 March and 25 April

[126] ROSE (ed.), *Missale Gothicum*, Introduction, p. 310, 312.

Feast	Date
Easter week Masses	flexible
Easter Octave	flexible
Invention of the Holy Cross	3 May
John, apostle and evangelist	early May (?)
Rogationes	flexible, three days before Ascension
Ascension	flexible
Pentecost	flexible
Ferreolus and Ferrucio	16 June
John the Baptist (nativity)	24 June
Peter and Paul	29 June
An apostle-martyr	30 June
Sixtus	6 August
Lawrence	10 August
Hippolyte	13 August
John the Baptist (passion)	29 August?
Cornelius and Cyprian	14 September
John and Paul	?
Symphorian of Autun	?
Maurice d'Agaune and his companions	22 September
Leodegar of Autun	3 October
Martin of Tours	11 November
Cecilia	22 November
Clement	23 November
Saturninus of Toulouse	29 November
Andrew	30 November

The prayers of Mass

The Gothic Missal is a sacramentary, comprising only those prayers for Mass that were recited by the celebrant, i.e. a priest or bishop. As such the book gives only limited insight into Mass as it was celebrated on an average Sunday or feast day throughout the liturgical year in late seventh- or early eighth-century Gaul. It offers no clues as to biblical readings, chants ordinary or proper, or the role of other ministers than the celebrant, such as the deacon.[127] The sacramentary also yields little information about the ritual elements that formed the structure and defined the performance of Mass, for example the processions that accompanied the introductory rites, the solemn entrance of the Gospel book and the offering of oblations at the beginning of the Eucharistic part of Mass. Rubrics concerning the performance of a particular ritual, such as Baptism at Easter (nos 258–263), are included only very rarely and pertain only to those ritual acts performed by the celebrant, as distinct from tasks that may have been executed by other ministers or the faithful.[128]

The Gothic Missal does familiarise us, however, with a very significant part of what is usually referred to as the 'Gallican' Mass: the style and content of its prayers and, thereby, the character and focus of the liturgical feasts. For further information we are dependent on other sources, which are limited in number. Even though the original sources representing the liturgy of Gaul from the fifth to the eighth centuries go to create a relatively rich picture,[129] they remain scarce in an absolute sense, while information about their date and place of origin is at best often fragmentary. This makes it difficult to reconstruct all details of the performance of Mass at a specific church or monastery, given the

---

[127] Concerning the role of the deacon, see below, section The performance of prayer.

[128] Some rubrics do however seem to indicate the role of the faithful, e.g. in singing the Sanctus and reciting the Lord's Prayer, see below, section The performance of prayer.

[129] Particularly in comparison to the liturgy of late antique and early medieval Rome, as is stressed by BERNARD, *Transitions*, p. 19. Bernard modifies the role that is often attributed to Rome in liturgical matters of the early Middle Ages (ibid., p. 15–22). This corresponds with Giles Constable's earlier and more general observation that 'Rome was only one microchristianity among others, each of which had its own religious culture and development'; the remark is equally adequate when one replaces 'religious' by 'liturgical'. GILES CONSTABLE, 'The Commemoration of the Dead in the Early Middle Ages', in JULIA SMITH (ed.), *Early Medieval Rome and the Christian West: Essays in Honour of Donald Bullough* (Leiden-Boston: Brill, 2000), p. 169–195, at p. 170.

fact that it is not possible to treat the different kinds of sources as pieces of a single jigsaw puzzle. The Church of early medieval Gaul has repeatedly been characterised as an acephalous entity: not a centralised organisation with a strong metropole, but rather a region in which individual bishops exercised considerable autonomy.[130] Even within episcopacies, differentiation could be considerable in liturgical matters. Service books from different regions reveal many similarities but also much diversity. Hence it is not possible to use one service book to fill gaps in the other. While the Bobbio Missal has many prayers in common with the Gothic Missal, its pericopes differ in many respects from the Lectionary of Luxeuil. Reconstruction of the biblical and hagiographic[131] readings for the Masses in the Gothic Missal would therefore be a perilous challenge. Should one choose a lectionary that is related geographically and chronologically, or one that is similar in choice and sequence of Masses?

It is not my purpose here to propose a full reconstruction of the Gallican Mass ordo. Many attempts have been made, while it remains questionable whether *the* Gallican Mass ordo ever existed as such. Twentieth-century scholarship tended to rely on the *Expositio missae*, transmitted in a manuscript from Autun (BM 184, f. 113–122) dated to the mid-ninth century, in order to reconstruct the outline of 'the' Gallican Mass and to sketch the ritual and textual context in which the prayers of a sacramentary like the Gothic Missal would once have functioned.[132] The title of the

[130] On the autonomy of late antique and particularly early medieval Gallic bishops, see RALPH MATHISEN, 'Church Councils and Local Authority: The Development of Gallic *Libri canonum* during Late Antiquity', in CAROL HARRISON et al. (eds), *Being Christian in Late Antiquity. A Festschrift for Gillian Clark* (Oxford: Oxford University Press, 2014), p. 175–193; YITZHAK HEN, 'The Church in Sixth-Century Gaul', in ALEXANDER MURRAY (ed.), *A Companion to Gregory of Tours*, Brill's Companions to the Christian Tradition 63 (Leiden: Brill, 2016), p. 232–255, esp. p. 238–239.
[131] The Gallican Mass included readings from saints' lives and martyrs' passions: GREGORY OF TOURS, *In gloria martyrum* 85, ed. MGH SRM 1.2, p. 95.
[132] SMYTH, *Liturgie oubliée*, p. 174, lists LOUIS DUCHESNE, *Les origines du culte chrétien* (Paris: Boccard, 1925³); HENRI LECLERCQ, 'Gallicane (liturgie)', DACL VI.1, col. 473–593, esp. col. 540–554 and id., 'Messe', DACL XI.1, col. 648–674; PIERRE BATIFFOL, 'L'*Expositio missae* attribuée à saint Germain de Paris',

first chapter of this document, which actually comprises two letters, attributes the text to Germain († 575), a monk originating
from Autun who later became bishop of Paris: *Germanus episco-
pus parisius scripsit de missa.*[133] More recent scholarship rejects the
attribution to Germain given the substantial influence of Isidore
of Seville's *De ecclesiasticis officiis*, which must be dated between
598–615.[134] Most experts agree with André Wilmart[135] that 'Germain' followed Isidore and not vice versa.[136] The most recent studies even consider the letters as a representation of the early reform
period of the Carolingian era, dating the source itself as late as
around 800.[137] Whatever the dating and origin of the *Expositio
missae*, as I will call this document henceforth, it can help us to

---

Études de liturgie et d'archéologie chrétienne (Paris: Gabalda, 1919), p. 245–290;
JEAN-BAPTISTE THIBAUT, *L'ancienne liturgie gallicane* (Paris: Bonne presse,
1929); KLAUS GAMBER, *Ordo antiquus gallicanus: Der gallikanische Messritus des
6. Jahrhunderts* (Regensburg: Pustet, 1965); FERNAND CABROL, *La messe en occident* (Paris: Bloud et Gay, 1932), p. 139–156; PHILIPPE BERNARD, *Du chant romain
au chant grégorien* (Paris: Cerf, 1996), p. 646–650. Smyth adds his own reconstruction in SMYTH, *Liturgie oubliée*, p. 176–177 with an explanation of the various
elements on p. 183–225. To this list, the reconstructions by Élie Griffe should be
added, who attempts a chronological overview from Justin Martyr to the fifth century: GRIFFE, 'Aux origines'. See further ROSE (ed.), *Missale Gothicum*, Introduction, p. 197–200; KING, *Liturgies of the Past*, p. 150–183; WILLIAM S. PORTER, *The
Gallican Rite*, Studies in Eucharistic Faith and Practice 4 (London: Alcuin Club,
1958), p. 19–46.

[133] *Expositio missae*, ed. PHILIPPE BERNARD, *Epistolae de ordine sacrae oblationis et de diversis charismatibus ecclesiae / Germano Parisiensi episcopo adscriptae*,
CCCM 187 (Turnhout: Brepols, 2007), p. 337. The editor considers this remark,
following André Wilmart, as a marginal gloss in the model of the extant copy,
which then became part of the main text; see p. 159–164; ANDRÉ WILMART, 'Germain (Lettres attribuées à saint)', DACL VI.1, 1924, col. 1050–1102, at col. 1061–
1065; BERNARD, *Transitions*, p. 37–38.

[134] ISIDORE OF SEVILLE: *De ecclesiasticis officiis*, ed. CHRISTOPHER M. LAW-
SON, CCSL 113 (Turnhout: Brepols, 1989), p. 13*-14*; translation and introduction
THOMAS L. KNOEBEL, *De ecclesiasticis officiis*, Ancient Christian Writers 61 (New
York: Newman Press, 2008).

[135] ANDRÉ WILMART, 'Germain', col. 1099–1102.

[136] Some authors adhere to the latter hypothesis: Leclercq, Van der Mensbrug-
ghe and Klaus Gamber, see SMYTH, *Liturgie obliée*, p. 175.

[137] ROSAMOND MCKITTERICK, *The Frankish Church and the Carolingian
Reforms, 789-895* (London: Royal History Society, 1977), p. 216; BERNARD, *Transitions*, p. 11.

imagine the celebration of Mass in the community that used the Gothic Missal in so far as it concerns elements common to both sources.

Not all Mass orders in the Gothic Missal contain the same prayers. There are elaborate Masses with a large number of prayers, such as Christmas and Easter, and very short ones, particularly the Masses for certain Roman martyrs and for Ascension Day and Pentecost. In the following, all prayers that occur in the Gothic Missal are discussed in order of appearance in the Mass ordo, not according to one specific Mass. Where necessary, missing elements will be added with the help of other sources, including the *Expositio missae*.

From the beginning of Christianity, the weekly celebration of the resurrection of Christ, normally on Sundays, is characterised by two central elements: the practice of reading from, meditating on and explaining the Holy Scriptures, and the celebration of a (ritual) meal. Traces of the first part of Mass are scarce in the Gothic Missal, a book for the celebrant who had no role in the readings and associated chants, at least in the earliest phase of the Gallican rite.[138] The celebrant's involvement was limited to the recitation of a collect following the *Prophetia*, the canticle chanted before the first reading from the Old Testament prophets,[139] and of the collect after the intercessory prayer at the end of the first part of Mass (*collectio post precem*). The scarce examples of the *collectio post prophetiam* and *collectio post precem* in the Gothic Missal are all this source tells us about the first half of Mass, the office of readings.

Collectio post prophetiam. In the Gothic Missal, the collect after the Prophecy occurs in two Masses only, those for Christmas Day (11) and Easter Day (273). Like the collect after the intercession (see below), it belongs to the first half of Mass rather than the Eucharist itself and relates to the appointed readings. The Gallican liturgy prescribed three readings, from the Old Testament (*Propheta*), the Epistles (*Apostolus*) and the Gospel (*Evangelium*)

---

[138] GRIFFE, 'Aux origines', p. 28.
[139] *Expositio missae* 4, ed. BERNARD, p. 340; GRIFFE, 'Aux origines', p. 25–27.

respectively. Before the Old Testament reading, the Canticle of
Zacharias (Luc. 1, 67–79) was sung, words uttered by Zacharias
upon the birth of his son John as 'the last of the Old Testament
prophets and the first Evangelist'.[140] Although the Gothic Missal
seems to imply that the *Prophetia* (or *Benedictus*, as it is called after its incipit) was reserved for the most solemn celebrations, other
Gallican sacramentaries give the collect *post prophetiam* for Sunday Masses as well,[141] and probably even for weekday Masses.[142]
Gregory of Tours also testifies to the inclusion of this chant on a
'normal' Sunday.[143]

The readings from the Old and New Testaments and their associated chants are followed by the homily.[144] Traces of these elements are absent in the Gothic Missal.

Collectio post praecem (Collect after the intercession).[145] The word
prex, often explained as 'litany',[146] refers to the intercessory prayers
that were originally part of the deacon's contribution to Mass in
dialogue with the faithful, after which the celebrant recited the
collect.[147] In the *Expositio missae* this element of dialogue is no
longer present: the *prex* is described as an intercessory prayer recited by the deacons (*leuite*) on behalf of the faithful, while the
prostrate celebrants (*sacerdotes*) intercede for the people.[148] The

[140] *Expositio missae* 4: *...Iohannes medius est, prophetarum nouissimus et euangelistarum primus*, ed. BERNARD, p. 340.

[141] SMYTH, *Liturgie oubliée*, p. 189 footnote 2 gives *Bobbio Missal* 448, 465, 474 for Sunday Masses; *Missale Francorum* 121, 139, 148 and probably 130 also for Sunday Masses.

[142] The Masses 19, 21 and 22 in the *Missale Francorum*, which also include a *post prophetia[m]*, are obviously Masses for weekdays (*incipient orationes et preces communes cotidianae cum canone*, ed. MOHLBERG, p. 26).

[143] GREGORY OF TOURS, *Historiae* 8.7 mentions the *prophetia* in the context of a Sunday Mass (*Adveniente die dominica*); ed. MGH SRM 1.1, p. 375.

[144] SMYTH, *Liturgie oubliée*, p. 193–195.

[145] ROBERT TAFT, *A History of the Liturgy of St. John Chrysostom, vol. 4: The Diptychs*, Orientalia christiana analecta 238 (Rome: Pontificium institutum studiorum orientalium, 1991), p. 26 translates 'prayer of the faithful'.

[146] GRIFFE, 'Aux origines', p. 27; BERNARD, *Transitions*, p. 145.

[147] SMYTH, *Liturgie oubliée*, p. 191.

[148] *Expositio missae* 12, ed. BERNARD, p. 343–344.

celebrant then recites the collect *post precem*.[149] In the Gothic Missal this prayer occurs only in the Mass for Christmas (12) and that for Easter (274), but other Gallican sacramentaries give the same collect for weekday Masses as well.[150]

The *prex* and the subsequent collect bring the first part of Mass to an end. At this point those not (yet) baptised are sent away, urged by the deacon to leave the church. The Gallican sacramentaries do not preserve a specific formula, nor do they provide a blessing, although other sources imply that such blessings did exist, particularly for the Lenten season when penitents would join the catechumens on their way out.[151] The *Expositio missae* makes a clear distinction between those allowed to stay and those expected to leave: 'Do not give what is holy to dogs; and do not throw your pearls before swine' (Matth. 7, 6).[152]

Once the catechumens have left the church, the Eucharistic ritual itself begins with additional prayers for the faithful and the procession accompanying the offerings to the altar. One Mass in the Gothic Missal includes an extra prayer which, given its position between the *collectio post precem* and the *praefatio missae*, clearly precedes the offertory procession: the *apologia sacerdotis* (Confession of the priest). Apologetic insertions, in which the minister confesses his unworthiness and requests forgiveness, can be found at several points in the order of Mass.[153] The Gothic Missal includes one example of this kind of prayer (275), namely in the Mass for Easter Day between the Collect after the intercession and the Preface to Mass. At this point the *apologia* marks

---

[149] *Expositio* 13: *...diceret sacerdos collecta post prece*, ed. BERNARD, p. 344.

[150] The *Missale Francorum* gives collects *post precem* for weekday Masses (140, 149); cf. the prayers *post prece* in the daily Mass given in the *Bobbio Missal* nos 29, 30, 31 (ed. LOWE, p. 15); cf. SMYTH, *Liturgie oubliée*, p. 192.

[151] SMYTH, *Liturgie oubliée*, p. 196.

[152] *Expositio* 13: *Nolite dare sanctum canibus neque mittatis margaritas uestras ante porcos*, ed. BERNARD, p. 344. BERNARD, *Transitions*, p. 148–149 interprets the departure of the catechumens or non-baptised as regular practice, not restricted to the period of preparation for Baptism during Lent. See also ibid., p. 153–156.

[153] JOANNE M. PIERCE, 'The evolution of the *Ordo Missae* in the Early Middle Ages', in LIZETTE LARSON-MILLER (ed.), *Medieval Liturgy. A Book of Essays* (New York: Garland, 1997), p. 3–24, at p. 10–11.

the transition to the Eucharistic part of Mass. It is explicitly designated as the confession of the priest (*sacerdotis*) to distinguish it from *apologiae* which other ministers might utter.[154] The *apologia* in the Gothic Missal is characteristic in view of its elevated and dramatic style, including several figures which reinforce its dramatic effect.[155] Joanne Pierce has qualified the *apologiae* as exemplary for the increasing 'privatisation' or 'clericalisation' of Mass in the early Middle Ages. It is true that the *apologia* in the Gothic Missal is a highly individualised text, focusing on the minister and his own unworthiness. Personal pronouns and verb inflections in the first person singular abound. Much depends, however, on the manner in which the prayer was executed. Were repeated pleas to be forgiven (*ignusce, ignusce mihi*), spared (*parce, parce, parce*) or heard (*exaudi, exaudi, exaudi me*) accompanied by gestures of humiliation and abasement? If that was the case, the prayer and its performance will doubtlessly have impressed the faithful and have brought them to reflect on their own unworthiness, especially if even a priest had to devote so many words to his own sinfulness.

Praefatio missae (Preface to Mass) and *Collectio sequitur* (following collect). The *praefatio missae*, recited by the celebrant, is the first of a number of *proprium* prayers accompanying the Eucharistic ritual of the second half of Mass. The term *praefatio* is commonly used in later Roman liturgical books as the title of the Eucharistic prayer itself. In the Gallican liturgy, however, the word retained its original meaning, referring simply to the 'beginning' of the actual Eucharist. It is not a prayer, but an exhortation to pray, addressed to the faithful (*fratres karissimi*).[156] The *praefatio* and *collect* formed respectively the introduction and conclusion to a second series of intercessory prayers for the faithful, but now in the absence of

---

[154] PIERCE, 'Evolution of the *Ordo Missae*', p. 11.
[155] On Irish influence possibly present in this text, see SMYTH, *Liturgie oubliée*, p. 79–81.
[156] The address is biblical and occurs in various Epistles: I Cor. 15, 58; Phil. 4, 1; Iac. 1, 16 and 2, 5; cf. ROSE (ed.), *Missale Gothicum*, Introduction, p. 158.

those not baptised.[157] There is no trace of this *oratio plebis* or prayers for 'various needs'[158] in the Gothic Missal, since the intercessory prayers were presumably recited by the deacon rather than the celebrant. Neither can it be excluded that they were not *proprium* but fixed prayers.[159] Thus, while the Gothic Missal suggests that the *praefatio* was directly followed by the collect, in actual fact the latter concluded the intercessory prayers by summarising them. As for the character of the intercessions, the group of prayers recited during the Easter Vigil (228–251) may give us an impression. What is more, the *praefatio missae* (no. 276) in the Mass for Easter Day illustrates their main topics.[160] The *praefatio missae* is a central text when it comes to our knowledge and appraisal of the themes of the feast days celebrated in the Gothic Missal, particularly with regard to Masses for saints. Besides the *immolatio* and *contestatio missae*, it appears to have been the appropriate moment to meditate on the significance of the feast in question.[161]

Collectio post nomina (Collect after the names). The fragmentary character of the sacramentary, providing the prayers but not the rituals performed by the celebrant, entirely obscures the integration in the offertory ritual of the recitation of the names of those who participate in the Eucharistic sacrifice; of this elaborate procedure there is no trace in the Gothic Missal.[162] This public recitation, both of the living and the dead, was performed by the deacon in the context of the solemn procession bringing the congregation's oblations to the altar. This position underlines the nature of the practice of reading the names aloud: while the faithful offered

---

[157] SMYTH, *Liturgie oubliée*, p. 333–345; BERNARD, *Transitions*, p. 158 and 166; see also PAUL DE CLERCK, 'Les prières d'intercession. Rapports entre Orient et Occident', *La Maison-Dieu* 183–184 (1990), 171–189.

[158] SMYTH, *Liturgie oubliée*, p. 334.

[159] SMYTH, *Liturgie oubliée*, p. 344.

[160] SMYTH, *Liturgie oubliée*, p. 335. No. 499 is comparable. On the content of the intercessory prayers proper, see SMYTH, *Liturgie oubliée*, p. 340–343.

[161] The *praefatio missae* is discussed in many of the analyses of individual saints' Masses in ROSE (ed.), *Missale Gothicum*, Introduction, Appendix B (p. 201–324).

[162] On the offertory ritual, see BERNARD, *Transitions*, p. 166–225. On the people's participation in the offertory and oblations, see section The performance of prayer.

themselves together with their gifts, they heard the names of their beloved departed for whom (*pro quibus*) they brought their offerings. The recitation of the names is therefore one of the strongest elements where the Eucharist is believed to connect the living and the dead, as two categories of the faithful participating in the one sacred celebration and attaining to its salutary effect (*effectus*).[163] The recitation of names in a Eucharistic context is often described as the ritual of 'the diptychs', referring to the physical form of the lists in the early Middle Ages.[164] As Fernand Cabrol has already emphasised, the names were not always carved in ivory; they were sometimes even engraved on the altar itself or written in the margins of a sacramentary. The late-eighth-century Sacramentary of Prague, with two lists of names on f. 83v, is possibly an example of the latter.[165] This practice could reflect the increasing practi-

[163] Cf. ISIDORE OF SEVILLE, *De ecclesiasticis officiis* 1.15: *Tertia [oratio] autem effunditur pro offerentibus siue pro defunctis fidelibus ut per eundem sacrificium ueniam consequantur*; ed. LAWSON, p. 17. On *effectus* in the liturgical concepts of the early Middle Ages, see ELS ROSE, '*Emendatio* and *effectus* in Frankish Prayer Traditions', in ROB MEENS et al. (eds), *Religious Franks: Religion and Power in the Frankish Kingdoms. Studies in Honour of Mayke de Jong* (Manchester: Manchester University Press, 2016), p. 128–147.

[164] BERNARD, *Transitions*, p. 226–232 presents four examples of early medieval (sixth- to eighth-century) liturgical diptychs that reused late antique consular diptychs, but contests the idea that such reuse was a general phenomenon. A copy of a consular diptych dated 406 is included in CAROLINE HUMFRESS, 'A New Legal Cosmos: Late Roman Lawyers and the Early Medieval Church', in PETER LINEHAN and JANET L. NELSON (eds), *The Medieval World* (London: Routledge, 2001), 557–575, p. 560. On the use of diptychs in ancient Greek and Roman as well as Jewish traditions, see OTTO STEGMÜLLER, 'Diptychon', in RAC 2, col. 1138–1149; see further PHILIPPE BERNARD, 'Les diptyques du monastère des Saints-Apôtres d'Arles au VIIᵉ siècle. Édition critique. Commentaire historique et liturgique', *Revue d'histoire de l'église de France* 89 (2003), 5–21; EDMUND BISHOP, 'Appendix. Observations on the Liturgy of Narsai', in RICHARD H. CONNOLLY, *The Liturgical Homilies of Narsai* (Cambridge: Cambridge University Press, 1909, reprinted 1967), p. 85–163, at p. 97–114; FERNAND CABROL, 'Diptyques (liturgiques)', in DACL 4.1, col. 1045–1094.

[165] At least as far as the second list is concerned, according to CARL I. HAMMER, 'The Social Landscape of the Prague Sacramentary: The Prosopography of an Eighth-Century Mass-Book', *Traditio* 54 (1999), 41–80, esp. p. 53–64 and 67. On the practice of writing names on altars and in sacramentaries, see BERNARD, *Transitions*, p. 243–244; LEO KOEP, *Das himmlische Buch in Antike und Christentum. Eine religionsgeschichtliche Untersuchung zur altchristlichen Bildersprache* (Bonn:

cal obstacle of reading the full lists of names in an ever-growing community:[166] putting the names in writing could take the place of their being read aloud.[167]

The only evidence of the practice of reading names aloud in the Eucharistic liturgy of the Gothic Missal is provided by the collect that follows the recitation of the names, the *collectio post nomina*. Otherwise than Bernard's assumption, in the Gothic Missal these texts are primarily prayers addressed directly to God or Christ, while only a smaller group are exhortations to prayer addressed to the faithful.[168] The majority of collects *post nomina* in the Gothic Missal include both living and deceased members of the community.[169] They give no insight into the ritual of the recitation itself,

Peter Hanstein Verlag, 1952), p. 103; for specific examples, see PATRICK GEARY, *Living with the Dead in the Middle Ages* (Ithaca-London: Cornell University Press, 1994), p. 88; OTTO G. OEXLE, 'Memoria und Memorialüberlieferung im früheren Mittelalter', *Frühmittelalterliche Studien* 10 (1976), 70–95, at p. 74–76.

[166] As signaled by YITZHAK HEN, *Culture and Religion in Merovingian Gaul A.D. 481–751* (Leiden-Boston: Brill, 1994), p. 48–49 and discussed by OEXLE, 'Memoria und Memorialüberlieferung', p. 77–79, who highlights the concerns of the community to have the names represented appropriately, despite practical obstacles.

[167] On the power of the written word in a performative context, see CLAUDIA RAPP, *Holy Texts, Holy Men, and Holy Scribes. Aspects of Scriptural Holiness in Late Antiquity*, in WILLIAM E. KLINGSHIRN et al. (eds), *The Early Christian Book* (Washington, D.C.: Catholic University of America Press, 2007), p. 194–222, at p. 219–220; ELS ROSE, 'Celebrating St Martin in Early Medieval Gaul', in PAUL POST et al. (eds), *Christian Feast and Festival: The Dynamics of Western Liturgy and Culture*, Liturgica Condenda 12 (Louvain: Peeters, 2001), p. 267–286; COURTNEY BOOKER, 'The Dionysian Mirror of Louis the Pious', *Quaestiones medii aevi novae* 19 (2014), 243–264, at p. 258, footnote 55.

[168] About two thirds of the collects *post nomina* are directly addressed to God or Christ, while one third are exhortations to prayer. Contra BERNARD, *Transitions*, p. 233: '...collecte *post nomina* [...] qui a pour principale caractéristique d'être adressée aux fidèles, non à Dieu'.

[169] Contra BERNARD, *Transitions*, p. 237, who assumes a tendency to simplify the *post nomina* collects in the Gothic Missal towards a single-theme prayer focusing on either the living or the dead. A closer study of the prayers reveals that the living and the dead are usually interconnected. Bernard's suggestion that the increasingly 'monothématique' *post nomina* prayers in the Gothic Missal indicate a Romanisation of the Gallican practice of the diptychs ('La seule différence avec la situation romaine est que ces diptyques réduits à des *memento* n'ont pas encore été intégrés à la prière eucharistique') does not hold. See also TAFT, *The Diptychs*, p. 28; ELS ROSE, 'Inscribed in the Book of Life: Liturgical Commemoration in

neither do they refer in any way to the role of the deacon as the reciter of the names,[170] the celebrant taking over for the concluding prayer. Even though there is much variety in the content and structure of the collects, their basic structure comprises three elements: a part that refers to the offering ritual and requests acceptance of the oblations, an intercession for the living and deceased members of the Eucharistic community, and a commendation of the names in the form of a supplication that they may be included in the Book of Life. The latter notion of a list or register of names in heaven is referred to in various ways, of which the 'heavenly book' and 'book of life' are the most frequent.[171]

The ritual of the names is one of the most distinctive characteristics of the Gallican Mass. In the mid-fifth century, Pope Innocent I expressed his displeasure about rites that differed from that of Rome in placing the ritual of the diptychs not in the heart of the Eucharistic prayer but rather before it, linked to the offertory ritual.[172] The Carolingian reformers of the late-eighth century followed Innocent's preferences, promoting the relocation of the ritual of the names to the Eucharistic prayer. The change was apparently not implemented wholeheartedly, as the repeated summons to follow Roman practice demonstrate.[173]

Merovingian Gaul', in BONNIE EFFROS and ISABEL MOREIRA (eds), *The Oxford History of the Merovingian World* (Oxford-New York: Oxford University Press, forthcoming 2017).

[170] BERNARD, *Transitions*, p. 233. Little is known about the exact performance of the ritual. Cabrol indicates that the number of names became too large for all of them to be recited during Mass. CABROL, 'Diptyques', col. 1050. See also footnote 166.

[171] See note 4 to collect 1.

[172] ROBERT CABIÉ, *La lettre du pape Innocent Ier à Décentius de Gubbio (19 mars 416)*, Bibliothèque de la RHE 58 (Louvain, 1973), with an edition of the text on p. 44–52; see further BERNARD, *Transitions*, p. 236; TAFT, *The Diptychs*, p. 28–29 and ROSE, 'Inscribed'.

[173] *Admonitio generalis* (789) 54, ed. HUBERT MORDEK, KLAUS ZECHIEL-ECKES and MICHAEL GLATTHAAR, *Die Admonitio generalis Karls des Großen*, MGH Fontes iuris germanici antiqui in usum scholarum separatim editi 16 (Wiesbaden: Harrasowitz, 2013), p. 206; *Synod of Frankfurt* (794), canon 51, ed. ALBERT WERMINGHOFF, MGH Concilia aevi Karolini I, p. 165–171, at p. 171.

Collectio ad pacem (Collect at the kiss of peace).[174] The exchange of the kiss of peace (*pax*) follows the offertory and immediately precedes the recitation of the Eucharistic prayer *stricto sensu*. A number of collects *ad pacem* in the Gothic Missal include elements that belong to the offertory prayer (*super oblata*) in the sense of commending the oblations.[175] While the collect *ad pacem* in the fifth Lenten Mass (189) appears to combine an offertory prayer with a collect at the kiss of peace, a great number of collects *ad pacem* seem to be composed rather as offertory prayers (*super oblata*) than as collects at the kiss of peace,[176] even if they double an element already present in the collect *post nomina*.[177]

The *Expositio missae* relates the exchange of the kiss as a sign of reconciliation to Matth. 5, 23–24, the exhortation to reconcile with a neighbour before bringing one's oblation to the altar.[178] This obvious relation is nevertheless rare in the Latin Mass commentaries, as Bernard has stressed.[179] The same document also relates the kiss of peace to its false counterpart, the kiss of the traitor (*proditoris*). Although Judas is not mentioned by name, the reference to Matth. 26, 49 is clear, as it is in the Gothic Missal (325), which mentions 'the fraudulent kiss of the traitor'.[180] In the collect that accompanies the actual exchange of the kiss,[181] emphasis lies

---

[174] For an overview of the ritual and its most important bibliography, see BERNARD, *Transitions*, p. 249–278.

[175] Cf. SMYTH, *Liturgie oubliée*, p. 362–363.

[176] Particularly nos 279, 315, 392, 412, 440, 445, 450, 491.

[177] As do nos 279, 450, 491.

[178] *Expositio missae* 19, ed. BERNARD, p. 349. On the early Christian background to this reconciliatory function of the kiss of peace, see KIRIL PETKOV, *The Kiss of Peace: Ritual, Self, and Society in the High and Late Medieval West*, Cultures, Beliefs, and Traditions 17 (Leiden-Boston: Brill, 2003), p. 13–14; SMYTH, *Liturgie oubliée*, p. 362–363.

[179] BERNARD, *Transitions*, p. 271.

[180] *fraudolentus osculos proditores*; cf. BERNARD, *Transitions*, p. 271–272.

[181] Scholars differ on the question whether the collect follows the kiss itself, or precedes it as an invitation, see BERNARD, *Transitions*, p. 250. The tenses of verbs expressing the actual exchange of kisses, which switch from present to perfect (*datur* 85, *profertur* 114, *praebet* 131, *inpenditur* 300; but *porrecta* 199, *inlegati fuerint* 120), give no decisive answer. Bernard seems to be on firmer ground when he concludes that the collect precedes the kiss. He does so on the basis of his analysis of marginal, sometimes Tironian notes in the manuscripts, among which the Gothic

on the sincerity of the kiss, not only as an outer ritual but also as an inner attitude. This is expressed a number of times by a litotes: *ut osculum quod in labiis datur, in cordibus non negetur*: 'that the kiss that is given with the lips will not be denied / will be confirmed by the hearts' (85).[182]

In a number of collects the ritual of the kiss of peace is described as a commandment. No. 151 uses the word *praecepto*: 'so that all who join together on [your] command at the kiss [of peace]'; no. 320 the verb *custodire iussisti*: '...the peace which you commanded [us] to preserve'; no. 475, again, the verb *praecepisti*: '...and give that peace which, according to your command, is enduring...' While no specific biblical quotation is given in the prayers, the notion of a commandment is explained more explicitly in the *Expositio missae* 19. It speaks of the commandment Christ gave to his disciples (*mandauit discipulis*) upon his ascension (*caelos ascendens*), and combines John 14, 27 (the gift of peace) with John 13, 35 (the new commandment of love by which Christ's disciples are recognised).[183]

While the kiss of peace is often associated with the kiss featuring prominently in the first verse of the Song of Songs (Song 1, 1: 'Let him kiss me with the kisses of his mouth'),[184] this happens only once in the Gothic Missal, in the context of Easter (269). The Easter season was already related to the Song of Songs in the Jewish tradition, in which the scroll was read during the fifty days between Easter and Pentecost.[185]

Missal (524 and 535), which indicate that the opening dialogue of the Eucharistic prayer followed immediately after the collect. This would imply that the kiss itself must have been exchanged before the collect. BERNARD, *Transitions*, p. 250–251.

[182] See also nos 114 and 465 for another use of the litotes in a collect at the kiss of peace; see also section Style and figures.

[183] *Expositio missae* 19, ed. BERNARD, p. 349.

[184] NICOLAS J. PERELLA, *The Kiss Sacred and Profane: An Interpretative History of Kiss Symbolism and Related Religio-Erotic Themes* (Berkeley CA: University of California Press, 1969), p. 52; LIEKE SMITS, *A Union Not Only of Bodies but of Spirits: The Image of the Kiss in the Commentaries on the Song of Songs of Bernard of Clairvaux and William of St. Thierry* (MA thesis Utrecht University, 2014), p. 12.

[185] On the relation between this verse from the Song of Songs and Matth. 5, 23–24, see PETKOV, *Kiss of Peace*, p. 16.

Immolatio or *contestatio missae* (Prayer of sacrifice). The fact that
the prayer of sacrifice follows immediately after the exchange of
the kiss of peace is indicated by the Tironian note added to the collect at the kiss of peace in the sixth Sunday Mass (525). Mohlberg
deciphered the note as reading: 'May the peace, fidelity and love of
our Lord Jesus Christ and of all the saints be always with you. Lift
up your hearts'.[186] The latter words, *sursum corda*, form the opening phrase of the tripartite dialogue between the celebrant and the
faithful which introduces the Eucharistic prayer. There is no further trace of this dialogue in the Gothic Missal, but other sources
testify to its use in the Gallican liturgy.[187] Moreover, indirect evidence testifies to the use of this dialogue in the community that
possessed the Gothic Missal, for the prayers of sacrifice begin with
the formulaic 'It is truly worthy and just...' (*Vere dignum et iustum
est*). These words refer to the final lemma of the dialogue, in which
the faithful respond to the celebrant's 'Let us give thanks to the
Lord our God' with the exclamation 'That is worthy and just'.[188]

The prayers of sacrifice in the Gothic Missal are both lauded
and loathed by various scholars for their extensive elaboration
on the nature of the feast and, in the case of a saint's day, on the
biographical particularities of the person in question. Whatever
the preference of the reader, the fact is that many of these prayers
offer detailed and often unique insight into the veneration of
saints in the community that used the Gothic Missal. The prayers
of sacrifice for saints' days, therefore, do not stand out for their
particular *laus dei* concentrating on the *mirabilia dei*, as Smyth
emphasises,[189] but for their characteristic *laus sancti*, focusing on
the *mirabilia sancti*.[190] The stylistic characteristics of these prayers
will be discussed under the heading Style and figures.

[186] MOHLBERG, *Missale Gothicum. Das gallikanische Sakramentar*, p. 28; ROSE
(ed.), *Missale Gothicum*, p. 542. Cf. BERNARD, *Transitions*, p. 283.
[187] e.g. the Mone Masses; cf. BERNARD, *Transitions*, p. 275 and Caesarius of
Arles in various sermons (ibid., p. 283).
[188] *Let us give thanks to the Lord – it is worthy and just.* See further section The
performance of prayer.
[189] SMYTH, *Liturgie oubliée*, p. 377–378.
[190] ELS ROSE, 'Hagiography as a Liturgical Act: Liturgical and Hagiographic
Commemoration of the Saints in the Early Middle Ages', in MARCEL BARNARD

The titles *immolatio* and *contestatio* are used as synonyms throughout the Gothic Missal, and are treated as such in the translation. This does not alter the fact that the two words have different semantic backgrounds and connotations. *immolatio* literally means 'sacrifice', and the verbatim translation of *immolatio missae* would be 'sacrifice of Mass'. As a prayer title, however, this makes little sense, hence my decision to translate it as 'prayer of sacrifice'. William Porter suggests that the word is formed 'from a misunderstanding of the Spanish name', *illatio*,[191] which basically translates the Greek word for the Eucharistic prayer: ἀνάφορα – literally 'bringing in'.[192] Although most authors and dictionaries refer to the word *immolatio* and its prayer text with the help of the term 'preface', thus approaching it through the perspective of the Roman Mass,[193] I prefer to describe it more independently as that part of the Eucharistic prayer which follows the *Sursum corda* dialogue and precedes the *Sanctus*.[194] The majority of 'prayers of sacrifice' (54 out of 69) are entitled *immolatio [missae]*, while the word (both the noun and forms of the verb *immolare*) also occurs in the prayers themselves. *contestatio*, on the other hand, is used in only fifteen 'prayers of sacrifice', and is employed exclusively in the technical context of the heading *contestatio* or *contestatio missae*. The word entails a supplication, while King relates its legal connotation of 'testimony, attestation' to the *Sursum corda* dialogue, confirming that the faithful *truly* 'have their hearts with the Lord' (*Habemus [sc. corda] ad dominum*).[195]

---

et al. (eds), *A Cloud of Witnesses. Saints and Role Models in Christian Liturgy*, Liturgia condenda 18 (Louvain: Peeters, 2005), p. 161–183.

[191] PORTER, *The Gallican Rite*, p. 3.

[192] KING, *Liturgies of the Past*, p. 173.

[193] Porter and King, as quoted in the previous footnotes; cf. ALBERT BLAISE, *Dictionnaire latin-français des auteurs chrétiens* (Turnhout: Brepols, 1954), s.v. *immolatio* (2); LEO F. STELTEN, *Dictionary of Ecclesiastical Latin* (Peabody MA: Hendrickson, 1995), s.v. *immolatio*.

[194] Cf. ROSE (ed.), *Missale Gothicum*, Introduction, p. 150 (*contestatio*) and 151 (*immolatio*).

[195] KING, *Liturgies of the Past*, p. 172.

Collectio post sanctus (Collect after the Sanctus[196]). The collect is a direct sequel and response to the sung *Sanctus*, which is announced by the standard incipit *Vere sanctus, vere benedictus*. It is characterised by Smyth as the embolism (interpolation) of the Sanctus, just as the *Pater noster* has its embolism in variant wording.[197]

Qui pridie (Who on the day before his suffering...). Most collects after the Sanctus end with the abbreviated formula *Qui pridie* or *Qui pridie quam pateretur*: 'Who on the day before his suffering...'[198] What followed is the institution narrative, which is nowhere in the Gothic Missal written out in full.[199] The *Irish Palimpsest Sacramentary*, conversely, gives a full account of the narrative, based on the Gospels (Matth. 26, 26–29; Luc. 22, 14–20) and Paul's Epistle to the Corinthians (I Cor. 11, 23–26).[200]

Collectio post mysterium or *post secreta* (Collect after the consecration). In the Gallican rite, the institution narrative, entailing the consecration of bread and wine, is followed by a proper collect, entitled *Collectio post mysterium* or *Collectio post secreta*. In

[196] On the Sanctus itself, see BRIAN SPINKS, *The Sanctus in the Eucharistic Prayer* (Cambridge: Cambridge University Press, 1991); ROBERT F. TAFT, 'The Interpolation of the Sanctus into the Anaphora: When and Where? A Review of the Dossier', Part I, *Orientalia christiana periodica* 57 (1991), 281–308 and Part II, *Orientalia christiana periodica* 58 (1992), 82–121.

[197] SMYTH, *Liturgie oubliée*, p. 210.

[198] On the variations in the formula and their backgrouds, see SMYTH, *Liturgie oubliée*, p. 409–410.

[199] This is not necessarily because the text was seen as an *oratio periculosa*; it was probably known by heart, like other texts referred to but not quoted in the Gothic Missal (e.g. *Pater noster*, dialogue preceding the prayer of sacrifice). Cf. SMYTH, *Liturgie oubliée*; on the narrative of institution as an *oratio periculosa,* see ARNOLD ANGENENDT, 'Sacrifice, Gifts, and Prayers in Latin Christianity', in TOM NOBLE and JULIA SMITH (eds), *The Cambridge History of Christianity vol. 3: Early Medieval Christianities c. 600-c. 1100* (Cambridge: Cambridge University Press, 2008), p. 453–471, at p. 457, without reference to sources.

[200] Ed. ALBAN DOLD and LEO EIZENHÖFER, *Das irische Palimpsestsakramentar im CLM 14429 der Staatsbibliothek München* (Beuron: Beuroner Kunstverlag, 1964), p. 15–16; cf. SMYTH, *Liturgie oubliée*, p. 407.

this context the word *mysterium* indicates the consecration.[201] The word *secreta* is, according to Smyth, a remnant of the Spanish phrase *missa secreta*. Scholars have previously interpreted this as an indication that the prayers accompanying the consecration were said in silence,[202] but this is contested by Smyth, who interprets *[missa] secreta* as *mysteria* in a theological, not a performative sense.[203] Various elements that are central to the Eucharistic prayer in all early Christian traditions come together in the collect *post mysterium*, most significantly the *anamnesis* (commemoration of Christ's passion and resurrection) and *epiclesis* (prayer for acceptance and blessing of the offerings).[204] The prayers not only request the Holy Spirit to be poured over (*infundere*) the gifts (e.g. 100, 431, 440, 505) but also over the faithful (e.g. 527).[205]

Colleccio ad panis fraccionum[206] (Collect at the breaking of the bread). There is only one example of a collect bearing this title: no. 272 in the Easter Vigil. Given the content of the prayer, Bernard is probably correct in suggesting that the prayer as such is not a new or unique phenomenon in the Gothic Missal, though the title is, and that the prayer in question may simply be a collect after

---

[201] ALBERT BLAISE, *Le vocabulaire latin des principaux thèmes liturgiques* (Turnhout: Brepols, 1966), p. 389 (section 341), footnote 7.

[202] KING, *Liturgies of the Past*, p. 175.

[203] SMYTH, *Liturgie oubliée*, p. 212.

[204] SMYTH, *Liturgie oubliée*, p. 427–448.

[205] In the light of evidence provided by the collects *post mysterium* and *post secreta* in the Gothic Missal, Louise Batstone's statement that 'It is hard to find clear evidence of an *epiclesis* anywhere in the Gallican liturgy, including the Bobbio Missal, with the exception of the rite of church consecration' is difficult to understand: LOUISE BATSTONE, 'Doctrinal and Theological Themes in the Prayers of the Bobbio Missal', in YITZHAK HEN and ROB MEENS (eds), *The Bobbio Missal. Liturgy and Religious Culture in Merovingian Gaul* (Cambridge: Cambridge University Press, 2004), p. 168–184, esp. p. 181–183. Precisely the prayers Batstone mentions with regard to the concept of *Eucharistia legitima* are marked by Lietzmann as *epiclesis* prayers: HANS LIETZMANN, *Mass and Lord's Supper. A Study in the History of the Liturgy* (transl. Dorothea H.G. Reeve, Leiden: Brill, 1979), p. 80.

[206] Read *fractionem*; cf. ROSE (ed.), *Missale Gothicum*, p. 454.

the consecration.[207] The actual breaking of the bread takes place after the Lord's Prayer and its embolism.[208]

Collectio ante and *post orationem dominicam* (Collect before and after the Lord's Prayer). In the Gallican Mass, the *Pater noster* was prayed after the ritual breaking of the bread (*fractio panis*, see previous prayer), not immediately after the prayer of sacrifice as in the Roman rite and the Frankish Mass from the Carolingian period onwards.[209] The importance of the participation of all the faithful in the recitation of the *Pater noster* is echoed by prescriptive documents such as the canons of church councils, or by narrative sources such as sermons and the lives of saints.[210] However, the Gothic Missal itself gives evidence of this practice through its palaeography, or more precisely through the rubrication of the first words of the prayer. The words *Pater noster* are generally executed either in coloured ink or in a different, capital-like letter, or both. This is represented in the translation by the use of small caps. The prayer itself is preceded and followed by a *proprium* collect, recited by the celebrant.

Benedictio populi (Blessing of the people). The blessing of the people, given before communion, was originally reserved for the bishop. The *Expositio missae* indicates a distinction between the elaborate blessing of a bishop (the *Expositio* quotes Num. 6, 24) and

[207] BERNARD, *Transitions*, p. 292.

[208] For a further discussion, see BERNARD, *Transitions*, p. 292–294.

[209] *Expositio missae* 22 (between the chapters on *Confractio et conmixtio* and *Benedictio populi*), ed. BERNARD, p. 350; see also BERNARD, *Transitions*, p. 309.

[210] SMYTH, *Liturgie oubliée*, p. 215 refers concerning early medieval Gaul to CASSIANUS, *Collationes* 9.22; PROSPER OF AQUITANIA, *De gratia dei et libero arbitrio* 15, and CAESARIUS OF ARLES, *Sermo* 73; in addition, see GREGORY OF TOURS, *De uirtutibus sancti Martini* 2.30, on a woman with a lame tongue who is miraculously cured in St Martin's basilica and is then able to join the other faithful in their recitation of the *Pater noster* (*sanctam orationem coepit cum reliquis decantare*), ed. KRUSCH, MGH SRM 1.2, p. 170. Bernard also gives a survey of sources: BERNARD, *Transitions*, p. 310–311; see further JOSEPH JUNGMANN, *Missarum sollemnia*, transl. Francis A. Brunner, *The Mass of the Roman Rite. Its Origins and Development* (New York, etc.: Benziger Brothers, 1959), p. 468.

that pronounced by a priest.[211] Augustine relates blessings to New
Testament epistolary greetings invoking God to bless the recipi-
ents of the letter.[212] The blessings in the Gothic Missal are entirely
proprium and, certainly in the case of feast days, go into great
detail concerning the nature and object of the commemoration.
While not all Masses in the Gothic Missal include a blessing,[213]
the feast of Circumcision has two (60 and 63), both before and
after communion. The meaning or function of this duplication
is unclear.[214] Similarly, it remains unexplained why some saints'
Masses include a blessing (e.g. Cecilia and Clement) while others do not (e.g. Agnes), and why some high feasts have a blessing
(Christmas, Epiphany) while Easter (both Vigil and Day) and the
days of the Easter Octave[215] do not, although the latter were surely
occasions when the bishop would have presided.

Collectio post communionem or *post Eucharistiam* and *collectio sequitur* or *consummatio missae* (Collect after communion / after
the Eucharist and Collect follows or Completion of Mass). Collects after communion are given for a select number of Masses:
the Christmas Vigil (9 and 10), Christmas Day (23 and 24), Stephen (35 and 36), James and John (44 and 45), Circumcision (61
and 62), Epiphany (92 and 93), Mary's Assumption (104 and 105),

---

[211] *Expostio missae* 23, ed. BERNARD, p. 350–351; BERNARD, *Transitions*, p. 311
and 330–331.

[212] SMYTH, *Liturgie oubliée*, p. 217 quotes AUGUSTINE, *Epistolae* 149.16 and
179.4.

[213] Masses in which a blessing before communion is given: Christmas Vigil (8),
Christmas Day (22), Stephen (34), James and John (43), *Infantes* (50), Circumcision
(60 and 63), Epiphany Vigil (81), Epiphany Day (91), Assumption of Mary (103),
Cecilia (116), Clement (122), Andrew (137), Peter's Chair (157), the Beginning of
Lent (169), Peter and Paul (379). In the Mass for the *nativitas* of John the Baptist
(373) a blessing is added in Merovingian minuscule.

[214] Bernard ascribes it to uncertainty among scribes and their commissioners
as to the exact place of the blessing, since the Gallican Mass ordo differed here
from the Roman rite, the latter always situating the blessing after communion.
BERNARD, *Transitions*, p. 332.

[215] The Council of Épaone (517), canon 55 even stressed the importance of an
episcopal blessing on the feasts of Christmas and Easter; cf. BERNARD, *Transitions*,
p. 337–338.

Beginning of Lent (167 and 168), Holy Thursday (214), and the six Sunday Masses (486 and 487, 497 and 498, 508 and 509, 519 and 520, 530 and 531, 541 and 542). The structure of these post communion prayers is variable, with roughly two alternatives. The most common is the combination of a *post communionem/eucharistiam*, phrasing an exhortation to prayer addressed to the faithful (*fratres karissimi*), with a collect addressed to God (*domine* or *deus*). This combination appears in the Masses for the Christmas Vigil, Christmas Day, Circumcision, and Epiphany. Five of the six Sunday Masses have a similar structure, although the collects *post communionem* usually have no explicit address but speak to the faithful in the exhortative, e.g. *deo patri omnipotenti gracias agamus* (497), *oremus patrem et filium* (508) and the like. The collect in these Masses is entitled *consummatio missae*, apart from the *item colleccio sequitur* in the fifth Sunday Mass (531). The second type gives two prayers as well, but both are addressed to God. In most cases (Stephen, Beginning of Lent, Sunday Mass IV) the second prayer is entitled *consummatio missae*, though the Masses for James and John and for Mary's Assumption give a *collectio sequitur*. There are two exceptions to the structure of an exhortative prayer followed by a collect. The first is the Mass for Holy Thursday, which gives a single *post communionem* addressed to God (214). The second exception is more puzzling: this is the combination of two exhortative prayers without a collect, found in the first Sunday Mass. Both the *post communionem* (486) and the *consummacio missae* (487) express an exhortation to pray, the first addressed to *fratres karissimi*, the second (*dipraecimor*) without a specific address.[216] Smyth suggests that the first prayer was no longer experienced as an exhortation, but this explanation is not satisfactory, for it would give rise to a structure with a full prayer, or a text experienced as such, followed by an exhortation to prayer. It is more probable that the second prayer (*consummacio missae*), which does not explicitly mention an address in contrast to the *fratres karissimi* spoken to in the first prayer, was perceived as a full prayer to conclude Mass. This unsolved matter at the end

[216] Cf. Smyth, *Liturgie oubliée*, p. 455.

of our survey of prayers relates to other questions concerning the actual performance of prayer which are discussed in the next section.

The performance of prayer

In the preceding section, the role of the various ministers involved in celebrating the Gallican Mass has been mentioned. Besides the celebrant, who by definition plays the leading role in a sacramentary, the deacon has been touched on several times, most notably in the context of the Exultet and the ritual of the names. Even though the Gothic Missal is primarily a textual source, it is possible to explore issues related to the performative context of its prayer texts, especially with regard to the participation of the faithful. There are numerous ways of approaching the role of the laity in the liturgy of Mass in early medieval Gaul, and to do them all justice would require a separate study. I aim to discuss certain issues here as they are brought forward by the prayers themselves, through both their wording and their palaeographical representation in codex Vat. reg. lat. 317.

Circumadstantes

The first issue to be addressed is the location of the people in the church building, brought forward by the use of the verb *circum(ad)stare* in three prayers: *circumstantem plebem* (94, *praefatio*), *circumstantem plebem* (137, *benedictio populi*), *pro salute regum ... et omnium circumadstancium* (272, *colleccio ad panis fraccionum*). In its original application by Christian authors, the term referred to the location of the faithful laity 'standing in a circle around the altar', and through their presence assisting at the celebration of Mass.[217] Even if the word becomes a more standard indication of 'the faithful', 'those attending Mass' as opposed to the clergy, this does not mean that the altar was not within reach

[217] LEWIS and SHORT, *Latin Dictionary*, s.v. *circumsto*; BLAISE, *Vocabulaire*, p. 201, section 84 and p. 523; see ROSE (ed.), *Missale Gothicum*, Introduction, p. 156.

of them once their number had considerably increased, as compared to the confined Christian community of the first centuries in which the word *circumadstantes* acquired its Christian meaning.[218] To be sure, this accessibility was relative.[219] The late-eighth-century *Ordo Romanus* 15 distinguishes between those who stood near the altar, and were therefore able to hear the prayers (of the canon) when recited quietly (*dissimile uoce*), and others who did not.[220] Ecclesiastical (functional), social and gender distinctions determined who were the *circumadstantes* closest to the altar. There is no evidence in Merovingian sources for a gender division in admittance to the altar, which is not to say that such regulations did not apply. Nevertheless, as Gisela Muschiol states, functional differences seem to have been more important than gender distinction in the question as to who was allowed to approach the altar and at what point.[221] Only the manner *in which* people approached the altar, mainly to receive communion, was subject to gender distinction.[222]

Whether or not the rather literal translation of *circum(ad)-stantes* which I have chosen for the prayers of the Gothic Missal ('the faithful standing around here', 94; 'all who are standing around here', 272) is justified, the placement of the laity was certainly not static. One of the main characteristics of the early medieval Mass was movement through the church building, of which the faithful were considered to be the 'living stones',[223] and in which 'specialised ritual spaces' were demarcated, as Éric Palazzo phrases it, in order to facilitate the many different elements of

[218] On the restricted social scope of the pre-Constantinian Christian community, see PETER BROWN, *The Ransom of the Soul: Afterlife and Wealth in Early Western Christianity* (Cambridge, MA: Harvard University Press, 2015), p. 41: 'The dead were thought to be as close to the living as the living were expected to be as close to each other'.

[219] For a succinct summary, see MUSCHIOL, *Men, Women and Liturgical Practice*, p. 203–206.

[220] Cf. EDWARD FOLEY, 'The Song of the Assembly in Medieval Eucharist', in LIZETTE LARSON-MILLER, *Medieval Liturgy. A Book of Essays* (New York-London: Garland Publishing, 1997), p. 203–234, at p. 208 and footnote 56.

[221] MUSCHIOL, 'Men, Women and Liturgical Practice', p. 205.

[222] MUSCHIOL, 'Men, Women and Liturgical Practice', p. 205–206.

[223] PALAZZO, 'Performing the Liturgy', p. 476, see also p. 479–482.

Mass, both of the first part of Mass and of the Eucharistic celebration.[224] This movement added to the deacon's burden, for throughout the service he was responsible for keeping order among the faithful.[225] The fact that he requested silence at various moments to catch their attention indicates that there must have been noise and disturbance at crucial moments. The first call to silence was at the beginning of the readings,[226] when the bishop greeted the faithful with the words *Dominus vobiscum* and the congregation was expected to answer *et cum spiritu tuo*; the second call was after the departure of the catechumens when the Eucharist itself commenced.[227]

The deacon's repeated call for silence among the faithful indicates that Mass could not be celebrated without their mindful attendance. What can be said, on the basis of the Gothic Missal, about the nature of their participation?

Acclamations

Whatever their physical location in the church building, the faithful had a distinctive role in the performance of prayers during Mass. From Origen until well into the ninth century the importance of the people's presence to assist in the performance of the liturgy was stressed in exegetical treatises, sermons, saints' lives and council canons.[228] What did this 'assistance' imply? In the first place, the presence of the faithful was required so that they could perform the various responses and acclamations.

At first sight, it seems difficult to determine from a sacramentary such as the Gothic Missal the extent to which the faithful engaged in the liturgy and took on an active role, such as in the acclamations assigned to them. At a closer look, however, if we turn from the textual to the palaeographical details of the manuscript,

---

[224] PALAZZO, 'Performing the Liturgy', p. 477–478.
[225] Cf. ALLAN DOIG, *Liturgy and Architecture from the Early Church to the Middle Ages* (Aldershot: Ashgate, 2008), p. 102.
[226] BERNARD, *Transitions*, p. 58–61; *Expositio missae* 2, ed. BERNARD, p. 338.
[227] BERNARD, *Transitions*, p. 164; *Expositio missae* 13, ed. BERNARD, p. 345.
[228] BERNARD, *Transitions*, p. 310–311.

some clear evidence does emerge. Throughout the sacramentary, certain words and short phrases are marked as being of a different level or character than the rest of the text. Just as the titles of Masses and prayers are executed in coloured ink to distinguish them from the text itself in a dark brown ink, there is also a marked distinction of ink, script or both in most occurrences of the word *Amen* after the different elements of the Blessing of the people, in the word *Sanctus* that ensues from the prayer of sacrifice, and in the incipit *Pater noster* that introduces the Lord's Prayer.[229] From corresponding evidence in narrative and prescriptive sources we can conclude that these words were intended as acclamations of the faithful in response to the celebrant. Such responses appear in various guises in the liturgy of Mass. They are generally short utterances in reaction to or as a sign of confirmation of prayers recited by the minister.[230]

From an early stage of Christianity, the use of the acclamation *Amen*, to be uttered by the faithful in order to conclude a liturgical prayer in a corporate setting, was considered vital. Marc Schneiders draws attention to the emphasis put on this element of the performance of Mass, more specifically in the Eucharistic prayer, by the second-century Justin Martyr.[231] Likewise, the anonymous commentary on the Epistles of Paul attributed to the pseudonymous Ambrosiaster, a Roman clergyman contemporary with Ambrose of Milan,[232] underlined the importance of the role of the faithful in

[229] Words and phrases to which this applies are marked by small caps in the translation.

[230] An adequate definition is given by MARC SCHNEIDERS, 'Acclamations in the Eucharistic Prayer', in CHARLES CASPERS and MARC SCHNEIDERS (eds), *Omnes circumadstantes. Contributions towards a History of the Role of the People in the Liturgy. Presented to Herman Wegman* (Kampen: Kok, 1990), p. 78–100: at p. 78; see also HANS B. MEYER, *Eucharistie: Geschichte, Theologie, Pastoral, Gottesdienst der Kirche*. Handbuch der Liturgiewissenschaft (Regensburg: Pustet, 1989), p. 128 and the classic article by THEODOR KLAUSER, 'Akklamation', in RAC, vol. 1 (Stuttgart: Hiersemann, 1950), col. 216–233.

[231] SCHNEIDERS, 'Acclamations', p. 80, referring to JUSTIN MARTYR, *Apologia* 65 and 67.

[232] ANDREAS MERKT, 'Wer war der Ambrosiaster? Zum Autor einer Quelle des Augustinus – Fragen auf eine neue Antwort', *Wissenschaft und Weisheit* 59 (1996), 19–33; DAVID G. HUNTER, 'Ambrosiaster', in ROBERT BENEDETTO

responding to the prayers of the celebrant with their acclamation *Amen*. Ambrosiaster took this acclamation most seriously, even considering the collective *Amen* as the fulfilment of the prayer:

> For an illiterate, listening to what he does not understand, does not know when the prayer ends and does not answer with *Amen*, that is 'It is true', so that the blessing be confirmed. For the confirmation of the prayer is fulfilled by those who answer with *Amen*, so that everything that is said is confirmed with a true testimony in the hearts and minds of those who listen.[233]

Though introduced into the liturgy of Mass at a later stage, the *Sanctus* is similarly a part of Mass assigned to the faithful.[234] While *Amen* is a mere word, the *Sanctus* is a more elaborate acclamation, chanted in response to the prayer of sacrifice (*immolatio* or *contestatio*). The *Sanctus* became part of the 'ordinary' (*ordinarium*) or standard components of Mass and includes not only the angelic song quoted from Is. 6, 3, but also the *Benedictus* based on Matth. 21, 9. An important witness to the role of the faithful in this part of Mass is the account of the healing of the girl Palatina given by Gregory of Tours in his *Liber de virtutibus sancti Martini* 2.14. Gregory tells how the lame girl spent three months praying at the

(ed.), *The New Westminster Dictionary of Church History*. vol. 1: The Early, Medieval and Reformation Eras (Westminster: John Knox Press, 2008), p. 20; WILHELM GEERLINGS, 'Ambrosiaster', in SIEGMAR DÖPP and WILHELM GEERLINGS (eds): *Lexikon der antiken christlichen Literatur* (Freiburg-Basel-Vienna: Herder, 1998), p. 12–13.

[233] AMBROSIASTER, *Commentarius in epistulas Pauli: ad Corinthias* 16: *Imperitus enim audiens quod non intelligit, nescit finem orationis, et non respondet: amen, id est verum; ut confirmetur benedictio. Per hos enim impletur confirmatio precis, qui respondent amen, ut omnia dicta veri testimonio in audientium mentibus confirmentur*, ed. HEINRICH I. VOGELS, *Ambrosiastri qui dicitur Commentarius in epistulas Pauli*, CSEL 81.2 (Vienna: Hoelder-Pichler-Tempsky, 1966–1969), p. 153–154.

[234] SCHNEIDERS, 'Acclamations', p. 80–81 refers a.o. to Gothic Missal 388; FOLEY, 'The Song of the Assembly', p. 207–209. Foley mentions the Council of Vaison (529), canon 3 as a reference to the introduction of the *Sanctus* in each Mass of the Gallican rite. He also states that this canon 'specifically note[s] that the people join the priest in singing the *Sanctus*' (footnote 47), but as far as I can see this is not the case. Council of Vaison (529), canon 3, ed. GAUDEMET and BASDEVANT, SChr 353, vol. 1, p. 190.

tomb of St Martin in Tours. On the feast day of the saint she was cured at the exact moment when Gregory recited the *contestatio* in commemoration of Martin's miracles:

> And when the prayer of sacrifice came to its end and all the people (*omnis populus*) proclaimed the *Sanctus* in praise of God, her stiffened nerves suddenly loosened, and she stood on her feet, while all the people watched her, and thus, with God's help, she proceeded to the holy altar in order to receive communion on her own strength, while no one was supporting her.[235]

A third example of an active role of the people, and almost as old as the Christian liturgy, is the Lord's Prayer, recited after the Eucharistic prayer. Although Bernard interprets the practice described in the late-eighth-century *Expositio missae* as that the recitation of the *Pater* was the prerogative of the bishop,[236] earlier sources, the Gothic Missal included, give evidence of a continuous lay participation in this part of Mass. Again, a miracle story in Gregory's *Liber de virtutibus sancti Martini* (c. 2.30) is illustrative, where Gregory tells of the healing of a mute woman, after which she was able to chant the *Pater noster* together with the others (*cum reliquis decantare*).[237] In his sermon 73, phrased as an exhortation to the people to be present in church when Mass is celebrated, Caesarius of Arles described the absence of people during Mass as a problem, for who would be there to exclaim, 'humbly and honestly': 'Forgive us our trespasses, as we forgive those who trespass against us'?[238] This and other sources indicate that in early Merovingian Gaul the faithful were expected to take their part in the celebration of Mass. Was this practice still alive in the community

---

[235] GREGORY OF TOURS, *De virtutibus sancti Martini* 2.14: *At ubi, expeditam contestationem, omnis populus* Sanctus *in laudem Domini proclamavit, statim dissoluti sunt nervi, qui legati erant, et stetit super pedes suos, cuncto populo spectante, et sic, propitiante Domino, usque ad altare sanctum ad communicandum propriis gressibus, nullo sustentante, pervenit*, ed. MGH SRM 1.2, p. 163.

[236] BERNARD, *Transitions*, p. 312: '...c'est le pontife qui procède seule à la proclamation du *Pater*'. The validity of Bernard's conclusion might well be questioned.

[237] GREGORY OF TOURS, *De virtutibus sancti Martini* 2.30, ed. MGH SRM 1.2, p. 170; see SMYTH, *Liturgie oubliée*, p. 215: 'Elle était récitée par tous'.

[238] CAESARIUS OF ARLES, *Sermo* 73, ed. MORIN, CCSL 103, p. 307; BERNARD, *Transitions*, p. 314.

that used the Gothic Missal more than a hundred years later? The palaeographical evidence in the codex indicates that it was, even though the situation changed in the late eighth century.[239]

The role of the people in the liturgy of Mass in early medieval Gaul is generally presented as confined, even 'very small',[240] but the above evidence indicates otherwise. Even if the Gothic Missal does not give the words of the dialogue *Sursum corda* preceding the *immolatio* or *contestatio*, Caesarius makes explicit that this part of the liturgy was entrusted to the people just like the Lord's Prayer,[241] and we may assume that the practice continued unchanged in the period in which the Gothic Missal was used.

Offertory

The question of the role of the people in the prayers of Mass, considered in various prayers as their 'sacrifice of thanksgiving' (*hostia laudis*[242]), can be extended to that of their role in the material sacrifice: the offering of oblations. The direct involvement of the faithful in the Eucharistic celebration consisted primarily of the preparation of the gifts of bread and wine for consecration. Until well into the Middle Ages, and certainly including the period in which the Gothic Missal was created and used, the faithful

---

[239] The *Sanctus* remained a song of the faithful in the Carolingian period; BERNARD, *Transitions*, p. 315–316; see also ANNE C. McGUIRE, 'Liturgy and Laity in the Ninth Century', *Ecclesia orans* 13 (1996), 463–494.

[240] SCHNEIDERS, 'Acclamations', p. 91: 'The number and extent of acclamations in the medieval western liturgy may be called meagre without qualification. Apart from Spain the people's role in the West has been very small' (Schneiders draws this conclusion in comparison with 'the East').

[241] CAESARIUS OF ARLES, *Sermo* 73: *Cum enim maxima pars populi, immo quod peius est, paene omnes recitatis lectionibus exeunt de ecclesia, cui dicturus est sacerdos: Sursum corda? Aut quomodo sursum se habere corda respondere possunt, quando deorsum in plateis et corpore simul et corde descendunt?* ed. MORIN, CCSL 103, p. 307. The text of the dialogue: *Dominus vobiscum* – ET CUM SPIRITU TUO. *Sursum corda* – HABEMUS AD DOMINUM. *Gratias agamus domino* – DIGNUM ET IUSTUM EST ('The Lord be with you – AND WITH YOU. Lift up your hearts – WE LIFT THEM UP TOWARDS THE LORD. Let us give thanks to the Lord – IT IS WORTHY AND JUST). The capitalised phrases are spoken by the faithful.

[242] Nos 15, 86, 469; cf. nos 110, 278, 357, 398, 418.

brought homemade bread and, depending on their means, wine into church, which were placed on the altar and consecrated during the Eucharistic prayer.[243] The motion of exchanging gifts is considered as one in which the faithful offer to God what they have accepted as the Creator's gift in the abundance of the earth, in order to regain it after the consecration as Christ's body and blood, the gifts of salvation.[244] This movement is expressed by the word (*sacrosanctum*) *commercium* which occurs in various prayers in the Gothic Missal (1, 355, 382). The role of the faithful in each Eucharistic celebration was not seen to be modest; the Council of Mâcon (585), canon 4, requires that everybody, men and women, contribute to the oblation each Sunday, in the form of 'both bread and wine'. Participation in this offering was believed to provide forgiveness of sins and to make those involved *consortes* of Abel and other celebrated performers of a rightful offering (*Abel uel ceteris iuste offerentibus*).[245] The contribution of the faithful did not go unnoticed, because the names of those who provided an oblation were recited during the offertory ritual, a rite that is concluded by the collect after the names, as we have seen in the previous section.[246]

Opinions differ on the date by which the practice of oblations contributed by the faithful was abandoned. Foley mentions a letter by Alcuin, dated 798, as a first indication of a tendency to use unleavened bread (*panis ... absque fermento*), which was required to be entirely pure (*mundissimus*) – does this imply that it could

---

[243] FOLEY, 'The Song of the Assembly', p. 210. The practice is already mentioned by Cyprian, who rebukes a wealthy woman for not having brought an oblation but taking, in the form of communion, from the offerings brought by the poor: CYPRIAN, *De opere et eleemosynis* 15, ed. MANLIO SIMONETTI, *Sancti Cypriani episcopi opera*, CCSL 3A (Turnhout: Brepols, 1976), p. 53–72, at p. 64; see GREGORY DIX, *The Shape of the Liturgy* (Westminster: Dacre Press, 1947), p. 115.

[244] Cf. IRENAEUS OF LYONS, *Aduersus haereses* 4.17.5 and 4.18.5–6, ed. ROUSSEAU, SChr 100.2, p. 590–592; 610–614.

[245] Council of Mâcon (585), canon 4, ed. GAUDEMET and BASDEVANT, SChr 354.2, p. 460–462; cf. SMYTH, *Liturgie oubliée*, p. 350.

[246] Smyth underlines the concrete character of the recitation of names in the Gallican liturgy, as opposed to the more abstract practice in the Roman canon. SMYTH, *Liturgie oubliée*, p. 350.

not be prepared by the hands of lay people?[247] Rosamond McKitterick suggests a continuation of the practice in the Carolingian period as well, stating that the oblation of the people in the form of homemade bread was 'the particular responsibility, even honour, according to most of the Carolingian episcopal statutes, of the people in each parish',[248] while Edmund Bishop even thought that the practice was maintained until the 'tenth or eleventh century'.[249] These observations imply that the practice of oblations brought in by the faithful would have been very much alive in the community that used the Gothic Missal. Narrative sources hint at a certain tension between rich and poor in this very palpable contribution of the faithful, indicating that rituals involving lay people in the performance of the liturgy also sharpened social divisions.[250] The reluctance of the rich to contribute their share, as Cyprian implies in his treatise on *Good works and alms*, is echoed by Caesarius of Arles in his sermon 14. Caesarius observes that there are many needy faithful who nevertheless bring their oblation to church, even if they barely manage, whereas there are rich people who bring nothing but take from the gifts offered by the poor: they take in judgment rather than salvation (cf. I Cor. 11, 29).[251] Gregory of Tours, on the other hand, seems to tell the opposite by referring to a rich woman who sends the best wine to the ritual offertory – perhaps in a desire to show off and gain prestige. If nothing else, Gregory's story testifies to possible abuse of the people's oblations by the clergy – as presumably happened with alms as well[252] – since in Gregory's account the sub-deacon

---

[247] ALCUIN, *Epistula* 137, ed. ERNST DÜMMLER, *Epistolae karolini aevi II*, MGH Epistolae 4 (Berlin: Weidmann, 1895), p. 210–216, at p. 211–212; cf. FOLEY, 'The Song of the Assembly', p. 210 and note 70.

[248] MCKITTERICK, *The Frankish Church*, p. 144.

[249] BISHOP, 'Appendix', p. 101.

[250] Cf. PETER BROWN, *The Rise of Western Christendom. Triumph and Diversity, A.D. 200–1000*, tenth anniversary revised edition (Chichester-Malden MA: Wiley-Blackwell, 2013), p. 33.

[251] CAESARIUS OF ARLES, *Sermo* 14.3, ed. MORIN, CCSL 103, p. 71; cf. SMYTH, *Liturgie oubliée*, p. 350.

[252] Cf. the Council of Arles (511), canon 5; ed. FRIEDRICH MAASSEN, MGH Conciliae aevi Merovingici (Hanover: Hahn, 1893), p. 4, which speaks of the lack of care for (royal) donations on the side of clerics.

replaced the good wine (*gazeti vini*) by a sour vinegar (*acetum ve-hementissimum*) and took the good wine for himself.[253]

In the cathedral rather than monastic setting where the Gothic Missal was probably used, the performance of prayer, even in the most sacred context of Mass, was not a prerogative of the clergy, as the above sketch of the participation of the faithful illustrates. The presence of the people, emphasised dramatically and repeatedly as indispensable by Caesarius of Arles in his sermon 73, was equally essential in this late Merovingian community that celebrated the liturgy with the Gothic Missal. The faithful were not simply expected to be present: their attendance implied that they *assisted* in the celebration of the Eucharist (*circumadstantes*), they were expected to provide the oblations that the deacon carried to the altar to be consecrated, after which the names of those who offered (*nomina offerentium*[254]) were recited, and they were requested to confirm the prayers by their acclamations. Without the endorsement of the faithful the prayers ended nowhere, and without their gifts the Eucharist could not take place. The final part of this Introduction will discuss the 'passive' participation of the faithful through the perspective of the language of prayer.

The language of prayer

Merovingian Latin: A 'grammar' of Vulgar Latin

The language of the late Merovingian period has had a negative ring ever since the early Carolingians characterised it in unambiguous terms as corrupted and corrupting, with a stab at the incompetence and ignorance of their (Merovingian) forefathers:

---

[253] GREGORY OF TOURS, *In gloria confessorum* 64, ed. BRUNO KRUSCH, MGH SRM 1.2 (Hanover: Hahn, 1885), p. 744–820, at p. 336; cf. GRIFFE, 'Aux origines', p. 31.

[254] A large number of collects *post nomina* in the Gothic Missal indicate that the names recited included the names of those who offered (*offerentum*): 53, 84, 130, 160, 177, 294, 299, 416, 427, 459, 474, 501, 534.

74

maiores nostri.[255] With this and similar tirades, damage was done to the esteem of the linguistic capacities and indeed, as Hans-Henning Kortüm convincingly argues, the moral qualities of the (late) Merovingians – a damage that has never been truly repaired until the present day.[256] That said, the question remains how the language of the Gothic Missal is to be interpreted, for it is certainly problematic for the modern reader trained in a classicist tradition. Since this is the topic of the main part of my introduction to the Latin edition,[257] some general remarks must suffice here. The remaining part of this section will discuss matters of style, while the principles and choices of the present translation are explained in a separate section preceding the actual translation.

The Gothic Missal is an essential source of what we usually call 'vulgar' Latin, despite protests against this prejudiced echo of the term and attempts to replace it by more neutral labels.[258] In its most impartial use, 'Vulgar Latin' refers to the spoken form of the Latin language as opposed to its written form, tied as the latter is to strict rules of grammar and style. In that sense, it is not merely the usage of the *vulgus* or *plebs*, since every person born into Lat-

---

[255] e.g. *Karoli epistola generalis*, ed. ALFRED BORETIUS, MGH Leges, CRF I, no. 30, p. 80.

[256] For an accurate description of the successful campaign to mix linguistic and moral qualities of the Merovingians in the past and (the most recent) present, see HANS-HENNING KORTÜM, 'Le style – c'est l'époque? Urteile über das 'Merowingerlatein' in Vergangenheit und Gegenwart', *Archiv für Diplomatik* 51 (2005), 29–48, esp. p. 31–38. Some recent examples of a similarly negative approach: SMYTH, *Liturgie oubliée*, who not only frequently rejects the language of Gallican prayers in the 'decadent' sources of the seventh and eighth centuries (see e.g. p. 205 on Gothic Missal 275 and p. 333 on *praefationes missae* in general), but also has a specific predilection for what is ancient: 'Il semble plutôt [...] que le *Monacensis* [= Irish Palimpsest Sacramentary], seule de son espèce en Extrême Occident, conserve ainsi un précieux archaïsme' (p. 355); PATRICK SIMS-WILLIAMS, *Religion and Literature in Western England, 600–800* (Cambridge: Cambridge University Press, 1990), p. 314: 'The Gallican style, though vapid and pleonastic – Edmund Bishop said it would not bear the test of translation into English – was also ostentatiously literary' and p. 316: 'the didactic manner and inflated style of the *Prefationes* and *Contestationes* of Gallican masses'.

[257] ROSE (ed.), *Missale Gothicum*, Introduction, p. 23–187.

[258] ROSE (ed.), *Missale Gothicum*, Introduction, p. 24–25; KORTÜM, 'Le style – c'est l'époque?' p. 34 footnote 14.

inity presumably made use of this form of the language at least in the private sphere and in colloquial conversation, whatever elevated rhetorical style he or she mastered in either public or written environments or both. In the course of the late antique and early medieval periods, the degree to which the spoken language visibly influenced written documents increased, as is already evident in the epigraphic sources of the first century BCE. This process was particularly strong in regions where the uniform educational system of the Roman Empire gradually declined, initially in regions where urban structures were less well preserved. This is not to say that education, or even classical education, disappeared entirely, since monastic centres cherished and transmitted the knowledge and teaching of the *artes liberales*, particularly the subjects of the trivium (*grammatica, retorica, dialectica*). Uniformity, however, was not the most prominent feature of educational practices in the post-imperial world, as is visible in linguistic categories such as spelling and morphology. Previous research has demonstrated the close relationship between the written form of texts and the regional pronunciation of Latin, which differed from province to province, as reflected in the plurality of the Romance languages that all emerged from the one Latin language.[259] The exchange of

[259] Seminal have been MICHEL BANNIARD, *Viva voce. Communication écrite et communication orale du IVe au IXe siècle en Occident latin*, Collection des Études augustiniennes: Série Moyen Âge et Temps Modernes 25 (Paris: Institut des études augustiniennes, 1992); MARC VAN UYTFANGHE, 'Le latin des hagiographes mérovingiens et la protohistoire du français. État de la question', *Romanica Gandensia* 16 (1976), 5–89. See also MICHEL BANNIARD, 'The Transition from Latin to the Romance Languages', in MARTIN MAIDEN et al. (eds), *The Cambridge History of the Romance Languages*, vol. 2 (Cambridge: Cambridge University Press, 2013), p. 57–106; MICHEL BANNIARD, 'Language and Communication in Carolingian Europe', in ROSAMOND MCKITTERICK (ed.), *The New Cambridge Medieval History*, vol. 2 (Cambridge: Cambridge University Press, 1995), p. 695–708. For an example of analysis of a text transmitted in a late Merovingian liturgical source, in which the influence of the spoken language is the most important key to its interpretation, see CHARLES WRIGHT and ROGER WRIGHT, 'Additions to the Bobbio Missal: *De dies malus* and *Joca monachorum* (fols. 6r–8v)', in HEN and MEENS (eds), *The Bobbio Missal*, p. 79–139, esp. p. 124–139 ('The language of *De dies malus* and the *Joca Monachorum* in the Bobbio Missal'). Further literature in ROSE (ed.), *Missale Gothicum*, Introduction, p. 24–25, and throughout the linguistic commentary.

vowels in writing (particularly e/i and o/u), and the disappear-
ance – and hypercorrect addition – of consonants at the end of
and within words, were catalysed by the increasing influence of
the spoken on the written language and by phonetic modifica-
tions that changed the Latin language from being defined by a
quantitative vowel system (long and short vowels) to a qualitative
distinction (vowels pronounced open or closed[260]).

Phonetic changes did not only affect spelling. The increasing
interchange of vowels in written documents ultimately made itself felt in the morphological system as well.[261] Phonetic change
and its orthographic reflection, increasing uncertainty about the
inflectional systems of noun and verb, and a growing tendency to
simplify particularly the nominal system, are the dynamics of the
Latin language in late antiquity and the early Middle Ages. They
go to explain the occurrence of morphological shifts in nouns and
verbs that may surprise the classically educated.

However, Vulgar Latin is not the only backcloth to the characteristic linguistic features of the Gothic Missal. This sacramentary is first and foremost a source of liturgical Latin, and as such
it is rooted in the biblical texts as they circulated in Latin from
the fourth century onwards. Early Latin Bible translations were
deeply influenced, in terms of both structure and vocabulary, by
the original languages of Scripture: Hebrew and Greek.[262]

Awareness of these shifts and changes in the Latin of the post-
classical and post-imperial period, and insight into the peculiari-
ties of the Latin tradition of Christian authors, help to explain the

---

[260] A brief introduction, based on the works by VEIKO VÄÄNÄNEN, *Introduction au latin vulgaire* (Paris: Klinksieck, 1981³) and József HERMAN, *Vulgar Latin*,
transl. Roger Wright (University Park, PA: Pennsylvania State University Press,
2000) is given in ROSE (ed.), *Missale Gothicum*, Introduction, p. 37–38. For an
analysis of the orthography in the Gothic Missal, see ibid., p. 37–66.

[261] The morphology of the Gothic Missal is analysed in ROSE (ed.), *Missale
Gothicum*, Introduction, p. 67–93; for a concise theoretical explanation, see HER-
MAN, *Vulgar Latin*, p. 49–80.

[262] The syntactic changes in the Gothic Missal that go back to the biblical languages are discussed in ROSE (ed.), *Missale Gothicum*, Introduction, p. 103–104,
while p. 105–181 offer an analysis of innovative vocabulary, both semantical and
lexicological.

features that distinguish the Gothic Missal, according to what becomes to some extent the regularity of irregularity. What is more, it must not be forgotten that the texts of the Gothic Missal were intended to be recited. Like sermons, liturgical prayers for use in the context of Mass were performative texts rather than texts for private meditation. We will never know how the words on the page sounded, or the extent to which they were adapted to the ears of the listeners, with their particular regional expectations of what Latin should sound like. Even if we were able to reconstruct the pronunciation of the prayers,[263] we cannot estimate how far the faithful were able to follow the highly complex rhetorical structures of the texts, with their rich and elevated style. The latter characteristic will be discussed below.

Style and figures

Style

From below the surface of orthographic and morphological irregularities that characterise the Gothic Missal, a language of prayer emerges that is related to the Latin tradition of late antiquity, the 'Golden Age' of liturgical composition, while in certain respects it bears a decidedly Gallic stamp. Whatever the origin of the prayers, whether copied from existing collections or written especially for the Gothic Missal or the models that precede Vat. reg. lat. 317,[264] a truly elevated style is encountered, incorporating not only the heritage of seven centuries of Christianity in all relevant languages (Hebrew, Greek, Latin and more), but also referring repeatedly to revered Latin authors of the pre-Christian

---

[263] On this problem, see ROGER WRIGHT, 'A Sociophilological Study of the Change to Official Romance Documentation in Castile', in MARY GARRISON et al. (eds), *Spoken and Written Language: Relations between Latin and the Vernacular Languages in the Earlier Middle Ages*, Utrecht Studies in Medieval Literacy 24 (Turnhout: Brepols, 2013), p. 133–147, at p. 137s.

[264] All categories are represented in the codex. About half of the prayers of the Gothic Missal are found in older and contemporary collections; see the concordance in ROSE (ed.), *Missale Gothicum*, p. 543–569.

period. Given the continuity of the educational programme of the *trivium* and the importance of classical authors as didactic material, their presence in texts of literary quality such as those of the Gothic Missal should not come as a surprise, even though earlier Christian authors, including the purist North African Tertullian, protested vehemently against 'pagan' usage in a Christian context.[265] Other sources from early medieval Gaul bear witness to a profound knowledge of the ancient authors, particularly Virgil, and the unabashed manner in which it was employed.[266]

Since an exhaustive analysis of the ancient authors that can be traced in the Gothic Missal would far exceed the scope of this introduction, a small number of examples must suffice, in addition to references in the notes to the translation. The most famous Virgilian quotation is the extensive text concerning the bee and her chaste conduct incorporated in the blessing of the paschal candle or *Exultet*. The Easter liturgy seems to be particularly prone to echo Virgil's work, as the expression *sol ... exortus est* (270) illustrates, though further references can be found throughout the sacramentary.[267]

Not all prayers divulge so easily the sources of their inspiration, be they classical or Christian. Quite some number are distinguished by their poetic tone, employing the symbolic language of these traditions without citing a specific author or source. An example is the preface in the Baptismal order of the Easter cycle, no. 255. The beginning of this prayer is poetic in its metaphors of maritime commerce. The faithful are imagined as standing at the

---

[265] CHRISTINE MOHRMANN, 'Le latin langue de la chrétienté occidentale', in MOHRMANN, *Études* I, p. 51–81, at p. 62–63; EAD., 'Observations sur la langue et le style de Tertullien', in MOHRMANN, *Études* II, p. 235–246.

[266] SABINE FIALON, 'L'imprégnation virgillienne dans l'imaginaire marin de deux passions africaines: la *Passio sanctae Salsae* et la *Passio sancti Fabii*', *Latomus* 72 (2013), 208–220; HELMUT REIMITZ, *History, Frankish Identity and the Framing of Western Ethnicity, 550–850* (Cambridge: Cambridge University Press, 2015), p. 86 on Gregory of Tours: 'Gregory of Tours knew his Virgil very well'; JEAN MEYERS, 'Les citations et reminiscences virgiliennes dans les *Libri Historiarum* de Grégoire de Tours', *Pallas* 41 (1995), 67–90.

[267] I am particularly grateful to Gerard Bartelink for pointing out other Virgilian passages in the prayers of the Gothic Missal, such as in nos 225 and 362.

seashore to draw 'new people' – a reference to Eph. 4, 21 here indicating the newly baptised – from the earth 'as merchants pull their
merchandise from the seashore'. The movement 'from the earth'
(*de terra*[268]) is unexpected, given the early Christian understanding of Baptism as a transfer through the waters *to* the dry land,
particularly in the context of Easter and certainly when a *uirga*
is mentioned, the same word that is used for the staff with which
Moses divided the Red Sea (Ex. 14). Here, the baptised are visual-
ised as new shipmates, who sail a new sea and beat it 'not with an
oar, but with the cross, not by a touch but with the mind, not with
a stick but with the sacrament'. It is clear that this prayer makes
use of traditional Christian imagery, such as the sea of faith, the
ship of the Church and the staff that symbolises trust in God, but
it combines them in an entirely new and original way.[269]

The use of turns of phrase that have their origin in a particular author, informative as they are, does not touch on the more
elaborate and complex issue of style, to which we will now turn.
The vocabulary of the Gothic Missal gives evidence of a poetic
style. Examples include the application of Latin neologisms, both
semantic and lexical, in order to avoid (Greek) loanwords (*nuntius*
for *angelus*, 205); the use of rare words that occur mainly in poetry
(*nemus*, 336); the use of plural forms where a singular would suffice (*atria*, 338; *natalium*, 418); the use of an abstract for a concrete
word (*infantiam*, 50; *deitatis*, 476); a personification to indicate an
abstract notion (*metuit gloriosa confessio*, 423).

In addition to singling out words and phrases, by bringing to
light the stylistic structure of the prayers we gain a real sense of
their elevated style. Several examples follow, and more are found
in the notes to the translated prayers. Although we must assume,
as indicated above, that the Gothic Missal as we know it through
Vat. reg. lat. 317 is a composite work, containing prayers by differ-

---

[268] *de terra* is translated as 'from the interior' by ALPHONSE NAPOLÉON
DIDRON, *Christian Iconography, or The History of Christian Art in the Middle Ages*,
transl. E.J. Millington (London: Bohn, 1851), vol. 1, p. 350–351.

[269] Cf. DIDRON, *Christian Iconography*, p. 350–351, who presents this prayer as
'a compendium of the scattered words of the primitive fathers' and as a source of
patristic sea imagery adopted by the medieval Church.

ent authors dating from approximately the late fourth to the late seventh centuries, certain stylistic elements nonetheless recur in a number of prayers of divergent origin. Just one example must suffice here, the *contestatio* in the Mass for Martin, in which the O-exclamations, the anaphoric use of *digne* and the parallelism in the *digne*-sentences are characteristic of the liturgical style of the entire sacramentary.[270]

The *contestatio* for the Mass for Martin (476) is marked by a closely-knit structure, determined by the parallel repetition of the O-exclamations in the first and final parts of the prayer: 'O blessed bounty with which God was clothed. O glorious division of the cloak...' These exclamations praise the elements of sanctity for which Martin is renowned: bounty, charity, the division of the cloak, generosity and virtuous strength. The O-exclamations embrace, as it were, the heart of the prayer, which explicitly explains why Martin is such a great saint and worthy of veneration, expressed by the repeated anaphoric *digne*: 'Rightly have you entrusted him...', 'Rightly was he not subjected...', 'Rightly ... did he not fear...' The structure of O-exclamations which embraces the *digne*-sentences is supported by three parallel *sic-ut* or *ita-ut* comparisons at the opening and close of the prayer: 'He was so perfect that he clothed Christ in the poor', 'He so carried out the office of the episcopate [...] that [...] he enforced obedience to doctrine', 'Through his apostolic strength he has granted a medicine to those who believed, such that he saved...'

O-exclamations are found in a number of Masses for saints: Agnes, Lawrence, Leodegar, Martin, Symphorian and Stephen, particularly in the prayers of sacrifice. They are also found in the *Exultet*, which was long attributed to Ambrose but is now generally considered as a composition originating in late-fourth- or

---

[270] See also ROSE (ed.), *Missale Gothicum*, Introduction, p. 205 (in relation to Stephen); 273 (in relation to Agnes), and ELS ROSE, 'Getroost door de klank van woorden. Het Latijn als sacrale taal van Ambrosiaster tot Alcuin', in GERARD ROUWHORST and PETRA VERSNEL-MERGAERTS (eds), *Taal waarin wij God verstaan. Over taal en vertaling van Schrift en traditie in de liturgie* (Heeswijk: Berne Media, 2015), p. 63–88.

fifth-century (southern) Gaul.[271] The most famous O-exclamation of Latin liturgical literature must be the paradox *O felix culpa*, for which this prayer is known and which is related to Ambrose's soteriology, marked by the idea of a *renovatio in melius*: restoration to a state better than the paradisiacal state.[272] The occurrence of O-exclamations in the prayers mentioned above indicates that this specific stylistic element marked the Gallic liturgical compositions over a long period from the late fourth or early fifth century (date of composition of the *Exultet*, probably also of the Mass for Martin[273]) to the very late seventh century (date of composition of the Mass for Leodegar).

The *contestatio* from Martin's Mass is illustrative of a clear desire to create structure by means of parallelism and strict composition. Other prayers stand out for their dramatic quality in a more emotional or eruptive manner. Examples are found in prayers for *Rogationes* emphasising the misery of fasting in a physical and explicit way, for example 332: 'lying in the mire of dregs and filthy garment of fasting'; 335: 'from those who lie down in the humility of fasting'; 338: 'the sinners who lie prostrate in the filth of their wretchedness'. Such texts almost breathe the stench of humiliation and indignity.

A similarly plastic, physical wording is chosen in the Mass for the Circumcision of the Lord, where, in the collect at the kiss of peace (54), the bodily circumcision is translated into a spiritual amputation of temptation, deceit, defilement and evil and physical longing. The ample use of synonyms for cutting, hewing and amputating adds to the vehemence with which this prayer rejects temptation and sin. This almost violent language is followed by the serenity of the subsequent *immolatio*, which speaks of continuous shelter for the faithful with God: 'For *in you we live, we move and have our being* (Act. 17, 28), and there is neither time nor moment to be spent without the blessings of your love'.

---

[271] FUCHS and WEIKMANN, *Das Exsultet*, p. 17.

[272] AMBROSE, *Explanatio Ps. 39.20*; see the footnotes to no. 225.

[273] ANDRÉ WILMART, 'Saint Ambroise et la Légende dorée', *Ephemerides liturgicae* 50 (1936), 169–202, at p. 202.

A third example that appeals to the emotions of humiliation and self-abasement is found in the Confession of the Priest (275). As we have seen above, the text – considered 'fort décadent' by some[274] – is an emotional outburst of the priest's awareness of his own unworthiness, which must have made no little impression on those present. The manifold repetition of single words expressing an almost desperate plea for salvation is as a continuous beating of the same weak spot until it hurts:

> Come, then, come to help, ineffable love, forgive, forgive me, wonderful Trinity. Spare, spare, spare, so I plea, O appeasable God. Hear, hear, hear me, so I ask, crying out to you...

Figures

Without attempting to be complete, several figures that frequently occur in the Gothic Missal, and the translation problems they pose, are discussed below.

Certain instances of *alliteration* could to some extent be retained in translation, for example the triplet 'triple title of the Trinity' (*trifario titulo trinitatis*, 273). Some prayers make frequent use of the figure, thus heightening the poetic effect, particularly in a performative setting.

The many cases of *asyndeton* are easier to translate, sometimes because the English does not need a conjunction in climactic sequences (3), sometimes because the figure strengthens a certain content, as in 479, where the 'burden of sin' is linked without conjunction to the 'darkness and punishments of hell' to accentuate the notion of repressing weight, or in 403, where the absence of a conjunction between 'palm of martyrdom' and 'perpetual life' marks the essential equality of the two. Certain asyndetic phrases are used to express the emotional content of the prayer. Examples are 481, where the asyndetic series of infinitives representing the faithful's 'inexpressible exultation' ('we praise, we bless, we worship you') makes audible the overflowing gladness that causes

---

[274] SMYTH, *Liturgie oubliée*, p. 205.

them to stammer in their praise; 484, where the asyndetic series of verbs ('you vivify us, sanctify us, prepare us for eternity') represents a climax of gifts of mercy or salvation; and the double asyndeton in 503, where the first series expresses God's ineffable nature ('ineffable, incomprehensible, eternal God'), and the second the response of the faithful in love, veneration, receptiveness and embrace. In other examples the conjunction is added between square brackets (13, 363).

The Gothic Missal contains some fine examples of *chiasmus*, occasionally even creating a sharp contrast between style and grammar. A good example is the collect after the names in the fifth Mass for Lent ('the fasting and prayers of a devoted heart and of the body', 188). Fasting seems to prompt an expression in chiastic oppositions, as we see in the collect after the names for the first Rogation Day ('time to eat ... time to fast': *tempus edendi ... ieiunandi tempus*, 329). The latter prayer is full of strong contrasts between eating and physical health, as opposed to fasting and spiritual well-being; unfortunately, the chiasmus *stricto sensu* is lost in translation.

The *litotes* is a favourite stylistic device in the Gothic Missal. In the present translation, almost all double negations are rendered as accentuated confirmations: *non negatur*, 3, 85, 114; 501; *non diffidimus*, 27; *non ambigua*, 142; *nec inmeritu*, 367; *non fictae*, 465; the related *neminem non pro uitae mori testantur* in 364. The complex example in 72 is further discussed in the section on translation principles.

Anaphoric repetition, finally, abounds in the prayers, as we have already seen in the discussion of the *contestatio* in Martin's Mass. Examples are too numerous to be listed, but it must be said that the figure occurs particularly in the prayers of festive Masses. In the Easter cycle, the phenomenon appears as the repeated *haec est dies* in the *immolatio* of the Easter Vigil (270), with a variant in the collect after the Sanctus in the Mass for Palm Sunday: *haec est sine fine felicitas, haec est beatitudo sine termino*. The *Exultet* not only employs the same phrase (*haec est enim nox, haec sunt festa paschalia*), but, remarkably, reverses the word order in the threefold *haec (igitur) nox est*.

The above examples demonstrate the possibilities and limitations in retaining stylistic characteristics in translation. It is the aim of the present translation to make the prayers of the Gothic Missal accessible to a broad public of interested readers, and the wish of the translator to give an impression of the rich and complex Latin that marks the period in which this sacramentary was created and used.

BIBLIOGRAPHY

Abbreviations

AASS   *Acta sanctorum* (Paris: Palmé, 1863–1940)

BHL   *Bibliotheca hagiographica latina antiquae et mediae aetatis* (Brussels: Via dicta 'des Ursulines', 1898–1901)

BnF   Bibliothèque nationale de France

CCCM   *Corpus christianorum continuatio mediaevalis* (Turnhout: Brepols, 1966-)

CCSA   *Corpus christianorum series apocryphorum* (Turnhout: Brepols, 1983-)

CCSL   *Corpus christianorum series latina* (Turnhout: Brepols, 1953-)

CLA   *Codices latini antiquiores. A Palaeographical Guide to Latin Manuscripts Prior to the Ninth Century*, ed. Elias A. Lowe, 11 vols. with a supplement (Oxford: Clarendon Press, 1934–1966)

CSEL   *Corpus scriptorum ecclesiasticorum latinorum* (Vienna: Hoelder-Pichler-Tempsky, 1866-)

DACL   *Dictionnaire d'archéologie chrétienne et de liturgie*, ed. Fernand Cabrol and Henri Leclercq (Paris: Letouzey, 1907–1953)

GCS — *Die griechischen christlichen Schriftsteller der ersten drei Jahrhunderte* (Leipzig: Hinrich, 1899–1955)

HBS — Henry Bradshaw Society

MGH — Monumenta Germaniae historica

AA — Auctores antiquissimi, 15 vols (Berlin: Weidmann, 1877-)

CRF — Capitularia regum Francorum (Hanover: Hahn, 1883-)

SRM — Scriptores rerum Merovingicarum (Hanover: Hahn, 1885–1979)

NRSV — The Bible. New Revised Standard Version Anglicized Edition (Oxford: Oxford University Press, 1995)

PG — *Patrologiae cursus completus series graeca*, ed. Jacques-Paul Migne (Paris: Garnier, 1857–1866)

PL — *Patrologiae cursus completus series latina*, ed. Jacques-Paul Migne (Paris: Siroune, 1844–1890)

RAC — *Reallexikon für Antike und Christentum* (Stuttgart, 1950-)

SChr — *Sources chrétiennes* (Paris: Cerf, 1941-)

Vulgate — *Biblia sacra Vulgata* (Stuttgart: Deutsche Bibelgesellschaft, 1994)

Manuscripts

MS Autun BM 184
MS Montpellier H 55
MS Paris, BnF lat. 10837
MS Vat. reg. lat. 317

Primary sources

Acts of Peter, transl. JAMES K. ELLIOTT, *The Apocryphal New Testament. A Collection of Apocryphal Christian Literature in an English Translation Based on M.R. James* (Oxford: Clarendon Press, 1993), p. 390–426

Admonitio generalis, ed. HUBERT MORDEK, KLAUS ZECHIEL-ECKES and MICHAEL GLATTHAAR, *Die Admonitio generalis Karls des Großen*, MGH Fontes iuris germanici antiqui in usum scholarum separatim editi 16 (Wiesbaden: Harrasowitz, 2013)

Adsumptio sanctae Mariae, ed. ANDRÉ WILMART, *Analecta reginensia. Extraits des manuscrits latins de la reine Christine conservés au Vatican* (Città del Vaticano: Biblioteca apostolica vaticana, 1933), p. 323–357

ALCUIN, *Epistulae*, ed. ERNST DÜMMLER, *Epistolae karolini aevi II*, MGH Epistolae 4 (Berlin: Weidmann, 1895)

AMBROSIASTER, *Commentarius in epistulas Pauli*, ed. HEINRICH I. VOGELS, *Ambrosiastri qui dicitur Commentarius in epistulas Pauli*, 3 vols., CSEL 81 (Vienna: Hoelder-Pichler-Tempsky, 1966–1969)

AMBROSIUS MEDIOLANENSIS, *De Noe*, ed. KARL SCHENKL, *Sancti Ambrosii opera*, CSEL 32.1 (Vienna: Tempsky, 1897), p. 411–497

AMBROSIUS MEDIOLANENSIS, *De paradiso*, ed. KARL SCHENKL, *Sancti Ambrosii opera*, CSEL 32.1 (Vienna: Tempsky, 1897), p. 265–336

AMBROSIUS MEDIOLANENSIS, *De sacramentis*, ed. OTTO FALLER, CSEL 73 (Vienna: Tempsky, 1955), p. 15–85

AMBROSIUS MEDIOLANENSIS, *De uirginitate*, ed. F. GORI, *Opera omnia di Sant' Ambrogio*, vol. 14.2 (Milano: Biblioteca Ambrosiana, 1989)

AMBROSIUS MEDIOLANENSIS, *Explanatio Psalmorum XII*, ed. MICHAEL PETSCHENIG, CSEL 64 (Vienna: Verlag der Österreichischen Akademie der Wissenschaften, 1954/1999)

AMBROSIUS MEDIOLANENSIS, *Expositio psalmi CXVIII*, ed. MARC PETSCHENIG, CSEL 62 (Vienna: Verlag der Österreichischen Akademie der Wissenschaften, 1913/1999 Michaela Zelzer)

AMBROSIUS MEDIOLANENSIS, *Expositio evangelii secundum Lucam*, ed. MARC ADRIAEN and PAOLO A. BALLERINI, *Expositio evangelii secundum Lucam*, CCSL 14 (Turnhout: Brepols, 1957)

AMMIANUS MARCELLINUS, *Rerum gestarum libri qui supersunt*, ed. WOLFGANG SEYFARTH (Stuttgart-Leipzig: Teubner, 1999)

Armenian Lectionary, ed. ATHANASE RENOUX, *Le codex arménien Jérusalem 121 I: Introduction aux origines de la liturgie hiérosolymitaine. Lumières nouvelles*, in FRANÇOIS GRAFFIN, Patrologia orientalis 35, vol. 1

(Turnhout: Brepols, 1969) and ID., *Le codex arménien Jérusalem 121 II: Édition comparée du texte et de deux autres manuscrits*, in FRANÇOIS GRAFFIN, Patrologia orientalis 36, vol. 2 (Turnhout: Brepols, 1971)

AURELIUS AUGUSTINUS, *De doctrina christiana*, ed. JOSEPH MARTIN, CCSL 32 (Turnhout: Brepols, 1962), p. 1–167

AURELIUS AUGUSTINUS, *De civitate Dei*, ed. BERNHARD DOMBAART and ALPHONS KALB, CCSL 47–48 (Turnhout: Brepols, 1955)

AURELIUS AUGUSTINUS, *Enarrationes in Psalmos*, ed. ELIGIUS DEKKERS and JEAN FRAIPONT, CCSL 40 (Turnhout: Brepols, 1966)

AURELIUS AUGUSTINUS, *Epistulae*, ed. ALOIS GOLDBACHER and JOHANNES DIVJAK, CSEL 34, 44, 57–58, 88 (Vienna: Tempsky, 1895–1981)

AURELIUS AUGUSTINUS, *In Iohannis euangelium tractatus*, ed. RADBOUD WILLEMS, CCSL 36 (Turnhout: Brepols, 1954)

AURELIUS AUGUSTINUS, *Sermo* 273, ed. JACQUES PAUL MIGNE, PL 38, col. 1250–1251

AURELIUS AUGUSTINUS, *Sermones*, ed. CYRIL LAMBOT, CCSL 41 (Turnhout: Brepols, 1966)

Breviarium apostolorum, in ANTOINE DUMAS and JEAN DESHUSSES (eds), *Liber sacramentorum Gellonensis*, CCSL 159 (Turnhout: Brepols, 1981), p. 489–490

CAESARIUS ARELATENSIS, *Sermones*, ed. GERMAIN MORIN, CCSL 103–104 (Turnhout: Brepols, 1953)

Calendar of 354, ed. HANS LIETZMANN, *Die drei ältesten Martyrologien* (Bonn: Marcus and Weber, 1911), p. 2–4

Calendar of Carthage, ed. HANS LIETZMANN, *Die drei ältesten Martyrologien* (Bonn: Marcus and Weber, 1911), p. 4–6

Calendar of Tours, GREGORIUS TURONENSIS, *Historiae* X.31, ed. BRUNO KRUSCH and WILHELM LEVISON, MGH SRM I.1 (Hanover: Hahn, 1951), p. 529–530

Calendar of Willibrord, ed. HENRY A. WILSON, *The Calendar of Willibrord*, HBS 55 (London: Henry Bradshaw Society, 1918)

CHROMATIUS AQUILEIENSIS, *Sermo* 17, ed. JOSEPH LEMARIÉ, *Chromatii Aquileiensis opera*, CCSL 9A (Turnhout: Brepols, 1974)

Conciliae, ed. JOSÉ VIVES, *Concilios Visigóticos e Hispano-Romanos* (Barcelona-Madrid: Consejo Superior de Investigaciones Científicas, 1963)

Conciliae, ed. FRIEDRICH MAASSEN, MGH Conciliae aevi Merovingici (Hanover: Hahn, 1893)

Conciliae, ed. JEAN GAUDEMET and BRIGITTE BASDEVANT, *Les canons des conciles mérovingiens (VIe–VIIe siècles)*, SChr 354 (Paris: Cerf, 1989)

Corpus benedictionum pontificalium, ed. EUGÈNE MOELLER, CCSL 162 (Turnhout: Brepols, 1971)

CYPRIANUS, *De opere et eleemosynis*, ed. MANLIO SIMONETTI, *Sancti Cypriani episcopi opera*, CCSL 3A (Turnhout: Brepols, 1976), p. 53–72

CYPRIANUS, *Epistulae*, ed. WILHELM HARTEL, CSEL 3.2 (Vienna: Geroldi, 1871)

CYPRIANUS, *Epistulae*, ed. GERARDUS F. DIERCKS, *Sancti Cypriani episcopi epistularium*, CCSL 3C (Turnhout: Brepols, 1996)

ENNODIUS, *Benedictio cerei*, ed. FRIEDRICH VOGEL, MGH AA 7, p. 18–20

Epistola Luciani ad omnem ecclesiam de revelatione corporis Stephani martyris. Transl. Avitus of Braga; ed. ÉTIENNE VANDERLINDEN, *Revelatio sancti Stephani*, in *Revue des Études Byzantines* 4 (1946), 178–217

Epistola presbyterum et diaconorum Achaiae, ed. MAXIMILIAN BONNET, *Acta apostolorum apocrypha* (Leipzig: Mendelssohn, 1898 / Hildesheim: Georg Olms, 1990), vol. 2.1, p. 1–37

Eucharist Sacramentary. North American Old Catholic Church (s.l., s.a.)

Expositio missae, ed. PHILIPPE BERNARD, *Epistolae de ordine sacrae oblationis et de diversis charismatibus ecclesiae / Germano Parisiensi episcopo adscriptae*, CCCM 187 (Turnhout: Brepols, 2007)

GREGORIUS MAGNUS, *Homiliae in euangelia*, ed. RAYMON ÉTAIX, CCSL 141 (Turnhout: Brepols, 1999)

GREGORIUS MAGNUS, *Moralia in Iob*, ed. MARC ADRIAEN, CCSL 143 (Turnhout: Brepols, 1979)

GREGORIUS NYSSENUS, *In Basilium fratrem*, ed. JACQUES PAUL MIGNE, PG 46, col. 787–818

GREGORIUS THAUMATURGUS, *Homily concerning the Holy Mother of God*, transl. (from the Armenian) by FREDERICK C. CONYBEARE, *The Expositor*, 5th series, vol. 3 (1896), p. 161–173

GREGORIUS TURONENSIS, *Libri historiarum X*, ed. BRUNO KRUSCH and WILHELM LEVISON, MGH SRM I.1 (Hanover: Hahn, 1951)

GREGORIUS TURONENSIS, *Libri IV de uirtutibus sancti Martini episcopi*, ed. BRUNO KRUSCH, MGH SRM 1.2 (Hanover: Hahn, 1885), p. 584–661

GREGORIUS TURONENSIS, *Liber in Gloria confessorum*, ed. BRUNO KRUSCH, MGH SRM 1.2 (Hanover: Hahn, 1885), p. 744–820

GREGORIUS TURONENSIS, *Liber in gloria martyrum*, ed. BRUNO KRUSCH, MGH SRM I.2 (Hanover: Hahn, 1885), p. 484–561

HIERONYMUS, *De uiris illustribus*. E.C. Richardson (ed.), *Texte und Untersuchungen zur Geschichte der altchristlichen Literatur 14/1a* (Leipzig: Hinrich, 1896)

HIERONYMUS, *Epistulae*, ed. JACQUES PAUL MIGNE, PL 30

HILARIUS PICTAVIENSIS, *Commentarius in Matthaeum*, ed. JEAN DOIGNON, *Sur Matthieu*, SChr 254, 258 (Paris: Cerf, 1978–1979)

INNOCENTIUS I, *Epistula ad Decentium*, ed. ROBERT CABIÉ, *La lettre du pape Innocent Ier à Décentius de Gubbio (19 mars 416)*, Bibliothèque de la RHE 58 (Louvain, 1973), 44–52

IRENAEUS LUGDUNENSIS, *Aduersus haereses*, ed. ADELIN ROUSSEAU and LOUIS DOUTRELAU, SChr 34, 100, 152–153, 210–211, 263–264, 293–294 (Paris: Cerf, 1952-...)

Irish Palimpsest Sacramentary, ed. ALBAN DOLD and LEO EIZENHÖFER, *Das irische Palimpsestsakramentar im CLM 14429 der Staatsbibliothek München* (Beuron: Beuroner Kunstverlag, 1964)

ISIDORUS HISPALENSIS, *De ecclesiasticis officiis*, ed. CHRISTOPHER M. LAWSON, CCSL 113 (Turnhout: Brepols, 1989)

ISIDORUS HISPALENSIS, *De ortu et obitu patrum*, ed. C. CHAPARRO GÓMEZ, *De ortu et obitu patrum* (Paris, 1985)

ISIDORUS HISPALENSIS, *De ecclesiasticis officiis*, transl. THOMAS L. KNOEBEL, *De ecclesiasticis officiis*, Ancient Christian Writers 61 (New York: Newman Press, 2008)

Itinerarium Egeriae, ed. PAUL GEYER et al., *Itineraria et alia geographica*, CCSL 175 (Turnhout: Brepols, 1965), p. 37–90

Karoli epistola generalis, ed. ALFRED BORETIUS, MGH Leges, CRF I, no. 30, p. 80

Lectionarium Luxouiense, ed. PIERRE SALMON, *Le lectionnaire de Luxeuil (Paris, ms. lat. 9427)* (Rome: Abbaye Saint-Jérome, 1944)

LEO MAGNUS, *Sermones*, ed. JEAN LECLERCQ and RENÉ DOLLE, SChr 22bis (Paris: Cerf, 1964)

Liber de miraculis beati Andreae apostoli, ed. JEAN-MARC PRIEUR, *Acta Andreae*, CCSA 6 (Turnhout: Brepols, 1989)

Liber mozarabicus sacramentorum, ed. MARIUS FÉROTIN (Paris: Firmin-Didot, 1912, repr. by ANTHONY WARD and CUTHBERT JOHNSON [Rome: CLV Edizioni liturgiche, 1995])

Liber pontificalis, ed. LOUIS DUCHESNE, *Liber pontificalis* (Paris: De Boccard, 1955–1957)

Liber Sacramentorum Engolismensis, ed. PATRICK SAINT ROCH, CCSL 159C (Turnhout: Brepols, 1987)

Liber Sacramentorum Gellonensis, ed. ALEXANDRE DUMAS and JEAN DESHUSSES, CCSL 159–159A (Turnhout: Brepols, 1981)

TITUS LIVIUS, *Ab urbe condita*, ed. WILHELM WEISSENBORN and H.J. MÜLLER, *Titi Livi Ab urbe condita libri* (Berlin: Weidmann, 1962)

Martyrologium Hieronymianum, ed. HIPPOLYTE DELEHAYE, *Commentarius perpetuus in Martyrologium Hieronymianum ad recensionem H. Quentin*. AASS novembris II.2 (Paris: Palmé, 1931)

Martyrologium Syriacum, ed. HANS LIETZMANN, *Die drei ältesten Martyrologien* (Bonn: Marcus and Weber, 1911), p. 7–15

Missale Gallicanum Vetus, ed. LEO C. MOHLBERG, Rerum ecclesiasticarum documenta, Series Maior, Fontes 3 (Rome: Herder, 1958)

Missale Gothicum, ed. GIUSEPPE M. TOMASI (ed.), *Codices Sacramentorum nongentis annis uetustiores* (Rome: ex typographia Angeli Bernabò, 1680)

Missale Gothicum, ed. HENRY M. BANNISTER, *Missale Gothicum: A Gallican Sacramentary* (London: Henry Bradshaw Society, 1917–1919)

Missale Gothicum, ed. LEO C. MOHLBERG, *Missale Gothicum (Vat. Reg. Lat. 317)*, Rerum ecclesiarcarum documenta, Series marior, Fontes 5 (Rome: Herder, 1961)

Missale Gothicum, ed. ELS ROSE, *Missale Gothicum e codice Vaticano Reginensi latino 317 editum*, CCSL 159D (Turnhout: Brepols, 2005)

Missale Gothicum, ed. LEO C. MOHLBERG, *Missale Gothicum. Das gallikanische Sakramentar (Cod. Vatican. Regin. Lat. 317) des VII.–VIII. Jahrhunderts. Facsimile und Kommentar* (Augsburg: Filser, 1929)

ORIGENES, *Contra Celsum*, ed. PAUL KOETSCHAU, GCS Origenes 1 (Leipzig: Hinrich, 1899)

PUBLIUS OVIDIUS NASO, *Tristia*, ed. JACQUES ANDRÉ, *Ovide, Triste. Texte et traduction* (Paris: Belles Lettres, 1968)

Passio Acaunensium, ed. BRUNO KRUSCH, MGH SRM III (Hanover: Hahn, 1896), p. 23–41

Passio Agnetis, ed. JACQUES PAUL MIGNE, PL 17, col. 735–742

Passio Andreae 'Conuersante et docente', ed. MAXIMILIAN BONNET, '*Passio sancti Andreae apostoli*', *Analecta Bollandiana* 13 (1894), 373–378

Passio Caeciliae, ed. HIPPOLYTE DELEHAYE, *Étude sur le légendier romain. Les saints de novembre et de décembre*, Subsidia hagiographica 23 (Brussels: Société des Bollandistes, 1936), p. 194–220

Passio Clementis, ed. FRANCISCUS XAVERIUS FUNK and FRANCISCUS DIEKAMP, *Patres apostolici*, vol. 2 (Tübingen: Laupp, 1913), p. 50–91

Passio Eulaliae, ed. ENRIQUE FLOREZ, *España sagrada* (Madrid: Antonio Marin, 1771–1908), vol. 13, p. 398–406

Passio Ferreoli et Ferrucionis, ed. *Acta Sanctorum Iunii IV*, vol. 24, p. 5–15

Passio Leudegarii I, ed. BRUNO KRUSCH and WILHELM LEVISON, MGH SRM V (Hanover-Leipzig: Hahn, 1910), p. 282–322

Passio Saturnini episcopi Tolosani et martyri, ed. THIERRY RUINART, *Acta primorum martyrum sincera et selecta* (Amsterdam, 1713²), p. 129–133

Passio Symphoriani, ed. THIERRY RUINART, *Acta primorum martyrum sincera et selecta* (Amsterdam, 1713²), p. 79–83

Passio sanctorum Xysti et Laurentii, in *Passio Polochronii*, ed. HIPPOLYTE DELEHAYE, 'Recherches sur le légendier romain', *Analecta Bollandiana* 51 (1933), 72–98

PRUDENTIUS, *Liber Cathemerinon*, ed. MAURICE P. CUNNINGHAM, *Carmina*, CCSL 126 (Turnhout: Brepols, 1966), p. 3–72

PRUDENTIUS, *Liber Peristephanon*, ed. MAURICE P. CUNNINGHAM, *Carmina*, CCSL 126 (Turnhout: Brepols, 1966), p. 250–389

Recognitiones, transl. PIERRE GEOLTRAIN and JEAN-DANIEL KAESTLI (eds). *Écrits apocryphes chrétiens*, vol. 2 (Paris: Gallimard, 2005), 1175–2003

Sacramentarium Bergomense, ed. ANGELO PAREDI, *Manoscritto del secolo IX della Biblioteca di S. Alessandro in Colonna in Bergamo. Trascritto da Angelo Paredi. Tavole comparative da Giusepe Fassi* (Bergamo: Monumenta Bergomensia, 1962)

Sacramentarium Gelasianum Vetus, ed. LEO C. MOHLBERG, *Liber sacramentorum romanae ecclesiae ordinis anni circuli* (Rome: Herder, 1968)

Sacramentarium Gregorianum Hadrianum, ed. JEAN DESHUSSES, *Le sacramentaire Grégorien: ses principales formes d'après les plus anciens manuscrits*, Spicilegium Friburgense, vols 16, 18, 24 (Fribourg: Éditions universitaires, 1971–1982)

Sacramentarium Veronense, ed. LEO C. MOHLBERG (Rome: Herder, 1994³)

SEDULIUS SCOTUS, *Carmen Paschale*, ed. JOHANN HUEMER, *Sedulii opera omnia*, CSEL 10 (Vienna: Geroldi, 1885), 1–146

SIDONIUS APOLLINARIS, *Epistulae*, ed. ANDRÉ LOYEN, *Sidoine Apollinaire*, vol. 2–3: *Lettres* (Paris: Belles Lettres, 1970)

SULPICIUS SEVERUS, *Dialogi*, ed. CHARLES HALM, CSEL 1 (Vienna: Gerold, 1866), p. 152–216

SULPICIUS SEVERUS, *Vita Martini*, ed. JACQUES FONTAINE, *Vie de Saint Martin*, SChr 133–135 (Paris: Cerf, 1967–1969)

Synod of Frankfurt (794), ed. ALBERT WERMINGHOFF, MGH Concilia aevi Karolini I, p. 165–171

TATIANUS, *Diatesseron*, transl. J. HAMLYN HILL, *The Earliest Life of Christ Ever Compiled from the Four Gospels: Being the Diatessaron of Tatian* (Piscataway NJ: Gorgias Press, 2006; facs. repr. of the original edition published in Edinburgh 1910)

TERTULLIANUS AFER, *De monogamia*, ed. PAUL MATTEI, SChr 343 (Paris: Cerf, 1988)

Transitus Mariae, MS Montpellier H 55, f. 97v–101r

VENANTIUS FORTUNATUS, *Pange lingua*, ed. GUIDO DREVES (ed.), *Analecta Hymnica Medii Aevi*, vol. 50 (Leipzig: Reisland, 1907), p. 70–73

VENANTIUS FORTUNATUS, *Vexilla regis*, ed. GUIDO DREVES (ed.), *Analecta Hymnica Medii Aevi*, vol. 50 (Leipzig: Reisland, 1907), p. 74–75

Secondary sources

EMILY ALBU, 'The Battle of the Maps in a Christian Empire', in CLAUDIA RAPP and HALL A. DRAKE (eds), *The City in the Classical and Post-Classical World. Changing Contexts of Power and Identity* (Cambridge: Cambridge University Press, 2014), p. 202–216

CLIFFORD ANDO, *Imperial Ideology and Provincial Loyalty* (Berkeley CA: University of California Press, 2000), p. 277–335

ARNOLD ANGENENDT, 'Sacrifice, Gifts, and Prayers in Latin Christianity', in TOM NOBLE and JULIA SMITH (eds), *The Cambridge History of Christianity vol. 3: Early Medieval Christianities c. 600–c. 1100* (Cambridge: Cambridge University Press, 2008), p. 453–471

ANTONIA ATANASSOVA, 'Did Cyril of Alexandria Invent Mariology?' in CHRIST MAUNDER (ed.), *Origins of the Cult of the Virgin Mary* (London-New York: Burns and Oates, 2008), p. 105–125

BARBARA BAERT, *A Heritage of Holy Wood. The Legend of the True Cross in Text and Image*, Cultures, Beliefs and Traditions 22 (Leiden: Brill, 2004)

JOHN BALDOVIN, *The Urban Character of Christian Worship. The Origins, Development, and Meaning of Stational Liturgy*, Orientalia christiana analecta 228 (Rome: Pontificium institutum studiorum orientalium, 1987)

MICHEL BANNIARD, *Viva voce. Communication écrite et communication orale du IVe au IXe siècle en Occident latin*, Collection des Études augustiniennes: Série Moyen Âge et Temps Modernes 25 (Paris: Institut des études augustiniennes, 1992)

MICHEL BANNIARD, 'Language and Communication in Carolingian Europe', in ROSAMOND MCKITTERICK (ed.), *The New Cambridge Medieval History*, vol. 2 (Cambridge: Cambridge University Press, 1995), p. 695–708

MICHEL BANNIARD, 'The Transition from Latin to the Romance Languages', in MARTIN MAIDEN et al. (eds), *The Cambridge History of the Romance Languages*, vol. 2 (Cambridge: Cambridge University Press, 2013), p. 57–106

GERARD BARTELINK, 'Denominations of the devil and demons in the *Missale Gothicum*', in NIENKE VOS and WILLEMIEN OTTEN (eds), *Demons and the Devil in Ancient and Medieval Christianity*, Supplements to Vigiliae Christianae 108 (Leiden: Brill, 2011), p. 195–209

PIERRE BATIFFOL, 'L'*Expositio missae* attribuée à saint Germain de Paris', *Études de liturgie et d'archéologie chrétienne* (Paris: Gabalda, 1919), p. 245–290

LOUISE BATSTONE, 'Doctrinal and Theological Themes in the Prayers of the Bobbio Missal', in YITZHAK HEN and ROB MEENS (eds), *The Bobbio Missal. Liturgy and Religious Culture in Merovingian Gaul* (Cambridge: Cambridge University Press, 2004), p. 168–184

STEPHEN BENKO, *The Virgin Goddess. Studies in the Pagan and Christian Roots of Mariology* (Leiden-New York-Cologne: Brill, 1993)

PHILIPPE BERNARD, *Du chant romain au chant grégorien* (Paris: Cerf, 1996)

PHILIPPE BERNARD, 'Les diptyques du monastère des Saints-Apôtres d'Arles au VIIᵉ siècle. Édition critique. Commentaire historique et liturgique', *Revue d'histoire de l'église de France* 89 (2003), 5–21

PHILIPPE BERNARD, *Transitions liturgiques en Gaule carolingienne. Une traduction commentée des deux 'lettres' faussement attribuées à l'évêque Germain de Paris* (Paris: Hora decima, 2008)

Bibliotheca hagiographica latina antiquae et mediae aetatis (Brussels: Via dicta 'des Ursulines', 1898–1901)

EDMUND BISHOP, 'Appendix. Observations on the Liturgy of Narsai', in RICHARD H. CONNOLLY, *The Liturgical Homilies of Narsai* (Cambridge: Cambridge University Press, 1909, reprinted 1967), p. 85–163

EDMUND BISHOP, *Liturgica historica: Papers on the Liturgy and Religious Life of the Western Church* (Oxford: Clarendon, 1918, repr. 1962)

SIBLE DE BLAAUW, *Cultus et decor. Liturgia e architettura nella Roma tardoantica e medievale* (Vatican City: Biblioteca apostolica vaticana, 1994)

ALBERT BLAISE, *Dictionnaire latin-français des auteurs chrétiens* (Turnhout: Brepols, 1954)

ALBERT BLAISE, *Le vocabulaire latin des principaux thèmes liturgiques* (Turnhout: Brepols, 1966)

ALBERT BLAISE, *Dictionnaire latin-français des auteurs du Moyen-Âge* (Turnhout: Brepols, 1975)

COURTNEY BOOKER, 'The Dionysian Mirror of Louis the Pious', *Quaestiones medii aevi novae* 19 (2014), 243–264

BERNARD BOTTE, '*Prima resurrectio*, un vestige de millénarisme dans les liturgies occidentales', *Recherches de théologie ancienne et médiévale* 15 (1948), 5–17

FRANÇOIS BOVON, *Das Evangelium nach Lukas vol. 1: Lk. 1,1–9,50*, Evangelisch-Katholischer Kommentar zum Neuen Testament III.1 (Zürich: Benziger Verlag, 1989)

PAUL BRADSHAW, *The Search for the Origins of Christian Worship*, 2nd edition (Oxford: Oxford University Press, 2002)

PETER BROWN, *The Rise of Western Christendom. Triumph and Diversity, A.D. 200–1000*, tenth anniversary revised edition (Chichester-Malden MA: Wiley-Blackwell, 2013)

PETER BROWN, *The Ransom of the Soul: Afterlife and Wealth in Early Western Christianity* (Cambridge, MA: Harvard University Press, 2015)

RÉGIS BURNET, *Les douze apôtres. Histoire de la réception des figures apostoliques dans le christianisme ancien* (Turnhout: Brepols, 2014)

FERNAND CABROL, 'Diptyques (liturgiques)', in DACL 4.1, col. 1045–1094

FERNAND CABROL, *La messe en occident* (Paris: Bloud et Gay, 1932)

BERNARD CAPELLE, 'La nativité de la Vierge dans le Missale Gothicum', *Revue Bénédictine* 58 (1948), 73–76

BERNARD CAPELLE, 'La messe gallicane de l'Assomption: son rayonnement, ses sources', in *Miscellanea liturgica in honorem L. Cuniberti Mohlberg*, 2 vols. (Rome: Bibliotheca 'Ephemerides liturgicae' 22 and 23, 1948–1949), vol. 2, p. 33–59

GILES CONSTABLE, 'The Commemoration of the Dead in the Early Middle Ages', in JULIA SMITH (ed.), *Early Medieval Rome and the Christian West: Essays in Honour of Donald Bullough* (Leiden-Boston: Brill, 2000), p. 169–195

OSCAR CULLMANN, *Saint Pierre, disciple, apôtre, martyr: histoire et théologie* (Paris: Delachaux and Nestlié, 1952)

PAUL DE CLERCK, *La prière universelle dans les liturgies latines anciennes. Témoignages patristiques et textes liturgiques*, Liturgiewissenschaftliche Quellen und Forschungen 62 (Münster: Aschendorff, 1977)

PAUL DE CLERCK, 'Les prières d'intercession. Rapports entre Orient et Occident', *La Maison-Dieu* 183–184 (1990), 171–189

BAUDOUIN DE GAIFFIER, 'A propos d'un passage du "Missale Gothicum".
S. Saturnin de Toulouse venait-il d'Orient?', *Analecta Bollandiana*
66 (1948), 53–58

WALTER DIEZINGER, *Effectus in der römischen Liturgie. Eine kultsprachliche Untersuchung* (Bonn: Hanstein, 1961)

ALPHONSE NAPOLÉON DIDRON, *Christian Iconography, or The History
of Christian Art in the Middle Ages*, transl. E.J. Millington (London:
Bohn, 1851), vol. 1

GREGORY DIX, *The Shape of the Liturgy* (Westminster: Dacre Press, 1947)

ALLAN DOIG, *Liturgy and Architecture from the Early Church to the Middle Ages* (Aldershot: Ashgate, 2008)

SIEGMAR DÖPP and WILHELM GEERLINGS, *Lexikon der antiken christlichen Literatur* (Freiburg i.Breisgau: Herder, 1998)

WOLFRAM DREWS, 'Jews as Pagans? Polemical Definitions of Identity in
Visigothic Spain', *Early Medieval Europe* 11 (2002), 189–207

CHARLES DU FRESNE SIEUR DU CANGE, *Glossarium mediae et infimae
latinitatis* (repr. Graz: Akademische Druck- und Verlagsanstalt, 1954)

JACQUES DUBOIS, *Les martyrologes du Moyen Âge latin*, Typologie des
sources du Moyen Âge occidental 26 (Turnhout: Brepols, 1978)

LOUIS DUCHESNE, *Les origines du culte chrétien* (Paris: Boccard, 1925³)

PETER VAN DER EERDEN, 'Engelen en demonen', in MANUEL STOFFERS
(ed.), *De middeleeuwse ideeënwereld, 1000–1300* (Heerlen-Hilversum
1994), p. 117–143

LEO EIZENHÖFER, 'Die Präfation für den Geburtstag der heiligen Agnes',
Archiv für Liturgiewissenschaft 11 (1969), 59–76

MARY PIERRE ELLEBRACHT, *Remarks on the Vocabulary of the Ancient
Orations in the Missale Romanum* (Nijmegen: Dekker & Van de Vegt,
1963)

EVERETT FERGUSON, *Baptism in the Early Church: History, Theology,
and Liturgy in the First Five Centuries* (Grand Rapids, MI-Cambridge:
William B. Eerdmans, 2009)

SABINE FIALON, 'L'imprégnation virgilienne dans l'imaginaire marin de
deux passions africaines: la *Passio sanctae Salsae* et la *Passio sancti Fabii*', *Latomus* 72 (2013), 208–220

EDWARD FOLEY, 'The Song of the Assembly in Medieval Eucharist', in
LIZETTE LARSON-MILLER, *Medieval Liturgy. A Book of Essays* (New
York-London: Garland Publishing, 1997), p. 203–234

GEORGES FOLLIET, 'La *spoliatio Aegyptiorum* (Exode 3: 21–23, 11: 2–3; 12:
35–36). Les interprétations de cette images chez les Pères et autres écrivains ecclésiastiques', *Traditio* 57 (2002), 1–48

YANIV FOX, *Power and Religion in Merovingian Gaul: Columbanian Monasticism and the Frankish Elites*, Cambridge Studies in Medieval Life and Thought: Fourth Series 98 (Cambridge: Cambridge University Press, 2014)

GUIDO FUCHS and HANS MARTIN WEIKMANN, *Das Exsultet. Geschichte, Theologie und Gestaltung der österlichen Lichtdanksagung* (Regensburg: Pustet, 1992)

KLAUS GAMBER, *Ordo antiquus gallicanus: Der gallikanische Messritus des 6. Jahrhunderts* (Regensburg: Pustet, 1965)

MARY GARRISON, 'The *Missa pro principe* in the Bobbio Missal', in YITZHAK HEN and ROB MEENS (eds), *The Bobbio Missal. Liturgy and Religious Culture in Merovingian Gaul* (Cambridge: Cambridge University Press, 2004), p. 187–205

PATRICK GEARY, *Living with the Dead in the Middle Ages* (Ithaca-London: Cornell University Press, 1994)

WILHELM GEERLINGS, 'Ambrosiaster', in SIEGMAR DÖPP and WILHELM GEERLINGS (eds): *Lexikon der antiken christlichen Literatur* (Freiburg-Basel-Vienna: Herder, 1998)

ANNE-VÉRONIQUE GILLES, 'L'évolution de l'hagiographie de saint Saturnin de Toulouse et son influence sur la liturgie', in *Liturgie et musique (IXᵉ–Xᵉ siècle)*, Cahiers de Fanjeaux 17 (Toulouse: Privat, 1982), p. 359–379

ANNE-VÉRONIQUE GILLES, 'Le dossier hagiographique de saint Saturnin de Toulouse', in MONIQUE GOULLET and MARTIN HEINZELMANN (eds), *Miracles, vies et réécritures dans l'Occident médiéval*, Beihefte der Francia 65 (Ostfildern: Thorbecke, 2006), p. 341–405

RÉMI GOUNELLE, *La descente du Christ aux enfers. Institutionnalisation d'une croyance* (Paris: Cerf, 2000)

ÉLIE GRIFFE, 'Aux origines de la liturgie gallicane', *Bulletin de littérature ecclésiastique* 52 (1951), 17–33

ÉLIE GRIFFE, *La Gaule chrétienne à l'époque romaine*, 3 vols. (Paris: Letouzey and Ané, 1964–1966)

CARL I. HAMMER, 'The Social Landscape of the Prague Sacramentary: The Prosopography of an Eighth-Century Mass-Book', *Traditio* 54 (1999), 41–80

PHILIP HARNONCOURT and HANS-JÖRG AUF DER MAUR, *Feiern im Rhythmus der Zeit* II.1, Gottesdienst der Kirche, Handbuch der Liturgiewissenschaft VI.1 (Regensburg: Pustet, 1983)

YITZHAK HEN, *Culture and Religion in Merovingian Gaul A.D. 481–751* (Leiden-Boston: Brill, 1994)

YITZHAK HEN, *The Royal Patronage of Liturgy in Frankish Gaul. To the Death of Charles the Bald (877)* (London: HBS, 2001)

YITZHAK HEN, 'The Liturgy of the Bobbio Missal', in YITZHAK HEN and ROB MEENS (eds), *The Bobbio Missal. Liturgy and Religious Culture in Merovingian Gaul* (Cambridge: Cambridge University Press, 2004), p. 140–153

YITZHAK HEN, 'Wilhelm Levison's Willibrord and Echternach', in MATTHIAS BECHER and YITZHAK HEN (eds), *Wilhelm Levison (1876–1947). Ein jüdisches Forscherleben zwischen wissenschaftlicher Anerkennung und politischem Exil*, Bonner historische Forschungen 63 (Siegburg: Franz Schmitt, 2010), p. 187–198

YITZHAK HEN, 'The Church in Sixth-Century Gaul', in ALEXANDER MURRAY (ed.), *A Companion to Gregory of Tours*, Brill's Companions to the Christian Tradition 63 (Leiden: Brill, 2016), p. 232–255

József HERMAN, *Vulgar Latin*, transl. Roger Wright (University Park, PA: Pennsylvania State University Press, 2000)

SAMANTHA KAHN HERRICK, *Imagining the Sacred Past. Hagiography and Power in Early Normandy* (Cambridge, MA: Harvard University Press, 2007)

SAMANTHA KAHN HERRICK, 'Apostolic Founding Bishops and their Rivals: The Examples of Limoges, Rouen, and Périgueux', in CHRISTINE BOUSQUET-LABOUÉRIE and YOSSI MAUREY (eds), *Espace sacré, mémoire sacrée: le culte des évêques dans leurs villes (IVᵉ–XXᵉ siècles)*, Hagiologia 10 (2015), p. 15–35

JEAN HILD, 'L'Avent', *La Maison-Dieu* 59 (1959), 10–24

JOYCE HILL, 'The *Litaniae maiores* and *minores* in Rome, Francia and Anglo-Saxon England: Terminology, Texts and Traditions', *Early Medieval Europe* 9 (2000), 211–246

PIET HOOGEVEEN, *Populus prior. Het Joodse volk in Karolingische Bijbelcommentaren* (PhD Dissertation Utrecht University, 2016)

MICHEL HUGLO, 'L'auteur de l'*Exultet* paschale', *Vigiliae christianae* 7 (1953), 79–88

CAROLINE HUMFRESS, 'A New Legal Cosmos: Late Roman Lawyers and the Early Medieval Church', in PETER LINEHAN and JANET L. NELSON (eds), *The Medieval World* (London: Routledge, 2001), 557–575

EDWARD D. HUNT, *Holy Land Pilgrimage in the Later Roman Empire. AD 312–460* (Oxford: Clarendon Press, 1982)

DAVID G. HUNTER, 'Ambrosiaster', in ROBERT BENEDETTO (ed.), *The New Westminster Dictionary of Church History*. vol. 1: The Early, Medieval and Reformation Eras (Westminster: John Knox Press, 2008)

PIERRE JOUNEL, 'L'été 258 dans le calendrier romain', *La Maison Dieu* 52 (1957), 44–58

JOSEPH JUNGMANN, *Missarum sollemnia*, transl. Francis A. Brunner, *The Mass of the Roman Rite. Its Origins and Development* (New York, etc.: Benziger Brothers, 1959)

BERNHARD JUSSEN, 'Liturgy and Legitimation, or How the Gallo-Romans Ended the Roman Empire', in BERNHARD JUSSEN (ed.), *Ordering Medieval Society. Perspectives on Intellectual and Practical Modes of Shaping Social Relations*, translated by Pamela Selwyn (Philadelphia: University of Pennsylvania Press, 2001), p. 147–199

THOMAS F. KELLY, *The Exultet in Southern Italy* (New York-Oxford: Oxford University Press, 1996)

BEVERLY M. KIENZLE, 'Penitents and Preachers: The Figure of Saint Peter and his Relationship to Saint Mary Magdalene', in LOREDANA LAZZARI and ANNA MARIA VALENTE BACCI (eds), *La figura di San Pietro nelle fonti del medioevo*, Atti del convegno tenutosi in occasione dello Studiorum universitatum docentium congressus (Viterbo e Roma 5–8 settembre 2000), Textes et études du moyen âge 17 (Louvain-la-neuve: FIDEM, 2001), p. 248–272

ARCHDALE A. KING, *Liturgies of the Past* (London: Longman, Green, 1959)

THEODOR KLAUSER, 'Der Übergang der römischen Kirche von der griechischen zur lateinischen Liturgiesprache', in LEO C. MOHLBERG (ed.), *Miscellanea Giovanni Mercati*, vol. 1 (Città del Vaticano: Biblioteca Apostolica Vaticana, 1946), p. 467–482

THEODOR KLAUSER, 'Akklamation', in RAC, vol. 1 (Stuttgart: Hiersemann, 1950), col. 216–233

LEO KOEP, *Das himmlische Buch in Antike und Christentum. Eine religionsgeschichtliche Untersuchung zur altchristlichen Bildersprache* (Bonn: Peter Hanstein Verlag, 1952)

HANS-HENNING KORTÜM, 'Le style – c'est l'époque? Urteile über das 'Merowingerlatein' in Vergangenheit und Gegenwart', *Archiv für Diplomatik* 51 (2005), 29–48

GERHART B. LADNER, *The Idea of Reform, its Impact on Christian Thought and Action in the Age of the Fathers* (Cambridge MA: Harvard University Press, 1959)

CÉCILE LANÉRY, 'La légende de sainte Agnès: quelques réflexions sur la genèse d'un dossier hagiographique (IVᵉ–VIᵉ s.)', in *Mélanges de l'École de Rome – Moyen Âge* 126 (2014), http://mefrm.revues.org/1702?lang=en

HENRI LECLERCQ, 'Gallicane (liturgie)', DACL VI.1, col. 473–593

HENRI LECLERCQ, 'Messe', DACL XI.1, col. 648–674

JEAN LECLERCQ, 'Aux origines du cycle de Noël', *Ephemerides liturgicae* 60 (1946), 7–26

J. LEROY, 'Un texte peu remarqué sur la fête de la nativité de Notre-Dame', in *Recherches de science religieuse* 28 (1938), 282–289

CARLTON LEWIS and CHARLES SHORT, *A Latin Dictionary* (Oxford: Clarendon Press, 1998)

HANS LIETZMANN, *Mass and Lord's Supper. A Study in the History of the Liturgy*, transl. Dorothea H.G. Reeve (Leiden: Brill, 1979)

FELICE LIFSHITZ, *The Name of the Saint: The Martyrology of Jerome and Access to the Sacred in Francia, 627–827* (Notre Dame, IN: Notre Dame University Press, 2006)

ELIZABETH A. LIVINGSTONE (ed.), *The Oxford Dictionary of the Christian Church* (Oxford: Oxford University Press, 1997)

ELIAS A. LOWE (ed.), *Codices latini antiquiores. A Palaeographical Guide to Latin Manuscripts Prior to the Ninth Century*, 11 vols. with a supplement (Oxford: Clarendon Press, 1934–1966)

ANNE C. MCGUIRE, 'Liturgy and Laity in the Ninth Century', *Ecclesia orans* 13 (1996), 463–494

ROSAMOND MCKITTERICK, *The Frankish Church and the Carolingian Reforms, 789–895* (London: Royal History Society, 1977)

ROSAMOND MCKITTERICK, 'Text and Image in the Carolingian World', in ROSAMOND MCKITTERICK (ed.), *The Uses of Literacy in Early Mediaeval Europe* (Cambridge: Cambridge University Press, 1990), p. 297–318

ROSAMOND MCKITTERICK, 'Royal Patronage of Culture in the Frankish Kingdoms under the Carolingians: Motives and Consequences', in *Committenti e produzione artistico-letteraria nell'alto medioevo occidentale*, Settimane di studio 39 (Spoleto: La sede del centro, 1992), vol. 1, p. 93–129

ROSAMOND MCKITTERICK, *Charlemagne: The Formation of a European Identity* (Cambridge: Cambridge University Press, 2008)

ROBERT MARKUS, *The End of Ancient Christianity* (Cambridge: Cambridge University Press, 1990)

RALF MATHISEN, '*Peregrini, barbari*, and *cives Romani*: Concepts of Citizenship and the Legal Identity of Barbarians in the Later Roman Empire', *American Historical Review* 111 (2006), 1011–1040

RALPH MATHISEN, 'Church Councils and Local Authority: The Development of Gallic *Libri canonum* during Late Antiquity', in CAROL

HARRISON et al. (eds), *Being Christian in Late Antiquity. A Festschrift for Gillian Clark* (Oxford: Oxford University Press, 2014), p. 175–193

ROB MEENS, *Penance in Medieval Europe 600–1200* (Cambridge: Cambridge University Press, 2014)

ANDREAS MERKT, 'Wer war der Ambrosiaster? Zum Autor einer Quelle des Augustinus – Fragen auf eine neue Antwort', *Wissenschaft und Weisheit* 59 (1996), 19–33

HANS B. MEYER, *Eucharistie: Geschichte, Theologie, Pastoral*, Gottesdienst der Kirche. Handbuch der Liturgiewissenschaft (Regensburg: Pustet, 1989)

JEAN MEYERS, 'Les citations et reminiscences virgiliennes dans les *Libri Historiarum* de Grégoire de Tours', *Pallas* 41 (1995), 67–90

GIUSEPPE MICUNCO, *Exultet I di Bari: parole e immagini alle origine della litteratura di Puglia* (Bari: Stilo, 2011)

CHRISTINE MOHRMANN, 'Exultent divina mysteria', *Ephemerides liturgicae* 66 (1952), 274–281

CHRISTINE MOHRMANN, 'Le latin langue de la chrétienté occidentale', in CHRISTINE MOHRMANN, *Études sur le latin des chrétiens*, vol. 1: *Le latin des chrétiens* (Rome: Edizioni di storia e letterature, 1958), p. 51–81

CHRISTINE MOHRMANN, 'Note sur doxa', in CHRISTINE MOHRMANN, *Études sur le latin des chrétiens*, vol. 1: *Le latin des chrétiens* (Rome: Edizioni di storia e letteratura, 1958), p. 277–286

CHRISTINE MOHRMANN, 'Observations sur la langue et le style de Tertullien', in CHRISTINE MOHRMANN, *Études sur le latin des chrétiens*, vol. 2: *Latin chrétien et médiéval* (Rome: Edizioni di storia e letterature, 1961), p. 235–246

CHRISTINE MOHRMANN, 'Les origines de la latinité chrétienne à Rome', in CHRISTINE MOHRMANN, *Études sur le latin des chrétiens*, vol. 3: *Latin chrétien et liturgique* (Rome: Edizioni di storia e letterature, 1965), p. 67–126

CHRISTINE MOHRMANN, 'Quelques observations linguistiques à propos de la nouvelle version latine du psautier', in CHRISTINE MOHRMANN, *Études sur le latin des chrétiens*, vol. 3: *Latin chrétien et liturgique* (Rome: Edizioni di storia e letteratura, 1965), p. 197–225

GERMAIN MORIN, 'Sur la provenance du "Missale Gothicum"', *Revue Bénédictine* 31 (1914), 326–332

GERMAIN MORIN, 'Une préface du *Missale Gothicum* supposant la fête de la nativité Notre-Dame en pays gallican dès le VIIe siècle', *Revue Bénédictine* 56 (1945–1946), 9–11

GISELA MUSCHIOL, 'Men, Women and Liturgical Practice in the Early Medieval West', in LESLIE BRUBAKER and JULIA M.H. SMITH (eds), *Gender in the Early Medieval World. East and West, 300–900* (Cambridge: Cambridge University Press, 2004), p. 198–216

OTTO G. OEXLE, 'Memoria und Memorialüberlieferung im früheren Mittelalter', *Frühmittelalterliche Studien* 10 (1976), 70–95

HUGHES O. OLD, *The Reading and Preaching of the Scriptures in the Worship of the Christian Church III: The Medieval Church* (Grand Rapids, MI-Cambridge: Eerdmans, 1999)

ÉRIC PALAZZO, *Histoire des livres liturgiques. Le Moyen Âge. Des origines au XIIIᵉ siècle* (Paris: Beauchesne, 1993)

ÉRIC PALAZZO, 'Performing the Liturgy', in THOMAS F.X. NOBLE and JULIA M.H. SMITH (eds), *The Cambridge History of Christianity vol. 3: Early Medieval Christianities, c. 600–c. 1100* (Cambridge: Cambridge University Press, 2008), p. 472–488

NICOLAS J. PERELLA, *The Kiss Sacred and Profane: An Interpretative History of Kiss Symbolism and Related Religio-Erotic Themes* (Berkeley CA: University of California Press, 1969)

PETER MEGILL PETERSON, *Andrew, Brother of Simon Peter: His History and His Legends* (Leiden: Brill, 1958)

KIRIL PETKOV, *The Kiss of Peace: Ritual, Self, and Society in the High and Late Medieval West*, Cultures, Beliefs, and Traditions 17 (Leiden-Boston: Brill, 2003)

JOANNE M. PIERCE, 'The evolution of the *Ordo Missae* in the Early Middle Ages', in LIZETTE LARSON-MILLER (ed.), *Medieval Liturgy. A Book of Essays* (New York: Garland, 1997), p. 3–24

JORDI PINELL, *Anamnesis y epiklesis en el antiquo rito galicano. Estudios y edición critica de las formulas galicanas de la 'Post Sanctus' y 'Post Mysterium'* (Lisbon, 1974)

JORDI PINELL, 'La Liturgia gallicana', in SALVATORE MARSILI (ed.), *Anàmnesis. Introduzione storico-teologica alla liturgia*, vol. 2: *La liturgia. Panorama storico generale* (Rome: Marietti, 1978), p. 62–67

MARCEL POORTHUIS, 'Moses' Rod in Zipporah's Garden', in ALBERDINA HOUTMAN et al. (eds), *Sanctity of Time and Space in Tradition and Modernity*, Jewish and Christian Perspectives Series 1 (Leiden: Brill, 1998), p. 231–264

WILLIAM S. PORTER, *The Gallican Rite*, Studies in Eucharistic Faith and Practice 4 (London: Alcuin Club, 1958)

CLAUDIA RAPP, *Holy Texts, Holy Men, and Holy Scribes. Aspects of Scriptural Holiness in Late Antiquity*, in WILLIAM E. KLINGSHIRN et al.

(eds), *The Early Christian Book* (Washington, D.C.: Catholic University of America Press, 2007), p. 194–222

HELMUT REIMITZ, *History, Frankish Identity and the Framing of Western Ethnicity, 550–850* (Cambridge: Cambridge University Press, 2015)

HANNEKE REULING, *After Eden. Church Fathers and Rabbis on Genesis 3, 16–21* (Leiden: Brill: 2005)

MICHAEL ROBERTS, *Poetry and Cult of the Martyrs: The Liber Peristephanon of Prudentius* (Ann Arbor: University of Michigan Press, 1993)

MICHAEL J. ROBERTS, *The Humblest Sparrow. The Poetry of Venantius Fortunatus* (Ann Arbor: University of Michigan Press, 2009)

SUSAN ROLL, *Toward the Origins of Christmas* (Kampen: Kok, 1995)

ELS ROSE, 'Celebrating St Martin in Early Medieval Gaul', in PAUL POST et al. (eds), *Christian Feast and Festival: The Dynamics of Western Liturgy and Culture*, Liturgia condenda 12 (Louvain: Peeters, 2001), p. 267–286

ELS ROSE, 'Apocryphal Traditions in Medieval Latin Liturgy. A New Research Project Illustrated with the Case of the Apostle Andrew', *Apocrypha* 15 (2004), 115–138

ELS ROSE, 'Hagiography as a Liturgical Act: Liturgical and Hagiographic Commemoration of the Saints in the Early Middle Ages', in MARCEL BARNARD et al. (eds), *A Cloud of Witnesses. Saints and Role Models in Christian Liturgy*, Liturgia condenda 18 (Louvain: Peeters, 2005), p. 161–183

ELS ROSE, 'Fasting Flocks. Lenten Season in the Liturgical Communities of Early Medieval Gaul', in RICHARD CORRADINI et al. (eds), *Texts and Identities in the Early Middle Ages*, Forschungen zur Geschichte des Mittelalters 12 (Vienna: Verlag der Österreichischen Akademie der Wissenschaften, Philosophisch-historische Klasse, Denkschriften 344, 2006), p. 289–301

ELS ROSE, *Ritual Memory. The Apocryphal Acts and Liturgical Commemoration in the Early Medieval West, c. 500–1215* (Leiden-Boston: Brill, 2009)

ELS ROSE, '*Virtutes apostolorum*: Origin, Aim, and Use', *Traditio* 68 (2013), 57–96

ELS ROSE, 'Liturgical Latin in Early Medieval Gaul', in MARY GARRISON et al. (eds), *Spoken and Written Language: Relations between Latin and the Vernacular Languages in the Earlier Middle Ages*, Utrecht Studies in Medieval Literacy 24 (Turnhout: Brepols, 2013), p. 303–313

ELS ROSE, 'The Cult of the Apostles in the Early Medieval West: From Eyewitnesses to Blood Witnesses', in KLAUS HERBERS and GORDON

BLENNEMANN (eds), *Vom Blutzeugen zum Glaubenszeugen? Formen und Vorstellungen des christlichen Martyriums im Wandel*, Beiträge zur Hagiographie 14 (Stuttgart: Franz Steiner, 2014), p. 57–70

ELS ROSE, 'The Apocryphal Acts of the Apostles in the Latin Middle Ages', in ELS ROSE (ed.), *The Apocryphal Acts of the Apostles in Latin Christianity. Proceedings of the First International Summer School on Christian Apocryphal Literature (ISCAL), Strasbourg, 24–27 June 2012* (Turnhout: Brepols, 2014), p. 31–52

ELS ROSE, 'Getroost door de klank van woorden. Het Latijn als sacrale taal van Ambrosiaster tot Alcuin', in GERARD ROUWHORST and PETRA VERSNEL-MERGAERTS (eds), *Taal waarin wij God verstaan. Over taal en vertaling van Schrift en traditie in de liturgie* (Heeswijk: Berne Media, 2015), p. 63–88

ELS ROSE, '*Emendatio* and *effectus* in Frankish Prayer Traditions', in ROB MEENS et al. (eds), *Religious Franks: Religion and Power in the Frankish Kingdoms. Studies in Honour of Mayke de Jong* (Manchester: Manchester University Press, 2016), p. 128–147

ELS ROSE, 'John the Disciple, Christianity Medieval Times and Reformation Era', in HANS-JOSEF KLAUCK et al. (eds), *Encyclopedia of the Bible and its Reception* (Leiden: Brill, 2017), col. 486–487

ELS ROSE, 'Inscribed in the Book of Life: Liturgical Commemoration in Merovingian Gaul', in BONNIE EFFROS and ISABEL MOREIRA (eds), *The Oxford History of the Merovingian World* (Oxford-New York: Oxford University Press, forthcoming 2017)

MICHELE RENEE SALZMAN, *On Roman Time. The Codex-Calendar of 354 and the Rhythms of Urban Life in Late Antiquity*, The Transformation of the Classical Heritage 17 (Berkeley CA: University of California Press, 1990)

MARC SCHNEIDERS, 'Acclamations in the Eucharistic Prayer', in CHARLES CASPERS and MARC SCHNEIDERS (eds), *Omnes circumadstantes. Contributions towards a History of the Role of the People in the Liturgy. Presented to Herman Wegman* (Kampen: Kok, 1990), p. 78–100

ANTHONY E. SIECIENSKI, *The filioque: History of a Doctrinal Controversy* (Oxford: Oxford University Press, 2010)

PATRICK SIMS-WILLIAMS, 'Thoughts on Ephrem the Syrian in Anglo-Saxon England', in MICHAEL LAPIDGE and HELMUT GNEUSS (eds), *Learning and literature in Anglo-Saxon England: Studies Presented to Peter Clemoes* (Cambridge-New York: Cambridge University Press, 1985), p. 205–226

PATRICK SIMS-WILLIAMS, *Religion and Literature in Western England, 600–800* (Cambridge: Cambridge University Press, 1990)

LIEKE SMITS, *A Union Not Only of Bodies but of Spirits: The Image of the Kiss in the Commentaries on the Song of Songs of Bernard of Clairvaux and William of St. Thierry* (MA thesis Utrecht University, 2014)

MATTHIEU SMYTH, *La liturgie oubliée. La prière eucharistique en Gaule antique et dans l'Occident non romain* (Paris: Cerf, 2003)

ALEXANDER SOUTER, *A Glossary of Later Latin to 600 A.D.* (Oxford: Clarendon Press, 1949)

BRIAN SPINKS, *The Sanctus in the Eucharistic Prayer* (Cambridge: Cambridge University Press, 1991)

OTTO STEGMÜLLER, 'Diptychon', in RAC 2, col. 1138–1149

EVINA STEINOVÁ, 'The Prehistory of the Latin Acts of Peter (BHL 6663) and the Latin Acts of Paul (BHL 6575). Some Observations about the Development of the *Virtutes apostolorum*', in ELS ROSE (ed.), *The Apocryphal Acts of the Apostles in Latin Christianity. Proceedings of the First International Summer School on Christian Apocryphal Literature (ISCAL), Strasbourg, 24–27 June 2012* (Turnhout: Brepols, 2014), p. 69–84

LEO F. STELTEN, *Dictionary of Ecclesiastical Latin* (Peabody MA: Hendrickson, 1995)

CHRISTOPH STIEGEMANN and MATTHIAS WEMHOFF (eds), *799. Kunst und Kultur der Karolingerzeit. Karl der Große und Papst Leo III. in Paderborn. Band 2. Katalog der Ausstellung Paderborn 1999* (Mainz: Von Zabern, 1999)

CAROL STRAW, *Gregory the Great. Perfection in Imperfection* (Berkeley-Los Angeles-London 1988)

RUDOLF SUNTRUP, '*Te igitur*. Initialen und Kanonbilder in mittelalterlichen Sakramentarhandschriften', in CHRISTEL MEIER and UWE RUBERT (eds), *Text und Bild: Aspekte des Zusammenwirkens zweier Künste in Mittelalter und früher Neuzeit* (Wiesbaden: Reichert, 1980), p. 278–382

ROBERT TAFT, *The Liturgy of the Hours in East and West. The Origins of the Divine Office and its Meaning for Today* (Collegeville MN: Liturgical Press, 1986)

ROBERT TAFT, *A History of the Liturgy of St. John Chrysostom, vol. 4: The Diptychs*, Orientalia christiana analecta 238 (Rome: Pontificium institutum studiorum orientalium, 1991)

ROBERT F. TAFT, 'The Interpolation of the Sanctus into the Anaphora: When and Where? A Review of the Dossier', Part I, *Orientalia christi-*

ana periodica 57 (1991), 281–308 and Part II, *Orientalia christiana periodica* 58 (1992), 82–121

THOMAS TALLEY, *The Origins of the Liturgical Year* (New York: Pueblo, 1986)

JEAN-BAPTISTE THIBAUT, *L'ancienne liturgie gallicane* (Paris: Bonne presse, 1929)

PAOLO TOMEA, 'La *Passio Agnetis* e il topos della *puella senex*', *Analecta Bollandiana* 128 (2010), 18–55

ACHILLE M. TRIACCA, 'Teologia dell'anno liturgico nelle liturgie occidentale antiche non romane', *Anàmnesis* 6 (1988), 311–363

VEIKO VÄÄNÄNEN, *Introduction au latin vulgaire* (Paris: Klinksieck, 1981³)

JOSEPH VAN DER STRAETEN, 'Les actes des martyrs d'Aurélien en Bourgogne', *Analecta Bollandiana* 79 (1961), 115–144

JOHN VAN ENGEN, 'Christening the Romans', *Traditio* 52 (1997), 1–45

MARC VAN UYTFANGHE, 'Le latin des hagiographes mérovingiens et la protohistoire du français. État de la question', *Romanica Gandensia* 16 (1976), 5–89

M.P. VANHENGEL, 'Le rite et la formule de la chrismation postbaptismale en Gaule et en Haute Italie du IVᵉ au VIIIᵉ siècle d'après les sacramentaires gallicans. Aux origines du rituel primitif', *Sacris erudiri* 21 (1972–1973), 161–222

CYRIL VOGEL, *Medieval Liturgy. An Introduction to the Sources* (Spoleto, 1983; transl. William G. Storey and Niels K. Rasmussen, Washington DC: Pastoral Press, 1986)

ANDRÉ WILMART, 'Germain (Lettres attribuées à saint)', DACL VI.1, 1924, col. 1050–1102

ANDRÉ WILMART, 'Saint Ambroise et la Légende dorée', *Ephemerides liturgicae* 50 (1936), 169–202

IAN WOOD, *The Merovingian Kingdoms, 450–751* (London-New York: Longman, 1994)

IAN WOOD, 'Liturgy in the Rhône Valley and the Bobbio Missal', in YITZHAK HEN and ROB MEENS (eds), *The Bobbio Missal. Liturgy and Religious Culture in Merovingian Gaul* (Cambridge: Cambridge University Press, 2004), p. 206–218

IAN WOOD, 'Topographies of Holy Power in Sixth-Century Gaul', in MAYKE DE JONG et al. (eds), *Topographies of Power in the Early Middle Ages*, The Transformation of the Roman World 6 (Leiden-Boston-Cologne: Brill, 2001), p. 137–154

CHARLES WRIGHT and ROGER WRIGHT, 'Additions to the Bobbio Missal: *De dies malus* and *Joca monachorum* (fols. 6r–8v)', in YITZHAK HEN and ROB MEENS (eds), *The Bobbio Missal. Liturgy and Religious Culture in Merovingian Gaul* (Cambridge: Cambridge University Press, 2004), p. 79–139

ROGER WRIGHT, 'A Sociophilological Study of the Change to Official Romance Documentation in Castile', in MARY GARRISON et al. (eds), *Spoken and Written Language: Relations between Latin and the Vernacular Languages in the Earlier Middle Ages*, Utrecht Studies in Medieval Literacy 24 (Turnhout: Brepols, 2013), p. 133–147

ISRAEL JACOB YUVAL, *Two Nations in Your Womb. Perceptions of Jews and Christians in Late Antiquity and the Middle Ages* (Berkeley CA: University of California Press, 2006)

HEINRICH ZWECK, *Osterlobpreis und Taufe. Studien zu Struktur und Theologie des Exultet und anderer Osterpraeconien unter besonderer Berücksichtigung der Taufmotive*, Regensburger Studien zur Theologie 32 (Frankfurt a.M.-New York: Peter Lang, 1986)

Online resources

Brepolis Vetus Latina database at http://apps.brepolis.net.proxy.library.uu.nl/vld/index.html

http://digi.vatlib.it/view/MSS_Reg.lat.317

http://gallica.bnf.fr/ark:/12148/btv1b60000332/f40.image.r=9428

http://mefrm.revues.org/1702?lang=en

http://www.tertullian.org/fathers/gregory_thaumaturgus_homily.htm.

TRANSLATION PRINCIPLES

The translation primarily aims to present a fluent English text reflecting as far as possible the stylistic and vocabulary opulence of the prayers. To this end, similar Latin words are not always translated with similar English terms. The main reason for this is simply that a single word can have different meanings. Thus, *uotum* may refer to a vow, offering something to God (41), or to a desire or wish, entreating something from God (13). Likewise, the complex word *uiscera* refers to human physicality in prayers that deal with fasting (333, 338) or the reception of the Eucharist (519, 530). In other contexts, however, *uiscera* refers to human spirituality or the imperishable soul (196, 257). In some cases, both interpretations seem to be possible (92). This multiplicity of meanings is further increased by the variety of chronological and geographical backgrounds to the prayers and their authors.

Irregularities in spelling and morphology are generally not reflected by the translation. Any attempt would undoubtedly result in an artificial, clumsy English, perhaps giving the reader a general impression of the idiosyncratic phenomena in the language, but lacking any analytic support. A full analysis of the language of the Gothic Missal is given in the introduction to the 2005 edition. The present Introduction and the notes to the translation rely on and refer to that study. Opportunities do arise, however, to show in the translation the lack of fluency in Latin, particular at points where the syntax flags. Examples are given below of texts where the translation reflects the irregularity of syntax, with a discussion of the choices made.

Prayers 46 and 47 in the Mass for the Holy Infants provide an example of syntax disruption. In both cases, the syntactical structure is similar. The prayers open with an address to God, using an anamnetic relative clause typical of the Latin (Eucharistic) prayer tradition: [God, who acted in the past, act to us in the present.][1] Both prayers in the Mass for the Holy Infants share this structure, with an anamnetic reference to the martyrs in general and to the children in particular (46), and to Rachel's distress and refusal to be comforted (47). However, the part of the prayer that focuses on the here and now, in both cases asking for fellowship and participation in the glory of the martyrs for the faithful present, is not organically linked to the address to God in the first sentence, but follows only after an interruption mentioning the children's fate (46) and Rachel's mixture of sorrow and joy over the children's pain and reward (47). In both instances, this produces a disruption in the syntax, after which a new vocative is introduced, repeating the vocative with which both prayers begin in order to complete the sentence with the actual plea. The situation in 48 is slightly different, since here the vocative is not repeated, and the prayer seems to go on smoothly despite the reflection on the children's happy fate (*felix mors eorum et beatificanda conditio...*). In all instances, the syntactic flow (or lack thereof) of the Latin is followed in the translation.

In prayer 72 a long and complex sentence occurs containing a number of double negations (*ne ... incertum teneat; ne ... deficiat; ne ... non pateat; ne ... non praebeat*). These could be interpreted as *litotes* and translated accordingly with a strong confirmation ('so that the darkness of ignorance is wholly absent from the illumination of faith', 'so that heaven is wide open to prayer'). The structure is not maintained throughout the prayer, however. The phrase *ne ... ignorantiae nox fidei inluminatione deficiat* requires an extra negation in order to prevent a nonsensical request: 'lest the night of ignorance is absent from the illumination of faith'.

---

[1] On this anamnetic structure see PAUL BRADSHAW, *The Search for the Origins of Christian Worship*, 2nd edition (Oxford: Oxford University Press, 2002), p. 43 and passim.

The prayer should state that the darkness of ignorance is *entirely absent* from the light of faith. This irregularity prompted me to translate as literally as possible, in order to retain the finesses of the prayer and its strong but not entirely impeccable parallelism.

In 89, a prayer preceding the Lord's Prayer, the participles *praesumentes* and *oboedientes* are not directly linked to the predicate *iubemur dicere*, although from the content it is clear that they should be related. The lack of a flowing line (unlike the almost identical no. 20) is mirrored by the translation.

Prayer 108 opens with an address to God, followed by a relative clause that has no main clause. Instead, the prayer is a succession of relative clauses linked to various antecedents. This yields an awkward sentence, which is reflected in the translation.

Syntactic unevenness occurs more often in compound sentences, of which prayer 138 is a telling example. Here, the double *ut* combined with a main verb to which the first *ut*-clause can be linked makes the sentence incomplete.

Prayer 185 is distinguished by its highly vulgar spelling, which is nevertheless rendered in normal English spelling, creating the impression of an equally regular Latin text – further details are given in the apparatus and the introduction to the edition. However, the syntactic presentation does preserve this irregularity where the English translation follows the Latin without correcting the fact that the relative clause linked to the addressed deity (*qui ... cognusceris*) is not followed, as one would expect, by a main clause expressing the intended prayer.

TRANSLATION

III ORDER OF MASS FOR THE VIGIL OF THE NATIVITY OF OUR LORD JESUS CHRIST

351

1 COLLECT AFTER THE NAMES.[a] Let the offering[1] of this feast day be pleasing to you, O Lord, so we ask, that by the favour of your grace through this holy exchange of gifts,[b] we may be found in the likeness of him in whom our being[2] is with you. Grant also to the souls[3] of our beloved that they, separated from the assembly of mortals, may be considered worthy to be inscribed in the heavenly record.[4] Grant this through our Lord Jesus Christ your Son, who lives and reigns with you [...][c]

---

[a] The types of prayer in the different Mass orders are discussed in the Introduction, section The prayers of Mass.

[b] On the nature of the gifts brought into church by the faithful, see Introduction, section The performance of prayer.

[c] Most formulas at the end of the prayers, expressing the praise of the triune God in what is technically called the doxology, are abbreviated in the manuscript. The most customary version would be *Per dominum nostrum Ihesum Christum filium tuum, qui tecum uiuit et regnat cum spiritu sancto in saecula saeculorum*, after which the congregation is expected to answer *Amen*. On the role of the people in the Gallican Mass through acclamations, see Introduction, section The performance of prayer.

115

2 COLLECT AT THE KISS OF PEACE.[5] Grant us, we pray, O Lord, that just as we first gathered in the vigil of this day to celebrate the venerable feast of the birth of your Son in the confession of your name, so we may also partake of his eternal gift. And deign to send your angel of peace, that he may join together our kisses with pure thoughts and reconcile us, purified of all stain of sin, with you. Through Jesus Christ our Lord, who is co-eternal with you.

3 PRAYER OF SACRIFICE.[6] It is worthy and just, truly worthy and just that we bring thanks to you Lord, holy Father, almighty and everlasting God, lovable Goodness,[7] tremendous Power, venerable Majesty.[a] You who amid the exultation of the angels have enriched this coming night, that must be revered by the entire world,[b] with the joy of heaven and the reward of earth, so that that which is above and that which is below[c] rejoice equally because our Lord Jesus Christ your Son is born in the flesh. Look on your servants[8] who beseech you, safeguard your people who resound with your praise, and make us so watchful during the solemn celebration of the coming night, that we may be considered worthy to receive the approaching birth of our Lord with a sincere heart. For through this [birth], the Invisible, coming forth from your being, has appeared visible in the flesh of our being, and He who is one with

352

[a] *domine ... maiestas*: asyndeton; see Introduction, section Style and figures.
[b] The phrase *per orbem terrarum* occurs in the Ambrosian hymn *Te deum laudamus*, and I follow the translation in the Book of Common Prayer ('throughout all the world' or, in this case, 'by all the world'). The expression has a background in Roman imperial rhetoric, where it is a synonym for *oikoumenē*, the inhabited world: EMILY ALBU, 'The Battle of the Maps in a Christian Empire', in CLAUDIA RAPP and HALL A. DRAKE (eds), *The City in the Classical and Post-Classical World. Changing Contexts of Power and Identity* (Cambridge: Cambridge University Press, 2014), p. 202–216, at p. 204–205; see also CLIFFORD ANDO, *Imperial Ideology and Provincial Loyalty* (Berkeley CA: University of California Press, 2000), p. 277–335, esp. 320–329. As such it is also translated as 'circle of the lands': RALF MATHISEN, '*Peregrini, barbari*, and *cives Romani*: Concepts of Citizenship and the Legal Identity of Barbarians in the Later Roman Empire', *American Historical Review* 111 (2006), 1011–1040, at p. 1037 footnote 178.
[c] *caelorum ... terrarum, superiora ... inferiora*: variatio; see Introduction, section Style and figures.

you, not born in time, not inferior in nature, has come to us, born in time. And through his birth, forgiveness of sins is granted and the resurrection is confirmed.[a] Therefore all the earth rightly worships and acknowledges you, while the heavens of heavens and the powers of the angels also praise you unceasingly, saying: HOLY, HOLY, HOLY.[b]

4 COLLECT AFTER THE SANCTUS. Truly holy, truly blessed is our Lord Jesus Christ your Son, who remains in heaven and has manifested himself on earth. For he, on the day before His suffering...[c]

5 AFTER THE CONSECRATION.[9] We do this, Lord, holy Father, almighty and everlasting God, commemorating and celebrating the Passion of your only Son Jesus Christ our Lord, who lives and reigns with you and the Holy Spirit for ever and ever.

6 BEFORE THE LORD'S PRAYER. We pray to you, God, almighty Father, with these supplications, with which our Lord Jesus Christ your Son taught us to pray, saying: Our Father [...][d]

7 AFTER THE LORD'S PRAYER. Deliver us from evil, almighty God, and keep us in what is good. Empty away our sins and fill us with virtues, and grant us the good of both the present and eternity, through our Lord Jesus your Son.

---

[a] *non negatur*: litotes; see Introduction, section Style and figures.

[b] The prayer of sacrifice moves on to the proprium chant *Sanctus/Benedictus*, the texts of which are found respectively in Is. 6, 3 and Matth. 21, 9. The incipit of this chant, usually the abbreviated word *Sanctus*, is regularly rubricated in the manuscript as an indication for its performance; see Introduction, section The performance of prayer.

[c] The Collect after the Sanctus introduces the Institution narrative, see Introduction, section The prayers of Mass.

[d] The implicit biblical reference is to Matth. 6, 5–15. In many cases, the incipit of the Our Father (*Pater noster*) is rubricated in the manuscript, to indicate that all participated in the recitation of the prayer. See Introduction, section The performance of prayer.

353   8 BLESSING OF THE PEOPLE. God, who decreed that the coming of your majesty be announced by the angel Gabriel before you descended. AMEN.[a]

You who without beginning are eternal, who deigned to illuminate the earth through the Virgin, to cleanse hell through the cross. AMEN.

Grant that, when this your people walk obediently according to your commandments, just as the birth from the Virgin is unique, so you will pour over them the shower of your blessings of the true light.[10]

And make that, girded with spiritual armour, they will overcome in your name the snares of temptations and the stings of the tempter, the temptations of the adversary and the allurements of the present life. AMEN.

And [grant] that they know that [this child] that is born is the Author of their first birth and of their being born again, and that they understand that they owe to you for what is holy. AMEN.

May you deign to grant this, who with the Father and the Holy Spirit lives and reigns [...]

9 AFTER COMMUNION. Strengthened by heavenly food and drink, most beloved brothers, let us bring praise and thanks to the almighty God, and pray that he who considers us worthy *to share in the body and blood of our Lord Jesus Christ, his only-begotten Son* (I Cor. 10, 16), may also consider us worthy of the heavenly reward. Through him, our Lord Jesus Christ, his Son.

10 COLLECT FOLLOWS. Let us keep in our hearts, Lord, what we have obtained with our mouth, and may a temporary gift become for us an eternal remedy.[b]

---

[a] The *Amen* responses in the Blessing of the people are rubricated in the manuscript, which indicates that they were not said by the celebrant but by the faithful in the form of an acclamation. See Introduction, section The performance of prayer.

[b] On the Eucharist as 'medicine of immortality', see SMYTH, *Liturgie oubliée*, p. 445–446, who links this notion to IGNATIUS OF ANTIOCH, *Letter to the Ephesians* 20.2.

IIII ORDER OF MASS FOR THE DAY OF THE NATIVITY OF OUR LORD JESUS CHRIST

11 COLLECT AFTER THE PROPHECY.[a] You have risen on our behalf as the true *sun of righteousness* (Mal. 4, 2), Jesus Christ. You have come from heaven as the Redeemer of the human race. *You have raised up for us a horn of salvation* (Luc. 1, 69), eternal Child of the exalted Father, born in the house of David according to the words of the ancient prophets, because you wished to save your own people[11] and *erase the written record of the old sin* (Col. 2, 14), in order to open up the triumph of eternal life. We therefore ask you now that *by your tender mercy* (Luc. 1, 78) you appear in our heart, O eternal Salvation, and that by snatching us away from the hostile enemy you make us practitioners of righteousness, so that we, with scorn for every erroneous path that leads to death, may serve you honestly while walking along the straight *way of peace* (Luc. 1, 79). Saviour of the world, who with the Father and the Holy Spirit lives, rules and reigns for ever and ever.

12 COLLECT AFTER THE INTERCESSION.[b] Hear your devoted servants, Lord, who on this day have gathered in the assembly of your Church for this feast of your birth, that they may set forth your praise. Give freedom to the prisoners, sight to the blind, forgiveness to sinners, for you have come to redeem us. *Look on* and illuminate your people *from your holy heaven* (Ps. 20, 6), whose souls,[12] full of devotion, trust in you, Redeemer of the world, who lives...

---

[a] The collect follows after the Prophecy or Canticle of Zacharias (Luc. 1, 67–79), also called *Benedictus* in the Gallican Mass; see Introduction, section The prayers of Mass. Many quotations and wordings in the prayer refer to this biblical passage.

[b] The word *prex* refers to the intercessions that took place between the liturgy of the Word and the celebration of the Eucharist. In the Gothic Missal, the *collectio post praecem* occurs only in the Masses for Christmas (12) and Easter (274); see further Introduction, section The prayers of Mass.

355   13 PREFACE TO MASS. Let us joyfully revere this holy day of the blessed birth, on which, through the birth of the Lord, the secrets of the Virgin's womb are revealed and the burden of that unspoiled body has flowed out for the relief of the world, as we have longed for this day through our prayers.[13] For this Newborn is more resplendent than day, more radiant than light. Let us therefore, most beloved brothers, humbly beseech almighty God, who for the sake of our redemption took upon him the earthly and fragile body, that he will protect us in eternal devotion just as he visited us through the birth of the body, taught us through his fellowship in our life, established the command of his preaching, redeemed us by his *tasting death* (Hebr. 2, 9), embraced us by his partaking of death [and] enriched us by pouring out the divine Spirit.[a] And grant that we persevere in this diligence of blessed service, who with the Father and the Holy Spirit lives and reigns, God, for ever and ever.

14 COLLECT FOLLOWS. *God, you who are [so] rich in mercy* (Eph. 2, 4), through which *you have restored us, dead through sin, to life* (Col. 2, 13) with Christ your Son, that he who formed all things *took on the form of a slave* (Phil. 2, 7), so that he who was in God was born in the flesh, that he who was worshipped in the stars *was wrapped in bands of cloth* (Luc. 2, 7), that he who reigns in heaven lay *in a manger* (Luc. 2, 7), mercifully grant us the ear of your majesty when we call upon you, and give this through the ineffable love of your mercy, so that we, rejoicing in the nativity of your Son, who was born of the Virgin and reborn of the Holy Spirit, may obey his commandments, which he has taught us to our salvation. Grant this through our Lord Jesus Christ your Son, who with you...

356   15 COLLECT AFTER THE NAMES. Accept, so we ask, O Lord Jesus, almighty God, this *sacrifice of thanksgiving* (Ps. 50, 14; Ps. 50, 23; Ps. 107, 22) dedicated to you, which is offered today for your Incarnation, and be so merciful through this, that you give life to the

---

[a] The long relative clause is an asyndeton; see Introduction, section Style and figures.

living and eternal rest to the dead.[a] Let the names of those who are united in our recitation be inscribed in eternity, for whom you have appeared in the flesh. Saviour of the world, who with the co-eternal Father lives and reigns.

16 COLLECT AT THE KISS OF PEACE. Almighty and everlasting God, you who have consecrated this day of your Incarnation and delivery of the blessed virgin Mary, and who as *cornerstone* (Ps. 118, 22) have united the old discord caused by the transgression against the ancient tree[b] with angels and humans through the mystery of your Incarnation: give to your servants that, through this celebration of joy, they who rejoice in your companionship through your vicinity in the flesh, are brought to the unity of the citizens of the highest place, above whom you have exalted your elevated body. And let them congregate together by means of an embrace that includes all, so that no break in the form of a quarrel may be exposed [for those] who rejoice that you, their Author, have come in their own nature by living with them[c] in the flesh. May you deign to grant this, who with the Father and...

17 PRAYER OF SACRIFICE. It is truly worthy and just, fair and salutary that we give thanks to you, Lord, holy Father, almighty and everlasting God, for today our Lord Jesus Christ deigned to visit the world. He proceeded from the shrine of the body of the Virgin and descended from heaven out of love. The angels sung *'Glory in the highest* (Luc. 19, 38; cf. Luc. 2, 14)'[d] when the hu-

---

[a] The Latin construction (*ut superstitebus uitam, defunctis requiem tribuas sempiternam*) allows for the adjective *sempiternam* to be linked to both *uitam* and *requiem*: living and dead share in the same eternal life and eternal rest. See also no. 27.

[b] *ligni ueteris*: in patristic writings *lignum uetitum* ('forbidden tree') is more regular, as it occurs in no. 174.

[c] The word *contubernium* has an association of tent or bed mates (in and outside marriage). For the use of this word in the context of the Incarnation, in which Christ shares life in the mortal body with humanity, see BLAISE, *Dictionnaire*, s.v *contubernium*.

[d] Although the Vulgate gives *gloria in altissimis* in Luc. 2, 14, many codices of the Vetus Latina give *gloria in excelsis*, as in Luc. 19, 38. See Brepolis Vetus Latina database at http://apps.brepolis.net.proxy.library.uu.nl/vld/index.html (consulted 10 September 2015).

357

man nature of the Saviour became manifest. The whole throng of angels shouted with joy because the earth received its eternal King. Blessed Mary has become a precious temple,[a] for she bore the Lord of lords. She indeed, for our sins, brought forth the splendid life, so that bitter death would be banished. For this womb,[b] which knew no human stain, was considered worthy to bear God. He was born in the world, who has always lived and lives in heaven, Jesus Christ your Son our Lord, through whom the angels praise your majesty.

18 AFTER THE SANCTUS. *Glory to God in the highest and on earth peace among those whom he favours* (Luc. 2, 14), *for our redemption has drawn near* (Luc. 21, 28). He has come, the age-old *expectation of the peoples* (Gen. 49, 10), he is near, the promised resurrection of the dead, and he already shines, the eternal expectation of the blessed, through Christ our Lord. For on the day before he suffered for the salvation of us all [...]

19 AFTER THE CONSECRATION. We believe, O Lord, in your coming, we commemorate your Passion.[c] Your body was broken for the remission of our sins, your holy blood was shed as a ran-

---

[a] Although according to I Cor. 3, 16–17, I Cor. 6, 19 and Eph. 2, 22 all faithful are 'the temple of the Holy Spirit', Mary was already singled out as the temple of God par excellence by the Greek *patres*, e.g. the third-century GREGORY THAUMATURGUS, *Homily concerning the Holy Mother of God* 11 and 13. The issue of Mary as temple of God became pressing in fifth-century Christological debates; cf. BENKO, *Virgin Goddess*, p. 229–262; ANTONIA ATANASSOVA, 'Did Cyril of Alexandria Invent Mariology?' in CHRIST MAUNDER (ed.), *Origins of the Cult of the Virgin Mary* (London-New York: Burns and Oates, 2008), p. 105–125. In the *Transitus Mariae* attributed to Melito of Sardes, Mary is indicated by a Jewish high priest as the *tabernaculum* that carried Christ (MS Montpellier H 55, f. 100r, l. 7); *Adsumptio Mariae* 39.2; ed. WILMART, p. 350 (see further nos 94–98).

[b] The word *uiscera* has many meanings, physical and spiritual, referring to the innermost parts of the body, the soul, but also to love and mercy; cf. ROSE (ed.), *Missale Gothicum*, Introduction, p. 148. Accordingly, the translation of the word varies according to context; see e.g. no. 126, where *uiscera* is translated with 'tenderness' in accordance with NRSV, and no. 220 where it is translated as 'mercy'.

[c] Smyth suggests that this phrase echoes the embolism to the narrative of Institution in the Milanese tradition: SMYTH, *Liturgie oubliée*, p. 420–422. See also nos 31 and 291.

som for our redemption. Who with the Father and the Holy Spirit lives and reigns for ever [...]

20 BEFORE THE LORD'S PRAYER. Not trusting our own merits, holy Father, but obeying the command of our Lord Jesus Christ your Son, we dare to say [...]

21 AFTER THE LORD'S PRAYER. Deliver us, almighty God, from all evil, from all peril, and keep us in all good work, perfect Truth and true Freedom, God, who reigns for ever and ever. 358

22 BLESSING OF THE PEOPLE. God, who has commanded the coming of your majesty to be announced through the angel Gabriel before you descended, who in a [worthy] manner[14] entered the human body, and whom the enlightened world[15] has received today from the womb of the Virgin. AMEN.
You, O Lord, bless these your servants, who rejoice over the solemn celebration of this day because of your coming. AMEN.
Grant peace to your people, whom you restored to life through the precious birth and whom you have redeemed from perpetual death through the endurance of your Passion. AMEN.
Bestow on them from your treasure the inexhaustible *riches of your kindness* (Rom. 2, 4). Fill them with knowledge, so that they follow you, the leader to righteousness whom they know as their Maker, with undefiled deeds and a pure heart. AMEN.
And, as in those days the faithlessness of Herod feared your coming in the world and the godless king disappeared from before the countenance of the great King, may also the solemn celebrations now in the present time break the bonds of sin. AMEN.
So that when you come again to judge, none of us will appear guilty before your seat of judgement, but that we may please your countenance when *the shroud of darkness* (II Petr. 2, 17) is struck from our hearts, and reach that land which your saints will possess in eternal rest. AMEN.

23 AFTER COMMUNION. Most beloved brothers, fed with heavenly food and revived through the drink from the eternal 359

cup, let us bring praise and thanks unceasingly to the Lord our God, and request that we, who have taken to us in the spirit the holy body of our Lord Jesus Christ, may be considered worthy, stripped of fleshly sins, to be made spiritual, through our Lord Jesus Christ, his Son.

24 COLLECT FOLLOWS. May that which we obtain from the blessing of your holy altar, so we ask you, O Lord, be for us a medicine of soul[16] and body, so that we, who are strengthened by partaking of such a great remedy, are not oppressed by any adversity, through our Lord Jesus Christ, your Son.[a]

V ORDER OF MASS FOR THE FEAST OF THE PROTOMARTYR[b] SAINT STEPHEN[c]

25 V PREFACE. Let us, most beloved brothers, now that we celebrate today the venerable and exalted passion of the most blessed protomartyr Stephen, pray to the God of the martyrs that, as he considered it worthy to give him the crown[d] after seeing his merits, he will lavish on us in all things his most bounteous mercy, moved through the prayers of Stephen. Through our Lord Jesus Christ his Son.

26 COLLECT FOLLOWS. God, you who have granted to the holy Stephen your martyr to be the first in ministry and martyrdom, as you have granted us the feast of this holy day for the commemoration of his passion, hear the humble prayers of your serv-

---

[a] The formulaic closing asks that the prayer be heard *per dominum* (Christ), while the prayer itself is addressed to *domine* (Christ).

[b] *protomartyris*: according to the biblical narrative (Act. 7, 54–60), the deacon Stephen was the first to be killed because he confessed Christ. See also ROSE (ed.), *Missale Gothicum*, Introduction, p. 201–202.

[c] On this Mass, see ROSE (ed.), *Missale Gothicum*, Introduction, p. 201–206.

[d] Although *corona* is a general image of the reward given to the martyrs (cf. Apoc. 2, 10), it is particularly apt in the case of Stephen, whose name in Greek (Στέφανος) signifies 'crowned'.

ants, so we ask, and give us the special protection of him whose   360
prayers for his enemies and sinners you affectionately accepted.
Grant also that he is our intercessor, who prayed for his own
persecutors.[a] Through our Lord Jesus Christ your Son, who lives
blessedly with you.

27 COLLECT AFTER THE NAMES. Almighty and everlasting God,
who, to adorn *the holy body of your Church* (Rom. 12, 4–5; cf. I
Cor. 12, 12–27) with the manifold virtue of the saints, dedicated
the blood of your glorious deacon Stephen as first-fruits of the
martyrs, grant us, that we celebrate the day of his birth with particular honour, because we fully trust[b] that he can support your
faithful, who as follower of the love of the Lord even prayed for his
own persecutors.[c] And give through his mediation, so we ask, that
the living may gain salvation and the dead eternal rest.[d] Grant this
through our Lord your Son.

28 COLLECT AT THE KISS OF PEACE. God, Giver[17] of love, God
who grants[18] us forgiveness, who gave abundantly to your holy
martyr Stephen during his passion that he received the rain of
stones mildly and prayed for those who threw them, we request
with prayers of trust your goodness, O Lord, that while we commemorate the passion of your martyr, through his intercession
we may be considered worthy to gain the safety of peace and the
forgiveness of our sins. Through our Lord Jesus Christ your Son,
who with you [...]

29 PRAYER[e] OF SACRIFICE.[19] It is worthy and just, fair and just   361
that we praise you and bless you, that we give thanks to you, al-

---

[a] This and the preceding sentence refer to Act. 7, 60 (Vulgate: Act. 7, 59).

[b] *non diffidimus*: litotes; see Introduction, section Style and figures.

[c] Cf. Act. 7, 60 (Vulgate: Act. 7, 59).

[d] In the Latin construction (*ut uiuentes salutem, defuncti requiem consequantur
aeternam*), the adjective *aeternam* can be linked to both *salutem* and *requiem*; see
also no. 15.

[e] On the stylistic characteristics of this prayer, see ROSE (ed.), *Missale Gothicum*, Introduction, p. 205 and Introduction, section Style and figures.

mighty and everlasting God. For you glory in the assembly of your saints, whom, chosen *before the foundation of the world* (Ioh. 17, 24), you have marked *in heaven with a spiritual blessing* (Eph. 1, 3), and whom you have joined with your only-begotten Son through his adoption of the flesh and the redemption of the cross. In them you have made your Holy Spirit reign, through whom they have come to the glory of blessed martyrdom through the favour of your goodness. It is therefore appropriate that this solemn feast is held for you, Lord of might, that this holy day is celebrated for you, [this day], which the blood of your first martyr the blessed Stephen, poured out as a testimony to your truth, has marked with the magnificent honour of your name. For he is the first confessor of this name *that is above every name* (Phil. 2, 9), in which you, holy Father, have placed the only protection of our salvation. He has gone before in your Church, as a splendid example of that one praise to strengthen the hearts of all. He was the first, after the Passion of our Lord Jesus Christ, to take possession of the palm of victory. As soon as he was consecrated in the ministry of deacon by the apostles through the Holy Spirit, he suddenly began to shine with a radiant snow-white colour, purple through the blood of martyrdom. O blessed *offspring of Abraham* (Ps. 105, 6; II Cor. 11, 22), who earlier than all others became a follower and witness to the teaching of the apostles and the cross of the Lord. *He* deservedly *saw the heavens open and Jesus standing at the right hand of God* (Act. 7, 55–56). It is therefore worthy and just that we praise such a person in the confession of your name. Almighty God, grant us by your goodness the help of him whom you deigned to call to such great glory. May such a person pray for this people, who rejoicingly received Christ when he came to Him[a] after the victory. May these eyes be opened for us to heaven, which, still in this *body of death* (Rom. 7, 24), in that hour of the passion saw the Son of God standing at the right hand of the Father. May he obtain this for us, who, when he was stoned, prayed to you, holy

362

[a] Personal and relative pronouns relating to divine persons are capitalised only incidentally to avoid confusion.

God, almighty Father, on behalf of his persecutors. Through our Lord Jesus Christ your Son, who deigned to be born in the flesh through the Virgin and to suffer death for our sins, so that through his example he taught his martyrs to suffer. To whom all the angels and archangels rightfully and unceasingly cry out, saying: HOLY, HOLY, HOLY.

30 COLLECT AFTER THE SANCTUS. Truly holy, truly blessed is our Lord Jesus Christ your only-begotten Son, who endowed his martyr Stephen with the company of the heavenly court, who took upon him the weakness of our body, [and] before he poured out his holy blood for the salvation of humankind instituted the mystery of the holy Eucharist.[20] Who on the day before his suffering [...]

31 AFTER THE CONSECRATION. Therefore we do this, Lord, we observe these commandments, we proclaim this passion of the sacred body through the holy sacrifice,[21] [and] we ask, almighty God, that we, as we now fulfil the truth of the heavenly sacrament, may partake of that true body and blood of the Lord. Through our Lord Jesus Christ your Son.

32 BEFORE THE LORD'S PRAYER. Taught by the examples of the glorious deacon and the lessons of the most blessed martyr Stephen, dear brothers, let us pour out our prayer in all humility to the eternal King and Father God, that, after he has given us the glow and the gift of faith, he will ignite us through the fire of his love to desire martyrdom, and will make us followers of him, who bore his passion not only for his own glory, but also as an example for our edification. And to whom he deigned to give strength in martyrdom, may he give the opportunity to be an intercessor for us. And may he permit [us] to say without hesitation the prayer that he deigned to teach us: OUR FATHER [...]

363

33 AFTER THE LORD'S PRAYER. Deliver us from evil, almighty God, and grant to us your supplicants that our soul may be so willing to suffer and die for your Christ, that it may be judged of

us that not we were lacking martyrdom, but that martyrdom was lacking us.[a] Through.

34 BLESSING OF THE PEOPLE. God, who so bound your martyrs through your love that they even wished to die for you in order not to be lost. AMEN.

And who so ignited in faith the blessed Stephen in his confession that he did not fear the rain of stones. AMEN.

Hear the prayer of your servants, which sounds up amid the festivities for your faithful friend.[22] AMEN.

May this voice reach you, while it intercedes for your people and which in martyrdom itself prayed for the enemies.[23] AMEN.

That the people, who have been acquired through mercy, while he claimed victory and you rewarded him, may come where he has seen you in glory while heaven was open.[b] AMEN.

May you deign to grant this.

35 COLLECT AFTER THE EUCHARIST. God, perpetual Salvation, inestimable Bliss, grant, so we ask, to all your people, that they who have taken the sacred and blessed may also be deemed worthy to be ever sacred and blessed. May you deign to grant this.

364   36 COMPLETION OF MASS. We bring thanks to you, O Lord, for your mercies which have been multiplied towards us, who saves us through the birth of your Son and sustains us through the prayer of the martyr Stephen. Through our Lord your Son.

---

[a] The phrase echoes the opening prayer of the Mass for Martin of Tours in the *Bobbio Missal* 363 (ed. LOWE, p. 109) and refers to both regret at not being able to shed one's blood for the faith and the notion of 'bloodless martyrdom' expressed by SULPICIUS SEVERUS, *Vita Martini*, *epistola* 2.12, ed. FONTAINE, p. 330. The longing for the opportunity to shed one's blood for the faith becomes a topos, expressed in this prayer and in no. 471, where the understanding of torture itself is spiritualised so that confessors can be equated with martyrs ('spiritually tortured'). Robert Markus speaks of an 'unsatisfied desire for martyrdom', leading to increased emphasis on asceticism as 'vicarious martyrdom': ROBERT MARKUS, *The End of Ancient Christianity* (Cambridge: Cambridge University Press, 1990), p. 70–71.

[b] Act. 7, 56 (Vulgate: Act. 7, 55).

VI MASS FOR THE FEAST OF THE APOSTLES
JAMES AND JOHN[a]

37 [PREFACE.] Now that we revere with the feast of this day James and John the holy apostles and martyrs[b] of God [in] the splendid testimony of the election by the Lord, the wonderful jewel of the company of the apostles and the heavenly proclamation of the truth of the Gospel, let us, dearest brothers, likewise pray to our Lord and God, that he who knew beforehand of their election because he called them himself,[c] may also confirm our calling through his election of the gifts. And that he who granted them the grace of apostleship and the crown of martyrdom, will give us perseverance in the fear of him. Through our Lord Jesus Christ his Son.

38 COLLECT FOLLOWS. O Lord, who foretold to your most blessed apostles James and John the glory of martyrdom by drinking your cup,[d] so that you not only confirmed the answer that a pure faith had openly declared, but also gave the strength that a devoted love had expected beforehand, be kindly disposed towards your Church, which solemnly celebrates this memorial of their passion. May the commemoration of the most blessed saints, so we ask, be of benefit to us in obtaining the listening ear of your compassion. May it be advantageous to celebrate anew the honour of the apostles, so that our prayer is able to incline the ears of your majesty. May it be of benefit to pray to the patrons, so that

365

---

[a] On this Mass, see ROSE (ed.), *Missale Gothicum*, Introduction, p. 206–210.

[b] On the question whether or not John was considered a martyr in the tradition reflected by this Mass, see ROSE (ed.), *Missale Gothicum*, Introduction, p. 209–210; see further ROSE, 'The Cult of the Apostles in the Early Medieval West'; EAD., 'The Apocryphal Acts of the Apostles in the Latin Middle Ages', in ELS ROSE (ed.), *The Apocryphal Acts of the Apostles in Latin Christianity. Proceedings of the First International Summer School on Christian Apocryphal Literature (ISCAL), Strasbourg, 24–27 June 2012* (Turnhout: Brepols, 2014), p. 31–52, at p. 50–51.

[c] The calling of James and John, the sons of Zebedee, is narrated in Matth. 4, 21–22.

[d] Reference to Matth. 20, 20–28.

you deign to hear us through their help. Saviour of the world, who with the eternal Father and the Holy Spirit lives and reigns.

39 COLLECT AFTER THE NAMES. Lord, whom the holy apostles James and John followed in complete faith when you called, and in pursuance of whom they were chosen by reason of their perfect love to be fishers of the world *after they relinquished the nets* (Matth. 4, 20) of the sea, *give ear to our prayer* (Ps. 17, 1), so we pray, and grant that, while we revere and worship the triumphs of the apostles, though we are not able to follow their deeds, we at least strain to live according to their admonitions. May you yourself deign to grant this, who with the Father and the Spirit.

40 COLLECT AT THE KISS OF PEACE. Eternal Lord, to whom it pleased to fulfil in your holy apostles James and John the secret of your divine grace, such that through the glorious example of their passion the one preceded the choir of apostles and the other sent it ahead, and that the blessed flock was gathered together between the two so that the one preceded the devotion of all and the other concluded it: have mercy on us and hear us, and grant that we, through the example of the first of your aforementioned martyrs and apostles, may retain the faith with which he was crowned, and through the instruction of the other may learn the love which he taught.[a] Through our Lord Jesus Christ your Son, who with you.

366   41 PRAYER OF SACRIFICE. It is worthy and just, truly fair and just that we bring you thanks and pay our vows,[24] Lord, holy Father, almighty and eternal God. For we live for you, all your works, and in their deeds[25] all *your faithful* (Ps. 145, 10), *whom you predestined to be conformed to the image of your Son* (Rom. 8, 29), praise and *bless you* (Ps. 145, 10). For in him *is raised up a horn of salvation* (Luc. 1, 69) for those who confess *his name, that is above every name* (Phil. 2, 9), with a free voice *in the presence of the kings* (Ps. 119, 46) and powers of this world. And they, after the example

---

[a] Implicit reference to I Ioh. 4, 7–21.

of their Lord and Saviour, through the yoke of punishment, triumphed over their persecutors and over the devil, and, by giving
their bodies as a sacrifice to God, were cut down for you by a precious death. And amid them stand out your most blessed apostles
and martyrs James and John, whose feast we celebrate today while
we implore your mercy, most compassionate and almighty God,
that you hear our prayers favourably through the merits of those
who pray for us. Through our Lord Jesus Christ your Son, who is
the power and the glory of all saints, the victory and crown of the
martyrs, the shepherd of the sheep and the sacrifice of the priests,
the redemption of the gentiles and the atonement of sins. Before
whose most holy seat stand the angels and archangels and proclaim unceasingly, saying: HOLY, HOLY, HOLY.

42 PRAYER AFTER THE SANCTUS. *Hosanna in the highest* (Matth.
21, 9), truly holy, truly blessed is our Lord Jesus Christ your Son,
who, holy amid the holy, deigned to give life for death, glory for   367
punishment, victory for the confession of faith. For he who on the
day before his suffering [...]

43 BLESSING OF THE PEOPLE. God who has prepared your apostles to be precious lights for the peoples, by appointing James and
John amid the vessels of the Church as candelabrums of the faith
to illuminate the souls. AMEN.
Give your people to imitate what the one has fashioned by praying
and the other by teaching. AMEN.
May in this people bear fruit what the one sowed through his
word and the other planted through his martyrdom. [AMEN.]
That through their mediation this crowd may be refreshed by the
sweetness of him, on whose breast reclined the beloved John.[a]
AMEN.
May you deign to grant this, who in the perfect Trinity...

44 AFTER COMMUNION. Replenished, O Lord, through the feast
of your apostles, we pray that we always praise you in the com-

---

[a] Reference to Ioh. 13, 23 and 25.

memoration of them, and that we obtain your mercy because they always pray [for us.] Through the Lord.

45 COLLECT FOLLOWS. Help us, O Lord, so we ask, through the intercession of your apostles, for joyful because of their commemoration we have received your holy gifts. Through the Lord.

368

VII MASS FOR THE FEAST OF THE HOLY INFANTS[a]

46 God, you who, as with flowers, have crowned your entire Church with the virtues of your precious martyrs, in order to receive through the triumphs of your witnesses both the glory of the solemn celebration and the examples of devotion, as on this day, on which you raise up the innocence of the infants to the merit of their martyrdom for our Lord Jesus Christ.[b] They died happily for Christ, but they will live even more happily with him in eternity; to this end they were born through human weakness to misery, to be born through the grace of God as martyrs to the crown.[c] Grant, almighty God, through the solemn ritual of this day, that, as you have given them the palms of victory, so you will give us eternal fellowship. Through our Lord Jesus Christ your Son, who lives with you [...]

[a] On this Mass, see ROSE (ed.), *Missale Gothicum*, Introduction, p. 210–216. The more common modern title of the feast is 'Holy Innocents' (Book of Common Prayer; Roman Missal), a designation based on the early Roman title *sancti innocentes*, while the Gallican tradition and the Gothic Missal speak of *infantes*; cf. BERNARD, *Transitions*, p. 123; ROSE (ed.), *Missale Gothicum*, Introduction, p. 214.

[b] Cf. IRENAEUS OF LYONS, *Aduersus haereses* 3.16.4, ed. ROUSSEAU and DOUTRELEAU, p. 304. On the influence of other patristic authors on this Mass, see ROSE (ed.), *Missale Gothicum*, Introduction, p. 215–216.

[c] The thrust of the prayer ('God, who has crowned your Church ... grant that we ...') is interrupted as it were by a further reflection on the fate of the infants ('They died happily for Christ' etc.). See Translation principles.

47 COLLECT FOLLOWS. Omnipotent and benevolent God, merciful and loving God, who gave to the people of Bethlehem and the town of the Lord eternal joy in place of temporary distress, so that the holy Rachel, who, weeping for her children, preferred the mourning of grief and refused the comfort of consolation[a] (for although she appeared bewildered by the temporary loss of her infants, yet she was happy, and sure of the eternity of the martyrs).[b] Grant to all who are present here, O Lord, and to your entire people of this place,[c] that they too may gain the palm of glory through the conduct of a holy life, as the little ones gained victory through their passion. Through our Lord Jesus Christ your Son, who lives with you [...]

48 COLLECT AFTER THE NAMES. God, you who make large through merit what appears to be small through infancy, you who glorify the beginning of your coming through the triumph of little children, you who raise them through the martyrdom of passion earlier than through increase of age – happy is their death and blessed is the condition through which they triumphantly[26] defeated the rage of the most cruel Herod and merited Christ as reward[27] – grant to this people, dedicated to your name, the honour of similar merits through the veneration of similar grace, so that those who celebrate this feast of the holy infants to the honour of your name may continually ascend to the blessedness of those same infants through the progress of faith. May you yourself deign to grant this, who [...]

369

49 PRAYER OF SACRIFICE. It is worthy and just, truly worthy and just that we always and everywhere bring thanks to you, Lord, holy Father, almighty and eternal God. Especially for these [infants] whose annual feast we celebrate again today by com-

[a] A paraphrase of Matth. 2, 18, quoting Ier. 31, 15.

[b] As in the previous prayer, the thrust of the prayer is interrupted by a reflection on Rachel's grief and happiness. See Translation principles.

[c] The Latin is not explicit, but the words *istius loci* refer to 'this place where we celebrate this feast day', whether it concerns a geographical location or the actual church where the celebration takes place.

memorating their martyrdom, who were dragged from the breasts of their nursing mothers by a servant of Herod. They are rightly called the flowers among the martyrs,[a] who, born[28] amid the coldness of unbelief, were struck down by a hoar frost of persecution just as they came into bud as the first blossoms of the Church,[b] while the founts of the town of Bethlehem coloured red. For the infants, who in view of their age could not speak, resounded the praise of the Lord with joy.[c] Killed, they proclaim what they could not in life. They tell with their blood what they were unable to do with their tongue. Martyrdom conferred praise on those to whom the tongue had refused the word. The infant Christ sent the infants ahead to heaven, he sent new gifts to the Father, and as a sacrifice of first-fruits he gave the first martyrdoms of young children, perpetrated by the crime of Herod, to the Creator. The enemy enriches the body while he harms it, he gave it a blessing while he ruined it. By dying they live, by falling they rise again, victory is achieved through destruction. Through his past mercies and through the present solemn celebration we praise you – because we can better bring immeasurable thanks for your goodness than requite something for you – with the holy angels and archangels with one voice, who rules as one God, distinct but not divided, threefold but not tripartite, alone but not solitary, saying: HOLY, HOLY, HOLY.

370

50 BLESSING OF THE PEOPLE. God, who has consecrated to you the first-fruits of the martyrs from the innocence of children. AMEN.

And [who] has joined the infants[d] to you, through their confession of faith, before their tongue learned to speak. AMEN.

---

[a] PRUDENTIUS, *Saluete flores martyrum*, in *Liber cathemerinon* XII, ed. CUNNINGHAM, p. 69.

[b] CAESARIUS OF ARLES, *Sermo* 222.2, ed. MORIN, CCSL 104, p. 879.

[c] Cf. LEO THE GREAT, *Sermo* 13.3, ed. JEAN LECLERCQ and RENÉ DOLLE, SChr 22bis (Paris: Cerf, 1964), p. 198. On the influence of this sermon on the prayers of this Mass, see ROSE (ed.), *Missale Gothicum*, Introduction, p. 212–213 and 216.

[d] *infantiam*: abstractum pro concreto; see Introduction, section Style and figures.

Grant that your people may be innocent through grace, even when in this time there are no more martyrdoms through the shedding of blood.[a] AMEN.

[And give], that this people will be protected, cleansed by Baptism,[b] who through blood has made it an innocence pleasing to you. AMEN.

So that the flock, through their[29] intercession, may through Baptism arrive where the happy children glory in being imbued with the dew of their shed blood. AMEN.

Through our Lord Jesus Christ your Son, who lives and reigns with you.

VIII ORDER OF MASS FOR THE CIRCUMCISION OF OUR LORD JESUS CHRIST[c]

51 [PREFACE.] Let us humbly pray to Christ our Lord, most beloved brothers, who has deigned for us to be born in the flesh, circumcised according to the law and baptised in the river, on this eighth day after his birth, the day on which he desired to undergo the sacrament of circumcision according to the form of the old law, that he, through a daily new recreation, may impart life to us, living within the womb of the Church, until his form appears in us, in which we may comprehend *the fullness of time* (Eph. 4, 13) perfected. And let us pray *that he will cut off* (Rom. 2, 29) *the foreskins of our heart* (Ier. 4, 4), which have grown through gentile sins, not with the knife but *with the Spirit* (Rom. 2, 29), until he, when the carnal growth, that is sin, has been cut away, will allow to live in our nature only what may serve and please him. May he deign to grant this, who with the Father and the Holy Spirit lives and reigns [...]

371

---

[a] For a similar expression of the notion of bloodless martyrdom, see no. 33.

[b] The notion of Baptism through martyrdom (for those who died before they could be baptised) is developed primarily by CYPRIAN, *Epistula* 72.21, ed. WILHELM HARTEL, CSEL 3.2 (Vienna: Geroldi, 1871), p. 794.

[c] On this Mass, see ROSE (ed.), *Missale Gothicum*, Introduction, p. 216–222.

52 COLLECT FOLLOWS. Holy, almighty and eternal God, *waken us to life by converting us* (Ps. 85, 6),[a] and may the gift of the knowledge of you release us, imprisoned in the error of heathendom, so that we are wakened to life through your eternal words after the sting of death (I Cor. 15, 56[b]) has been destroyed, so that *as we have served injustice and iniquity as slaves in the weakness of the flesh, now, freed from sin, we may serve righteousness in sanctification* (Rom. 6, 17–18). Through our Lord Jesus Christ, your Son.

53 COLLECT AFTER THE NAMES. Now that the names of those who offer have been heard, most beloved brothers, let us pray to Christ the Lord that we, just as we celebrate this feast by reason of his fleshly circumcision, may rejoice in the victory over the deception of *the demons* (Eph. 6, 12),[c] while his love grants us that these offers are as beneficial to the correction[d] of the living as they help the dying to find rest. Through our Lord Jesus Christ his Son, who with him lives and reigns eternally in the unity of the Holy Spirit for ever and ever.

372

54 COLLECT AT THE KISS OF PEACE. God, who loves the *circumcision of the heart* (Rom. 2, 29[e]) more than that of the body,[f] and who does not allow *circumcision of the foreskin executed according to the letter* (Rom. 2, 29), but [according] to love united with faith and good works:[g] you cut away our ears that they do not listen to blood, our hearts that they do not cling to deceit, our eyes that they do not steal what belongs to another. You cut

---

[a] The word *conuersus* in the Vulgate and in this quotation is lacking in the NRSV. Vulgate: Ps. 84, 7.

[b] *aculeo mortis*: although the Vulgate gives *stimulus mortis* in I Cor. 15, 56, *aculeus mortis* is common in many codices of the *Vetus Latina* (Itala). See Brepolis Vetus Latina database at http://apps.brepolis.net.proxy.library.uu.nl/vld/index.html (consulted 11 September 2015).

[c] NRSV gives 'the spiritual forces of evil'.

[d] On the early Christian use and meaning of the word *emendatio*, see GERHART B. LADNER, *The Idea of Reform, its Impact on Christian Thought and Action in the Age of the Fathers* (Cambridge MA: Harvard University Press, 1959).

[e] Cf. Deut. 10, 16; Leu. 26, 41; Ier. 4, 4 (cf. no. 51); Ez. 44, 9; Act. 7, 51.

[f] *corporis*: the Vulgate gives *carnis* in Rom. 2, 28.

[g] On faith and good works, see Iac. 2, 14–26.

away in our hands what defiles, in our feet what leads to evil, in our foreskins what longs for things of the flesh. You cut away what tears, strike away what wounds, hew off what mutilates, cut off what increases umbrage, so that when wickedness is amputated, only charity can increase in us. Through our Lord Jesus Christ, your Son.

55 PRAYER OF SACRIFICE. It is worthy and just, truly fair and just that we bring you thanks and bless you unceasingly, almighty, everlasting God. For *in you we live, we move and have our being* (Act. 17, 28), and there is neither time nor moment to be spent without the blessings of your love. During these days, which the remembrance of your deeds and gifts has marked with several reasons for salutary celebrations, we acknowledge – since joy renews both the time of past gladness and the time of eternal goodness – and exalt all the more profusely that we live again through the remembrance of the hallowed grace, as in the recent joy.[a] Thus we commemorate, according to the appointed commemoration, the present day, the eighth after the day of the birth that brings salvation, which is marked by the lawful circumcision of the Lord, born of the flesh, and we honour the sacrifice of peace with solemn prayers, and we revere the work of such grace in the merciful humility of the Lord most high. For as he took upon him our mortality to devour death, so he also took upon him the yoke of the law in his flesh in order to remove the yoke of the devil from our neck. He is circumcised in the flesh of our body so that we, cleansed in heart by the Word of his Spirit, without wound in the flesh would be circumcised in the spirit,[b] so that the spiritual circumcision is beneficial to both men and women, since he had come as the Redeemer of the entire human race. Thus through the mystery of the Incarnation he also encompassed the two genders, because he accepted man born out of woman. Grant therefore, Lord, to look mercifully upon us, who through the hallowed ceremony humbly offer the sacrifice of circumcision, out of joy of

373

[a] *sc.* of Christmas.
[b] Cf. Rom. 2, 29 and the references given in the previous prayer (54).

our immortality, and hear mercifully the prayers of us who bring the sacrifice. Through Christ our Lord, through whom the angels praise your majesty [...]

56 AFTER THE SANCTUS. Truly holy, truly blessed is our Lord Jesus Christ, your *Son, who has come to seek and save what was lost* (Luc. 19, 10). For he, on the day before his suffering [...]

57 AFTER THE CONSECRATION. While we, Lord, uphold these institutions and precepts, we humbly pray that you deign to acknowledge this sacrifice and bless and sanctify it, so that the lawful Eucharist[a] in the name of you and of your Son and the Holy Spirit becomes for us a transformation of the body and blood of our Lord God, Jesus Christ your only-begotten Son. Through whom you create all things, bless the created, sanctify the blessed and bountifully give the sanctified, God, who in the perfect Trinity lives and reigns for ever and ever.

58 BEFORE THE LORD'S PRAYER. Let us pray to the almighty and eternal Lord, that he, who has granted that the beginning and completion of all the faith is in the circumcision of our Lord Jesus Christ, grants that we may be counted in his part, in whom consists the highest perfection of all the salvation of humanity. And may he allow us to say with confidence the prayer that our Lord has taught us: Our Father [...]

374

59 AFTER THE LORD'S PRAYER. Deliver us from evil, almighty God, and grant that when the mass of sin has been cut away, only the growth of virtue will increase in us, through our Lord Jesus Christ, your Son.

---

[a] Smyth analyses the use of the expression *eucharistia legitima* in the earliest centuries of Christianity, in particular the work of Ignatius of Antioch, who understands *eucharistia legitima* as a sacrament performed as 'true', 'authentic', i.e. in line with Christ's institution and presided over by a bishop: SMYTH, *Liturgie oubliée*, p. 510–511, particularly in relation to no. 271 below.

60 BLESSING OF THE PEOPLE. God, Ruler and Maker of all things, by whom all that you made is filled with majesty, ordered with wisdom and protected with love. AMEN.

Grant to behold these your servants,[30] who through the service of our mouth desire the gifts of your blessings. AMEN.

Fill them with the knowledge of your will, so that in all things they serve the authority of your commands with the duty of reverence. AMEN.

Avert from them the dishonouring and repulsive ignominy of lust. Avert from them the lighthearted and noxious delights of the body. Avert from them the envy that is inimical to all your blessings and to all that is good. AMEN.

So that they, growing *in all patience and long-suffering* (Col. 1, 11), called by you, cross over to the Father of eternal light in the realm of hereditary[a] glory.[31] AMEN.

May you deign to grant this, who with the Father and the Holy Spirit lives and reigns for ever and ever. AMEN.

61 COLLECT AFTER COMMUNION. Restored by spiritual food and revived by heavenly drink, most beloved brothers, let us pray to almighty God, that he, who has redeemed us through the participation in his body and the shedding of his blood, will order us to be placed[32] in eternal rest. Through our Lord Jesus Christ his Son.

62 COLLECT FOLLOWS. We humbly implore your mercy, O Lord, that this your sacrament may be for us not a charge leading to retribution, but a salutary intercession leading to forgiveness. May you deign to grant this.

375

63 BLESSING OF THE PEOPLE UPON THE CIRCUMCISION OF THE LORD. May the almighty Lord bless you and fortify your heart through the abundance of his mercy. AMEN.

---

[a] Since the faithful share in the inheritance of the Son, they also share in his glorification: Rom. 8, 17 *coheredes, conglorificemur*.

May he sanctify your spirit, may he lengthen your life, may he grace your purity and ever edify your senses through good works. Amen.

May he give you prosperity, may he grant you peace, may he bestow upon you salvation, may he nourish your rest, may he fortify your love and always defend you against all diabolical and human snares through his protection and strength. Amen.

And may he accept your devotion so mercifully, that whatever you ask of him he will grant with mildness. Amen.

May he take away all the evil that you committed and grant the grace that you requested. Amen.

Through our Lord Jesus Christ his Son.

VIIII HERE BEGIN THE PREFACES WITH THE COLLECTS FOR THE EPIPHANY VIGIL[a]

64 PREFACE. Let us revere with due exultation, most beloved brothers, the beginning of the miracles that our Lord Jesus Christ deigned to carry out in his new state of adopted flesh. For already when he appeared as God in the human womb, he took care of the fulfilment of our salvation. As man he was invited to a wedding, and what he revealed at the wedding has proved that he is God. And although we cannot fully express his exaltation on the grounds of these first principles of his wondrous deeds, we join in the audacity to proclaim his praise while we are astonished by the glory of such great things. Let us through a humble prayer therefore ask that admittance to eternal life is given to us by him, through the light of whose birth the entire earth is illuminated. May he deign to grant this, who in the perfect Trinity lives and reigns for ever and ever.

65 COLLECT FOLLOWS. Almighty and merciful God, answer in your loving kindness your people who humbly pray to you, whom

376

---

[a] On Epiphany in the Gallican liturgy, see Introduction section The liturgical year.

you see celebrating with faithful devotion on this day on which our Lord and God, after he had excepted true humility, revealed his *form as a slave* (Phil. 2, 7) in the world in such a merciful manner that in heaven he wondrously manifested his divine power. For he who for us was a young boy, led the wise men to himself with the help of the star that went before.[a] We therefore pray for your mercy, Lord, so that as you have allowed them to know your Christ as their true God in the true flesh, you will protect in this time all your faithful too, whom your holy Church bears in her motherly womb, with the help of your invincible power, and that in the future they may obtain the eternal reward of your heavenly kingdom. Through him our Lord, Jesus Christ your Son, who lives blissfully with you [...]

66 PREFACE. Let us pray together with the highest prayers to the almighty Lord, most beloved brothers, and to Jesus Christ his Son and our Saviour, who has manifested himself on earth with such strength and has revealed such great miracles among the peoples, that he *who has cured the sick and raised the dead, cleansed the lepers* (Matth. 10, 8), has given light to the blind, and with five loaves and two fish has satisfied five thousand people,[b] that he[33] who brought this about on earth also deigns to be favourably inclined to us in all sin. Saviour of the world, who with the eternal Father lives and reigns [...]

377

67 COLLECT FOLLOWS. Almighty and everlasting God, Creator and Ruler of the world, you who have consecrated the coming solemn celebration of this day[34] with the firstborn of the election of the gentiles, fill the world with your glory and appear with the light of your light to the peoples who are subject to you, so that your salvation rises, wondrous by reason of a new heavenly clarity, to renew our hearts continuously. Through our Lord Jesus Christ [your] Son, who lives and reigns with you [...]

---

[a] Cf. Matth. 2, 1–11.

[b] The Feeding of the Five Thousand (Marc. 6, 30–44; Ioh. 6, 1–13; see also Marc. 8, 1–21) was a central theme during the Epiphany cycle in the Gallican rite; see Introduction, section The liturgical year.

68 PREFACE. Most beloved brothers, let us pray to almighty God, who granted us the feast of this night, that he also gives us purity of heart, so that as the wise men have found our Lord Jesus Christ while the star preceded them and have attained the coveted joy, and, *after they had opened their treasure-chests, offered him gifts of gold, frankincense and myrrh* (Matth. 2, 11) – thus we, his servants, strengthened by the help of this our Saviour, may be considered worthy to enter into *the promised land*[35] (Hebr. 11, 9), so that we rejoice in being enriched by the eternal possession of the heavenly kingdom. Through our Lord Jesus Christ his Son, who lives and reigns with him for ever.

69 COLLECT FOLLOWS. God, who has announced the Incarnation of your Word through the testimony of a most clear star, on seeing which the wise men adored your majesty by offering gifts, grant that the knowledge of your star always appears in our hearts and that our treasure[a] is in the confession of you. Through our Lord Jesus Christ your Son.

378

70 PREFACE. Let us pray with a humble prayer to the almighty, everlasting Lord, most beloved brothers, whose mercy is not smaller than his might, who, though he exceeded [in greatness] the esteem of all his deeds, through his love himself surpassed the greatness of his deeds[b] by sending us Jesus Christ his Son, our Lord, *whose burden is light and whose yoke is easy* (Matth. 11, 30). For he, begotten of the womb of the Virgin, has to this end given over to us the yoke of salvation, that he would raise us all up to the Kingdom. [Let us therefore pray] that he will expel from our senses the darkness of bad thought, so that we, upon whom the radiance of his love has shone, will hereafter not be darkened by any stains of sin. Through our Lord Jesus Christ his Son, who with him [...]

[a] Cf. Matth. 6, 21 and Luc. 12, 34. Cf. also AMBROSE, *De uirginitate* 18: *cuius in ore thesaurus erat, cum Christum in confessione loqueretur* (on the martyr Stephen: *martyr ... primus*), ed. F. GORI, *Opera omnia di Sant' Ambrogio*, vol. 14.2 (Milano: Biblioteca Ambrosiana, 1989), p. 96.
[b] The Latin varies not in word choice but in word order: *operum suorum ... suorum operum*. See Introduction, section Style and figures.

71 COLLECT FOLLOWS. Hear us, our Saviour, and kindly accept this annual devotion of our solemn celebration,[36] so that, as the star has shone brightly to expose the path of salvation to the wise men, thus you pour out the light in our hearts through the grace of your gift, so that we who acknowledge you may under your protection walk *the way of truth* (Ps. 119, 30;[a] II Petr. 2, 2[b]). Through our Lord Jesus Christ your Son.

72 PREFACE. While we proclaim the praise of the Lord, his mighty deeds and the wonders that he has done, most beloved brothers, when he divided the sea before his people,[c] held before them the light, carried before them the fire,[d] *opened the doors of heaven* (Ps. 78, 23) and served them *the bread of angels* (Ps. 78, 25):[e] let us ask that he also encloses us with a similar watch of his mighty works, lest the fury of this world envelops us, and the path of life keeps an uncertain course, and the darkness of ignorance is [not] absent from the illumination of faith, and access to heaven is not open to prayer, and the living bread, by renouncing itself, does not provide life.[f] May he in truth grant what he bestowed in a mystery, *toward redemption of the people that he acquired for himself and to the praise of his glory* (Eph. 1, 14).[g] Through our Lord Jesus Christ his Son, who lives and reigns.

379

73 COLLECT FOLLOWS. The power of your works, O Lord, is as admirable as your mercy towards the wise men is loveworthy. For at your command the star provided guidance to the wise men and

---

[a] NRSV gives 'way of faithfulness'.

[b] Here, NRSV gives 'way of truth'.

[c] Cf. Ex. 14.

[d] Cf. Ex. 13, 21–22.

[e] Cf. Ex. 16.

[f] The sentence is complex and contains a number of double negations (litotes: *ne ... non pateat; ne ... non praebeat*), which could be translated with a strong confirmation ('so that the darkness of ignorance is wholly absent from the illumination of faith', 'so that heaven is wide open to prayer'). I have opted for the original uniformity, however, as explained in the Translation principles.

[g] BLAISE, *Dictionnaire*, s.v. *acquisitio*, gives this text as an example, with reference to Eph. 1, 14.

led them with a sure direction to Christ, whose true humanity in the flesh was such that his true majesty was resplendent in his work.[a] For he was shown as a child to the servants of stars and he was worshipped as a small child by the wise men. We therefore ask you, O Lord, that you will also mercifully correct our sins and lead us to the salutary vision of your truth, while the illumination of your mercy precedes us. Through our Lord Jesus Christ your Son.

74 PREFACE. Beloved brothers, let us pray to God, who sanctified the stream of the Jordan[b] and blessed the bond of marriage,[c] that we merit the forgiveness of sins only through the grace of him whose wonders we celebrate again every year. May he deign to grant this, who with the Father and the Holy Spirit lives and reigns [...]

380   75 COLLECT FOLLOWS. Hear us, O Lord, in the vigil of this solemn celebration, and we ask that you deign to kindly support with your wonders[37] the hearts[38] of this people, who celebrate the vigil dedicated to you, and that you who deigned to sanctify the waters of the Jordan[d] will also make us appear holy and unstained before you. Who with the Father and the Holy Spirit lives and reigns [...]

X MASS FOR THE EPIPHANY VIGIL

76 PREFACE. Let us pray, most beloved brothers, to our Lord and God of the benefactions of the unspoiled things of nature, that we who at Epiphany, that is the day of his revelation, are gathered for the sacred celebration of the vigil, believing that the light of his Incarnation, the birth from the Virgin, the Baptism at the Jordan and the miracles at Cana are a sign given for our salvation, are made such that we demonstrate in our deeds that we are enlightened in our confessions through the immeasurableness of his

---

   [a] Variatio in word order: *humanitas uera ... uera maiestas*; see Introduction, section Style and figures.

    [b] On Christ's Baptism in the river Jordan, see Matth. 3, 13–17.

    [c] On the Wedding at Cana, see Ioh. 2, 1–11.

    [d] Cf. Matth. 3, 13–17.

benefactions. Through our Lord Jesus Christ his Son, who lives with him [...]

77 COLLECT FOLLOWS. God, you who through your only-be-gotten Son Jesus Christ our Lord have given the sanctification of eternal salvation because the waters[39] procure regeneration,[a] and who yourself have come through the Holy Spirit when the spiritual dove descended on his head,[b] grant, so we ask, that that blessing may come upon this entire Church of yours, so that it may continuously protect all, bless each individual unceasingly, direct the way to those who follow you and open the door of the heavenly kingdom to all who expect him.[40] Through our Lord Jesus Christ your Son, who lives and reigns with you for ever.

381

78 COLLECT AFTER THE NAMES. Grant, almighty God, through the ineffable love of your mercy, that he whose power and majesty have shone through the diversity of your miracles, will also begin to shine in the purification of our hearts. Come down therefore into the offering present here, such that it supplies a medicine to the living and consolation to the deceased. And let the destiny of those whom the preceding reading has interwoven be included among the elect.[41] Through our Lord Jesus Christ your Son.

79 AT THE KISS OF PEACE. God, Illuminator of all peoples, grant to your own people that they rejoice in perpetual peace, and pour this radiant light into our hearts, that you instilled in the hearts of the three wise men. Through our Lord Jesus Christ your Son who lives with you.

80 PRAYER OF SACRIFICE. It is worthy and just, truly worthy and just that we praise you, almighty and everlasting God. For *you have displayed your might among the peoples* (Ps. 77, 14[c]) and you have

---

[a] On *regeneratio* and Baptism, see ROSE (ed.), *Missale Gothicum*, Introduction, p. 112.
[b] Cf. Matth. 3, 16.
[c] Vulgate: Ps. 76, 15.

382

revealed *your saving power among all nations* (Ps. 67, 2[a]), while you appointed the present day so that on it a star, clearer than all stars, incited men from all parts of the world to worship the infancy of the true King, and so that a ray of your light revealed the Lord of heaven and earth, born in the flesh to the salvation of all. Therefore the entire world rejoices throughout all the world,[b] now that joy has been poured out, and the heavenly powers too sing together a hymn of praise to your glory, saying unceasingly: HOLY, HOLY, HOLY.

81 BLESSING OF THE PEOPLE. God, you who deigned to hold the present day in such esteem that you chose to glorify it with so many miracles. AMEN.

You who have deigned, in the form of your creation, to descend as fount of living water for our salvation into the fount of the Jordan. AMEN.

And on this [day] the star taught the wise men to worship you and the pallid water produced wine. AMEN.

Be for your servants *light itself on their path* (Ps. 119, 105[c]), you who, with the star as sign, are glorified as the King of salvation. AMEN.

Convert the confounded hearts of humans to you, to seek you, you who at the wedding feast turned water into wine.[d] AMEN.

That the people, joined with the angels in heaven and protected by them, sing glory to you, God. AMEN.

Grant this, Saviour of the world, who with the Father and the Holy Spirit lives.

[a] Vulgate: Ps. 66, 3.

[b] *per orbem terrarum*: see no. 3.

[c] *lux itineris*: the Vulgate has *lumen semitae* (Psalterium Gallicanum) or *lux semitae* (iuxta Hebraeos). The Vetus Latina database gives no examples of the use of *iter* in this context: See Brepolis Vetus Latina database at http://apps.brepolis.net. proxy.library.uu.nl/vld/index.html (consulted 25 November 2015).

[d] *falernum*: BLAISE, *Dictionnaire*, s.v. *falernum* refers to the Gothic Missal for the use of this word, indicating a 'vin de qualité'. Both Prudentius (*Liber cathemerinon* IX.28) and Gregory of Tours (*Liber de virtutibus sancti Martini* 2.16 and 2.26) use the word in the context of Epiphany; see ELS ROSE, 'Liturgical Latin in Early Medieval Gaul', in MARY GARRISON et al. (eds), *Spoken and Written Language: Relations between Latin and the Vernacular Languages in the Earlier Middle Ages*, Utrecht Studies in Medieval Literacy 24 (Turnhout: Brepols, 2013), p. 303–313, at p. 309.

XI MASS FOR THE HOLY DAY OF EPIPHANY

82 PREFACE. Most beloved brothers, let us celebrate the venerable day of Epiphany and, in the light of his miracles, the first day
on which our Redeemer and Lord, from the years of his infancy,
demonstrated his miraculous strength and the power of his Father, through the obedient prayers of our worship and through
a solemn celebration, while we ask in devoted prayer that he who
has changed water into wine will now turn the wine of our offering into his own blood. And may he who has granted to others the
plenitude of unmixed wine, sanctify us through our drinking of
him and through the outpouring of the Holy Spirit the Comforter. Through our Lord Jesus Christ his Son, who lives with him [...]

383

83 COLLECT FOLLOWS. God, you who through the wondrous
signs of your miraculous strength have made known the way to
our salvation, and have granted to the wise men, who made their
way while a star shone forth before them, to worship and propiti-
ate before you, eternal King and everlasting Lord, with mystical
gifts, who in our body, through the sacrament of wondrous Baptism, cleanse us who are regenerated of the Spirit, by making us
to be born again, and through the gift of your ineffable power,
by today changing water into wine, have revealed your divinity
to your disciples: hear us, your suppliants, by reason of the day of
the most holy feast, and grant that we, illuminated[a] by your glory,
may die for the world [and] live for you, Christ the King, Saviour
of the world, who with the Father and the Holy Spirit lives and
reigns for ever.

84 COLLECT AFTER THE NAMES. Now that we have heard the
names and prayers of those who bring the offering, most beloved
brothers, let us appeal to the compassion of the almighty God

---

[a] *inluminati* and the derived noun *illuminatio* have the connotation of receiv-
ing the light of Baptism; see ROSE (ed.), *Missale Gothicum*, Introduction, p. 151.
In the Gallican rite it was common to administer Baptism during Epiphany, see
Introduction, section The liturgical year.

the Father, that he, who today through his Son has most wondrously changed the essence of water into wine, likewise deigns to convert the offerings and prayers of all into a divine sacrifice and to thankfully accept them, as he also thankfully accepted the gifts of his *righteous Abel* (Matth. 23, 35) and the offerings of his patriarch Abraham.[a] And may he command[42] that the destiny of those whose names the preceding reading has interwoven may be included[43] among the elect.[44] Through our Lord Jesus Christ his Son, who lives and always reigns with him.

384   85 COLLECT AT THE KISS OF PEACE. Lord Christ Jesus, you who are exalted in majesty and subject to power when you obeyed the orders of the mother in the strength of the Father, in order to reveal yourself as the son of man through obedience and at the same time to manifest yourself as God through wondrous deeds, who, for the sake of the cleansing of all peoples, went down into the bed of the Jordan to sanctify it, in order to wash away our sins and purify our consciences: visit your Church and hear the prayers of us all. Grant peace also to those who do not request it, so that the kiss that is given with the lips will be confirmed[b] by the hearts. May you deign to grant this, who with the Father and the Holy Spirit lives and reigns [...]

86 PRAYER OF SACRIFICE. It is truly worthy and just, fair and just that we always and everywhere bring thanks to you, Lord, holy Father, almighty and everlasting God, who for us made a

---

[a] On the typological interpretation of the sacrifice of Abel and Abraham in the early medieval West, see RUDOLF SUNTRUP, '*Te igitur.* Initialen und Kanonbilder in mittelalterlichen Sakramentarhandschriften', in CHRISTEL MEIER and UWE RUBERT (eds), *Text und Bild: Aspekte des Zusammenwirkens zweier Künste in Mittelalter und früher Neuzeit* (Wiesbaden: Reichert, 1980), p. 278–382; PALAZZO, *Le Moyen Âge*, p. 80–81; ROSAMOND MCKITTERICK, 'Text and Image in the Carolingian World', in ROSAMOND MCKITTERICK (ed.), *The Uses of Literacy in Early Mediaeval Europe* (Cambridge: Cambridge University Press, 1990), p. 297–318, at p. 306, and see the illuminated initial in the *Sacramentary of Drogo of Metz* (Paris, BnF lat. 9428, f. 15v) at http://gallica.bnf.fr/ark:/12148/btv1b60000332/f40.image.r=9428 (consulted 14 April 2016).

[b] *non negetur*: litotes; see Introduction, section Style and figures.

voice like thunder sound from heaven over the beds of the Jordan. To point out the Saviour of the world and to reveal the Father of eternal light you opened heaven, blessed the air, purified the fount and affirmed your only Son through the dove of the Holy Spirit.[a] Today the founts have received your blessing and carried away our condemnation, such that they provide purification of all sins to the faithful, and through rebirth to eternal life make those created to temporal life by a fleshly birth into children of God.[b] For those whom death through transgression had taken away are called back by eternal life to the kingdom of the heavens, by receiving them back from death. We therefore join our voices with the praises of the angels in due exultation, and we offer *the sacrifice of our thanksgiving* (Ps. 50, 14; Ps. 50, 23; Ps. 107, 22) by venerating your glory through the wondrous sacrament during the celebration of this day, by reason of the apparition of Jesus Christ our Lord and because of the beginning of our vocation. Through this our Lord, through whom the angels praise your majesty [...]

87 COLLECT AFTER THE SANCTUS. Truly holy, truly blessed is   385
our Lord Jesus Christ your Son, who as a sign of the heavenly birth today gave these wonders of his majesty to the world, so that he showed the star to the wise men to worship it, and with the passage of time changed water into wine, and through his Baptism sanctified the stream of the Jordan, Jesus Christ our Lord, who on the day before his suffering [...]

88 AFTER THE CONSECRATION. Pay merciful heed to the sacrifices presented, so we ask, O Lord, through which [sacrifices] gold, frankincense and myrrh are no longer offered, but with these same gifts [our oblation] is signified, offered, sacrificed, received.[c] Through our Lord Jesus Christ your Son, who lives with you and with the Holy Spirit.

[a] Cf. Matth. 2, 1–11.

[b] References to Baptism administered on this day.

[c] *declaratur, offertur, immolator, sumitur*: the four verbs have no subject; I suggest that they should be linked to the sacrifice of the Eucharist. The series of verbs is asyndetic.

89 BEFORE THE LORD'S PRAYER. Not presuming our own merit, Lord, but obeying the command of our Lord Jesus Christ your Son, whom you sent to liberate us *from the darkness and shadow of death* (Luc. 1, 79; Is. 9, 2; Ps. 107, 10).[45] For *we are not worthy to be called your children* (Luc. 15, 21), but are commanded to say: OUR FATHER.

90 AFTER THE LORD'S PRAYER. Deliver us from evil, almighty, everlasting God, and rule over us, [you] who for us repelled the dominion of death, so that we, O Lord, are always mindful of your commandments with eagerness, of your judgements with fear, of your promises with joy. Through him who lives, rules and reigns with you, God in the unity of the Holy Spirit for ever and ever.

386

91 BLESSING OF THE PEOPLE. Almighty Creator, who have made yourself known often with so many wonders, but today with remarkable ones. AMEN.
Who on the returning feast first multiplied as shepherd the wine in the casks, then the bread in the baskets.[a] AMEN.
Over the heads of your manservants and maidservants, let your Holy Spirit descend from your throne, you who were seen to descend in bodily form in the dove, while John baptised in the Jordan. AMEN.
Fill their souls with the wine of righteousness, who today through your Word have changed the taste of the water. AMEN.
Safeguard your people, who venerate you with singular devotion through the holy mysteries. AMEN.
Lay on a feast, Shepherd, by which, when the hunger of this world has been overcome, the souls will feed lavishly on the food of eternity. [AMEN.]
Pour over them also the gifts of spiritual virtues, so that the enemy in no way can enter into them by force or mislead them with deceit. AMEN.

---

[a] A reference to the miracles of the Wedding at Cana and the Feeding of the Five Thousand (Marc. 6, 30–44; Ioh. 6, 1–13; see also Marc. 8, 1–21).

But may, through perseverance in good conduct, those *who are called through adoption as children* (Rom. 8, 15; Eph. 1, 5) be considered worthy *to enter into the possession of the heirs* (Rom. 8, 17). AMEN.

That when they are required to pass away[46] from here by departing, they will be given to be admitted there, from where the star, admired by the wise men, has worshipped you as God, while it stood at the crib. AMEN.

May you deign to grant this, who lives, rules and reigns in the perfection of the Trinity. AMEN.

92 AFTER THE EUCHARIST. Let us entreat in harmonious prayer, most beloved brothers, the mercy of God, that these salutary sacraments, received by our hearts, purify our soul and sanctify our body, and confirm our heart[a] and soul equally in the hope of heavenly things. May he deign to grant this, who lives and reigns [...]

387

93 COLLECT FOLLOWS. Look favourably, Lord, on your people, and release that people, which[47] you grant to benefit from the divine sacraments, from all sins. Through our Lord Jesus Christ your Son [...]

XII MASS FOR THE ASSUMPTION OF THE BLESSED MARY, MOTHER OF OUR LORD[b]

94 PREFACE. The inexplicable mystery of the noble day of the mother of the Lord is all the more worthy to be celebrated the more it is exceptional among humankind by reason of the assumption of the Virgin. For through her the integrity of life has obtained a Son and death has found no equal example.[c] And the

---

[a] *uiscera*: I interpret the word here as 'heart' in view of the prayer for confirmation in hope; a physical interpretation, on the other hand, would be justified on the basis of the stylistic structure (*animam corpusque ... uiscera et corda*: chiasmus).

[b] On this Mass, see ROSE (ed.), *Missale Gothicum*, Introduction, p. 223–232.

[c] In addition to the Assumption, other Marian themes are mentioned in this Mass, especially Mary's divine motherhood and the birth of Christ. See ROSE (ed.), *Missale Gothicum*, Introduction, p. 225.

blessed one caused no less wonder through her departing than exultation through the birth of her only child. [She is] not only admirable because of the pledge she received through faith, but [also] laudable because of the death through which she departed. Let us pray, dear brothers, with particular joy, with all-embracing love, with a faithful prayer and an attentive heart, that we will be assisted and protected through the support of her who is praised as fertile virgin, as blessed through her offspring,[a] as illustrious through her merit, as happy through her departure, while we implore the mercy of our Redeemer, that he deigns to lead the faithful standing around here[b] to the same place where he has taken the blessed mother Mary to glory while the apostles served her.[c] May he deign to grant this, who with the Father and the Holy Spirit lives and reigns, God for ever [...]

388

95 COLLECT FOLLOWS. God, who, because you do not allow that that work of the creation of the world that you have created alone

[a] The word *partus* may signify 'delivery' or '(giving) birth', as well as the infant resulting from childbirth.

[b] The verb *circumstare* literally means 'to stand around in a circle', while the participle *circumstantes* signifies 'bystanders': LEWIS and SHORT, *Latin Dictionary*, s.v. *circumsto*, (2) *circumstantes*. In patristic writings and liturgical texts, where the variants *circumadstare* and *circumadstantes* are found (BLAISE, *Dictionnaire*, s.v. *circumadsto*), the verb refers to those attending Mass, who 'were present standing at the celebration of the holy sacrifice': BLAISE, *Vocabulaire*, p. 201, section 84. On the participation of the faithful in the Gallican Mass, see Introduction, section The performance of prayer.

[c] Two Latin versions of the ancient Greek apocryphal narratives of the assumption of Mary must have circulated in early medieval Gaul: the anonymous *Adsumptio sanctae Mariae* (ed. WILMART, *Analecta reginensia*, p. 323–357, see no. 17) and the *Transitus Mariae* attributed to Melito of Sardes, of which the earliest manuscript goes back to the eighth century (Montpellier H 55, f. 97v–101r; cf. MIMOUNI, *Dormition*, p. 264). Capelle demonstrated that the Pseudo-Melito text was of greater influence in the Gothic Missal than the *Adsumptio* edited by Wilmart, which Gregory of Tours presumably used in his *In gloria martyrum* 1.4: BERNARD CAPELLE, 'La messe gallicane de l'Assomption: son rayonnement, ses sources', in *Miscellanea liturgica in honorem L. Cuniberti Mohlberg*, 2 vols. (Rome: Bibliotheca 'Ephemerides liturgicae' 22 and 23, 1948–1949), vol. 2, p. 33–59, at p. 57. Both texts describe the presence of the apostles at Mary's death, as they were called back from their missionary tasks in all corners of the world. *Adsumptio Mariae* 19, ed. WILMART, p. 338; *Transitus Mariae*, Montpellier H 55, f. 99r, l. 10–12.

on command of your authority go to waste, have built a house for yourself in the womb of the Virgin,[a] and have revealed unheard secrets to the world, lest the people fashioned by you were lost, so that the little womb of a modest maiden could contain him whom the heights of the heavens [could] not grasp: we humbly ask you to allow those from whom and for whom you took on the mortal body, through the intercession of your blessed mother Mary, to gain the victory, having conquered the desire for worldly honour. Saviour of the world, who with the eternal Father lives and reigns, God, in unity with the Holy Spirit, God for ever [...]

96 COLLECT AFTER THE NAMES. By pouring out our prayers, most beloved brothers, let us invoke the Lord, the inhabitant of the virgin hospice, the bridegroom of the blessed *wedding canopy* (Ps. 19, 5),[b] the Lord of the tabernacle, the King of the temple, who conferred that innocence on the mother from which the incarnate deity deigned to be begotten. And this spirit, conscious of nothing of this world and only attentive to prayer, retained purity in her behaviour, which she had received in her womb through the blessing of the angel.[c] And through her assumption, she who carried the Author of life did not experience the stain of death. Let us therefore invoke the Lord, that by his mercy the dead may be liberated from hell to that place where the body of the blessed Virgin was taken from her tomb.[d] May he deign to grant this, who lives in the perfect Trinity.

[a] *domum tibi in aluum uirginis fabricasti*: on Mary as a *templum praeciosum*, see no. 17.

[b] Vulgate: Ps. 18, 6.

[c] On the purity of Mary, see IRENAEUS OF LYONS, *Aduersus haereses*, 4.33.11, ed. ROUSSEAU, SChr 100, p. 830.

[d] According to the tradition of the *Transitus Mariae*, Christ announced to his mother the transfer of her body to paradise while he came down to take her soul to heaven (Montpellier H 55, f. 99r, l. 29–30). After the assumption of her soul (Montpellier H 55, f. 99v, l. 5–6), the apostles buried her body at Gethsemane in the new tomb that Christ had indicated to them (Montpellier H 55, f. 99v, l. 4; *Adsumptio Mariae* 28.2, ed. WILMART, p. 315). A cloud appeared in which angels were seated to carry Mary's body heavenward (Montpellier H 55, f. 99v, l. 30–32).

389   97 COLLECT AT THE KISS OF PEACE. God, Father of the whole world, you who have lived spiritually in the saints and even bodily in the Virgin mother, who,[48] enriched with the fertility of your abundance, flowering in gentleness, strong in love, joyful through inner peace, outstanding in faith, praised *by the angel as 'full of grace'* (Luc. 1, 28), *by Elizabeth as 'the blessed one'* (Luc. 1, 42), *by the peoples rightly as 'the blissful one'* (Luc. 1, 48), whose faith has given us a mystery, whose delivery[a] joy, whose life profit and whose decease this feast: we humbly ask that you will generously grant to all, now at the solemn celebration, the peace that you have given to your disciples at the assumption of your mother.[b] Saviour of the world, who lives with the Father and the Holy Spirit.

98 PRAYER OF SACRIFICE. It is worthy and just, almighty God, to duly give great thanks to you at this most festive time, on the day that must be revered more than all others, on which the faithful people of Israel came out of Egypt,[c] on which the Virgin mother of God departed from this world to Christ. For she is not infected with sin through corruption and has not endured decomposition in the tomb, she is free from defilement, glorious through her child, untroubled through her assumption, exalted through the gift of paradise. She did not know the injury of coition, she accepted the promises concerning her child, not subjected to the pains of childbirth, nor to the toils of death. And her life was not annulled by will, nor her death by power of nature. [She is] *the beautiful wedding canopy from which a worthy bridegroom comes forth* (Ps.

---

[a] On the different meanings of the word *partus* (both delivery and infant), see no. 94.

[b] *Transitus Mariae*, Montpellier H 55, f. 99r, l. 4; cf. *Adsumptio Mariae* 24, ed. WILMART, p. 343. A second exchange of peace is recorded when Christ arrived to carry Mary's soul to heaven (Montpellier H 55, f. 100v, l. 20–21; *Adsumptio Mariae* 47.3), and a third one before he actually returned to heaven, when angels had come to carry Mary's body to paradise (Montpellier H 55, f. 101r, l. 10–11).

[c] A reference to the antiphon Peter began to sing when the apostles buried Mary: *Exiit Israel de Aegipto alleluia* (cf. the Easter antiphon *In exitu Israel de Aegypto*, based on Ps. 114 (Vulgate 113), 1): *Transitus Mariae*, Montpellier H 55, f. 99v, l. 28; *Adsumptio Mariae* 34, ed. WILMART, p. 348.

19, 5),[a] *light to the nations* (Is. 42, 6; 49, 6), hope of the faithful, robber of the demons,[b] confusion of the Jews, vessel of life, tabernacle of glory, heavenly temple. And the merits of this young girl are praised [still] higher when the examples of the old Eve are offered for comparison.[c] For the one brought life to the world, the other introduced the law of death, the latter sent us to death by collaborating with the enemy, the former saved us by generating life,[d] the latter, through the apple from the tree, struck us in the very root, *but from this shoot a flower has emerged* (Is. 11, 1) to restore us with its scent and to heal us with its fruit. The latter begets a curse consisting of grief,[e] the former confirms a blessing[f] that entails salvation. The perfidy of the latter consented with the serpent, deceived her husband, damned her offspring, but the obedience[g] of the former reconciled the Father, merited the Son and absolved posterity. The latter gives bitterness to drink from the juice of the apple,

390

[a] Vulgate: Ps. 18, 6. The phrase *Speciosus thalamus,* etc. also occurs in a sermon attributed to Hildefonsus of Toledo, as indicated by EDMUND BISHOP, *Liturgica historica: Papers on the Liturgy and Religious Life of the Western Church* (Oxford: Clarendon, 1918, repr. 1962), p. 176–178. Sims-Williams argues that Hildefonsus took it from the Gothic Missal: SIMS-WILLIAMS, *Religion and Literature,* p. 315 and ID., 'Thoughts on Ephrem the Syrian in Anglo-Saxon England', in MICHAEL LAPIDGE and HELMUT GNEUSS (eds), *Learning and Literature in Anglo-Saxon England: Studies Presented to Peter Clemoes* (Cambridge-New York: Cambridge University Press, 1985), p. 205–226, at p. 217.

[b] Gerard Bartelink has demonstrated how the word *praedo,* a general indication of the devil as plunderer, is now turned against the devil, presented here as the booty: GERARD BARTELINK, 'Denominations of the Devil and Demons in the *Missale Gothicum*', in NIENKE VOS and WILLEMIEN OTTEN (eds), *Demons and the Devil in Ancient and Medieval Christianity,* Supplements to Vigiliae Christianae 108 (Leiden: Brill, 2011), p. 195–209, at p. 205–206.

[c] On Mary as the new Eve, parallel to the presentation of Christ as the new Adam in I Cor. 15, 22 and 45, see IRENAEUS OF LYONS, *Aduersus haereses* 3.22.4, ed. ROUSSEAU and DOUTRELEAU, SChr 211, p. 438–444.

[d] *ista generando saluauit*; cf. IRENAEUS OF LYONS, *Aduersus haereses* 3.22.4, ed. ROUSSEAU and DOUTRELEAU, SChr 211, p. 440.

[e] *maledictione*: cf. Gen. 3, 16. On the reception of this 'curse' in patristic (and rabbinic) literature, see HANNEKE REULING, *After Eden. Church Fathers and Rabbis on Genesis 3, 16–21* (Leiden: Brill: 2005).

[f] *benedictione*: cf. Luc. 1, 28 (*benedicta tu*).

[g] *oboedientia*: see IRENAEUS OF LYONS, *Aduersus haereses* 3.22.4, ed. ROUSSEAU and DOUTRELEAU, SChr 211, p. 440.

the former exudes an eternal sweetness through the fount of her Son. The latter, through the sour taste, has deterred the teeth of her children, the former has fashioned the food of delight from the very sweetest bread. For, depending on her, nobody will perish except those scornful of sating their throats with this bread. But let us now change the old moans into new joys. We therefore turn back to you, fruitful[49] virgin, untouched mother, woman in labour without having known a man, woman of honour through your Son, unsoiled, happy, through whom inspired joys[50] have succeeded one another for us. For as we have rejoiced in her birth and celebrated her delivery,[a] so we glory in her departure. It were perhaps insufficient if Christ had sanctified you through his entry alone, if he had not also honoured so excellent a mother through her departing.[b] You were rightly taken up through the assumption by him whom you took up devotedly by receiving him through faith, so that the earth[c] could not keep you enclosed as you did

---

[a] On the double meaning of the word *partus*, see nos 94 and 97.

[b] The two preceding sentences (*Cuius sicut gratulati ... ardonasset egressu*) create several interpretative problems. The beginning of the first sentence ('For as we rejoice in her birth') seems to refer to the birth of Mary herself as a joyful event, celebrated by the Christian community on the appointed day (8 September) in the same manner as Christmas (*partu*, on 25 December) and Mary's Assumption (*transitum*, 18 January – concerning the date of Mary's assumption in the Gallican sacramentaries, see ROSE (ed.), *Missale Gothicum*, p. 223–224). However, the word *ortus* is rarely used to indicate a mortal's birth. It could also refer to Christ's birth, which is regularly indicated by this word, as in other prayers in the Gothic Missal (II, 13). Scholars who in the past understood *ortus* as a reference to Mary's birth, assumed that the prayer refers to it a second time in the phrase *Parum fortasse fuerat, si te Christus solo sanctificasset introitu* ('It were perhaps insufficient if Christ had sanctified you through [his] entry alone...'). Leroy ('Un texte peu remarqué sur la fête de la nativité de Notre-Dame', in *Recherches de science religieuse* 28 [1938], 282–289) and Morin ('Une préface du *Missale Gothicum* supposant la fête de la nativité Notre-Dame en pays gallican dès le VIIᵉ siècle', in *Revue Bénédictine* 56 [1945–1946], 9–11) interpreted *introitu* as referring to Mary's birth ['your entry'], while I follow Capelle ('La nativité de la Vierge dans le Missale Gothicum', *Revue Bénédictine* 58 [1948], 73–76), as the translation shows ('his entry'), in the latter's assumption that *introitu* refers to Christ's entrance into the human body: the Incarnation. For a more detailed discussion with reference to relevant literature, see ROSE (ed.), *Missale Gothicum*, p. 227–229.

[c] *rupes*, meaning rock or cavern, refers to the burial place of Mary's body, from which it was taken to paradise. See no. 96.

not belong to it. O soul, truly adorned with different crowns of honour, to whom the apostles render their holy service, the angels their chant,[a] Christ his love, the cloud its vehicle,[b] the assumption paradise and glory the place of honour amid the choirs of virgins. Through Christ our Lord, to whom the angels and archangels unceasingly [sing, saying: Holy, holy, holy...]

99 COLLECT AFTER THE SANCTUS. Truly holy, truly glorious is your only-begotten Son our Lord Jesus Christ, who, although he was of himself equal to the Father, became of our [being],[c] still *lower than the angels* (Hebr. 2, 9), and while from his Father's side he had immortality, from his mother's side he assumed[51] that which must die, so that in himself he would liberate humankind from hell, while death did not keep him in the tomb.[d] For he, on the day before his suffering [...]

391

100 AFTER THE CONSECRATION. Let, O Lord, the co-eternal and co-operating Comforter, the Holy Spirit, descend in this sacrifice of your blessing, so that we accept the offering that we bring to you from your fertile ground, after you have sanctified it through a heavenly reward, so that when the bread is changed into the body and the cup into the blood, that which we have offered for our sins contributes to our merits. Grant this, almighty God, who lives and reigns for ever.

101 BEFORE THE LORD'S PRAYER. Almighty and everlasting God, hear your people who beseech you by reason of the honour of the most blessed mother Mary. And be so bounteous to our prayers that we may be considered worthy to say with confidence the prayer that our Lord Jesus Christ your Son taught us to pray, saying: [OUR] FATHER [...]

---

[a] *Transitus Mariae*, Montpellier H 55, f. 99v, l. 32–33.

[b] *Transitus Mariae*, Montpellier H 55, f. 99r, l. 30–31.

[c] The possessive pronoun *nostra* is not accompanied by a noun.

[d] On Christ's humanity, which he received from his mother Mary, see IRENAEUS OF LYONS, *Aduersus haereses* 3.22, ed. ROUSSEAU and DOUTRELEAU, SChr 211, p. 430–444.

102 AFTER THE LORD'S PRAYER. Deliver us from all evil, from every sin, Author of all good and God the Creator, and defend us through the intercession of your blessed mother Mary with daily protection against the snares of the daily enemy. Saviour of the world, who with the Father and the Holy Spirit lives and reigns.

103 BLESSING OF THE PEOPLE. God, who, while the heavens do not hold you captive, has deigned to be enclosed in the sanctuary of the Virgin's womb. AMEN.

392   So that the untouched mother bore fruit through the Holy Spirit and attained incorruptibility through her child.[a] AMEN.
Give your people the angel as guardian, who foretold to Mary the Son that faith would receive [in her]. AMEN.
May that blessing, which without human seed formed the Redeemer in the Virgin's womb, sanctify your flock. AMEN.
So that under your protection the Church rejoices in the congregated people, as Mary is considered worthy to glory in her child. AMEN.
May you deign to grant this, who with the Father and the Holy Spirit lives and reigns, God for ever and ever. AMEN.

104 AFTER THE EUCHARIST. Safeguard your faithful, so we ask, O Lord, so that what they have faithfully adopted with soul and body may protect them through the intercession of the blessed Mary. May you deign to grant this, who with the everlasting Father lives and reigns for ever.

105 COLLECT FOLLOWS. We ask, O Lord our God, that through the intervention of the blessed Mary, the holy mysteries which we have received actively may also be pursued mindfully, and that the comfort thus given to us may confer on us eternal life. Through him who with you and the Holy Spirit lives and reigns.

---

[a] On the double meaning of *partus*, see nos 94, 97 and 98.

XIII MASS FOR THE FEAST OF SAINT AGNES, VIRGIN AND MARTYR[a]

106 PREFACE. On the feast of the birth[b] of the blessed martyr Agnes, most beloved brothers, let us be present before the Lord with great joy and a devoted heart. For truly worthy of honour is the feast of her who was born for the world such that she was reborn for heaven, who was begotten *under the law of death* (Rom. 8, 2) such that she crushed the author of death, who was made in the weak gender so that[c] she looked down on the tortures that are terrifying for strong men, who was made in such a fragile condition that, as a girl,[d] she triumphed over virgins and powers. O true nobility, that so came forth from the earthly race that it has come to the fellowship of divinity. Let us therefore pray that she who stands worthy before the divine countenance intervenes for us with her prayers. May he deign to grant this, who with the Father and the Holy Spirit lives and reigns.

107 COLLECT FOLLOWS. God, Helper and Reward of the conqueror Agnes, hear us through her intervention now that we celebrate the feast of her passion. For you have granted Agnes the grace of such a great gift, that she crushed at her young age and overcame in the weakness of her gender the devil, who through Eve had overthrown the entire human race, that she struck him down through her confession of the truth, while clearly showing that she was not only a martyr of perpetual virginity and would remain a virgin, but that she [also] deserved to become

393

---

[a] On this Mass, see Rose (ed.), *Missale Gothicum*, Introduction, p. 272–277.

[b] While the word *natale* is commonly used for the anniversary of a saint's death, the word *natalicia* in this prayer seems to refer to Agnes's earthly birth. Likewise, the presence of many references to birth and life on earth seem to imply that the prayer is related to a feast commemorating Agnes's earthly birth. See Rose (ed.), *Missale Gothicum*, Introduction, p. 273–275.

[c] On the *sic-ut* structure of this prayer, completed with an O-exclamation, see Rose (ed.), *Missale Gothicum*, Introduction, p. 273–274. For a more extensive discussion, see Introduction, section Style and figures.

[d] On Agnes as a *puella* (*senex*), see Paolo Tomea, 'La *Passio Agnetis* e il topos della *puella senex*', *Analecta Bollandiana* 128 (2010), 18–55.

the bride of the *unblemished Lamb* (Ex. 12, 5; Leu. 23, 12), purely on the grounds of her name.[a] Accept therefore the offering of this sacrifice with joy, you who have crowned the virgin, glorious through such great merits. Through our Lord Jesus Christ your Son.

108 COLLECT AFTER THE NAMES. God, who renews the flower of virgins through Mary's womb by returning to us in the Virgin mother what was lost through the intemperate mother.[b] And by following [Mary], the holy virgins have come into your wedding canopy[c] with the palm of martyrdom. One of them is the blessed martyr Agnes, whose passion is solemnly celebrated today, who has roused us to the joy of her piety. For her feast is truly worthy of honour, who so came forth from the earthly race that through the consecration of her virginity she came to the fellowship of the divinity.[d] Through our Lord.

394

[a] The lamb that the Israelites offered on their exodus from Egypt is indicated in Ex. 12, 5 as *agnus absque macula* (NRSV: 'lamb without blemish'). Augustine gives a twofold etymology of Agnes's name, relating it to the Latin word indicating a female lamb ('*agnam*') and to the Greek word for 'chaste' ('ἀγνή'). Thus Agnes 'was what she was called' (*Erat quod vocabatur*). AUGUSTINE, *Sermo* 273, PL 38, col. 1250–1251; see CÉCILE LANÉRY, 'La légende de sainte Agnès: quelques réflexions sur la genèse d'un dossier hagiographique (IVᵉ–VIᵉ s.)', in *Mélanges de l'École de Rome – Moyen Âge* 126 (2014), footnote 12, http://mefrm.revues.org/1702?lang=en (consulted 15 September 2015). Given the emphasis on Agnes's virginity, which is as inherent as her proper name (see also no. 108), it may not be too far-fetched to apply the Irenaean model of the virgin Mary as a new Eve to this virgin as well (cf. no. 98).

[b] The relative clause *Deus qui ... renouas* has no main clause: the prayer is indeed a succession of relative clauses. See Translation principles. On the image of Mary as the new Eve ('the intemperate mother'), see nos 107 and 98.

[c] In the *Passio Agnetis* BHL 156, dated in the first or second decade of the sixth century (LANÉRY, 'La légende de sainte Agnès', section 17–19), Agnes states that her heavenly bridegroom has spread her a wedding bed (*thalamus*), ed. PL 17, col. 735–742, at col. 736B.

[d] On the intrinsic connection between virginity and martyrdom, see LANÉRY, section 4 and 6–7.

109 AT THE KISS OF PEACE.[a] May the feast of your blessed martyr Agnes always greet us joyfully, so we ask, O Lord, so that she[b] may pour the joy of her glorification and the purity of peace into us, and make us people who are pleasing to you. Through our Lord.

110 PRAYER OF SACRIFICE. It is truly worthy and just [that we praise you.] For it is for you, O Lord, that the solemn celebration is held, for you the sacred day is celebrated, which the blood of the blessed virgin Agnes, shed as a testimony to your truth, has marked with the magnificent honour of your name. Although she was as yet of a tender body and not yet of the mature blossom of a girl, to the glorification of your grace you gave her this virtue of faith and strength of patience, so that the constancy of the virgin did not yield to the cruelty of her persecutor, so that through this the crown of martyrdom would be all the more glorious, since amid the bitter suffering this could not be snatched away from her gender or her age. And now that we today celebrate the day of her passion with devotion, we offer you a sacrifice of thanksgiving,[c] O Lord our God, as you are glorified

---

[a] This and the following prayer (no. 110) incorporate parts of early Roman prayers for Agnes and other martyrs as collected in the *Sacramentarium Veronense*, see ROSE (ed.), *Missale Gothicum*, Introduction, p. 276–277 and LEO EIZENHÖFER, 'Die Präfation für den Geburtstag der heiligen Agnes', *Archiv für Liturgiewissenschaft* 11 (1969), 59–76. Agnes's *natale* on 21 January is mentioned in the oldest Roman list of bishops and martyrs, the *Depositio episcoporum et martyrum*, included in the Calendar of 354, ed. LIETZMANN, *Die drei ältesten Martyrologien*, p. 3.

[b] The relative *quae* could also refer to the feast (*festivitas*) rather than to Agnes. In the latter interpretation, *suae* accompanying *glorificationis* ('her glorification') is an example of the use of a reflexive possessive pronoun instead of an indicative pronoun (*eius*), see ROSE (ed.), *Missale Gothicum*, Introduction, p. 88–89. The translation would be 'May the feast of your blessed martyr Agnes always greet us joyfully, so we ask, O Lord, so that it may pour the joy of [Agnes's] glorification and the purity of peace into us, and make us people who are pleasing to you'. Since the celebration of a saint's feast consists of a Mass, it would therefore follow that through the feast itself the faithful are rendered pleasing to God.

[c] *uictimam laudis*; Ps. 49, 14 and 23 and Ps. 106, 22 (all Vulgate numbering) have *sacrificium laudis* as in no. 15, 86, 469. Ps. 115, 8 (Vulgate) and Hebr. 13, 15 have *hostiam laudis* (as in nos 278, 357, 398, 418). The combination *uictimam laudis* does not occur in the Vulgate, and for Ps. 49, 14 not in the Vetus Latina either.

395 in the fellowship of joy by the *dominions, rulers and powers*, the heavens and *the powers of the heavens* (Eph. 1, 21; Luc. 21, 26), and the blessed seraphim with the angels and archangels,[a] while you rule in glory with your Son our Lord and with the Holy Spirit, saying: HOLY [...]

XIIII MASS FOR THE FEAST OF THE HOLY VIRGIN CECILIA[b]

111 [PREFACE.] Let us pray to God the Keeper of all things, most beloved brothers, now that we celebrate with faithful devotion the venerable and exalted passion of the blessed martyr Cecilia and the sacred ceremony, that he favourably attends the faithful prayers of his Church and that, as he has given her the crown to-day, he also generously grants us mercy. Through our Lord Jesus Christ his Son, who lives with him [...]

112 COLLECT FOLLOWS. Almighty and everlasting God, who *chooses what is weak in the world to confound all that is strong* (I Cor. 1, 27), grant us that we rejoice with fitting devotion in the feast of the holy martyr Cecilia, so that we praise your power in her passion and gain the help that is foreseen for us. Through our Lord Jesus Christ your Son.

---

[a] The fifth-century Pseudo-Dionysius the Areopagite is the oldest source of a division in three choirs of three angelic orders: *Seraphin, Cherubin, Throni; Dominationes, Virtutes, Potestates; Principatus, Archangeli, Angeli.* Gregory the Great changed the order by switching *Virtutes* and *Principatus*, a tradition which is echoed here. Cf. PETER VAN DER EERDEN, 'Engelen en demonen', in MANUEL STOFFERS (ed.), *De middeleeuwse ideeënwereld, 1000–1300* (Heerlen-Hilversum 1994), p. 117–143, at p. 125–126, with reference to PSEUDO-DIONYSIUS AREOPAGITA, *De caelesti hierarchia 7–9* and GREGORY THE GREAT, *Homiliarum XL in evangelia libri duo*, XXXIV; see also CAROL STRAW, *Gregory the Great. Perfection in Imperfection* (Berkeley-Los Angeles-London 1988), esp. p. 35–36.

[b] On this Mass, see ROSE (ed.), *Missale Gothicum*, Introduction, p. 277–279.

113 COLLECT AFTER THE NAMES. Look upon your people, we ask you, O Lord, rejoicing in the glorification of the holy martyr Cecilia, and grant that obedience of the hearts sanctified to you that pleases [you], so that those who continually honour you in your saints may acquire the perpetual abundance of your gifts. And may they invisibly embrace what they visibly offer, so that as the merits of Cecilia are pleasing, the offices of our worship may be rendered agreeable [to you.] Through our Lord Jesus your Son.

396

114 COLLECT AT THE KISS OF PEACE. Grant Lord, that we are cherished by the supplications of your holy martyr Cecilia, so that we are recommended by the intercession and merits of her whose venerable feast we anticipate with the ceremony. And grant, so we ask Lord, that the peace expressed with the lips may be confirmed[a] by the hearts. Through.

115 PRAYER OF SACRIFICE. It is worthy and just, fair and salutary that we always bring thanks to you, almighty and everlasting God, who *makes your power perfect in weakness* (II Cor. 12, 9). For the blessed and glorious Cecilia, striving for heavenly fellowship by despising the marriage of this world, was not impeded by the capriciousness of her age, nor held back by fleshly enticements, nor deterred by the frailty of her gender, but amid her youthful years, amid the delights of the world, amid the punishment of her persecutors, she gained as a chaste virgin and martyr a multiple victory, and to yet greater triumph she led her Valerianus, whose bride she had been, to the heavenly kingdom.[b] And she merited the crown of chastity such that she entered the wedding canopy of the King[c] not only as a virgin

---

[a] *non negetur*: litotes; see Introduction, section Style and figures.

[b] The prayer refers to the *Passio Caeciliae*, dated to the end of the fifth century (ed. DELEHAYE, *Étude sur le légendier romain*, p. 194–220).

[c] *regium thalamum*: Ps 44, 16 (iuxta Hebraeum). In the *Passio Caeciliae*, the word *thalamus* is used to indicate the wedding of Cecilia and Valerianus (c. 3, ed. DELEHAYE, p. 196); for 'bedroom' the word *cubiculum* is used (c. 4, ed. DELE-HAYE, p. 196).

397 but also as a martyr. Through Christ our Lord, through whom
your majesty is praised by the angels and worshipped by the dominions.[a]

116 BLESSING OF THE PEOPLE. Most high, most excellent,
most merciful God, bless your manservants and maidservants.
AMEN.
Grant them, through the mediation of the holy virgin Cecilia, a
heart concerned with love for you, devoted to fear of you and perfect in honour of you. AMEN.
Give them tranquil times, health of the body and salvation of the
soul. AMEN.
Let them be considered worthy to seek you through the faith, to
find you through their deeds and to please you through grace.[52]
AMEN.
And, with you as witness, let them do those things with diligence
that, with you as judge, will be worthy of reward. AMEN.
May you deign to grant this, who lives, rules and reigns in the perfect Trinity.

XV MASS FOR THE FEAST OF THE HOLY
BISHOP CLEMENT[b]

117 [PREFACE.] Let us venerate with due service, most beloved
brothers, this day of the glorious passion of the holy and venerable
bishop Clement, through whom the superstitious heathenism of

---

[a] On the tradition of *dominationes* as part of the heavenly hierarchy, see no. 110.
[b] On this Mass, see ROSE (ed.), *Missale Gothicum*, Introduction, p. 279–282.
See also recent work by Samantha Herrick on the role of Clement as a disciple of
the apostles and the continuation of this apostolic tradition in the later medieval
West, most notably SAMANTHA KAHN HERRICK, 'Apostolic Founding Bishops
and their Rivals: The Examples of Limoges, Rouen, and Périgueux', in CHRISTINE
BOUSQUET-LABOUÉRIE and YOSSI MAUREY (eds), *Espace sacré, mémoire sacrée:
le culte des évêques dans leurs villes (IVe–XXe siècles)*, Hagiologia 10 (2015), p. 15–35
and EAD., *Imagining the Sacred Past. Hagiography and Power in Early Normandy*
(Cambridge MA: Harvard University Press, 2007), p. 54–55.

the Jews[a] collapsed and the catholic faith has shone in the hearts of the people, now that the circle of the year has passed round, while we pray for the mercy of the Lord, that he, who gave him as a light to the darkest ignorance[b] of heathendom, [he], *the dawn from on high, will break upon us* (Luc. 1, 78) with his light. That he who placed him at the head of the holy Church[c] deign to sustain us, who groan under the rod of worldly sorrows, upon Clement's supplications. Through our Lord Jesus Christ his Son, who lives with him [...]

118 COLLECT FOLLOWS. Christ, almighty Lord, who led the blessed bishop Clement, by reason of your name immersed in the storm of the heathen [and] in the depth of the sea,[d] out in glory after the wars, when the arena was opened up just as you had tested him in the combat of war: we ask your goodness, that, plucked from the storm of desire, you present us, innocent, before the glory of the Father. Saviour of the world who lives and reigns with the eternal Father, God in the unity of the Spirit.

398

[a] The reference to Clement's mission to Jews and pagans is derived from the *Passio Clementis* I.1, ed. FRANCISCUS XAVERIUS FUNK and FRANCISCUS DIEKAMP, *Patres apostolici*, vol. 2 (Tübingen: Laupp, 1913), p. 50–91; see ROSE (ed.), *Missale Gothicum*, Introduction, p. 281. *[...] per quem* [sc. *Clementem*] *superstitiosa gentilitas conruit Iudaeorum*: Jews are considered here as pagans (*gentilitas*), although in patristic writings the term *gentilitas* is used as opposed to Judaism: BLAISE, *Dictionnaire*, s.v. *gentilitas* (2). ISIDORE, *Etymologiae* VIII.10.2 characterises the *gentiles* primarily as those not (yet) baptised, in which sense the term seems to be used here; see WOLFRAM DREWS, 'Jews as Pagans? Polemical Definitions of Identity in Visigothic Spain', *Early Medieval Europe* 11 (2002), 189–207, esp. p. 196 and p. 200, footnote 40: ' When the Jews were regarded as an *incredula gens*, they could eventually be reckoned as *gentilitas*'. *superstitio* is connected to Jews e.g. by ISIDORE, *Etymologiae* VIII.4.9: *Iudaeis ... quorum superstitio*, see DREWS, 'Jews as Pagans?' p. 200–201.

[b] The reference to darkness and ignorance (blindness) echoes the *Passio Clementis* V.2-XIV.3 (ed. DIEKAMP, *Patres*, p. 55–67), where the story is told of Sisenius, who was first struck by blindness and then converted after Clement cured him. See ROSE (ed.), *Missale Gothicum*, Introduction, p. 281–282.

[c] A reference to Clement's role as successor to Peter as the fourth bishop of Rome. See also no. 121 and ROSE (ed.), *Missale Gothicum*, Introduction, p. 281.

[d] The image of the sea may be prompted by Clement's martyrdom at sea (*Passio Clementis* XXIII, ed. DIEKAMP, p. 77–79); cf. ROSE (ed.), *Missale Gothicum*, Introduction, p. 281.

119 COLLECT AFTER THE NAMES. Now that the list of names of the deceased has been recited, let us, most beloved brothers, humbly pray for the mercy of almighty God, that through the mediation of his holy bishop and martyr Clement he grants absolution to the deceased and salvation to the living. Let us also commemorate Clement's most faithful [converts] Sisenius and Theodora,[a] that God grants them, in whom he sowed faith to believe in him through the blessed martyr, a share of the kingdom of paradise. Through our Lord Jesus Christ his Son, who lives with him [...]

120 COLLECT AT THE KISS OF PEACE. God, Harmoniser[53] of discord and Origin of eternal fellowship, undivided Trinity, who through the holy bishop Clement subjected the disbelief of Sisenius, cut off from the unity of the Church, to the catholic faith and wove [it] into eternal love: hear our prayers and grant us that *peace which you once left to your apostles when you were about to ascend into heaven* (cf. Ioh. 14, 27). And let those who through the impression of the lips are now joined[54] by a kiss, remain in peace under your protection in the future. May you deign to grant this, who lives, rules and reigns in the perfect Trinity.

399

121 PRAYER OF SACRIFICE. It is worthy and just, truly worthy that we bring thanks to you, Lord, holy Father, almighty and everlasting God, on the solemn celebration of your holy martyr Clement, who left his relatives and his fatherland and, following the fragrance of your name,[b] travelled across lands and seas and in self-

[a] Sisenius and Theodora occur in the *Passio Clementis* as converts of the martyr. Cf. *Passio Clementis* V–XIV, ed. DIEKAMP, p. 55–67; Rose, *Missale Gothicum*, Introduction, p. 281.

[b] *odor nominis tui*: Augustine uses the image of the fragrance of Christ's name to signify the salvation of the world. AUGUSTINE, *De civitate dei* 16.37, ed. BERNHARD DOMBAART and ALPHONS KALB, CCSL 47–48 (Turnhout: Brepols, 1955), vol. 48, p. 542.

renunciation took upon him the cross of foreignness[a] to follow you in the footsteps of your apostles. According to the promise of your Son,[b] O Lord, you have requited him, both in the present world and in the future one, the hundredfold reward of what was given. For you give[c] back in foreign regions the parents he had lost in his fatherland, when he had soon surrendered himself to the teaching of the most blessed Peter. Those of his earthly family whom he had lost, you give back as partakers of divine nature. Then you appoint him, by asking him as successor to his teacher, to be the primate of the city of Rome, the honour of which he had despised on your behalf. And in exchange for this transitory renown you

[a] BLAISE, *Dictionnaire*, s.v. *peregrinatio*, gives this prayer as an example of the meaning 'départ (du missionnaire) pour l'étranger'. It is not certain whether this is what Clement's *peregrinatio* entailed according to the author of this prayer. Gregory of Tours does indeed count Clement among the Roman missionaries who arrived in Gaul: GREGORY OF TOURS, *In gloria martyrum* 35 and 36. However, the passage could also refer to an older Clementine tradition represented by the 'Pseudo-Clementine' *Recognitiones* and dated to the fourth century: GEOLTRAIN and KAESTLI (transl.), *Écrits apocryphes chrétiens*, vol. 2, p. 1186, in which Clement's search for the Christian faith is narrated. Clement leaves Rome in search of acceptable answers, but ironically he only finds them after becoming a pupil of Peter and finally succeeding him as bishop of Rome: *Recognitiones*, transl. GEOLTRAIN and KAESTLI, p. 1627–2003. For the motif of 'the parents he had lost in the fatherland', see *Recognitiones* VII.5–11, transl. GEOLTRAIN and KAESTLI, p. 1857–1862. Against that background, *peregrinatio* would not refer to a missionary endeavour, but to a journey abroad or a spiritual quest. I also take into account that this prayer occurs in the *Sacramentarium Veronense* and is, therefore, certainly older than the work of Gregory and probably older than the Gallic Clementine legend dated in the fifth century, see GRIFFE, 'Origines chrétiennes'; ID., *La Gaule chrétienne*, vol. 1, p. 104–115. For the dating of *Sacramentarium Veronense* 1190, see Mohlberg (ed.), *Sacramentarium Veronense*, p. lxx–lxxiv. The *Passio Clementis* is dated to the fourth or fifth century, see ELIZABETH A. LIVINGSTONE (ed.), *The Oxford Dictionary of the Christian Church* (Oxford: Oxford University Press, 1997), p. 360; SIEGMAR DÖPP and WILHELM GEERLINGS, *Lexikon der antiken christlichen Literatur* (Freiburg i.Breisgau: Herder, 1998), p. 131. I reconsider my interpretation in ROSE (ed.), *Missale Gothicum*, Introduction, p. 280–281, where I interpreted the entire passage as referring to Clement's exile to the mines of Cherson at the Black Sea, as recounted in the *Passio Clementis*.

[b] Cf. Matth. 19, 29 and Marc. 10, 30.

[c] Where this prayer addresses God with reference to the hagiographic narrative of Clement's life and deeds, it employs the present tense instead of the more common perfect tense. I follow the original tenses in the translation.

make him illustrious in heavenly honour. Finally you bring him, elevated by the glory of his martyrdom and in exchange for his temporal deeds, to the eternal crown. Through Christ our Lord, through whom the angels praise your majesty and the archangels cry out unceasingly, saying: HOLY, HOLY, HOLY.

122 BLESSING OF THE PEOPLE. Custodian of the priesthood, Consecrator[55] of martyrdom, Palm of triumph, God, bless your manservants and maidservants. AMEN.
Grant through[56] this martyr that they live virtuously, act prudently and behave such that they can be saved.[57] AMEN.
So that under his authority they do those things that are considered worthy upon your judgement, and are found unworthy to be subjected to punishment. AMEN.
May you deign to grant this, who lives and reigns in the perfect Trinity.

400

XVI MASS FOR THE FEAST OF THE HOLY BISHOP AND MARTYR SATURNINUS[a]

123 [PREFACE.] Let us humbly pray to God, most beloved brothers, who has steeped the imperishable palms of the glorious martyrs with the blood of victory and has dedicated the blessed celebration of this day to those of his who claimed victory for him: that he who has given the celebration of this day will also give the full accomplishment[58] of this feast. And let he who has given that which the celebration of the feast encompasses grant that we follow this with the affection of devotion. And may that which benefited on this day the glory of his holy man and most blessed martyr Saturninus be of service to our salvation. Through our Lord Jesus Christ his Son, who with him and with the Holy Spirit.

124 COLLECT FOLLOWS. Almighty and everlasting God, we bring due thanks to Jesus Christ our Lord, in whose likeness the most

[a] On this Mass, see ROSE (ed.), *Missale Gothicum*, Introduction, p. 292–296.

blessed Saturninus, while he offered his sacrifice, himself became the sacrifice, and, while exercising the office of bishop to which he was elected, fulfilled his martyrdom full of devotion, so that through the eminence of his righteousness and his victory he became both martyr and bishop.[a] And when the magnitude of his faith increased,[59] while he accepted the holy chair he seized the crown of martyrdom.[b] We therefore humbly pray to your majesty, Lord, that you who gave him such great endurance in your name grant this congregation, through his intercession, forgiveness of its sins. Through our Lord Jesus Christ your Son.

125 COLLECT AFTER THE NAMES. It is a great and always festive [good] to us, most beloved brothers, to faithfully pray with supplications for which remuneration has already been made through the merits of the bishop and martyr Saturninus. For by observing the precepts of our Saviour he not only merited the episcopate and a blessed life,[60] but also consecrated this such honourable service through his blessed martyrdom.[c] And let us pray through his merits to the almighty God, that he transfer the souls of the deceased from hell to there where, by reason of[61] his love, he has deigned to take him up after his victory. Through our Lord Jesus Christ his Son, [who lives] with him [...]

401

[a] The resemblance between the Latin words for martyr (*testis*) and bishop (*antistes: et testis fieret et antestis*) is lost in the translation. The vulgar spelling *antestis* (for *antistes*), common in the Gothic Missal, only adds to the wordplay, see ROSE (ed.), *Missale Gothicum*, Introduction, p. 39. The *Passio Saturnini* underlines the double crown (*corona geminata*) of episcopacy and martyrdom with which Saturninus was crowned: *Passio Saturnini episcopi Tolosani et martyri* 1, ed. THIERRY RUINART, *Acta primorum martyrum sincera et selecta* (Amsterdam, 1713²), p. 129–133, at p. 130; see ROSE (ed.), *Missale Gothicum*, Introduction, p. 293–294. On the edition by Ruinart, see ANNE-VÉRONIQUE GILLES, 'Le dossier hagiographique de saint Saturnin de Toulouse', in MONIQUE GOULLET and MARTIN HEINZELMANN (eds), *Miracles, vies et réécritures dans l'Occident médiéval*, Beihefte der Francia 65 (Ostfildern: Thorbecke, 2006), p. 341–405, at p. 363.

[b] Here, as in the phrase *et testis fierit et antestis*, a reference is made to the concurrence of Saturninus's episcopate and martyrdom.

[c] On this prayer as a further testimony of Saturninus's *corona geminata*, see ROSE (ed.), *Missale Gothicum*, Introduction, p. 294.

126 COLLECT AT THE KISS OF PEACE. God, who crowns your saints in exchange for their merits with *the tenderness of your mercy* (Luc. 1, 78) and with your abundant richness, such that you bring wranglers' souls to peace through their intercession: we ask through the intervention of the holy bishop and your martyr Saturninus that you separate the appeased people, gathered for his feast, from all rivalry, so that you deign to consider them as perfect before your countenance. Through our Lord Jesus Christ your Son.

127 PRAYER OF SACRIFICE. It is worthy and just, it is very good and it is a privilege for us to extol with particular devotion your omnipotence, Trinity God, through the service of the supplicant tongue, in exchange for the triumphant martyrdom of all, but particularly at this time to greet with due honour the blessed Saturninus, the illustrious witness of your awe-inspiring name.[a] For when the crowd of gentiles drove him out of the temple they brought him into heaven.[b] Indeed, this your bishop, from eastern parts,[c] was sent from Rome to the town of Toulouse, and, as substitute for your Peter, he has in turn accomplished both the office of bishop and martyrdom on the Garonne. We therefore bless you, O Lord, in all your works and we implore that the spiritual desires of the Christian people will be solemnly fulfilled, and that the mercy [which we] ask of you will be quickly obtained through

[a] *tremendi nominis tui*; *nomen terribile* occurs more frequently in the Vulgate (Deut. 28, 58; Ps. 110, 9).

[b] From this point the *contestatio* follows the *Passio Saturnini* rather closely, see ROSE (ed.), *Missale Gothicum*, Introduction, p. 294–296.

[c] According to De Gaiffier the words *ab orientis partibus* are the result of confusion with a prayer for Advent, with which Saturninus's feast on 29 November often coincided: BAUDOUIN DE GAIFFIER, 'A propos d'un passage du "Missale Gothicum". S. Saturnin de Toulouse venait-il d'Orient?', *Analecta Bollandiana* 66 (1948), 53–58. According to Anne-Véronique Gilles this confusion gave rise to later hagiographic traditions situating Saturninus's origin 'in the East': ANNE-VÉRONIQUE GILLES, 'L'évolution de l'hagiographie de saint Saturnin de Toulouse et son influence sur la liturgie', in *Liturgie et musique (IXᵉ–Xᵉ siècle)*, Cahiers de Fanjeaux, 17 (Toulouse: Privat, 1982), p. 359–379, at p. 363–364; EAD., 'Dossier hagiographique', p. 352; see also ROSE (ed.), *Missale Gothicum*, Introduction, p. 294–296.

the supplications of your holy Saturninus, so that you will grant
the reward of our merits when the glory of your majesty will have
appeared over us. Through Christ our Lord, to whom all angels   402
and archangels and also the cherubim and seraphim rightly proclaim unceasingly, saying: HOLY, HOLY, HOLY.

XVII MASS FOR THE FEAST OF THE HOLY
APOSTLE ANDREW[a]

128 PREFACE. Most beloved brothers, let us honour with eager
awareness and with our entire heart[b] the day of the apostle, so in-
vigorating for the world, on which the so famous fisher Andrew,[c]
after the illumination of Achaea through his preaching,[d] has honoured that land with his blessed martyrdom and has brought the
sacrifice of his own body by embracing the sign of the cross,[e] while

---

[a] On this Mass, see ROSE (ed.), *Missale Gothicum*, Introduction, p. 262–271.

[b] *uisceribus*: interpreted here as a spiritual faculty.

[c] Cf. Matth. 4, 18 and Marc. 1, 16.

[d] The tradition of Andrew's mission to Achaea is transmitted in early Latin
sources, both lists of apostles, such as the *Breviarium apostolorum*, in ANTOINE
DUMAS and JEAN DESHUSSES (eds), *Liber sacramentorum Gellonensis*, CCSL 159
(Turnhout: Brepols, 1981), p. 489; ISIDORE OF SEVILLE, *De ortu et obitu patrum*,
69, ed. C. CHAPARRO GÓMEZ, *De ortu et obitu patrum* (Paris, 1985), p. 203 and
narrative sources, most notably the Latin apocryphal Acts of Andrew, transmitted
as the *Liber de miraculis beati Andreae apostoli* (BHL 430) and generally – though
not undisputedly – attributed to Gregory of Tours, ed. JEAN-MARC PRIEUR, *Acta
Andreae*, CCSA 6 (Turnhout: Brepols, 1989), p. 569. See further ROSE, '*Virtutes
apostolorum*: Origin', p. 61–64 on the Latin lists of apostles, and 65–68 on the debate concerning the attribution of the *Liber de miraculis* to Gregory.

[e] The phrase refers to Andrew's salutation of the cross as narrated in the apocryphal Acts of Andrew, and is indicative of the influence of this narrative tradition
in the liturgical prayers of the Gothic Missal. Other such elements are found in
the collect at the kiss of peace (131) and the prayer of sacrifice (132). For an analysis of narrative sources, both Latin and Greek, that transmit the Acts of Andrew,
and their relation to the liturgical prayers in commemoration of Andrew, see ELS
ROSE, 'Apocryphal Traditions in Medieval Latin Liturgy. A New Research Project
Illustrated with the Case of the Apostle Andrew', *Apocrypha* 15 (2004), 115–138.
On the relation between the apocryphal Acts of the Apostles and liturgical texts in
general, see EAD., *Ritual Memory. The Apocryphal Acts and Liturgical Commemoration in the Early Medieval West, c. 500–1215* (Leiden-Boston: Brill, 2009).

we pray for the renowned mercy of almighty God, that he command this people, forewarned by the sign of His cross[62] and supported by the faith, to go where the martyr went before when he had completed combat. May he deign to grant this, who with the Father and the Holy Spirit lives and reigns.

129 COLLECT FOLLOWS. Lord Christ, glorious cross-bearer, who in battle so fortified the steadfastness of the blessed apostle Andrew, crucified on account of the glory of your name, that you exalted him through his martyrdom:[63] hear this humble company of faithful present here and grant that we, who now pay the due interest to his solemn feast, preserve in the coming time, with his help, the manner of a most chaste life. Through you, O Christ, Saviour of the world, who lives, rules and reigns with the eternal Father, God in the unity of the Holy Spirit, for ever and ever.

130 COLLECT AFTER THE NAMES. Let us pray to the almighty God and our Lord, most beloved brothers, that he commends to himself the solemn ceremony of this day, which we have undertaken for the feast of his most blessed apostle and martyr Andrew. And that, as he has today protected Andrew, taken prisoner for preaching his Word, in the bonds of the dungeon and during scourging and crucifixion,[a] and has given him the crown because of his noble martyrdom, he deigns through Andrew's intervention also in all temptations to protect us who believe in Him, who are wearied by the oppressions of this world and the snares of the adversary, and to give bountifully of His mercy. And that through the intercession of his apostle he sanctifies the names that have been recited of those who offer and of those who have passed away. Through our Lord Jesus Christ his Son, who lives with him [...]

131 COLLECT AT THE KISS OF PEACE. Almighty and everlasting God, who have bound to you the blessed apostle Andrew through such great love, that through your help he defeated the storms of this world, crushed the affections of the flesh and did not fear the

403

---

[a] *Liber de miraculis* 36, ed. PRIEUR, CCSA 6, p. 649.

assaults of the shining sword, whom the cross received as a humble man[a] to give him back as victor: give peace, so we ask, to these servants gathered for his solemn celebration, that, while they give a kiss to their neighbours, they are lenient to those by whom they have been offended and obtain forgiveness for their sins. Through our Lord Jesus Christ your Son, who with you […]

132 PRAYER OF SACRIFICE. It is worthy and just, fair and just to bring thanks to you for your ineffable love, almighty, everlasting God, and to proclaim with inestimable joy the passion of your saints, through Christ our Lord. For he has given faith to the blessed Andrew in his first calling,[b] and has granted him victory in his martyrdom. The blessed Andrew had received these two matters. He therefore had perseverance in his preaching and endurance in his martyrdom. For after the unjust lashes, after the enclosure of the dungeon, he offered himself, bound to the cross, as a pure sacrifice to you, God.[c] Most meekly, he stretched out his arms to the heavens, he embraced the banner of the cross, he kissed the cross, he became acquainted with the secrets of the Lamb. And then, when he was led to the cross [and] was crucified, he suffered in the flesh and spoke in the spirit, he forgot the torments of the cross, while from that cross he preached Christ. As indeed his body was stretched on the wood, so Christ was glorified by his tongue, for hanging on the cross he gave thanks that he

404

[a] *quem crux eleuata suscepit humilem*: reference to the texts *Conuersante et docente* (BHL 429), ed. MAXIMILIAN BONNET, '*Passio sancti Andreae apostoli*', *Analecta Bollandiana* 13 (1894), p. 373–378, at p. 376 and *Epistola presbyterum et diaconorum Achaiae* (BHL 428) 10, ed. MAXIMILIAN BONNET, *Acta apostolorum apocrypha* (Leipzig: Mendelssohn, 1898 / Hildesheim: Georg Olms, 1990), vol. 2.1, p. 1–37, at p. 24–26. See ROSE (ed.), *Missale Gothicum*, Introduction, p. 267–268.

[b] The words *in prima vocatione* refer to the tradition that emphasises Andrew as the first disciple (cf. Matth. 4, 18–22 and Marc. 1, 14–20). The epithet Πρωτόκλητός, granted to Andrew in the Byzantine tradition, is primarily based on Ioh. 12, 20–34; see PETER MEGILL PETERSON, *Andrew, Brother of Simon Peter: His History and His Legends* (Leiden: Brill, 1958), p. 5.

[c] The relation of this prayer to the early-sixth-century *Passio Conuersante et docente* (BHL 429) and, to a lesser extent, the *Epistola presbyterum et diaconorum Achaiae* (BHL 428), both quoted fairly literally, is discussed in ROSE (ed.), *Missale Gothicum*, Introduction, p. 267–270.

was united with Christ. He did not allow himself to be freed from the cross, lest his struggle waned as time passed. The crowd looks on and laments for him, and demands that he whom they know as the saviour of their heart[a] be released from his bonds, and calls for the just one to be freed, lest the people be destroyed by this sin. Meanwhile the martyr gives up the spirit in order to gain possession of the kingdom of the eternal Judge. Grant us through his merits, almighty God, that, safe and protected against all evil, we will always bring praise and thanks to you, our Lord, God of the martyrs and Prince of the apostles,[b] with the angels and archangels who do not cease to proclaim your glory, saying [...]

133 COLLECT AFTER THE SANCTUS. *Hosanna in the highest* (Matth. 21, 9), truly holy, truly blessed, truly glorious is our Lord Jesus Christ your Son, who consecrated the blessed apostle Andrew first through his election[c] and then through his strife. For he, on the day before [...]

134 COLLECT AFTER THE CONSECRATION. We worship you, Lord, who humbly underwent your Passion for the salvation of the world, but we believe that in the Father you always remain powerful. We pray that we who participate at your altar will glory in God[64] with the blessed apostles. Grant this, Saviour of the world, who lives with the eternal Father and the Holy Spirit.

135 COLLECT BEFORE THE LORD'S PRAYER. God, you who have commanded that your holy apostles, taken away from the storms of this world, would be attached to the company of angels, whom you as most loving exhorter have also taught how they should pray to you, adhering to your instructions: we humbly ask that you, who have nourished them to their salvation[d] with a joyful ad-

405

---

[a] On the phrase *reparatorem mentis* and the general approach to the apostle as mediator of salvation, see ROSE, 'Apocryphal Traditions', p. 126–128.

[b] The epithet *princeps/principes apostolorum* is traditionally reserved for Peter (and Paul), see BLAISE, *Vocabulaire*, p. 219 and 225 (sections 98 and 104).

[c] Matth. 4, 18 and Marc. 1, 16.

[d] Implicit reference to Luc. 11, 1–4.

dress,[65] permit us with full trust to proclaim that same prayer and to say: OUR FATHER.

136 COLLECT AFTER THE LORD'S PRAYER. Rescue us from all evil, almighty God, and grant that, because the radiant light of the apostles surrounds us, we reject the mole of sin and the vanity of the world. Through our Lord Jesus Christ your Son.

137 BLESSING OF THE PEOPLE. Lord, almighty God, who, seated in glory above the stars, have bequeathed to us your blessed apostles as a caring star, of whom beforehand you first elected on their merit a splendid cohort, strong through a happy light, to predestine them for the kingdom. AMEN.
Give mercifully that the people gathered here[a] are protected by the sign of your cross, so that they overcome each attack of the enemy power. AMEN.
Let the doctrine of the apostle pour into their senses, so that they contemplate you with a serene heart. AMEN.
So that in that terrifying time of judgement they are defended by the help of those whose teaching they have followed. AMEN.
May you deign to grant this, who with the Father and the Holy Spirit lives and reigns, God [...]

XVIII MASS FOR THE FEAST OF THE HOLY VIRGIN EULALIA[b]

138 [PREFACE.] Let us, most beloved brothers, [pray] to almighty God, who with the crown of glory[c] so consecrated the wise virginity[d] joined with faith, that through him who brought Mary moth-

406

---

[a] On the meaning of the word *circumstantem*, see no. 94.
[b] On this Mass in honour of Eulalia of Mérida, see ROSE (ed.), *Missale Gothicum*, Introduction, p. 309–312.
[c] The wording *apice gloriae* corresponds to the *Passio Eulaliae* 1, ed. ENRIQUE FLOREZ, *España sagrada* (Madrid: Antonio Marin, 1771–1908), vol. 13, p. 398–406, at p. 398; cf. ROSE, (ed.), *Missale Gothicum*, Introduction, p. 311.
[d] Cf. Matth. 25, 1–13.

erhood, Eulalia became a martyr.[66] The one was blessed through the result of giving birth, the other through dying, the one because she fulfilled the duty of Incarnation, the other by seizing the example of martyrdom, the one believed the angel, the other resisted the enemy, the one [was] elected so that through her Christ was born, the other so that through her the devil was conquered. Let us ask with a humble prayer that he hears the blessed Eulalia when she prays for us, and that we who are impeded in all things because sin turns against us, are rescued from all stain of sin through her help. Through our Lord Jesus Christ his Son, who with him [...]

139 COLLECT FOLLOWS. God, who granted glory to your holy martyr Eulalia in exchange for punishment, life in exchange for death, strength in exchange for weakness, the crown in exchange for martyrdom: grant that we may so rejoice in your mercy as she delights in glory, and that we may be considered worthy to obtain forgiveness in eternity by your grace. Through our Lord Jesus Christ your Son, who with you [...]

140 COLLECT AFTER THE NAMES. Let us humbly pray to God, most beloved brothers, who has granted the glorious and imperishable crown of martyrdom to his holy servant Eulalia, that we, who do not deserve glory, may with the help of divine mercy obtain forgiveness through her prayers. And that he also deigns to grant to our beloved, who have gone before us in the sleep of peace, the beatitude of everlasting life and the grace of perpetual light. Through our Lord Jesus Christ his Son, who lives with him [...]

141 COLLECT AT THE KISS OF PEACE. God, Dissipator[67] of enmities, Seeker of peace, whose goodness tends to join together what is disjoined as your love tends to peacefully maintain what is pure: grant, Lord, that when we obey the teaching of your apostles, you connect us with peace, adorn us with love and sanctify us with purity. And may we who are deemed worthy to take as our example the martyrdom of the blessed virgin Eulalia be considered worthy to obtain the victory over wrath so overcome. Through our Lord Jesus Christ your Son, who lives with you [...]

407

142 PRAYER OF SACRIFICE. It is worthy and just, fair and salutary that we always and everywhere bring thanks to you, Lord, holy Father, almighty and everlasting God, and that we praise you in all your deeds. For through the gift of your grace you have adorned your servant Eulalia with a noble mark of the spirit, so that unharmed in herself she preserved the beauty of your image. She was truly a worthy companion of your Son,[a] as, though of the weaker gender, she entered strongly into combat and, above what could be expected from human strength, she surrendered herself to undergo punishment in the fervour of love for you. For she shed her blood as a precious salve under the testimony of the good confession, and offered her unspoiled body to the flames to become a fragrance of the sweetest incense. She went to the judgement seat of the bloodthirsty ruler: not because she was sought [but] to gain the Kingdom, out of contempt for punishment, to find what she sought, to behold him whom she had confessed, without fear of judgement, convinced[b] of the crown, not weakened by the tools of torture, not distrustful of the reward. She was questioned and she acknowledged you, and through a remarkable miracle your majesty received the exhaled spirit of the virgin, which [your majesty] took from the flame, in the form of a dove, so that she ascended into heaven as virgin and martyr under this sign through which you, Father, had revealed your Son on earth.[c] Through whom the angels praise your majesty and the archangels do not cease to proclaim, saying [...]

[a] On Eulalia as Christ's bride (*sponsa*), see *Passio Eulaliae* 4, ed. FLOREZ, p. 400; ROSE (ed.) *Missale Gothicum*, Introduction, p. 311.

[b] *non ambigua*: litotes in the sense that *ambiguus* is negative: uncertain; see Introduction, section Style and figures.

[c] A direct reference to the fifth- or sixth-century *Passio Eulaliae* 8 (ed. Florez, p. 405), a passage based on PRUDENTIUS, *Peristephanon* 3, v. 161–165, ed. CUNNINGHAM, p. 283. The image also occurs in GREGORY OF TOURS, *In gloria martyrum* 90, ed. KRUSCH, p. 548; see ROSE (ed.), *Missale Gothicum*, Introduction, p. 311–312.

408 ## XVIIII MASS FOR THE CONVERSION OF SAINT PAUL[a]

143 God, who everywhere spreads the fame of the honour of the blessed apostle Paul, grant, so we pray, that we are always cherished by his teaching and merit. Through [...]

144 COLLECT FOLLOWS. Splendour of the saints, Remunerator of the righteous, God, *who is above all and through all and in us all* (Eph. 4, 6), for whom *a contrite heart is a sacrifice* (Ps. 51, 17) and *a prayer a* pure *burnt offering* (Ps. 141, 2),[b] grant us, through the intercession of the most blessed apostle Paul, sanctification of the heart, ardour of the spirit and purity of the body, so that when mortal sin has been put to death we always bring you offerings of praise with our spirit and body undefiled. May you deign to give [...]

145 [COLLECT AFTER THE NAMES.] God, on this day of his calling you have changed the heart and name of your apostle Paul, insolent towards the piety of Christ's name,[68] and struck [down] by a heavenly voice and by fear. First the Church dreaded him as a persecutor, now she rejoices in having him as teacher of the heavenly commandments. You have therefore struck him with outer blindness to make him see within, and you removed for him the darkness of cruelty and conferred on him knowledge of divine law in order to summon the gentiles. But you also rescued him from the peril of death at sea *when he was shipwrecked for the third time* (cf. II Cor. 11, 25) for *the faith he had fought*
409 *against* (cf. Gal. 1, 23), when he was already a devoted man: grant, so we pray, that we too, who revere his conversion and faith, after the blindness of sin may behold you in heaven, who illuminated[c] Paul on earth. And may you willingly accept the gifts present

---

[a] On this Mass, see ROSE (ed.), *Missale Gothicum*, Introduction, p. 232–236.
[b] Vulgate: Ps. 140, 2.
[c] *inluminasti*: on the spiritual meaning of this verb and its noun *illuminatio*, see no. 83 and ROSE (ed.), *Missale Gothicum*, Introduction, p. 151.

here, that they may be acceptable to you through the prayers of
your apostle.

146 COLLECT AT THE KISS OF PEACE. God, who writes with
your finger the laws of righteousness[a] *in the hearts of the faithful*
(cf. II Cor. 3, 3), and who, on the present day of his calling, so
writes in Paul from heaven the fervour of your charity, *not with
ink but with your living Spirit* (II Cor. 3, 3), that he surrendered
his body to be broken for the members of your Church who once
had crushed the members of that same Church: grant us fellowship in sincere brotherly charity through the mediation of this
instructor and teacher of the faith, and deign to grant [us] just
one spark from the multiple flame of your love, which he possessed, so that through fervent love we follow the teacher, whose
passionate ardour we continue to celebrate through the precept
of charity.

147 PRAYER OF SACRIFICE. It is worthy and just, truly fair and
just that we bring thanks to you, Lord, holy Father, almighty
and everlasting God, who, in order to show that you wish to forgive the sins of all, converted the persecutor of your Church on
one word of your calling, and at once made for us a teacher out
of the persecutor. For he who had accepted letters from others
for the destruction of the churches,[b] began to write his own [let-
ters] for the restoration of those same churches, and to show that
from a Saul he had become a Paul, *as a wise architect he* hastily
laid a foundation (I Cor. 3, 10), so that your holy catholic Church   410
rejoices in him as builder by whom she was previously destroyed,
and that he became such a great defender of her that he did not
fear all punishments of the body or even death of the body. For
he has become the head of the Church who had shattered the
members of the Church, he surrendered the head of his mortal
body to receive Christ as head of all his members.[c] For which he

[a] Cf. Ex. 31, 18 and Deut. 9, 10, where the two tablets of the covenant are said to
have been written with the finger of God.
[b] Cf. Act. 9, 2.
[c] Cf. Col. 1, 18; Eph. 1, 22–23.

was even considered worthy to be *a chosen instrument* (Act. 9, 15), who has received the same our Lord Jesus Christ your Son in the dwelling of his heart. Through whom [the angels] praise your majesty [...]

XX MASS FOR SAINT PETER'S CHAIR[a]

148 [PREFACE.] While we celebrate the highly honourable day of the laudable celebration, on which, through an outstanding faith, the *Son of the highest God* (cf. Matth. 16, 16)[b] is revealed through the mouth of Peter,[c] and on which he truthfully confessed in the presence of his fellow apostles on the question by Christ concerning himself and who He was,[d] when the blessed *Bariona* (Matth. 16, 17) was chosen through the Word of the Redeemer by reason of his devoted faith so that *on*[69] *this rock* (Matth. 16, 18) of Peter the foundation of the Church was laid,[e] [let us pray], most beloved brothers, that the Creator of beatitude himself, who elevated the faith of Peter with such glorious praise, strengthens his people. Through our Lord.

149 COLLECT FOLLOWS. God, who on this day gave the blessed Peter as head of the Church after you, when he truthfully confessed you and was worthily elevated by you, we humbly pray that you, who gave a shepherd so that no sheep be lost,[f] save [us], so that the flock escapes errors, through the intercession of him whom you appointed at the head. And may you deign [...]

411

---

[a] On this Mass, see ROSE (ed.), *Missale Gothicum*, Introduction, p. 236–244.
[b] *filius excelsi dei*: the Vulgate gives *filius dei vivi*. The repeated references to Matth. 16, 13–20 in this prayer make it plausible that the pericope was read on this day, as is the case in contemporary Gallican Mass books like the *Bobbio Missal* (ed. LOWE, p. 36) and the *Lectionary of Luxeuil*, ed. SALMON, p. 67–68 (with Ioh. 21, 15–19).
[c] Reference to Matth. 16, 13–15.
[d] Implicit reference to Matth. 16, 13–15.
[e] Cf. Matth. 16, 17–18.
[f] Cf. Ioh. 21, 15–17.

150 AFTER THE NAMES. Let us invoke God with supplications, who conferred on the blessed disciple Peter such power that, if he will have bound, no other will loose, and what he will have loosed on earth will be loosed in heaven:[a] that, when the souls of the deceased are led out of hell, *the gates of Hades*, which the Church believes will be overcome by the faith of the apostles,[b] *will not prevail* (Matth. 16, 18) through sin over those who are buried. Through our Lord Jesus Christ.

151 COLLECT AT THE KISS OF PEACE. Most merciful Creator, who set the disciple on fire with such great love that he leapt out of the boat and quickly hastened to you bare-footed across the sea,[c] and because you saw this love and *gave him the keys to heaven* (Matth. 16, 19): look mercifully on the voices[d] of those who implore you, so that all who join together on [your] command at the kiss [of peace] expel envy from the heart and are led through grace to where Peter is the gate watcher of heaven.[e] Grant this, Saviour of the world.

152 PRAYER OF SACRIFICE. It is worthy and just [that we bring thanks to you], who in your profusion, with the copious gift of your infinite clemency, deign to raise up the handiwork of

[a] Cf. Matth. 16, 19.

[b] Although one could interpret the text as a reference to the authority of the apostles to forgive sins, based on Matth. 16, 18–19 as referred to here and confirmed in Matth. 19, 24, related prayers indicate that it is not 'sins' (*crimina*) that are believed to be overcome by the apostles, but the gates of Hades (*infernae portae*). As far as the wording of the text is concerned, I indeed assume that the relative *quas* in line 5 of the Latin edition refers to *portae* and is not written instead of *quae* to refer to *crimina*. This prayer is also found in the *Bobbio Missal* 119 (ed. LOWE, p. 36) in the context of St Peter's Chair, with the same wording and orthography. The Mass for Peter and Paul in the Gothic Missal corroborates this interpretation through the phrase *Hic [sc. Petrus] portas inferni … uicit* (no. 378).

[c] Cf. Matth. 14, 29.

[d] The sentence combines a visual verb (*inspice*) and an auditive noun (*voces*).

[e] The notion of Peter as the gatekeeper of heaven (*ianitor caeli*) occurs in HILARY OF POITIERS, *Commentarius in Matthaeum* 16, ed. JEAN DOIGNON, *Sur Matthieu*, SChr 258 (Paris: Cerf, 1978–1979), p. 54 and in AUGUSTINE, *Epistula* 36, ed. ALOIS GOLDBACHER, *Sancti Augustini epistulae*, CSEL 34.2 (Vienna: Tempsky, 1895–1898), p. 50.

412

your creation such that you had compassion for the little slave of clay, entrusted *the keys of heaven* (Matth. 16, 19) to a person of earthly making and, *to judge the tribes* (Matth. 19, 28), installed the throne of the supreme seat in the highest. The present day is a witness that the chair of the episcopacy of the blessed Peter is established, this day on which the apostle by merit of his faith was appointed as head of the Church[a] because he confessed the mystery of the revelation of the Son of God.[b] On his confession stands the foundation of the Church: *against this rock the gates of Hades cannot prevail* (Matth. 16, 18), the serpent[c] disappears without trace and death does not triumph.[d] But the praise and glory which blessed Peter received in the course of time, what voice, what tongue, who could describe it? Hence it is that, with a firm foot he trampled the shaking sea and with a hovering foot he walked between the waves of water.[e] He[70] turned his foot to the Beautiful Gate where the lame sat, and the crippled, touched by the fingers of Peter, no longer needed a staff.[f] Hence, when he was sleeping while in prison, Christ watched with him and, detained in prison, he came outside again through the help of an angel.[g] Hence he raised up the lame who lay ill in bed and

---

[a] The word *praelatus*, according to Blaise, is used in the general sense of 'head' ('chef') among patristic authors, including Gregory the Great (BLAISE, *Vocabulaire*, p. 518, section 381). Later on it is also used to indicate a bishop (ALBERT BLAISE, *Dictionnaire latin-français des auteurs du Moyen-Âge* (Turnhout: Brepols, 1975), s.v. *praelatus*). I interpret it here as 'head (of the Church)', given the special position of Peter, again based on Matth. 16, 18–19. However, in the context of the feast commemorating Peter's episcopacy it is tempting to translate it as 'bishop'.

[b] Cf. Matth. 16, 16–17.

[c] A number of biblical associations arise, primarily Gen. 3 and Luc. 10, 19. Act. 28, 3–6 seems to be closest, where Paul shakes off a viper into the fire, particularly in combination with the following part of the sentence, which refers to Paul's Letter to the Corinthians.

[d] Cf. I Cor. 15, 54–55.

[e] Cf. Matth. 14, 29.

[f] Cf. Act. 3, 1–10.

[g] Cf. Act. 12, 7–9.

he made the crippled walk through his word.[a] Hence he called the woman Tabitha back from death, and, at the command of his wondrous strength, [death] was not empowered to take [her] away.[b] Hence he aspired to such a great gift of faith amid the apostles that he healed all illnesses when he passed by, and the dead lived again when his salutary *shadow* (Act. 5, 15) touched them. Through Christ our Lord. To whom rightfully [the angels sing ...]

153 AFTER THE SANCTUS. Accept, O Lord, amid the service[71] of the voice of the angels, also the obedience of our worship.[72] Through Christ.

154 AFTER THE CONSECRATION. We therefore offer these most holy gifts for our salvation, in obedience of your commands, praying that you deign to join your Holy Spirit with these ritual offerings, so that [this sacrifice] becomes for us a lawful Eucharist[c] in the name of you and your Son and the Holy Spirit through the transformation of the body and blood of our Lord Jesus Christ your only-begotten Son, so that [this Eucharist] will grant everlasting life to us who eat of it and the eternal kingdom to us who drink of it. Through the same Lord.

413

[a] Cf. Act. 9, 33–34. The central role of the miracles of healing performed by Peter, as reported in the canonical book of Acts of the Apostles, is also reflected in the narrative tradition of the apocryphal Acts of the Apostles, recited in the liturgy of the Hours. Thus, the introductory sections of the *Virtutes Pauli* (BHL 6575) refer to the healing miracles performed by both Peter and Paul according to the canonical book of Acts of the Apostles; cf. EVINA STEINOVÁ, 'The Prehistory of the Latin Acts of Peter (BHL 6663) and the Latin Acts of Paul (BHL 6575). Some Observations about the Development of the *Virtutes apostolorum*', in ELS ROSE (ed.), *The Apocryphal Acts of the Apostles in Latin Christianity. Proceedings of the First International Summer School on Christian Apocryphal Literature (ISCAL), Strasbourg, 24–27 June 2012* (Turnhout: Brepols, 2014), p. 69–84, at p. 77. It is uncertain whether such passages from the book of Acts were taken as the epistle pericope for the feast day in the church where the Gothic Missal was in use. The Bobbio Missal gives I Petr. 1, 3–4 as reading from the Epistles (ed. LOWE, p. 35–36), whereas the Lectionary of Luxeuil gives Act. 12, 1–17 relating Peter's release from prison (ed. SALMON, p. 66–67).

[b] Cf. Act. 9, 36–43.

[c] *legitima eucaristia*: see no. 57.

155 BEFORE THE LORD'S PRAYER. Taught by divine instruction and formed by divine education we dare to say: OUR FATHER.

156 AFTER THE LORD'S PRAYER. Deliver us [from evil], eternal Love and true Liberty, and do not allow those who long to be owned by you to be seized by the enemy.[a] Almighty [God], who lives [...]

157 BLESSING. You who are seated above the hosts of heaven,[73] you who contain the entire orb of the earth[b] in your hand,[74] hear those who will celebrate the solemn rituals on this day. AMEN.
So that we who celebrate the festivities of our holy patron[c] and your apostle Peter will please you through his intercession. AMEN.
Grant this for ever in the heart of priests, kings and all your servants: that the sins committed by our people, who confess you and praise you as the true God, will be forgiven. AMEN.
And, as you had us emerge pure from the holy font,[d] let us thus be eternally united within the everlasting borders with the assembly of saints. [AMEN.]
May you deign to grant this, who with the Father [...]

[a] On *inimicus* as a proper name for the devil in the Gothic Missal and elsewhere, see BARTELINK, 'Denominations of the Devil and Demons', p. 204.

[b] *toto orbe terrarum*: see no. 3.

[c] The use of the term *patroni nostri* implies that the community for which this prayer or the Gothic Missal as a whole was compiled maintained a special veneration for the apostle Peter. However, more saints are addressed as *patronus noster* in this sacramentary, and Morin ('Sur la provenance') even hypothesised that the book had its origin in Gregorienmünster (Alsace) in view of the address to Gregory the Great in nos 351 and 352. See ROSE (ed.), *Missale Gothicum*, Introduction, p. 16–17.

[d] The reference to Baptism suggests a close proximity between this feast and Epiphany, an important moment in the Gallican year to administer this sacrament; see Introduction, section The liturgical year.

XXI ORDER OF MASS AT THE BEGINNING OF LENT[a]

414

158 Almighty and everlasting God, grant that we commence this solemn forty-day fast with appropriate obedience and celebrate it with works pleasing to you. Creator and Redeemer of the human race, mercifully grant that, through an upright way of life, we practise the abstinence that leads to our salvation and which is considered as your gift. May [you deign] to grant this [...]

159 COLLECT FOLLOWS. God of abstinence, God of purity, who is gladly appeased by the humility of those who fast and who kindly inclines to the prayers of the mortified, hear our prayers on this day when we commence a fast of forty days, and through your benevolence pour upon us abstinence from sin, when the storm of the different temptations that afflict us is struck down.[b] Saviour of the world.

160 COLLECT AFTER THE NAMES. Now that the names of those who offer have been enumerated,[75] let those who, through fasting of soul and body, pray to the Lord for the gifts of humility dedicated to the altar, obtain [them] by reason of the merit of devoted sanctification. Through.

161 COLLECT AT THE KISS OF PEACE. God of abstinence, God of love and peace, you who incline yourself to the prayers of the mortified, have mercy on us, hear us, and, after you have calmed the storm of all kinds of agonies, bestow on us the serenity of your peace. And if we have lost that peace through the abundance of our sins, may we acquire it once more through the grace of your mercy. Through our Lord Jesus.

415

[a] On the observation of Lent in Merovingian Gaul, see Introduction, section The liturgical year and ROSE, 'Fasting Flocks'.

[b] *tempestate discussa*: cf. TITUS LIVIUS, *Ab urbe condita*, 42.20.1, ed. WILHELM WEISSENBORN and H.J. MÜLLER, *Titi Livi Ab urbe condita libri* (Berlin: Weidmann, 1962), vol. 9, p. 95–96.

162 PRAYER OF SACRIFICE. It is truly worthy and just, fair and salutary that we [bring] thanks to you, O Lord, holy Father, almighty and everlasting God, through Christ our Lord, who is your only-begotten Son and who abides in your glory, in whom the faith of those who fast is fed, hope is carried forward and love strengthened. For he is the *living and true bread, who descended from heaven* (Ioh. 6, 51; Ioh. 6, 32–33) and always abides in heaven, who is an eternal being[76] and the food of virtue.[a] Indeed your Word, *through which everything came into being* (Ioh. 1, 3), is not only the food of human hearts but is also *the bread of the angels themselves* (Ps. 78, 25). With the nourishment of this bread your servant Moses fasted *for forty days and nights* (Ex. 34, 28) when he received your law, and he abstained from the food of the flesh[b] in order to be more receptive to your sweetness, living from your Word. He lived in the spirit from the sweetness of [your Word] and on his face he received the light of [your Word.][c] Therefore he felt no physical hunger and forgot the food of the earth, because the sight of your glory brightened him and the Word of God, infused through the Spirit, fed him. Deign, O Lord, to give us this Bread[d] during these forty days, which we enter today by beginning with the mortification of the forty-day abstinence, and enkindle us, so that we thirst for it unceasingly. When we eat his [*sc.* Christ's] body, which is sanctified by you, we are strengthened, and when we drink his blood with a longing gulp, we are cleansed. Through Christ our Lord, through whom.

163 AFTER THE SANCTUS. *Blessed is the one who comes in the name of the Lord* (Matth. 21, 9), *God the Lord of knowledge* (I Sam. 2, 3), who gives his wonders and *orders all things well* (Sap. 8, 1), *who*

---

[a] *esca uirtutis*: on this spiritual food, see also AMBROSE, *De paradiso*, 14.71, ed. KARL SCHENKL, *Sancti Ambrosii opera*, CSEL 32.1 (Vienna: Tempsky, 1897), p. 329.

[b] Cf. Ex. 34, 28.

[c] Cf. Ex. 34, 29–35.

[d] *Hunc panem*: meaning Christ, who is called 'the living and true bread' at the beginning of this prayer (*Ipse est enim panis uiuus et uerus*). The subsequent relative clause *Cuius carne* clearly refers to Christ's body; to apply it literally to *panis*, bread, would yield an incomprehensible phrase.

rides upon the clouds, the Lord is his name (Ps. 68, 4).[a] May he, *the living and true bread, who descended from heaven* (Ioh. 6, 51; Ioh. 6, 32–33) to give food to *the hungry* (Is. 58, 7), indeed what is more, to be himself the food for the living, come into being for us *in this bread, through which the hearts are strengthened* (Ps. 104, 15), so that through the power of this bread we are able to fast during these forty days without the impediment of flesh and blood.[b] Now that we have the Bread himself [sc. Christ], who *nourishes the poor with loaves* (Ps. 132, 15),[c] who consecrated the forty-day fast through Moses and Elijah when they fasted for forty days,[d] who later, in his own fasting for us, marked the same number of days with the solemn practice of fasting,[e] let us strive to imitate what the Lord himself accomplished for us in the weakness of our body in 40 days without interruption, albeit little by little with the same calculated number of days by observing the arrangement of the evening meals. Through [our Lord Jesus Christ] who on the day before [his suffering...]

164 AFTER THE CONSECRATION. May the offering of our devotion be acceptable to you, O Lord, so that by your grace it sanctifies our fasting and acquires for us the mercy of your comfort. Through him.

165 BEFORE THE LORD'S PRAYER. Not because we have come to know our merit but your command, O Lord, because you have deigned to assign it to us, we dare to say: [...]   417

[a] Vulgate: Ps. 67, 5.

[b] The prayer contrasts the bliss of Christ's flesh and blood (*carne et sanguine*, see the wording in no. 162, lines 19–20) with mortal flesh and blood (*carnis et sanguinis*, no. 163 line 7; line numbers as in ROSE (ed.), *Missale Gothicum*, p. 415–416) by which the faithful are hindered.

[c] Vulgate: Ps. 131, 15 (and not 133, 15 as indicated in ROSE (ed.), *Missale Gothicum*, p. 416).

[d] Moses: Ex. 34, 28; Elijah: I Sam. 9, 8.

[e] Cf. Matth. 4, 2.

166 AFTER THE LORD'S PRAYER. Safeguard, O Lord, your faithful and preserve from earthly dangers those whom you teach through your heavenly sacraments. Saviour of the world [...]

167 AFTER THE EUCHARIST. Grant, O Lord, so we pray, that through the sum of good deeds we are raised up, you, who do not withhold from us all that is good for us, as you also have given us these gifts. Through our Lord Jesus Christ.

168 COMPLETION OF MASS. God of the heavenly powers, who gives *more than we ask* (Eph. 3, 20) or deserve, grant, so we pray, that your mercy will be bestowed on us, for we cannot trust our own merits. Through our Lord Jesus Christ.

169 BLESSING OF THE PEOPLE AT THE BEGINNING OF THE FAST. Keep watch over your flock, Shepherd of souls, you who do not know what sleeping is.[a] AMEN.
And sanctify [your flock] with your invisible touch, so that it will not be harassed by the terrors of the night. AMEN.
418 Strengthen the weak, raise up the contrite and give strength to the sick, lift up through your goodness, edify through your love, cleanse through your purity, illuminate through your wisdom, preserve through your mercy. AMEN.
May the perseverance of love for you, the temperance of behaviour, the mildness of mercy and the discipline of deeds be to the benefit of the vigilant faith.[77] AMEN.
So that you do not cast away from the greatness of your promise [the flock] that you have adopted to be your own by your grace,[b] through the granted kindness of your mercy, but lead it to forgiveness. AMEN.
Through the Lord.

[a] Cf. Ps. 121, 4.
[b] Cf. Eph. 1, 5, even if here as in all Paul's references to adoption, the adopted are imagined as children (*filiorum*) rather than sheep (*gregem*).

XXII LIKEWISE A MASS FOR LENT [II]

170 Almighty and everlasting God, who in the observation of fasting and alms sowed for us the seed as remedy for our sins, grant, so we pray, that we are always devoted to you in the work of soul and body.[78] May you [deign] to grant this.

171 COLLECT FOLLOWS. God, Creator of human salvation, grant us that we exercise fasting appropriately, through which, in your providence, you gave the perpetual remedy[a] of our being.

172 COLLECT AFTER THE NAMES. God, who commands us not only to fast from fleshly food but [also] from pleasures harmful to the soul itself, grant us such help from your forgiveness, so we pray, that by fasting from illicit temptations we grow to heavenly matters. And may you command that the names that are recited are inscribed in the heavenly Book.[b] Through [...]

419

173 COLLECT AT THE KISS OF PEACE. Grant to us, almighty God, that through the annual exercise of the sacrament of the forty-day fast we advance in our understanding of the mystery of Christ and pursue his love through a worthy way of life, so that you give us true peace. Through our Lord Jesus Christ.

174 PRAYER OF SACRIFICE. It is truly worthy and just that we always and everywhere bring thanks to you, O Lord, holy Father, almighty and everlasting God, [and] that we dedicate our fast to you, which you have taught us to observe from the foundation of the world. For in this gift you bestowed great grace on the body, since if that mother of the human race had respected that the tree was forbidden to her[c] she would have retained both immortality and her fatherland.[d] But forgive through our fast, so we pray, the

---

[a] *sempiterna remedia*: see no. 10.

[b] *caelesti pagina*: see note 4.

[c] Cf. Gen. 2, 17.

[d] The designation of paradise with *patria* occurs more often in patristic texts, e.g. the sermons of Caesarius of Arles (ed. Morin, nos 58, 78, 151, 171).

sins of the ancient mother, which she committed through the illicit misuse of the forbidden wood, and let us, who fell from paradise because we did not abstain, now return [to] that same place through fasting. Through Christ our Lord, through whom [...]

XXIII LIKEWISE ANOTHER MASS FOR LENT [III]

175 God, who through the providence of your profound wisdom have instituted the sacred fast for mortals, through which the hearts of the weak would be healed to their salvation, purify our soul and body, Saviour of the soul and body and bounteous Giver of eternal felicity. Through him who is co-eternal [...]

420

176 COLLECT FOLLOWS. God, you who for the healing of souls have commanded to chastise the body through the devotion of fasting, grant, so we pray, that our heart is able to exercise the commands of your love such that we can always abstain from all sin. Through our Lord Jesus.

177 COLLECT AFTER THE NAMES. We ask, O Lord, that your protection sustain the humble, and that it will always protect those who trust in your mercy with the necessary things that the human race cannot do without. And may the gifts of immortality overcome them, and may you command that the recited names of those who bring the offering will be inscribed with the heavenly handwriting[a] in the Book of Life.

178 COLLECT AT THE KISS OF PEACE. Look upon our weakness, so we pray, O Lord, and come quickly to help us with your love, we who find ourselves in the suffering of fasting, so that

---

[a] *cyrographo*: the word is used in a negative manner in no. 11, the Mass for Christmas, in imitation of Col. 2, 14: the written record of the old sin. In the present prayer it is used in a positive sense, as also in no. 182 in the following Mass. ROSE (ed.), *Missale Gothicum*, Introduction, p. 166.

we grow to the heavenly things and you grant us sincere peace. Through [...]

179 PRAYER OF SACRIFICE. It is worthy and just that we here and everywhere bring thanks to you, O Lord, holy Father, almighty and everlasting God, and that we dedicate our fast to you, which you have taught us to observe for the healing of the soul and chastisement of the body, since the souls are fed when the bodies are restricted, and that which mortifies the outer person opens wide the inner self. Be mindful through our fasting, O Lord, of your mercies, which you granted to sinners who always fast faithfully, that by abstaining not only from food but also from all sin we please you through fasting that is gratifying to you, in which our wishes will prove to correspond with your will. Through Christ our Lord, before whose [...]

421

XXIIII LIKEWISE ANOTHER MASS FOR LENT [IIII]

180 Almighty and everlasting God, who has created humankind such that, as a better being equipped through earthly benefits, you raised him towards heavenly gifts: grant, so we pray, that as we have fallen from the conceded region of beatitude through illicit desires, so, through the nourishment dispensed by your gift, our transitory humanity is supported and lost eternity restored. Through [...]

181 COLLECT. May, O Lord, so we ask, the salutary abstinence educate us at all times, so that it makes us who are intent on fasting purer and procures for us your gifts. Through [...]

182 COLLECT AFTER THE NAMES. May, O Lord, your venerable mercy not only exercise us through holy fasting, but make us more suitable for the heavenly rites. And may you command that the

422

recited names are inscribed with the heavenly handwriting[a] in the Book of Life. Through [...]

183 COLLECT AT THE KISS OF PEACE. Grant us, almighty God, that since our mortality is subject to sin and quarrels, through the present fast your medicine will purify us through sincere love. Through our Lord.

184 PRAYER OF SACRIFICE. It is worthy and just that we praise you together as Author and Sanctifier of our fast, through which you deliver us from the debts of our sins. Favourably accept, therefore, the prayers of those who fast, and we ask you: forgive us our sins, through which we are rightly afflicted, so that you snatch us away mercifully from all evil. Through Christ our Lord.

185 PRAYER AFTER THE SANCTUS DURING LENT.[79] God, Founder and Creator of all things, who is recognised as one in Trinity and three in unity, whose magnitude the human tongue is too deficient to tell, whom the angels unceasingly proclaim holy, and therefore we your most undeserving servants raise up, though with an unworthy mouth, not three holy persons but the three-times holy of our herald's voice, so that a harmonious chant[80] is proclaimed and your praise is repeated threefold. We therefore pray for your love, most merciful Lord, that you give us what we desire and grant us what we expect, so that we are considered worthy, when the cloud of sin has been wiped away, to praise your splendour with a pure and free conscience. Saviour [...]

423

XXV LIKEWISE A MASS FOR LENT [V][b]

186 Grant, so we ask, O Lord our God, that the nourishment we refrain from on account of the mortification of the flesh through

---

[a] *cyrographo*: see no. 177.
[b] The absence of any closing formulas to the prayers in this Mass (apart from the *immolatio*) is striking.

fasting, we bestow on the poor with the goodwill granted by you by giving bountifully. For only then the observation of fasting will prove fruitful, if our heart is purer than the senses of the body through the restraints of chastity, and if love makes the awareness of our dedication fruitful.

187 COLLECT FOLLOWS. Grant us, almighty God, that nourished in spirit by fasting from physical food, we are satiated with strength, and by abstaining from food and sin alike, we rise up stronger in virtue against all enemies.

188 COLLECT AFTER THE NAMES. Bestow on us, O Lord, so we pray, the help of your grace, so that we are delivered from the enemies of our vices, duly intent on the fasting and prayers of a devoted heart and of the body.[81] And you who have deigned to grant this fast, so that through abstinence and bodily chastisement we may be found strong in faith and effective in deeds, receive from those who fast the prayers and offering of this day, and, propitiated by [our sacrifice], may you thus deign, while you grant consolation to the dead and forgiveness to the living, to engrave with a perpetual inscription the names of those who have been individually mentioned.

424

189 COLLECT AT THE KISS OF PEACE. May this offering of our fasting be acceptable to you, so we pray, O Lord, so that, by reconciling us through the gift of your love, it makes us susceptible to uprightness, and, through it united, leads us to the eternal promise. And pour favourably into our hearts, intent on the mortification of fasting, through the pure brotherly kisses, love for you and purity with regard to our neighbour,[82] so that resting through abstinence from earthly quarrels and injuries, we may the more willingly reflect on heavenly things.

190 PRAYER OF SACRIFICE. It is worthy and just that we always bring thanks to you, O Lord, holy Father, almighty and everlasting God, so that you, when regarding the measure of [our] earthly weakness, in your anger do not rebuke us for our bad-

425 ness, but in your immeasurable goodness purify, teach, comfort us.[a] For because we can do nothing without you that may please you, your grace alone will help us to live a salutary way of life. Through Christ our Lord, through whom [the angels praise] your majesty.

XXVI LIKEWISE A MASS FOR LENT [VI]

191 O Lord God, you who are rightly angry with your people and mercifully forgive them, incline your ear to our prayers, so that we who in the supplications of your fasting[b] confess you with all our senses, do not experience your judgement but your mercy. Through [...]

192 COLLECT FOLLOWS. Deign, O Lord, to sanctify the gifts we have offered and placed on your altar, and reconciled through these gifts, forgive our sins, so we ask, on the day of our fasting, mindful of the human condition, and turn away from us what we deserve as retribution for them. Through our Lord.

193 AFTER THE NAMES. God, Inspirer and Teacher of good deeds, who gives to our hearts the knowledge of you when the pleasures are restrained through the abstinence of bodily fasting, grant us growth of *faith, hope and love* (I Cor. 13, 13), so that through the sanctification of fasting your temple may be in us,[c] which may become eternal through your grace. And may you command that the names, remembered by their designation for this transitory age, are marked with the title of eternity.

426 194 AT THE KISS OF PEACE. Almighty and merciful God, hear the humble supplications of those who fast, and favourably grant

---

[a] *purifices, erudias, consoleris*: asyndeton; see Introduction, section Style and figures.

[b] i.e. 'the fasting instituted by you'.

[c] An inversion of the customary image of the people as God's temple; see no. 17.

the gift of your mercy when all conceit has ceased, so that through the union of peace we serve you with steadfast hearts when all rivalry has been suppressed. Through [...]

195 PRAYER OF SACRIFICE. It is truly worthy and just that we [always] and everywhere bring thanks to you, almighty and everlasting God, who rightly punishes and leniently forgives, in both matters merciful, because you rule us according to that law, that by punishing you do not allow us to be lost in eternity and by sparing you give room to amend. Through Christ.

XXVII MASS FOR THE TRANSMISSION OF THE CREED[a]

196 The obedience of our worship, O Lord, embraces this day in order to revere it in two respects, because of both the sanctified rite of the fast and your wondrous signs which have shone on this day. [The day] on which you have brought Lazarus back from hell,[b] when he emerged to your thunderous voice[c] and, by rousing it, you brought back to life the corpse of him *who already stank for four days* (Ioh. 11, 39).[83] And *the crowd* (Ioh. 12, 12; Matth. 21, 8) from Bethany, astonished at the wonder, ran to meet you as king, rejoicing [and] bearing *palm branches* (Ioh. 12, 13). Hear us in this

---

[a] On this Mass, see Introduction, section The liturgical year; on its title (*In symbuli traditione*), see also ROSE (ed.), *Missale Gothicum*, Introduction, p. 154. The word *symbolum*, referring to any sign of recognition, was already used among Christians of the first century to indicate the profession of faith: BLAISE, *Dictionnaire*, s.v. *symbolum*. The title does not cover the full content of the Mass, which is centred on two pericopes: Ioh. 12, 12-19 (the Entry into Jerusalem) and Ioh. 11 (the death and resurrection of Lazarus, see below). Though palm branches feature frequently in the prayers, the term *dominica in ramis palmarum* itself ('Palm Sunday') does not occur in the Merovingian service books.

[b] The notion of Lazarus's resurrection from hell (*tartara*) is present in Sedulius's fifth-century *Carmen Paschale*, 4.284-290, ed. JOHANN HUEMER, *Sedulii opera omnia*, CSEL 10 (Vienna: Geroldi, 1885), 1-146, at p. 110-111 as a prefiguration of Christ's resurrection, see ROBERTS, *Humblest Sparrow*, p. 151-152.

[c] Cf. Ioh. 11, 43.

427

double supplication of our servitude, and grant mercifully and favourably that our souls, shut away in the tomb of sin and decayed through the deadly filth of wounds, live again through your visitation of our inner self, as the soul[a] of Lazarus too was brought back to life by your voice. Saviour.

197 COLLECT FOLLOWS. Good Redeemer our Lord, who, as the meek one sitting on the back of the meek donkey,[b] of your own will draw near to the Passion for the sake of our salvation, while the road is eagerly covered with tree branches for you and the people come to meet you rejoicing with triumphant palm branches: we beseech your divine majesty that you favourably accept the confession of our mouth and the humiliation of our body in fasting. Grant that we bear the fruit of vigour,[c] so that as they came out to meet you with tree twigs, we are thus considered worthy to run out to meet you, rejoicing with palm branches of victory, when you return in your second Advent. Saviour of the world.

198 COLLECT AFTER THE NAMES. Behold, O Lord, for the prophecy concerning you from the high priest Caiaphas, which was unknown to him, has come true for the peoples, [namely] that you alone would die for the people so that not all would be killed at the same time,[d] and that you would die as a single grain in the ground so that a great harvest would spring forth.[e] We humbly beseech you, who were killed as offering for the salvation of the world, that from your side you grant us forgiveness, you who

---

[a] *uiscera*: interpreted here as 'soul' in view of the parallel with *animae*.

[b] Cf. Matth. 21, 5, quoting Zach. 9, 9. Cf. Ioh. 12, 15, where the word *mansuetus* is not included.

[c] *uiriditatis*: used here in the patristic sense of spiritual power, sprouting and bearing fruit through grace in the Church and the individual believer; combined with *fructus* in AMBROSE, *De paradiso*, 13.66, ed. SCHENKL, CSEL 32.1, p. 324. In the context of the present prayer the word is well chosen in view of its metaphoric use, combined with the implicit reference to the green leaves of the palm trees, which play a central role on this Sunday. Blaise does not include the word in his dictionaries or in the liturgical vocabulary.

[d] Cf. Ioh. 11, 50.

[e] Cf. Ioh. 12, 24.

offered yourself for us. And those whom the recitation has commemorated before the holy altar, who have already been carried
across from these bodily bonds to your peace,[84] we ask, O Lord,
that they have you as Liberator, whom through Baptism they were
able to have as Redeemer. But we also ask, O Lord our God, that
you command that those who prepare themselves amid those
present for the sacrament of salutary Baptism, immersed in faith,
taught in their mind, confirmed in grace,[a] prepare themselves[85] to
receive the fullness of your grace through the gift of your Spirit,
so that they are considered worthy to be reborn from the fount of
holy Baptism, for which they have longed. And may you deign.

428

199 COLLECT AT THE KISS OF PEACE. Ruler of all things, you
who [are] the Creator, and from your creation in a particular manner the Beloved and the Lover, for whom Martha busied herself,[b]
of whom Mary washed the feet,[c] with whom Lazarus, after he
was brought back to life, sat at table[d] – truly the entire house was
in love. Grant to your people that they so exercise in love, that
through peace they may remain united in you. Bring about in us
those tears that Mary brought forth by reason of her great love,
and let our prayer be scented as the pure ointment of Mary was
scented, poured out over the blessed feet, so that through our
kisses which we give to one another, we attain the peace acquired

---

[a] *inbutos in fide, instructos in sensu, confirmatos in gratia*: asyndeton.

[b] Cf. Luc. 10, 38–42.

[c] Cf. Ioh. 12, 3–8.

[d] Cf. Ioh. 12, 2, though the twofold mention of tears later on in this prayer
indicates that this passage is merged with the meal scene in the house of Simon the
Pharisee in Luc. 7, 36–49. Here, the tears and kisses of the (anonymous) woman
are mentioned, which John does not record. The question whether this is one event
told by different evangelists, or different events in the various gospels, is discussed
by a number of scholars, see FRANÇOIS BOVON, *Das Evangelium nach Lukas vol. 1:
Lk. 1,1–9,50*, Evangelisch-Katholischer Kommentar zum Neuen Testament III.1
(Zürich: Benziger Verlag, 1989), p. 387–389. In the early Christian Gospel Harmony (*Diatessaron*) by Tatian (AD 120–173), no tears are mentioned: J. HAMLYN
HILL, *The Earliest Life of Christ Ever Compiled from the Four Gospels: Being the
Diatessaron of Tatian* (Piscataway NJ: Gorgias Press, 2006; facs. repr. of the origi-
nal edition published in Edinburgh 1910), p. 157.

by Mary when she kissed the feet of her Redeemer.[a] Saviour of the world.

200 PRAYER OF SACRIFICE. It is truly worthy and just that you, Lord, are praised[86] by each gender, age and sense on this day of fasting and of your praise,[87] with the triumphant hymn of victory with which multitudinous crowds of people came to meet you from Jerusalem and Bethany, while they cried out with one voice: *'Hosanna [to] the Son of David, blessed is the one who comes in the name of the Lord!'* (Matth. 21, 9) For the leaves of the trees served you with the tongue when the sand paths were full of young branches. And the cloak of the people was spread out for your feet and the road was covered while the men took their clothes off:[b] the people gave you the triumph as the new victor. All that clamour becomes raised to praise, the voices of those who cried out penetrate into the temple, saying: *'Blessed is the one who comes in the name of the Lord!'* (Matth. 21, 9). *Behold, Jerusalem, how your King approaches you, the humble one seated on a donkey* (cf. Matth. 21, 5). Come, so we ask, and appear in our midst, and you who once redeemed us through the cross, redeem us who are fallen again through this offering of bread and blood, so that when we feel you entering our hearts we come out towards you and with those heavenly powers cry out, saying: HOLY [...]

201 AFTER THE SANCTUS. This is felicity without end, this is unbound beatitude, to cling so unceasingly to God, that he himself is hope, is rest, that in him exertion holds vigil and in him rest takes repose. Bread and wine are thus granted to us such that what he first depicted for us in mysteries he returns in rewards. Through Christ our Lord. Who on the day before [...]

202 AFTER THE CONSECRATION. Behold these gifts from heaven, righteous Consoler, you who are always willing to grant grace. And may you sanctify these things, which are offered with devo-

[a] Cf. Luc. 7, 36–49.
[b] Cf. Matth. 21, 8.

429

tion, with the majesty that is yours by nature, you who are perpetually holy and generously give holy things. May [you deign] to
grant this [...]

203 BEFORE THE LORD'S PRAYER. Taught by the revered precepts and encouraged by the gift of love, we humbly beseech you,
who do not despise the tears of weeping Mary, who deign to give
the name of brother to Lazarus, who with the mouth of grace call
the offspring of the Church *co-heirs* (Rom. 8, 17), and say: [OUR]
FATHER.

204 AFTER THE LORD'S PRAYER. Exercise in us, Liberator, the   430
ability of special law, you who rewarded Lazarus's virtue, Mary's
piety and Martha's toil, you who rouse the zeal of your people and
are glorified with the Father in one voice. Almighty God, who in
the Trinity [...]

XXVIII MASS FOR OUR LORD'S SUPPER[a]

205 [PREFACE.] As we celebrate the most holy solemn ritual of
the Easter feast, beginning today, and the salutary image of the
sacrifice of the Lord in a spiritual offering, while Christ himself
offers, an image which is poured out no longer in the bitterness
of unleavened bread[b] *nor in the yeast of the old malice* (I Cor. 5, 8),
but in *a new and pure dough* (I Cor. 5, 7), and while we offer unblemished[c] offerings on the holy altar, let us, most beloved brothers, pray to almighty God, through his only-begotten Son our
Lord Jesus Christ, that he who deigned to bless and sanctify these
things through the offering of his holy body and blood, will so
bless the sacrificed gifts of his servants who bring their offering,

---

[a] The title *Caena domini* refers to the Last Supper and the institution of the
Eucharist commemorated on this day; see further Introduction, section The liturgical year.

[b] The Old Testament prescriptions concerning unleavened bread are found in
Ex. 12.

[c] *inmaculatas*: the Old Testament pesach lamb is *absque macula*; cf. Ex. 12, 5.

that through the illumination of the Holy Spirit a sweet fragrance[88] rises up while the angels[a] take [it with them.] Through our Lord Jesus Christ [his] Son.

431   206 COLLECT FOLLOWS. God of holiness and Lord of the heavenly powers, hear our prayers and answer this blessed people, *redeemed through the blood* (Apoc. 5, 9) of our Lord Jesus Christ, from your holy seat of *unapproachable light* (cf. I Tim. 6, 16). Through him who is co-eternal.

207 AFTER THE NAMES. Now that the gifts, different yet with one devotion to faith, are gathered on the holy altar, let us in turn bring forth prayers of mutual concern, while we ask of the love of the Lord that he purifies the hearts of all who offer to *a sacrifice of reasonableness and sanctification pleasing to him* (cf. Rom. 12, 1), that he deigns to gather the souls of the deceased *in Abraham's bosom* (Luc. 16, 23), and that he admits them *to share in the first resurrection*[b] (cf. Apoc. 20, 6). Through our Lord.

208 PRAYER AT THE KISS OF PEACE. God, who, when you were about to take up him who had become man into heaven, *left* among the most important of your commands *peace to* our fathers *the apostles* (Ioh. 14, 27): grant also to us your servants, as successors to those same apostles, peace of the inner self through the kiss of the outer person. May you [deign ...]

---

   [a] *nuntiis*: the use of the classical word instead of *angelis* is poetic; cf. ROSE (ed.), *Missale Gothicum*, Introduction, p. 140 and see Introduction, section Style and figures.

   [b] The quotation refers to the belief that the righteous would be resurrected first to live in the thousand years (*millennium*, hence 'millenialism') that would precede the second, general resurrection: SMYTH, *Liturgie oubliée*, p. 483–485. On the integration of this belief in the liturgical prayers of the Latin West, see BERNARD BOTTE, '*Prima resurrectio*, un vestige de millénarisme dans les liturgies occidentales', *Recherches de théologie ancienne et médiévale* 15 (1948), 5–17; BLAISE, *Vocabulaire*, section 410, p. 547. Tertullian recommended the prayer for the beloved dead, that they might be given *refrigerium* and 'a share in the first resurrection' (*in prima resurrectione consortium*): TERTULLIAN, *De monogamia* 10.4.5, ed. PAUL MATTEI, SChr 343 (Paris: Cerf, 1988), p. 176.

209 PRAYER OF SACRIFICE. It is worthy and just [that we thank you] through Jesus Christ your Son our Lord, who, *girded with a towel, washed the feet of his disciples* (cf. Ioh. 13, 5), and when   432
he was about to depart from this world, left them an example of humility. For through his deeds the most righteous Master teaches those whom he had often instructed with his salutary admonishments. But is it a wonder that he girded himself with a linen cloth, who by taking on *the form of a slave became equal to man* (Phil. 2, 7), or is it a wonder that *he poured water into a basin to wash the feet of his disciples* (cf. Ioh. 13, 5), who shed his blood on earth to wash away the impurity of sinners? *With the towel that was tied around him he then wiped the feet that he had washed* (cf. Ioh. 13, 5), who encouraged the feet of the evangelists with the flesh with which he was covered.[a] The Lord thus washed the feet of his disciples, but of those whose feet he washed on the outside, on the inside he cleansed the souls with the hyssop of forgiveness. O admirable sacrament, O great mystery! Peter is in confusion when he sees the example of such great humility in the King of such great majesty:[b] humankind trembles with fear because God deigned to bow over its feet. But if God, humiliated, would not bow to man, man would never stand erect before God, for from the moment that God deigned to show the light of his humanity in the land of mortals,[c] from that moment man began to seek *the land of the living* (Ps. 142, 5).[d] Before whose [countenance...]

---

[a] i.e. through his Incarnation. The phrase 'Is it a wonder ... with which he was covered' (*Sed quidni mirum si praecinxit ... uestigia confirmauit*) is taken from AUGUSTINE, *In Iohannis euangelium tractatus* 55.7, where the final phrase ('With the towel ... with which he was covered') constitutes a rhetorical question: *quid mirum si linteo quo erat praecinctus, pedes quos lauerat, tersit, qui carne qua erat indutus, euangelistarum uestigia confirmauit?* Ed. RADBOUD WILLEMS, CCSL 36 (Turnhout: Brepols, 1954), p. 466.

[b] Cf. Ioh. 13, 6–10.

[c] The phrase *regio mortalium* is less common in patristic literature; it is found as a synonym for *regio vivorum* (Ps. 116, 9; Vulgate Ps. 114, 9) in Augustine (*Sermo* 279); Prosper of Aquitaine (*Expositio psalmorum, Psalmus 114*), Quoduultdeus (*Sermo* 3) and Arnobius (*Commentarii in psalmos, psalmus 114*).

[d] Vulgate: Ps. 141, 6.

210 AFTER THE SANCTUS. O Lord, you are truly holy and just, you are truly great and good, who sent your Son our Lord Jesus Christ for us as a light to earth from the highest stronghold of heaven, as a Redeemer of the imprisoned bodies. For he himself who [...]

433   211 AFTER THE CONSECRATION. *Lamb of God, who takes away the sins of the world* (Ioh. 1, 29), give heed to us and have mercy on us. Guard us whom you have redeemed, for you who are the priest have become for us the sacrifice, you have become the ransom who are the Redeemer from all evil,[a] Saviour [of the world...]

212 BEFORE THE LORD'S PRAYER. Now that we are about to take of the food of the *living bread* (Ioh. 6, 51) and the gifts of the holy blood, let us strengthen our minds and hearts through the Lord's prayer. May the Most High recognise the voice of His Son and may the cry of the united people lift up the words of Christ to the ears of the Father and say: [OUR] FATHER.

213 AFTER THE LORD'S PRAYER. Deliver us, O Lord, deliver us from all evil and from the strongest adversaries: the devil, and defend us against that death[89] that is stronger than all things, through the protection of your power and of your right hand.

214 AFTER COMMUNION. Grant us, almighty God, that as we are restored by the temporary supper of your Passion, so we may be considered worthy to be satisfied by the eternal [Supper.]

[a] Cf. I Tim. 2, 6.

XXVIIII THE PRAYERS FOR GOOD FRIDAY AND HOLY SATURDAY BEGIN HERE[a]

215 Grant[b] us, O Lord, for whom your Only-begotten, *smeared with spit, received both slaps in the face[c] and fist blows* (cf. Matth. 26, 67), that we receive the gift of perpetual blessing. Who with you [...]

216 THEN A PRAYER FOR THE SIXTH HOUR. Look mercifully on these your servants, O Lord, for whom our Lord Jesus Christ did not hesitate to deliver himself into the hands of sinners and endure the torment of the cross.[d] Through him.

217 THEN A PRAYER FOR THE NINTH HOUR. God, who for our redemption accepted the blood of Jesus Christ, scatter the work of the devil and shatter all snares of sin, so that no contagion of the old condition[e] may blemish the creature of rebirth.[90] Through.

434

218 PRAYER FOLLOWS. God, from whom both Judas the traitor received the punishment for his guilt[f] and the thief obtained the reward of his confession,[g] grant us an answer[91] to our faithful prayer, that our Lord Jesus Christ, as during his Passion he gave different retribution[92] to both according to merit, will generously

---

[a] *biduana*: the term is a remnant of the time in which Lent was restricted to two days: KING, *Liturgies of the Past*, p. 137. Blaise translates the technical term in a concrete manner: '*orationes in biduana*, 'oraisons pour le Vendredi et le Samedi-saints': BLAISE, *Dictionnaire*, s.v. *biduana*, and I follow him here, although in no. 219 I translate 'two-day fast' for the sake of brevity. On the prayers for Good Friday and Holy Saturday, see Introduction, section The liturgical year.

[b] The prayer lacks a title; it might be a prayer for the third hour, in line with *Missale Gallicanum Vetus* 116, ed. MOHLBERG, p. 30.

[c] BLAISE, *Dictionnaire*, s.v. *palma* (2), translates 'soufflet': slap in the face, referring to Matth. 26, 67.

[d] Cf. Matth. 26, 2.

[e] *uetustatis*: cf. Rom. 7, 6.

[f] Cf. Matth. 27, 3–10.

[g] Cf. Luc. 23, 39–43.

grant the mercy of his resurrection after he has taken away the sin of the old condition.[a] Through our Lord Jesus.

219 LIKEWISE PRAYERS FOR THE TWO-DAY FAST[b] ON THE SATURDAY AT THE SI[XTH HOUR.][93] Most beloved brothers, let us humbly pray to almighty God, Father, Son and Holy Spirit, one Creator of the universe, on this great morning of the great Sabbath, namely the resting [day] of the body of the Lord, that his Son, who mercifully rescued Adam from the depths of the mire of hell,[c] through his mercy alone saves us at our cry from the dirt of this impurity to which we cling. For we call and pray *that the pit of hell will not threateningly raise his mouth over us [and] that we, saved from the mire of sin, do not get stuck in it* (Ps. 69, 14–15[d]). Through the Lord.

435

220 COLLECT FOLLOWS. O Lord Christ Jesus, righteous God, hear us and grant, so we pray, the things we request with the heart. And we ask this, that we may please you, that we cling to you unceasingly, so that we always give thanks to you, for you, O Lord, have redeemed us to eternal life from eternal death. You who descended into the pit to lead the prisoners from hell,[e] descend now, so we pray, through the mercy of your love, to release us from the bonds of sin in which each of us is confined. Saviour.

---

[a] *uetustatis*: cf. Rom. 7, 6.

[b] *in biduana*: see footnote a on p. 203.

[c] On the theme of Christ's descent into hell, see Introduction, section The liturgical year.

[d] Vulgate: Ps. 68, 15–16.

[e] On hell as a prison, see MICHAEL ROBERTS, *Poetry and Cult of the Martyrs: The Liber Peristephanon of Prudentius* (Ann Arbor: University of Michigan Press, 1993), p. 82–83; in his reference to the Gothic Missal in the context of Venantius Fortunatus's Easter poem (*Carmina* 3.9), Roberts omits the present prayer despite the vocabulary parallel to the work of Venantius: ROBERTS, *Humblest Sparrow*, p. 150 footnote 106.

XXX

221. PREFACE AT THE VESPER PRECEDING EASTER.[a] Most beloved brothers, *born again of water and the Spirit* (cf. Ioh. 3, 5) through the mercy of the Lord and freed from countless bonds by the manifold care of the Father's love, let us pray to the Lord, the Author of this divine grace, *now that the sacrifice of evening prayer has been ignited* (cf. Ps. 141, 2) and erected through the Spirit on a heavenly platter. And let us pray, now that the fire, of which he desires that it be ignited in us, solemnly burns with the glow of prayer, that he will forgive the sins of [our] entire life, the stains of daily sin and the debts of human weakness, in this Holy Week of the Forty Days of this year and particularly on the day on which his body rested in the sepulchre. And that he may also allow us to come out of Egypt in the crowd of the true Israel,[b] and that when the enemies are defeated, while we celebrate in the one catholic Church the gift of the peace of the Lord, and the doorposts of our bodies are sprinkled with the blood of the unblemished lamb,[c] he will defend us during the solemn celebration of this venerable night from death, which is about to destroy the world, while we pray. Through the Lord.

436

---

[a] It remains unclear whether the word *vespera* should be translated as vespers in the technical sense or rather as a particular evening service preceding the Easter vigil. Normally the Latin word for vespers is plural: *vesperae*. Moreover, the first prayer clearly links this service to Holy Saturday rather than to the day of the resurrection: *[in] sepulti corporis sui sabbato*. On the other hand, the (implicit) references to the offering of incense to accompany the evening prayer (*incensu uespertinae praecis sacrificio*) and the lighting of the candle (*igne illo, quem ipse in nobis accendi desiderat*) link the prayer to the ritual practices that have from the earliest period belonged to the service of vespers as eve of the following feast day, and from which the lighting of the paschal candle takes its origin; see ROBERT TAFT, *The Liturgy of the Hours in East and West. The Origins of the Divine Office and its Meaning for Today* (Collegeville MN: Liturgical Press, 1986), p. 37 ('...the lucernarium of the Easter vigil derives from that of vespers, not vice-versa'). See also Ex. 12, 6, where the sacrifice of the pesach lamb is appointed *ad vesperam* (NRSV: 'at twilight'); FUCHS and WEIKMANN, *Das Exsultet*, p. 81.

[b] Cf. Ex. 12.

[c] Cf. Ex. 12, 7.

222 COLLECT FOLLOWS. Christ Jesus, grant that through the evening offering, accomplished through the cross, we will be new sepulchres for your body in the evening of the world.[a] Saviour.

223 PREFACE AT THE BEGINNING OF THE HOLY EASTER NIGHT. Most beloved brothers, let us venerate with all praise the Author of light, the Prince of light, the Examiner of hearts, the Redeemer of the faithful, that now that the day draws to a close he hears the voices of our calling and illuminates the approaching darkness of the night with the brilliance of his light, that there is not a single occasion in us for temptation and affliction. And may he who is the Giver of the true light be our Defender against darkness, so that we are always in his light, we who glorify the Lord Christ as our Author. Through.

224 PRAYER FOLLOWS. Guide us, O Lord, during the alternating turns of the times, and keep us during the different successions of days and nights, so that we who have passed this day through the gift of your mercy, aided by the prayers of your saints, may pass this night with a purity of soul and body that is pleasing to you. Through our Lord Jesus Christ your Son, resurrected from death.

437

225 BLESSING OF THE CANDLE OF THE HOLY BISHOP AUGUSTINE, WHICH HE WROTE AND SANG WHEN HE WAS A DEACON.[b] Let the heavenly choir of angels now rejoice, let the divine servants[94] rejoice, and let the trumpet of salvation ring out on account of the victory of the great King. Let [the earth too] be glad, illuminated

---

[a] The entombment of Christ is also set in the evening, cf. Matth. 27, 57.

[b] The Gallican sacramentaries traditionally attribute the hymn accompanying the blessing of the paschal candle to Augustine: *Bobbio Missal* 227, ed. LOWE, p. 69; *Missale Gallicanum Vetus* 132, ed. MOHLBERG, p. 35; see KELLY, *Exultet*, p. 50. An excellent running commentary to the Gallican *Exsultet* is offered by FUCHS and WEIKMANN, *Exsultet*, p. 38–101, which I refer to here in as far as it is relevant in the context of the Gothic Missal and for clarification of the present translation.

by such a radiant light, and let the whole world, lightened by the splendour of the eternal King, perceive that it has laid off darkness. Let Mother Church too be joyful, adorned by the brilliance of such great light, and let this sanctuary resound to the loud voices of the faithful. Therefore invoke, so I ask, most beloved brothers,[a] you who are present in the so wonderful clarity of this holy light, together with me the mercy of almighty God, that he who deigned to accept me, not because of my merits,[b] in the company of his servants,[c] commands me to fulfil the praise of this candle while the grace of his light is poured out. Through his resurrected Son.

BLESSING OF THE CANDLE. It is worthy and just,[d] indeed it is truly worthy and just to sing the praises of the invisible God and almighty Father and his only-begotten Son our Lord Jesus Christ, with all the love of our heart and mind and with the service of our voice, who paid for us the debt of Adam to the eternal Father and wiped away the bond of the old sin with his precious blood.[e] For

---

[a] According to FUCHS and WEIKMANN, *Das Exsultet*, p. 48, only the clergy are addressed by this *fratres karissimi*. The grounds for this interpretation, however, remain unclear, and it is in contradiction with the statement that the deacon 'letzlich nur als Sprecher der versammelten Gemeinde fungiert' (p. 51; cf. also p. 80: 'die feiernde Gemeinde [wendet sich] durch den Diakon'; p. 96).

[b] This expression of unworthiness is comparable to the *Apologia* for Easter Day, no. 275; see FUCHS and WEIKMANN, *Das Exsultet*, p. 49.

[c] The word *sacerdos* usually signifies 'priest' or 'bishop'. Here, it is translated more neutrally because the *Exultet* is traditionally sung by the deacon; see FUCHS and WEIKMANN, *Das Exsultet*, p. 17; KELLY, *Exultet*, p. 3, 7–9 and passim. The modern text on which the commentary by Fuchs and Weikmann is based (*Missale Romanum* 1970) changes *sacerdotum* into *leuitarum*; the translation of this same version by Kelly ('priests' for *levitarum*, p. 32) is confusing.

[d] The opening of the prayer implies that the 'Blessing', the prayer proper, is preceded by the dialogue between the deacon and the faithful, which also occurs in the prayer of sacrifice. The wording (*Dignum et iustum* instead of *Vere dignum est*) indicates Gaul as the origin of the *Exultet*, as is remarked by MICHEL HUGLO, 'L'auteur de l'*Exultet* paschale', *Vigiliae christianae* 7 (1953), 79–88, at p. 80–81; cf. KELLY, *Exultet*, p. 52.

[e] FUCHS and WEIKMANN, *Das Exsultet*, p. 51–52 refer to Rom. 5; Hebr. 9 and 10; Col. 2; and Ps. 51, 4, though no explicit quotations are included.

these are the Paschal celebrations,[a] on which he, the true Lamb, was slaughtered[b] and his blood dedicated to the doorposts,[c] on which[95] you once took our fathers, the children of Israel, when you led them out of Egypt, through the Red Sea with dry feet.[d] This then is the night[e] that has purged the darkness of sin through the light of the *pillar* (Ex. 13, 21) of fire. This is the night that today,[f] through the entire world, returns those who believe in Christ, separated from the vices of the world and the darkness of sin, to mercy [and] weds [them] to holiness. This is the night in which Christ nullifies the bonds of death[g] and ascends from hell as Victor. For there was no benefit in our birth if there had been no benefit in our redemption.[h] O wonderful grace of your love towards us.[i] O inestimable love of your benevolence, that you handed over

438

---

[a] *Haec sunt enim festa paschalium*: FUCHS and WEIKMANN, *Das Exsultet*, p. 53 rightly point to the plural form as expressing the multilayered function of the celebration: Easter as the 'feast of feasts'; Easter as a feast that implies at least the eight days of the Octave but even more precisely the fifty days of Eastertide; Easter as a feast with a variety of contents, with its connection to the Old Testament, to the Resurrection, to Baptism, and to eschatological expectation.

[b] Implicit reference to I Cor. 5, 7.

[c] *postibus*: the image of the marked doorposts of Ex. 12 is interpreted in patristic exegesis as a prefiguration of Baptism; FUCHS and WEIKMANN, *Das Exsultet*, p. 57–58 refer to AUGUSTINE, *In Iohannis euangelium tractatus*, ed. WILLEMS, CCSL 36, p. 463–464.

[d] References to Ex. 12–14. FUCHS and WEIKMANN, *Das Exsultet*, p. 59 link the reference to the children of Israel as 'our fathers' to I Cor. 10, 1–2.

[e] *Haec igitur nox est*: FUCHS and WEIKMANN, *Das Exsultet*, p. 58 refer to Christmas as a parallel without mentioning its introit Ps. 118 (117), 24: *Haec est dies...*

[f] *hodie*: the phrase refers to the sacrament of Baptism administered in this night; the addition of *hodie* marks the turn from the prefigurative past of the Old Testament to the universal Christian present: FUCHS and WEIKMANN, *Das Exsultet*, p. 60.

[g] On hell as a prison, see no. 220.

[h] AMBROSE, *Expositio euangelii secundum Lucam* 2.41, ed. MARC ADRIAEN and PAOLO A. BALLERINI, *Expositio evangelii secundum Lucam*, CCSL 14 (Turnhout: Brepols, 1957), p. 49; FUCHS and WEIKMANN, *Das Exsultet*, p. 64–65.

[i] On the O-exclamations in the *Exultet* and in other prayers in the Gothic Missal, see Introduction, section Style and figures.

the Son to redeem the slave.[a] O truly necessary sin of Adam,[b] wiped away by the death of Christ. O happy fault, deigned worthy to merit so good and great a Redeemer. O blessed night, that alone merited to know the time and hour at which Christ rose again from hell.[c] This is the night of which is written: *'And the night will be lightened as the day'* (Ps. 139, 12), and: *'The night is my light[d] in my delight'* (Ps. 139, 11).[e] For the holiness of this night chases away sins, settles debts, returns innocence to the fallen[f] and joy to the sad,[g] banishes hate, produces concord and bows the powers. Accept then,[h] holy Father, in the grace of this night, *the evening sacrifice[i] of this incense*[96] (cf. Ps. 141, 2), which the holy Church, through the solemn offering of the candle, returns to you by the hands of your servants[97] from the work of the bees. But we already

[a] FUCHS and WEIKMANN, *Das Exsultet*, p. 66 refer to Rom. 8, 32 and Gal. 4, 4–7.

[b] *O certe necessarium Adae peccatum*: the thought is understood against the background of the *renovatio in melius*: salvation is not the restoration of the situation before the Fall, but an improvement to a state that is better than paradise. This notion is also applicable to the exclamation 'O happy fault'; cf. AMBROSE, *Explanatio Psalmorum XII* 39.20, ed. MICHAEL PETSCHENIG, CSEL 64 (Vienna: Verlag der Österreichischen Akademie der Wissenschaften, 1954/1999), p. 225; see FUCHS and WEIKMANN, *Das Exsultet*, p. 65–67 and endnote 56 on p. 135.

[c] Cf. Matth. 24, 26; Matth. 25, 13; Marc. 13, 32; FUCHS and WEIKMANN, *Das Exsultet*, p. 71–75.

[d] *inluminacio*: Baptism resounds in this word; see no. 83.

[e] The wording of these quotations from Ps. 139 led Michel Huglo to assume that the *Exultet* originated in Gaul, where the use of the Gallican Psalter was common; HUGLO, 'L'auteur', p. 84–85. On the christological interpretation of these verses in patristic exegesis, see FUCHS and WEIKMANN, *Das Exsultet*, p. 72–73.

[f] FUCHS and WEIKMANN, *Das Exsultet*, p. 76–77 link this passage to the renewed admission of the penitents to the Easter communion.

[g] FUCHS and WEIKMANN, *Das Exsultet*, p. 77 read this as a reference to the completion of the Lenten fast.

[h] *igitur*: FUCHS and WEIKMANN, *Das Exsultet*, p. 80–81 link this to the *Te igitur* in the *canon missae*; see e.g. no. 481. It remains unclear whether the object of *suscipe* is the sacrifice of praise or a material offering of wax. See the discussion in FUCHS and WEIKMANN, *Das Exsultet*, p. 82–87.

[i] *sacrificium uespertinum* is echoed by *lucifer matutinus* at the end of the hymn; FUCHS and WEIKMANN, *Das Exsultet*, p. 81.

know the praise of this pillar of fire,[a] which the glowing red fire ignites[98] to the honour of God. For although it is divided into parts, it does not encounter damage when light is taken from it. It is fed by melting wax, which mother bee brought forth to the substance of this precious lamp.[b] The bee surpasses other animals that are subjected to man.[c] Although she has a tiny little body, a vast vitality flows through her narrow breast; she is weak in strength but strong in craft. For as soon as the change of seasons has taken place, when the snow-white winter lays off its greyness and the mildness of spring has wiped away icy old-age,[d] then for her follows immediately the concern to start work. And spread across the fields, while their wings slightly glide in balance and their little legs hang freely, they get ready to pluck flowers with the mouth. Burdened by their food, they return to the hive. And there, according to an incomparable art, some build little cells with strong glue. Some press together tightly the liquid honey, others turn the flowers into wax, some shape little ones with the mouth, yet others shut away the nectar from the collected leaves. O truly blessed and admirable bee, whose genitals are not violated by males and not shattered by bearing, and whose chastity is not destroyed by children, just as holy Mary received as a virgin, gave birth as a vir-

439

[a] Here, the *columna* refers to the paschal candle (i.e. Christ). Alternatively, the pillar of fire in Ex. 13, 21 and the paschal candle as symbol for Christ merge; FUCHS and WEIKMANN, *Das Exsultet*, p. 60 and 87.

[b] The sentence is full of Christology: *lampadis* is probably inspired by Is. 62, 1, read as a prophecy of Christ's coming. The lamp (Christ) is brought forth by mother bee (Mary – for this reason the translation is literal instead of the more common 'queen bee'); *substantia* refers to the human nature of Christ; FUCHS and WEIKMANN, *Das Exsultet*, p. 90 and endnote 147 on p. 140.

[c] The 'praise of the bee' is based on VIRGIL, *Georgica*, book 4. For precise references, see FUCHS and WEIKMANN, *Das Exsultet*, p. 140 endnote 149. See also HEINRICH ZWECK, *Osterlobpreis und Taufe. Studien zu Struktur und Theologie des Exultet und anderer Osterpraeconien unter besonderer Berücksichtigung der Taufmotive*, Regensburger Studien zur Theologie 32 (Frankfurt a.M.-New York: Peter Lang, 1986). The insertion of a long Virgilian passage in a Christian prayer text was not appreciated by all: see Jerome's protest in his *Epistula* 18, PL 30, col. 182D-183C; cf. FUCHS and WEIKMANN, *Das Exsultet*, p. 94.

[d] Early Christian authors interpreted the congruence of Easter and spring as 'divinely willed', see ROBERTS, *Humblest Sparrow*, p. 147, with reference to ENNODIUS, *Benedictio cerei*, ed. FRIEDRICH VOGEL, MGH AA 7, p. 18–20, at p. 20.

gin and remained a virgin. O truly blessed night that *plundered the Egyptians* (cf. Ex. 12, 36)[a] [and] enriched the Jews, night in which the heavenly world is joined to the earthly. We pray to you, O Lord, that this candle, consecrated to the honour of your name to destroy the darkness of this night, will persevere unfailingly, and that, pleasant through a sweet fragrance, it mingles with the lights of heaven. May the morning star[b] find its light, that morning star, I say, that knows no decline, that [star] which, after his return from hell,[c] was a clear light for the human race. We pray then, O Lord, that you deign to grant to us your manservants and maidservants, to all the clergy and most faithful people, together with our father this most blessed man *N*,[d] peace of the times, and to keep us in this Easter joy. Through our Lord your Son, resurrected from the dead.

226 COLLECT AFTER THE BLESSING OF THE CANDLE. Holy Lord, almighty God, who for our sight in the darkness has commanded these candles to shine forth in the obscurity of this world, grant, while we hasten to that day of eternity and to the meeting with your Only-begotten, that, undisturbed by sins, we walk by this temporary light that you have prepared for the darkness while we pass through this night. Through the Resurrected.

440

227 COLLECT AFTER THE CANDLE HYMN. God, Temple of eternal fire, God, Dwelling of the true light, God, Seat of eternal clarity, while we celebrate for you, O Lord, the solemn offer-

---

[a] *nox, quae expoliauit Aegyptios*: see GEORGES FOLLIET, 'La *spoliatio Aegyptiorum* (Exode 3: 21–23, 11: 2–3; 12: 35–36). Les interprétations de cette images chez les Pères et autres écrivains ecclésiastiques', *Traditio* 57 (2002), 1–48; FUCHS and WEIKMANN, *Das Exsultet*, p. 95.

[b] *lucifer matutinus*: strictly speaking, the addition *matutinus* is redundant; FUCHS and WEIKMANN, *Das Exsultet*, p. 98 interpret it as an echo of *sacrificium uespertinum* (see footnote i on p. 209).

[c] On the *descensus ad inferos*, see no. 219.

[d] *una cum patre nostro beatissimo uiro* illo: the prayer on behalf of the bishop emphasises that the deacon, rather than the bishop (who presides over the Easter Vigil), recites the *Exultet*.

ing of the completion of the day and the beginning of the night, and, now that the lights of your altar are ignited, while we offer the temporary light, we pray that you generously grant to your manservants and maidservants[99] the true and perpetual light. Through the Resurrected.

XXXI TWELVE EASTER PRAYERS WITH AS MANY COLLECTS[a]

228 PRAYER FOR THANKSGIVING.[100] PREFACE. Most beloved brothers, now that we have obtained the expected and desired day of Easter, let us bring thanks to almighty God the Father, because he called us to eternal salvation on this day through his Son our Lord Jesus Christ, whom he gave as an offering for us. Let us therefore praise him with a faithful prayer of thanksgiving, let us bless him, let us honour the blessed and blissful name of God the Father in the Son, and [the name] of the Son in the Father and the Holy Spirit, for ever and ever.

229 PRAYER FOLLOWS. Holy Lord, almighty Father, hear, protect and sanctify your people, strengthened by the sign of the cross, purified by Baptism, anointed with chrism, [the people] that you have gathered to celebrate the blessedness of the feast of this day, and mercifully pour on all the knowledge of you through participation in your Holy Spirit. Through.

441

230 PRAYER FOR THE EXILES. PREFACE. In accord and in one body in the Spirit of God the Father the almighty Lord, let us pray for mercy for our brothers and sisters who are far away through captivities, who are detained [in] prisons, who are assigned to the mines, that for them the Lord is a helper, protector and consoler, and that he does not forget those who persevere in him in faithful innocence.

---

[a] On the Easter intercession, see Introduction, section The liturgical year.

231 PRAYER FOLLOWS. Grant, O Lord, to the exiles a fatherland, to the fettered release, to the captives freedom, so that your people in this and the future world is freed through the gift of your mercy. Through.

232 PRAYER FOR THE PRIESTS.[101] PREFACE. Admitted to the holiest of holies and made participants in the eternal priesthood of the heavenly altar, let us pray for the mercy of God the almighty Father, that he fills his priests and servants with gifts of spiritual grace.

233 PRAYER FOLLOWS. O Lord God of the powers, justify and sanctify the shepherds and leaders of your sheep, so that our adversary the devil, overcome by their faith and holiness, does not dare to attack and violate the Lord's flock. Through the Resurrected.

234 PRAYER FOR THE VIRGINS. PREFACE. Let us pray in unity to the God of uncorrupted eternity and the Lord of unviolated nature, while we plea for our brothers who have dedicated body and soul to glorious virginity, that the Spirit of mercy[102] accompanies them until the completion of their intention.[a] Through.

442

235 PRAYER FOLLOWS. Look, O Lord, upon the consecrated virgins and voluntary eunuchs, the precious pearls of the Church, that they watch over their bodies and spirit with the immaculate conscience of chastity and similar esteem. Through the Resurrected.

236 PRAYER FOR THOSE WHO GIVE ALMS. PREFACE. Most beloved brothers, let us pray in supplication to the holy and blessed God of retribution, while we plea for our brothers and sisters, through whose service and generosity those in the Church who suffer poverty do not feel their need: that the Lord imparts spiritual wealth to those who share the means of earthly matter with the need of faithful souls. Through the Resurrected.

[a] *propositum* refers particularly to the intention to live the dedicated life of a monk: BLAISE, *Dictionnaire*, s.v. *propositum*.

237 PRAYER FOLLOWS. Grant the devout prayers of your servants, merciful Lord, that all those who, mindful of the heavenly
commandments, supply the poor with that which is needed, are
crowned with the incorruptible and heavenly glory of your compassion and mercy. Through.

238 PRAYER FOR TRAVELLERS.[a] PREFACE. Let us pray to God the
almighty Father, most beloved brothers, the Lord of the heavenly,
earthly and infernal things, that the almighty God with his aid as
companion [and] helper will bring back and protect all our brothers
and sisters who are subjected to the necessities of travels. Through.

443

239 COLLECT FOLLOWS. Return,[b] O Lord, to the travellers the
ground of the fatherland which they long for, so that through
the contemplation of your mercy, while for this life they give
thanks for your benefits, they eagerly desire to be *fellow citizens of
the saints and members of your household* (Eph. 2, 19). Grant this
through the Resurrected.

240 PRAYER FOR THE SICK. PREFACE. Let us pray to the God
of all salvation and the Lord of all strength for our brothers and
sisters who are tormented according to the flesh by different sorts
of sicknesses, that the Lord grants them the heavenly gift of his
healing. Through.

241 PRAYER FOLLOWS. O Lord, for whom it is easy to bring the
dead back to life, restore those who are sick to the former health, so
that those who pray for the remedy of your heavenly mercy do not
desire the remedy of an earthly medicine. Through the resurrected.

---

[a] The words *peregrinatio* and *peregrinor* can refer to pilgrims, but also in a more
general sense to those who travel for whatever reason; see BLAISE, *Dictionnaire*,
s.v. *peregrinatio*. The word can also be understood in a more spiritual sense, as illustrated by the *immolatio* of the Mass for Clement (no. 121).

[b] The verb *restitue* ('restitute, restore') makes the prayer ambivalent. It seems to
qualify the *peregrinatio* as a mundane journey or pilgrimage, expressing the travel-
ler's longing to be back home again; yet at the same time the *patria* mentioned is to
be understood as a pilgrim's linear goal: the celestial fatherland (cf. no. 174) which
will provide co-citizenship with the saints in heaven.

242 PRAYER FOR THE PENITENTS. [PREFACE.] As we acknowledge the God of goodness and mercy, who prefers the penitence
of sinners to their death, let us pray with communal prayers and
lamenting for our brothers and sisters for the mercy of the Lord,
that he does not repel those who confess the offences of their sin   444
from the forgiveness of his goodness. Through.

243 PRAYER FOLLOWS. King of glory, who *has no pleasure in the*
death of the wicked but that he turns from his ways and lives (Ez. 33,
11), grant penitence to us who are stained with the blemish of sins, so
that *we may weep together with those who weep and grieve, and rejoice*
with those who rejoice (Rom. 12, 15). Through the Resurrected.

244 PRAYER FOR UNITY. PREFACE. Most beloved brothers,
let us pray to *the one God and Father, from whom are all things,*
and to our one Lord Jesus Christ, through whom [are] all things
(I Cor. 8, 6), that he confirms the unity of his Church through
the united will of our gathering. Through his Son the Resurrected.

245 COLLECT FOLLOWS. Almighty Lord, who is a *God of good-*
ness and of all consolation (II Cor. 1, 3), we humbly pray to you
that you snatch away the heretics and unfaithful from the perpetual flames of hell through the manifestation of your truth, for
you desire that everyone be saved and come to the knowledge of the
truth (I Tim. 2, 4). Through.

246 PRAYER FOR THE PEACE OF KINGS.[a] PREFACE. Most belov-   445
ed brothers, let us in unity pray in supplication to *the Lord of lords*
and King of kings (Apoc. 19, 16),[b] that he deigns to give to us his

---

[a] On the prayers *pro pace regum* in the Merovingian tradition, see MARY GAR-
RISON, 'The *Missa pro principe* in the Bobbio Missal', in HEN and MEENS (eds),
The Bobbio Missal, p. 187–205; BERNARD, *Transitions*, p. 242 and additional bib-
liography in footnote 84; on the votive Mass for kings and the kingdom, see HEN,
Royal Patronage, p. 39–41.

[b] Cf., with slightly different wording, I Tim. 6, 15, also quoted in no. 249 (*solus*
potens).

people peace between kings, so that when their minds are soothed the peace of this gathering persists for us. Through.

247 COLLECT FOLLOWS. Creator[103] of all flesh [and] spirits and Protector of all worldly kingdoms, grant to the eminence of kings the prosperity of faith and peace, so that while we yet remain on earth it is possible for us to freely serve your heavenly kingdom. Through the Resurrected.

248 PRAYER FOR THE SOULS OF THE DEAD.[104] PREFACE. Most beloved brothers, let us pray to God the Judge of the universe, to the God of heavenly, earthly and infernal things, for the souls of our beloved who have gone before us in the peace of the Lord, that the Lord will gather them in his rest and raise them from the dead *to share in the first resurrection* (Apoc. 20, 6). Through.

249 PRAYER FOLLOWS. Jesus Christ, our life and our resurrection, give to our fellow priests and our beloved who have come to rest in your peace the consolation of the heavenly abode for which they longed. And if some of them, misled by the trickery of demons, have stained themselves with many blemishes of sin, you, O Lord, who only are mighty,[a] forgive their sins,[b] so that the devil sighs over the fact that those whom he gloated over in becoming participants of his damnation, through your mercy [have become] companions of your blessedness. Saviour.

446

250 PRAYER FOR THE CATECHUMENS. [PREFACE.] Most beloved ones, let us in unity support the prayer of hope of our brothers, so that when they go to the font of his blessed rebirth, the almighty Lord accompanies them with the help of all his mercy.[105]

251 COLLECT FOLLOWS. Creator of all things, O Lord, and fount of living water,[c] wipe away through the bath of Baptism the sins of

---

[a] *qui solus potens es*: cf. I Tim. 6, 15; see also no. 246.
[b] 'And if some of them ... forgive their sins': cf. I Ioh. 2, 1–2.
[c] Cf. Ioh. 4, 1–30.

those to whom you have already given faith in the resurrection, so that they do not fear the death of this world. Fill them with your Holy Spirit, so that they rejoice *that Christ gains form* and lives *in them* (Gal. 4, 19). Through.

XXXII AT BAPTISM[a]

252 O Lord, deign to bless this child your servant *N*,[106] for nobody is turned away, not on the grounds of condition nor on the grounds of age, as your most beloved Son our Lord says: *'Do not stop the little children from coming to me'* (Matth. 19, 14). But let these, O Lord, before they know good and evil, be marked with the seal of your cross, and let those who need God[107] be considered worthy to come to Baptism in your holy name. Through the Lord.

447

253 LIKEWISE A COLLECT. Receive the seal of Christ, accept the divine words, be illuminated[b] by the Word of the Lord, for today you are restored by Christ.[c] Through the Lord.

254 LIKEWISE A COLLECT. I mark you in the name of the Father, the Son and the Holy Spirit, so that you are a Christian. Your eyes, that you see the light of God, your ears, that you hear the voice of the Lord, your nose, that you smell the sweetness of

---

[a] *Ad christianum faciendum*: the title is descriptive, 'to be made a Christian'.

[b] On Baptism as illumination, see no. 83. Drews does not mention this ancient Christian imagery when he describes Christianisation as Enlightenment: DREWS, 'Jews as Pagans?' p. 201–202.

[c] *confessus es a Christo*: the phrase can only be read literally if it is assumed that the deponent form *confiteor* is used as an active verb: 'you are acknowledged by Christ' (on the active use of deponent verbs, see ROSE (ed.), *Missale Gothicum*, Introduction, p. 90). The meaning of this phrase is neither clear nor convincing. Reading *confessus es* as a deponent verb (e.g. in the amendation *confessus es a Christo [possideri]*) creates the problem that it ascribes a confession of faith to an infant, who is by definition unable to speak. I opt for a third possibility, namely to replace *confessus* by *conversus* in the meaning given by ALEXANDER SOUTER, *A Glossary of Later Latin to 600 A.D.* (Oxford: Clarendon Press, 1949), s.v. *conuerto*: '(*of God*) restore to favour, pardon'.

Christ, [your mouth],[a] that you are converted and confess the Father and the Son and the Holy Spirit, your heart, that you believe in the inseparable Trinity. Peace be with you, through Jesus Christ our Lord, who lives with the Father and the Son and the Holy Spirit.

XXXIII COLLECT FOR THE BLESSING OF THE FONT

255 [PREFACE.] Standing on the bank of the clear fount, most beloved brothers, pull hither *new people* (Eph. 4, 24) from the earth, as merchants pull their merchandise from the seashore.[108] And let each, when they set sail, beat one at a time on a new sea, not with an oar but with the cross,[b] not by a touch but with the mind, not with a stick but with the sacrament.[c] This place, although small, yet full of grace, is well steered by the Holy Spirit. Let us therefore pray to our Lord and God that he sanctifies this font, that for all[109] who will descend into this font he makes it a bath of the most blessed rebirth for the remission of all sins.[110] Through the Lord.

448

256 COLLECT FOLLOWS. God, who has sanctified the river Jordan for the salvation of souls, may the angel of your blessing descend on these waters, so that your servants, poured over with it, receive remission of sins and, *reborn of water and the Holy Spirit* (Ioh. 3, 5), serve you devotedly in eternity. Through the Lord.

[a] *[Signo] ... conuersus ut confitearis patrem et filium et spiritum sanctum*: an object parallel to *oculos, aures, nares, cor* is lacking. In line with the call to confession it makes sense to add *os* or *linguam* here, as suggested by MOHLBERG (ed.), *Missale Gothicum*, p. 65.

[b] On the power of Moses's (and Aaron's) staff (*uirga*), see Ex. 4, Ex. 7, Ex. 9, Ex. 10, and esp. Ex. 14, 21 where the raised staff of Moses divides the Red Sea; see also Num. 17 and, conversely, the failure of Moses's trust in Num. 20, where he strikes the rock to provide water for the people.

[c] On this passage, see Introduction, section Style and figures.

257 PRAYER OF SACRIFICE. It is worthy and just [that we praise you], O Lord, holy Father, almighty and everlasting God, Initiator of the sacred chrism, Father and Giver of a new sacrament through your only Son our Lord and God. For you mildly give to the waters to carry your Holy Spirit,[a] prior to the riches of the world, you procure the waters of Bethsaida while the angel administers healing,[b] you sanctify the bed of the Jordan because your Son Christ deigns to do so.[c] Look upon these waters, O Lord, which are prepared to wash away the sins of humankind. Grant that the angel of your love is present at this holy font, [that] it washes away [the sins] of the former life and sanctifies the poor dwelling for you, taking care that the soul[d] of those who will be reborn blossoms eternal and that the newness of Baptism is truly[111] restored. Bless, O Lord our God, this creation water and let your strength descend on it. Pour out on it your Holy Spirit the Comforter, the angel of truth. Sanctify, O Lord, the waves of this water, as you have sanctified the streams of the Jordan, so that those who descend into this font in the name of the Father and the Son and the Holy Spirit may be considered worthy to obtain forgiveness of sins and imbuement with the Holy Spirit. Through our Lord Jesus Christ, who is blessed with the Father and the Holy Spirit for ever and ever.

449

Then you make a cross with chrism and you say:
258 I exorcise you, creature water, I exorcise you, all the army of the devil, all power of the adversary, all shadow of demons. I exorcise you in the name of our Lord Jesus Christ the Nazarene, who became flesh of the virgin Mary, to whom the Father *has subjected all things* (I Cor. 15, 27[e]) in heaven and on earth. Fear and tremble, you and all your wickedness. Make way for the Holy Spirit, so that for all[112] who will descend into this font it may be a bath of the Baptism of rebirth for the remission of all sins.[113] Through our

[a] Cf. Gen. 1, 2.
[b] Cf. Ioh. 5, 1–18.
[c] Cf. Matth. 3, 14–17 and no. 74 above.
[d] *uiscera*: interpreted spiritually in view of the prayer for 'eternal bloom'.
[e] Vulgate: I Cor. 15, 26.

Lord Jesus Christ, who will come to judge you, enemy, *on the seat of the majesty of his Father* (Matth. 19, 28) with his holy angels, and the world with fire, for ever and ever.

Then you blow three times on the water and you pour chrism in it in the form of a cross and you say:
259 The infusion of the salutary chrism of our Lord Jesus Christ *may make [this fount] to be a fount of living water* for all who descend into it, *to eternal life* (Ioh. 4, 14).[a] Amen.

450   *While you baptise you question him and you say:*
260 I baptise you, *N*, in the name of the Father and the Son and the Holy Spirit, for the remission of sins, that you may have eternal life. Amen.

While you annoint him with chrism you say:
261 I anoint you with chrism of holiness, as with a tunic of immortality, which our Lord Jesus Christ received as first when this was handed over by the Father, that you wear it unharmed and unblemished until before the seat of judgement of Christ and that you live for ever and ever.[b]

While you wash his feet you say:[c]
262 I wash your feet, as our Lord Jesus Christ did to his disciples.[d] May you do this to guests and strangers, that you have everlasting life.

---

[a] The emphasis on chrism as representing eternal life is expressed in AMBROSE, *De sacramentis* 2.24, ed. OTTO FALLER, CSEL 73 (Vienna: Tempsky, 1955), p. 36; see also no. 261. On Ambrose's (contested) authorship of *De sacramentis*, see SMYTH, *Liturgie oubliée*, p. 39–41, who situates it in Milan around the time of Ambrose.

[b] See the previous footnote.

[c] The custom of washing the feet of the newly baptised is part of all Western liturgies outside Rome. It is described in AMBROSE, *De sacramentis* 3.4–7 (ed. FALLER, p. 39–41) as a *mysterium* of sanctification, granting the newly baptised to share with Christ ('Unless I wash you, you have no share with me', Ioh. 13, 8). *De sacramentis* 3.5 (ed. FALLER, p. 40) emphasises that Rome did not know or maintain this custom; see also SMYTH, *Liturgie oubliée*, p. 475–478.

[d] Cf. Ioh. 13, 1–20.

While you put the [Baptism] garment on him you say:
263 Receive the white garment, that you may wear it unstained until before the seat of judgement of our Lord Jesus Christ. Amen.

264 COLLECT. Let us pray, most beloved brothers, to our Lord and God for his newborn[114] who have just been baptised, that the Saviour, when he will come in his majesty, makes those *he has made to be born again of water and the Holy Spirit* (Ioh. 3, 5) clothed with the salvation of eternity. Through the Lord.

265 LIKEWISE ANOTHER [COLLECT.] Now that they have been baptised by asking for the chrism[115] and have been crowned in Christ, whom the Lord has deigned to endow with rebirth, we pray to almighty God that until the end they will bear unstained the Baptism which they have received. Through the Lord.

451

XXXIIII MASS FOR THE VIGIL OF THE HOLY FEAST OF EASTER

266 [PREFACE.] Delivered from the darkness of the world through the grace of this most holy night, and elected to the promised grace of righteousness and heavenly light, let us pray, most beloved brothers, to the indefatigable goodness of the almighty God the Father through Christ his Son, that through the continuous protection of his majesty he guards his holy catholic Church, spread throughout the world,[a] which he acquired through the Passion and most glorious blood of his most beloved Son, and that he [keeps] it safe and defended against all snares of the world and gives it tranquil times in eternity. Through the Resurrected.

267 COLLECT. *You have redeemed us* (Apoc. 5, 9), O Lord God, through the bath of rebirth and the blood of the cross, so that that flesh, which had first become mortal in Adam, through the Passion of your majesty was again called back to heaven. Saviour.

[a] See no. 3.

452

268 AFTER THE NAMES. Let us pray for those who offer the most holy spiritual gifts to the Lord our God, for themselves and for their beloved, and for the souls of their beloved in commemoration of the holy martyrs, that the Lord our God deigns to mercifully hear their prayers. Through the Resurrected.

269 AT THE KISS OF PEACE. Fulfil, O Lord, the prayers of those who supplicate, hear the weeping of the sinners, *let* the Master and Creator of peace *kiss us with the kiss of his mouth* (Song 1, 1), so that we who receive this sacrifice[116] have in us the peace for which we hope. Through.

270 PRAYER OF SACRIFICE. It is worthy and just, fair and just that we here and everywhere bring thanks to you, speak praise to you and offer sacrifices and praise your mercies, O Lord, holy Father, almighty and everlasting God. *For you are great and do wondrous things, you alone are God* (Ps. 86, 10).[a] *You made the heavens by understanding* (Ps. 136, 5), *you spread out the earth on the waters* (Ps. 136, 6), *you made the great lights* (Ps. 136, 7), *the sun to rule over the day* (Ps. 136, 8), *the moon and stars to rule over the night* (Ps. 136, 9). *You made us and not we ourselves* (Ps. 100, 3), *do not forsake the work of your hands* (Ps. 138, 8). *Yours is the day, yours also the night* (Ps. 74, 16), *by day you commanded your steadfast love* (Ps. 42, 8)[b] *and at night you revealed [it]*,[c] which during today's vigil we celebrate through the feast of this light. For this is the night [that is] witness to the secrets of salvation, the night in which you grant forgiveness to sinners, in which you make new men of old, in which you make old people, nearly at their end, to mature chil-

[a] The entire prayer is noteworthy for the high density of psalm citations and, in the final part, quotations from the Gospel.

[b] Vulgate: Ps. 41, 9.

[c] Ps. 41, 9 according to a number of manuscripts of the Vetus Latina, esp. Itala; see Brepolis Vetus Latina database at http://apps.brepolis.net.proxy.library. uu.nl/vld/index.html (consulted 22 September 2015). This version was also known to Augustine, see AUGUSTINE, *In Iohannis euangelium tractatus* 93.4, ed. WILLEMS, p. 561; see also GREGORY THE GREAT, *Moralia in Iob* praef. 2.6, ed. MARC ADRIAEN, CCSL 143 (Turnhout: Brepols, 1979), p. 12. The Vulgate gives *et nocte canticum eius apud me*, cf. NRSV: 'and at night his song is with me'.

dren, which you draw forth from the holy font, reborn to a new
creation. This night reborn people are begotten for the eternal day,   453
the halls of the heavenly kingdom are unlocked, and through a
blessed law human offerings are exchanged for divine gifts. For[a]
this is that *night which is made a light in my pleasures* (Ps. 139, 11),[b]
in which you have so greatly *gladdened us, O Lord, by your work*
(Ps. 92, 4[c]). This is the night in which hell is opened, the night in
which Adam is released,[d] the night in which the coin that was lost
is found again,[e] the night in which the lost sheep is carried back on
the shoulders of the good shepherd,[f] the night in which the devil
fell and Christ rose as the *sun of righteousness* (Mal. 3, 4),[g] and in
which, after the bonds of hell were unbound and the bolts broken, *many bodies of the saints, torn from the tombs, entered into the
holy city* (Matth. 27, 52–53). O truly blessed night, which alone deserved *to know the time and hour* (Matth. 24, 42) at which Christ
was resurrected, as already prophesied in the psalm: for 'the night
is as bright as the day' (Ps. 139, 12).[h] [This is] the night in which the
resurrection was born for all eternity. For you, almighty God, are
praised by the multitude of heavenly creatures and the innumerable choirs of angels without ceasing, saying: Holy [...]

271 AFTER THE SANCTUS. At your command, O Lord, all
things *in heaven and on earth were made, in the sea and all deeps*

---

[a] From here to the quotation from Ps. 139, 12 in the antepenultimate line, the
text quotes the *Exultet*, no. 225; cf. KELLY, *Exultet*, p. 53.

[b] For the English translation, see Ps. 139, 11 as given on http://www.latinvul-
gate.com/lv/verse.aspx?t=0&b=21&c=138 (consulted 11 May 2015). Iuxta Hebraeos: *si dixero forte tenebrae operient me nox quoque lux erit circa me*; Iuxta Gallicanum: *et dixi forsitan tenebrae conculcabunt me et nox inluminatio in deliciis meis.*
The quotation in the prayer here is incomplete, it should probably be *Haec est enim
nox illa, quae facta est inluminatio in diliciis* (as in no. 225).

[c] Vulgate: Ps. 1, 5.

[d] On the *descensus ad inferos*, see no. 219.

[e] Cf. Luc. 15, 8–9.

[f] Cf. Luc. 15, 4–5.

[g] The phrase combines biblical (*sol iusticiae* according to Mal. 3, 4) and Virgilian wording (*exoriens sol*, VIRGIL, *Georgica* 1.438; see LEWIS and SHORT, *Latin
Dictionary*, s.v. *exorior*). See also Introduction, section Style and figures.

[h] 'O truly blessed night ... bright as the day': cf. no. 225.

454

(Ps. 135, 6). To you the patriarchs, prophets, apostles, martyrs, confessors and all the saints bring thanks, and while we too do this, we pray that you will willingly lend your ear to these spiritual offerings and sincere sacrifices. We pray to you that you bless this sacrifice with your blessing and sprinkle it with the dew of your Holy Spirit, so that it is a lawful Eucharist[a] for all. Through Christ our Lord. Who in the night before [...]

272 COLLECT AT THE BREAKING OF THE BREAD. Look upon this oblation, almighty God, which we offer to you in honour of your name, for the salvation of kings and their army[b] and of all who are standing around here,[c] and grant that whoever will partake of this will receive health of mind, soundness of body, the protection of salvation, understanding of the knowledge of Christ, the security of hope, strength of faith and the eternity of the Holy Spirit. Grant this through him who lives and reigns with you.

XXXV MASS FOR THE FIRST DAY[d] OF THE HOLY FEAST OF EASTER[117]

273 COLLECT AFTER THE PROPHECY.[e] Most high and almighty God, who raised up *the horn of our salvation* (Luc. 1, 69) in the mystery of your cross, so that *in the house of your servant David* (Luc. 1, 69) you would elevate us with a royal dignity in which, through the triple title of the Trinity,[f] the manifested unity would also be revealed to us in all its splendour, namely a Saviour in man, indeed priest in chrism, certainly a king according to the flesh through birth: we lay our prayers before your majesty, imploring that you

---

[a] *legitima eucharistia*: see no. 57.

[b] The central position of kings and their armies is in harmony with the prayers for *Biduana*; see nos 246 and 247.

[c] *circumadstantes*: see no. 94.

[d] The days of Easter week are indicated by numbers rather than their ferial names; see ROSE (ed.), *Missale Gothicum*, Introduction, p. 135.

[e] On the place and meaning of this prayer in the Gallican Mass, see no. 11.

[f] *trifario titulo trinitatis*: alliteration, see section Style and figures.

grant that those, whom you have deigned to consecrate in your name *through the bath of rebirth* (Tit. 3, 5), while *they serve you, O Lord, in holiness and righteousness* (Luc. 1, 74–75), also preserve invulnerably the unity of faith through the imbuement of your Holy Spirit and, while they hasten with free steps along *the way of peace* (Luc. 1, 79) ascend the heavenly kingdom. Through the Resurrected. 455

274 AFTER THE INTERCESSION. O God, who, after you tore out the thorns of superstition, planted in your Church the cuttings of faith with a deep root, hear the prayer of your people, *look down from heaven, and see; have regard for this vine* (Ps. 80, 14[a]), and grant that through your irrigation it receives fruit in abundance, while it receives growth in the bud because you plant it.[b] Through the Resurrected.

275 CONFESSION OF THE PRIEST.[c] Before the countenance of your immeasurableness and before the eyes of your ineffableness, O marvellous majesty, indeed before your holy countenance, great God, of your great love and power, almighty Father, I come as an exceedingly worthless supplicant, not without due reverence yet without any dignity of office, and I stand here as a guilty witness of my conscience. What should I ask, then, since I do not merit it? But be it said in faith – not without the peace of God – that he who should be the mediator for sin is instead an accuser of [his own] sins. I therefore accuse myself before you and I do not excuse myself, but in the presence of witnesses I confess my injustice before you, O Lord my God. I confess, I say, I confess among witnesses the injustice of my impiety, so that you remit the impiety of my sin. I confess it, but if you do not forgive me, then punish me properly. You have me here before you, a sinner who confesses his sins, but who – I know it – does not amend them, unless with words. For I try to appease you with words, but I offend you with my deeds. I feel guilt, but I put off amendment. Come, then, come 456

[a] Vulgate: Ps. 79, 15.
[b] Cf. Ps. 80, 15 (Vulgate: Ps. 79, 15–16).
[c] On this prayer, see Introduction, sections The prayers of Mass and Style and figures.

to help, ineffable love, forgive, forgive me, wonderful Trinity. Spare, spare, spare, so I plea, O appeasable God. Hear, hear, hear me, so I ask, crying out to you[118] with these words of that son of yours: '*Father, eternal God, I have sinned against heaven and before you, I am no longer worthy to be called your son, treat me like one of your hired hands* (Luc. 15, 18–19)'. And now, merciful Father, I desire the only haven of your mercy, with Christ's favour, that you deign to accept through him what is worthless through me. Through him who lives and reigns with you in the Trinity.

276 PREFACE TO MASS. Most beloved brothers, now that we have reached the salutary day of Easter, so expected and desired by us and the entire human race, let us bring thanks to almighty God with a unified and faithful prayer, while we ask for his mercy on this [day] of the resurrection of our Lord Jesus Christ his Son, that he grants us quiet times, peace-loving rulers, mild judges, weak enemies, healthy bodies, a mild climate, a favourable year, a fruitful harvest, penitence for reconciliation of schisms, calling of the gentiles and unity for the Church, and that through the sanctification with his Comforter he illuminates the congregation to a peaceful and pure gathering. May he preserve in all the chastity of the virgins and the glorious and blessed intention of abstinence, devoted and dedicated to him, and may he cherish with his mercy the onerous abstinence of the widows and grant the help of [his] fatherly love to the orphans. Through our Lord, resurrected from the dead.

457

277 COLLECT FOLLOWS. Almighty God, hear your people who on this day are gathered in your name in honour of the resurrection of our Lord Jesus Christ your Son, and send your humbly entreated majesty from today's feast to eternal happiness, and transmit it from the exultation of today's solemn celebration to uncorrupted joys. Through the Resurrected.

278 AFTER THE NAMES. Accept, so we ask, O Lord, our *offering of appeasement* and *praise* (Hebr. 13, 15), and mercifully accept these gifts from your manservants and maidservants which we offer today on the day of the resurrection of our Lord Jesus Christ accord-

ing to the flesh. And grant through the intercession of your saints consolation *in the land of the living* (Ps. 116, 9ᵃ) to our beloved who rest in Christ. Through [...]

279 AT THE KISS OF PEACE. Grant to your supplicants, so we ask, O Lord, that this offering of our servitude confers on us salvation and peace on the day of the resurrection of our Lord Jesus Christ. Through the Resurrected.

280 PRAYER OF SACRIFICE. It is truly worthy and just, fair and salutary that we always here and everywhere bring thanks to you, O Lord, holy Father, almighty and everlasting God, but on this day of the resurrection of our Lord Jesus Christ your Son an even greater jubilation springs up in our hearts. For this is the day on which the cause of perpetual joy was born for us, this is the day of the resurrection of humanity and the birth of everlasting life, this is the day on which *we are satisfied in the morning with your steadfast love* (Ps. 90, 14), on which he, *the blessed one, our God, who comes to us in the name of the Lord has given us light* (cf. Ps. 118, 26–27). For this our Lord Jesus Christ your Son, fulfilling the prophecies, *visited us after two days at the appointed time [and] rose again on the third day* (cf. Os. 6, 2).ᵇ For this is the day that is marked by the blessing of such a great gift, and which is celebrated through the entire world with today's feast, while mortals rejoice because the death of all is annulledᶜ by the cross of Christ, and in his resurrection the life of all has risen. And now, O Lord, holy Father, almighty and everlasting God, we implore that you deign to bless and sanctify this offering. Through Christ our Lord.

458

281 AFTER THE SANCTUS. This voice accompanies you, O Lord, with a mysterious light, which, while it sings the perennial praise

---

ᵃ Vulgate: Ps. 114, 9.

ᵇ Os. 6, 2 has a different perspective: 'After two days he will revive us; on the third day he will raise us up' (Vulgate: Os. 6, 3).

ᶜ *mors perimpta* (for *perempta*): the expression is found in an early-fifth-century sermon by CHROMATIUS OF AQUILEIA, *Sermo* 17, ed. JOSEPH LEMARIÉ, CCSL 9A (Turnhout: Brepols, 1974), p. 76.

of the Lord in the heights, introduced on earth too the celebration of such a great name, so that *if the people were silent, stones would acclaim* (Luc. 19, 40) such a person. Hell *has seen you,*[a] O God, Hell *has seen you and feared* (cf. Ps. 77, 16[b]) *the crash of your thunder* (Ps. 77, 18[c]) when it said: *'Death has been swallowed up in your victory. Where, O death, is your sting?'* (cf. I Cor. 15, 54–55). The sufferings of the wretched, astonished, have briefly stopped, and the tortures had no torment. And punishment itself feared for its judge, because the nature of the terrible darkness, ruled by the presence of your radiance, was then already afraid to be judged.

459

The faithful[d] *exult in glory, singing for joy on their couches* (Ps. 149, 5), because they recognised the Author of the light promised to them, and you, O Lord, surrounded by their crowd and bathed in a splendour known only to you, sanctify the offerings instituted by you, not through the merits of him who invites,[e] but through the example of Him who sanctifies, so that when all is ceremoniously completed and our Saviour has already returned from hell, death understands that it is conquered and life is called back. Through Christ our Lord, who on the day before his suffering [...]

XXXVI EASTER MORNING MASS FOR THE ENTIRE EASTER WEEK, FOR THE NEWLY BAPTISED.[f] ON THE MONDAY[g]

282 God, who multiplies the people who believe in you through the abundance of your mercy, look graciously on your elect, so

---

[a] On the *descensus ad inferos*, see no. 219.

[b] Vulgate: Ps. 76, 17.

[c] Vulgate: Ps. 76, 19.

[d] *sancti*: translation based on NRSV.

[e] i.e. the priest.

[f] The 'newly baptised' are described as children: the little ones that are reborn. This does not necessarily imply that they were infants (daily Masses to initiate them would hardly be appropriate for this category); rather, the author of the text follows the imagery of I Petr. 2, 2: *sicut modo geniti infantes* ('like newborn infants').

[g] *secunda feria*: second day of the week.

that those who have been reborn through holy Baptism may be considered worthy to enter the heavenly kingdom, through the Lord.

283 COLLECT. Grant, O Lord, that your servants, who have been called to your mercy, be unceasingly protected by your help, so that those who have been reborn through divine Baptism may never be torn out of the power of your kingdom. Through [...]

284 AFTER THE NAMES. Hear our supplications, O Lord, and ac-   460
cept benevolently and favourably the oblations of your manservants and maidservants, which we offer to you. Through [...]

285 AT THE KISS OF PEACE. Grant, so we ask, almighty God, that we may follow in our behaviour the Easter feast, which we cherish with devotion [...]

286 PRAYER OF SACRIFICE. It is truly worthy and just [that we give thanks...], for he is the true *Lamb* that was *sacrificed* (I Cor. 5, 7) for us, who by dying has overthrown our death and by rising again has restored our life, Jesus Christ our Lord. To whom all angels rightly [sing: Holy...]

XXXVII LIKEWISE AN EASTER MASS. ON THE TUESDAY[a]

287 God, you who have made that all who are reborn in Christ are *a royal and priestly race* (cf. I Petr. 2, 9), give us that we desire and are able to do what you command, so that the people, called to eternity, has one faith in its heart and one love in its deeds. Through [...]

---

[a] *tercia feria*: the third day.

461   288 COLLECT. Almighty and everlasting God, through whom redemption and adoption[a] is given to us, look upon the works of
your love and preserve what you deigned to give, that to those reborn in Christ may be given eternal inheritance and true liberty.
Through [...]

289 AFTER THE NAMES. Accept, O Lord, the gifts offered in your
name, which the universal Church, acquired through his blood,
offers on the day of the resurrection of your Son who triumphs in
glory. Through [...]

290 AT THE KISS OF PEACE. Almighty and everlasting
God, who through your only-begotten Son have unlocked for
us the entrance to your eternity after death was completely
overcome, arouse the hearts of the faithful towards you, that
all who are *reborn* in Christ *of water and the Holy Spirit* (Ioh. 3,
5) are considered worthy to enter into the kingdom of heaven.
Through.

291 PRAYER OF SACRIFICE. It is worthy and just to give thanks
to you, almighty and everlasting God, through Jesus Christ,
your Son our Lord, through whom you, calling the human race
into being, instructed that the Pesach already be celebrated
by your servants Moses and Aaron through the offering of a
lamb, [and] commanded that, in the time that followed until
the coming of our Lord Jesus Christ, who was led as a lamb to
be sacrificed,[b] this same custom[c] be observed in [his] remem-
462   brance. He is the unblemished Lamb[d] which was sacrificed at

---

[a] On the adoption of the faithful as children of God through Christ, see Gal.
4, 5; Rom. 8, 23, Eph. 1, 5: BLAISE, *Dictionnaire*, s.v. *adoptio* (2). The connection
with redemption is given primarily in Gal. 4 and Rom. 8.

[b] Cf. Is. 53, 7, although the wording is different in the Vulgate version.

[c] *consuetudinem*: the ritual connotation of the word as it is used here is not
mentioned by BLAISE, *Dictionnaire*, s.v. *consuetudo*, who focuses on its use with
regard to specific monastic practices and rules.

[d] *agnus inmaculatus*: Ex. 12, 5 gives *agnus absque macula*.

the first Pesach of the first people,[a] he is the ram on top of the high mountain, brought forth from the thorn-bush and destined for sacrifice,[b] he is the *fatted calf* (Luc. 15, 23, 27, 30) that was sacrificed in the tabernacle of our father Abraham in honour of the guests.[c] We celebrate his Passion, death and resurrection and expect his coming.[d] And therefore we cry out with the angels and archangels, saying [Holy ...]

XXXVIII LIKEWISE AN EASTER MASS. ON THE WEDNESDAY[e]

292 God, who after the passage through the river Jordan led your holy people into the land of your promise,[f] grant, so we request, that we too may always experience divine benevolence through the revelation of the mystery of your majesty. Through.

293 COLLECT. Grant us, so we ask, O Lord, that just as we celebrate the solemn mysteries of the resurrection of our Lord Jesus Christ, so we may also be considered worthy to rejoice with all the saints at his coming.[g] Through.

---

[a] Cf. Ex. 12. *prioris populi*: often used in patristic literature from Origen onwards. In the context of the Jewish people the notion is not necessarily positive, indeed it has an explicitly negative connotation in e.g. CAESARIUS OF ARLES, *Sermo* 104.4, ed. MORIN, CCSL 103, p. 431. See also PIET HOOGEVEEN, *Populus prior. Het Joodse volk in Karolingische Bijbelcommentaren* (PhD Dissertation Utrecht University, 2016), p. 14, who refers to the tendency in Carolingian exegesis to explain the precedency of the Jewish people in relation to the biblical reversal of the first who will be last (Matth. 19, 30). A similar thought is expressed in no. 321: *Ille* (Adam) *quidem prior, sed iste* (Christ) *melior*. See also ISRAEL JACOB YUVAL, *Two Nations in Your Womb. Perceptions of Jews and Christians in Late Antiquity and the Middle Ages* (Berkeley CA: University of California Press, 2006), p. 14–15.

[b] Cf. Gen. 22.

[c] Cf. Gen. 18. The calf of Abraham's sacrifice is *tenerrimum et optimum*: 'tender and good' (Gen. 18, 7).

[d] On this phrase see no. 19.

[e] *quarta feria*: the fourth day.

[f] Cf. Ios. 3 and 4.

[g] Cf. I Thess. 3, 13.

294 AFTER THE NAMES. Now that the names of those who offer have been heard, and the commemoration of the most blessed apostles and martyrs and all the saints has been completed with due reverence, let us commemorate the names of those who offer and those who have departed, so that included in the eternal Book,[119] they may be added to the multitude of saints. Through.

463

295 AT THE KISS OF PEACE. God, through whose mouth was made known that you gave peace to all and left the statutes of peace,[a] pour into our hearts the zeal for peace and the desire for good will, so that we, purged of the blemish of all sin, may with unstained hearts preserve the peace which we pursue with lips and mouth.[b] Through.

296 PRAYER OF SACRIFICE. It is worthy and just that we always bring you praise and thanks, almighty and everlasting God, through Jesus Christ, your Son our Lord, *who was led for us as a sheep to the slaughter, and as a lamb that before its shearers is silent so he did not open his mouth* (Is. 53, 7; Act. 8, 32). For he is *the Lamb of God*, your only-begotten Son,[c] *who takes away the sins of the world* (Ioh. 1, 29), who does not cease to offer himself for us, and who defends us before you with a perpetual plea, for he never dies even if he is sacrificed, but he always lives even if he is killed. *For our paschal lamb, Christ, has been sacrificed* (I Cor. 5, 7) so that *we no longer offer by means of the old yeast or the blood of fleshly sacrifice, but through the unleavened bread of sincerity and the body of truth* (cf. I Cor. 5, 8), through Christ our Lord.

[a] The prayer refers to Ioh. 14, 27 (*pacem relinquo uobis*), but the expression *pacis statuta* is not found there.
[b] *labiis ore*: asyndeton.
[c] *unigenitus filius*: cf. Ioh. 1, 18; 3, 16; 3, 18.

XXXVIIII LIKEWISE AN EASTER MASS. ON THE THURSDAY[a]

464

297 God, who on the solemn feast day of Easter mercifully prepares heavenly medicines for the world, continue the benefit of[120] the gifts of this annual festivity, so that through the temporal celebration [this] is conducive for us to life everlasting. Through.

298 COLLECT. God, who is the Author of our freedom and salvation, hear the voices of those who make supplication to you, and grant that they whom you redeemed by the outpouring of your blood may live through you and rejoice in you with perpetual immunity. Saviour.

299 AFTER THE NAMES. Now that the names of those who offer have been heard, let us pray to the Lord of eternity,[121] that in us the fear of him, purity of heart and *love that has no end* (I Cor. 13, 8) may remain steadfast. For this is the salutary offering, this is the true, this is the pleasing[b] sacrifice, these are the pure drink offerings, offered for us and for the peace of the dead *with broken and contrite hearts* (cf. Ps. 51, 19[c]).[d] Through.

300 AT THE KISS OF PEACE. Grant, O Lord, that in all servants of your redemption the ardour of unbroken love overflows such that a disturbance of hateful feelings in no manner prevails over these desires, but that the outer sign of the kiss, given by way of the perfection of an enduring peace, is henceforth not deceived by any error of enmity. Saviour.

465

---

[a] *quinta feria*: the fifth day.

[b] Cf. Leu. 3, 3. The word *pinguis*, 'fat', occurs in the context of oblations (incense) in OVID, *Tristia* 5.5.11, ed. JACQUES ANDRÉ, *Ovide, Triste. Texte et traduction* (Paris: Belles Lettres, 1968), p. 141 (LEWIS and SHORT, *Latin dictionary*, s.v. *pinguis*), and in the Old Testament, where Num. 18 prescribes that the best, i.e. the fattest part (vs. 30: *praeclara et meliora*; vs. 32: *egregia et pinguissima*), be reserved for the offering.

[c] Vulgate: Ps. 50, 17.

[d] On this prayer as an example of the importance of a perfect offering, see Introduction, section The performance of prayer.

301 PRAYER OF SACRIFICE. It is truly worthy and just that we profusely pray in harmony and concord to the almighty God and his only Son the Lord Jesus Christ our Saviour, who freed his Church from *the second death* (Apoc. 2, 11; Apoc. 20, 6 and 14; Apoc. 21, 8) when his blood was shed over the cross. Through him we ask you, almighty God, that you increase your Church in faith, preserve it in hope and protect it in love, and that you deign to willingly accept our offerings with glory and honour. And we therefore praise you with the angels and archangels, saying [Holy...]

XL LIKEWISE AN EASTER MASS. ON THE FRIDAY[a]

302 God, you who restore us to everlasting life through the resurrection of Christ, grant that we taste the heavenly things and abstain from earthly desires. Through.

303 COLLECT. God of glory, *whom it has pleased that all the fullness dwelled in your Only-begotten* (cf. Col. 1, 19), [whom it has pleased] *to disarm*[b] *all rulers and powers* (Col. 2, 15) *and to reconcile all things in him* (cf. Col. 1, 20) *through whom you had created the universe* (cf. Col. 1, 16): look upon the festive vigil of the congregation submitted [to you], receive the prayers devoted to Easter supplications, and you who have given us the victory of the resurrection through the turn of the tides,[c] grant us the joy of this feast through the sanctification of [our] works. Through.

304 AFTER THE NAMES. Grant, merciful Lord, that we truly participate in the resurrection of our Lord Jesus Christ. Through.

466

[a] *sexta feria*: the sixth day.

[b] The Vulgate gives *expolians*, but many manuscripts of the Vetus Latina give *exuans*, see Brepolis Vetus Latina database at http://apps.brepolis.net.proxy.library.uu.nl/vld/index.html (consulted 22 Sepember 2015).

[c] i.e. the seasons of the liturgical year.

305 AT THE KISS OF PEACE. God, who made your people partaker in your redemption, grant us, so we ask, that we perpetually rejoice over the day of the resurrection of the Lord. Through.

306 PRAYER OF SACRIFICE. It is worthy and just that we bring thanks to you, O Lord, holy Father, almighty and everlasting God, through Jesus Christ your Son our Lord, whom you wished to be handed over as a sacrifice for us all. O wonderful grace of your love towards us. O ineffable love of charity, that you handed over the Son to redeem the slave. O truly necessary sin of Adam, wiped away by the death of Christ. O happy fault, deemed worthy to merit such good and great a Redeemer.[a] For we would never know how great the love of your mercy towards us was if we would not experience [it] on the grounds of the death of your only and co-eternal Son, our Lord and God Jesus Christ. The grace of your love has defeated the malice of the devil, *for where sin abounded, grace abounded even more* (Rom. 5, 20). But your mercy has given us back more than the envious enemy took away. He begrudged us paradise, you gave us the heavens. He inflicted on us temporal death, you gave us perpetual life. Therefore the entire world rejoices throughout all the world[b] with profuse joy, and the heavenly powers too join in singing without end the hymn of your glory, saying [Holy...]

467

XLI MASS FOR THE SATURDAY[122] OF THE OCTAVE OF EASTER

307 Protect your servants, O Lord, whom you kindly redeemed *of water and the* Holy *Spirit* (Ioh. 3, 5), so that *while we strip off the old self with its practices* (Col. 3, 9[123]), we live in the manner of life of him to whose being you have brought us through this celebra-

---

[a] 'O wonderful grace ... Redeemer': cf. the notes to no. 225 (*Exultet*), also concerning authorship and figurative language.
[b] *in orbe terrarum*: see no. 3.

tion of the Paschal mysteries during the eight days of your resurrection. Through.

308 COLLECT. Almighty and everlasting God, make that what we celebrate with the Paschal services during the eight days of your resurrection, we may at all times experience as fruitful. Saviour.

309 AFTER THE NAMES. God of eternal mercy, who through this return of the Easter feast inflames the faith of the people devoted to you, increase the grace that you have given, so that all comprehend with worthy understanding through which Baptism they are cleansed, through which Spirit they are reborn, through which blood they are redeemed. Through.

468

310 AT THE KISS OF PEACE. God, who through your Only-begotten unlocked for us the entrance to eternity by entirely overcoming death, lead us to participation in the heavenly joys, that, *reborn of your Holy Spirit* (cf. Ioh. 3, 5), you let us enter into your kingdom. Through the Resurrected.

311 PRAYER OF SACRIFICE. It is worthy and just, necessary and salutary that the entire human race reveres you with all its heart[a] as Lord and God, marvellous King Christ, now that your condemnation to the bonds of hell is absolved, the multitude of believers rejoices over the signs of freedom. Now that you are truly manifested to the world as *a lion of the tribe of Judah* (Apoc. 5, 5), all the earth rejoices that *the lion, the devil, the devourer of souls is destroyed* (I Petr. 5, 8).[124] And you let yourself be nailed to the stake of the cross by the fixtures of the nails, so that it was a powerful strength which[125] the evil one once greatly feared. The earth trembled at his loud cry when *he gave up his spirit* (Matth. 27, 50), heaven feared, the day fled, *the sun was obscured* (Luc. 23, 45) and the stars all departed at the same time while they concealed their rays.[126] Hell mourned at

---

[a] *uisceribus*: interpreted as a spiritual faculty in view of the verb *ueneretor* (for *ueneretur*).

his descent[a] because its doors were shattered, and at his resurrection the angels rejoiced and earth sprang up for joy with its inhabitants. At this triumph the threat[127] is seen that was promised through the mouth of the prophet: *I will be your death* (Os. 13, 14 Vulgate), O Hell, *where then is your victory?'* (I Cor. 15, 55) And death could be devoured by nothing other than Life, who[b] through his descent[c] gave back those held by death to the heavenly spheres by rising again from the dead, so that his resurrection was confirmed by the witness of the living and the dead. Therefore, holy Father, almighty and everlasting God, glory to you forever through Jesus Christ your Son our Lord, who is always in you and coming forth from you and with you. Through him [the angels] praise you [...]

469

XLII MASS TO CONCLUDE THE EASTER FEAST

312 [PREFACE.] Most beloved brothers, let us humbly pray to God, who because of the fall of the entire world deigned to *send his only Son* (cf. Ioh. 4, 9) after he [had] assumed the form of true man from the flesh of the Virgin,[128] that as he raised us with him from perpetual death on this [day] of his resurrection, so too, through the gift of his love, while he protects us against all the tricks of the enemy, he leaves [us] unharmed in the bosom of the Mother Church, and that, just as he joins to him through the devotion of this moment those who eternally[129] rejoice with a pure conscience over the rebirth of the firstborn of the Church, he also joins them with him through reconciliation in eternity. May he deign to bless these gifts of his people. Saviour.

313 COLLECT. God, Creator and Moderator of all light, whom heavenly things admire and earthly things fear, for whom hell trembles, whom the squadrons of angels and armies of archangels serve, [you

470

---

[a] On the *descensus ad inferos*, see no. 219.

[b] The Latin text links the male relative pronoun *qui* to the female noun *vita*: apparently *vita* is a personification of Christ, in line with Ioh. 11, 25 and Ioh. 14, 6.

[c] On Christ's descent into hell, see no. 219.

have come] not to conquer the world which you made yourself, but to bring down the sins of the world which the devil devised. *For you deigned to so love this world that you handed over your Only-begotten* (Ioh. 3, 16) for our salvation. For through his cross we are redeemed, through his death we are brought to life, through his Passion we are saved, through his resurrection we are glorified. We therefore call you through supplication to him, that you deign to support these servants in all things, as you supported our fathers who hoped for your mercy. Grant also to help them all, so that in their senses there is the fear of love for you, in their hearts faith, in their work justice, in their doing love, in their speaking truth, in their manners discipline, so that they worthily and rightly deserve to obtain for themselves the reward of immortality. Through.

314 AFTER THE NAMES. Grant, so we ask, almighty God, that we who celebrate the solemn ceremonies of the resurrection of the Lord, rise again from the death of the soul through the renewal of your Spirit. Through.

315 AT THE KISS OF PEACE. Hear us, O Lord, holy Father, almighty God, and join together with these offerings and prayers, received by you, the presence of your strength, so that what each has individually offered to the honour of your majesty will contribute to the salvation of all. Through the Resurrected.

471   316 PRAYER OF SACRIFICE. It is worthy and just, necessary and salutary that we bring thanks to you, almighty God, [and], although the limbs of mortals are not consistent with your glory, proclaim the praises of our redemption. When the bonds of darkness tied [down] the human race to the seats of hell, as a slave subjected to death, the Word of the Spirit, *through which in the beginning all things were made* (cf. Ioh. 1, 1 and 3), came down to Mary. And while she, a virgin, marvelled at her giving birth,[a] she brought

[a] *miratur*: *miro* occurs as an active verb in later Latin alongside the deponent *miror*. One could also read *partu suo*: 'and while she, a virgin, was admired because of her son…' On the double meaning of *partus* ('giving birth'; 'offspring'), see no. 94.

forth the man she confined to the world as God. And yet, even before he was born, O most high and almighty God, she knew that
he was yours, for she also knew that [he] was the beginning of the
world. Out of free will, for the sake of the redemption of the human race, he climbed the cross to triumph over the enemy tyrant,
and after briefly leaving the temple of his body, by breaking the
locks of hell,[a] he gave back [the human race] to the former life, as
it had been before. And it would not have sufficed that he only
amended sin as man, but he was also reborn through heavenly
ablution, and, returning to his origin through a relived and new
manner of birth, he led us to the heavenly kingdom. O counsel
of divine providence. O inestimable help of redemption. Through
the Virgin is restored for us the glorious life which seemed extin-
guished by reason of the disobedience[b] with regard to the tree. The
sins of the world are washed away by the water, through which the
world itself had previously experienced its shipwreck.[c] And thus,
most high Creator, we offer with pure devotion an immaculate offering, and *by lifting up our hands* (Ps. 141, 2) we celebrate a devout
sacrificial meal according to the order of your Son Jesus Christ.
Through Christ our Lord.

XLIII MASS FOR THE INVENTION OF THE HOLY CROSS[d]

472

317 [PREFACE.] *Let us glory in the cross of our Lord Jesus Christ*
(cf. Gal. 6, 14), most beloved brothers, and let us rejoice with
a joyful heart, and let us celebrate the feast of this day with
great reverence and spiritual joy. For on this cross our Lord and
Saviour hung for our salvation and triumphed over the devil.[e]

---

[a] On the *descensus ad inferos*, see no. 219.
[b] Cf. IRENAEUS OF LYONS, *Aduersus haereses* 3.22.4, ed. ROUSSEAU and
DOUTRELEAU, SChr 211, p. 438–444.
[c] Cf. Gen. 6–8.
[d] On this Mass, see Introduction, section The liturgical year; on the invention
of the relics of the 'true' cross by the Empress Helena, see BAERT, *Heritage*.
[e] On the cross as a sign of triumph, see BAERT, *Heritage*, p. 59 and 71–72.

Now through this cross the bitterness of gall has restrained the appetite of evil longing which the sweetness of the tree has enticed, and the sharpness of the sour wine has curbed the desire of gluttony which the sweetness of the apple has entrapped.[a] Saviour [...]

318 COLLECT. Grant us, almighty Father, through the mystery of the cross of your Only-begotten, that the venom of the old serpent, with which he tried to give the faithful to drink, can be washed out of the hearts of the faithful through that medicine which flowed from Christ's side, and that the confession of the name of Christ recreates those who were driven out of paradise by trespassing the command.[b] Saviour [...]

473

319 AFTER THE NAMES. Lord Jesus Christ, who, hung on the beam of the cross *in the form of a slave which you had accepted* (cf. Phil. 2, 7), *cried out* to the Father *why he had forsaken you* (cf. Matth. 27, 46), and pleaded to him to grant forgiveness to the persecutors,[c] we humbly implore your compassion, that you deign to grant what you were then seen to ask the Father in exchange for the humility of Incarnation, now that you remain in the power of the divine which is always connected to the Father. Saviour [...]

320 AT THE KISS OF PEACE. God, who never abandons your catholic Church which you have redeemed through your holy blood, and who mercifully grants us, unworthy, gathered in the Church, forgiveness of sins, and who deigned to justify the con-

---

[a] These implicit references to the tree of paradise from which Adam and Eve ate the forbidden fruit relate to the typological tradition that considered the tree of paradise as a prefiguration of the cross; BAERT, *Heritage*, p. 289–349; MARCEL POORTHUIS, 'Moses' Rod in Zipporah's Garden', in ALBERDINA HOUTMAN et al. (eds), *Sanctity of Time and Space in Tradition and Modernity*, Jewish and Christian Perspectives Series 1 (Leiden: Brill, 1998), p. 231–264.

[b] Again the cross is linked to paradise, although the tree is not explicitly mentioned.

[c] Cf. Luc. 23, 34.

fession of the thief[a] who hung with you on the cross,[b] we ask you to increase [and] multiply the faith of all who believe in you, and that you deign, with your customary love, to keep undiminished in us the peace which you commanded [us] to preserve. Saviour [...]

321 PRAYER OF SACRIFICE. It is worthy and just, almighty God, that we pay the vows of offerings to you and that we incessantly exalt you in the proclamation of our praise, and set forth the examples of the two Adams, namely of the one, the inhabitant of paradise, and of the other, the Redeemer of the human race.[c] For the one was earlier, but the other was better,[d] the one earthly, the other heavenly, the one made of clay, the other conceived from the Word. Then Eve was misled by the persuasion of the devil, now Mary is made illustrious through the message of the angel. Then man who was created was destroyed by the envy of the serpent, now man who was lost is freed by the mercy of the Redeemer. Then man, because he did not keep the commandment, was expelled from paradise,[e] now the thief merits paradise through his confession of Christ the Lord.[f] We therefore implore you, most merciful Father, by reason of the ineffable mystery of the illustrious cross and the admirable kingship of our Lord Jesus Christ your Son, that we all honour this day, on which we celebrate the feast of his cross, with spiritual joy and modest exultation, and that you, amid the heavenly powers, accept the praise and the voices of our humility, while we say with manifold praise: HOLY [...]

474

[a] *latronis*: NRSV gives 'criminal' (Luc. 23, 39).

[b] Cf. Luc. 23, 39–43.

[c] The prayer of sacrifice concentrates on the typologies of Christ as the new Adam and Mary as the new Eve, the former based on I Cor. 15, 22 and 45, and both central in IRENAEUS OF LYONS, *Aduersus haereses* 3.22.3–4, ed. ROUSSEAU and DOUTRELEAU, SChr 211, p. 438–444.

[d] Cf. no. 291 on *prior populus*.

[e] Cf. Gen. 3.

[f] Cf. Luc. 23, 39–43.

XLIIII MASS FOR THE HOLY APOSTLE AND EVANGELIST JOHN[a]

322 Almighty and everlasting God, you who have made the feast of this day to the joy of the blessed evangelist John, grant to your Church that it loves what he believed and preaches what he taught. Through our Lord Jesus Christ your Son [...]

323 COLLECT. God, who through the mouth of the blessed evangelist John revealed the secrets of your Word,[b] grant, so we ask, that what he poured into our ears in an elevated manner, we may understand with the corresponding knowledge of our intelligence. Through [...]

475

324 AFTER THE NAMES. Grant, almighty God, that *the Word made flesh* (Ioh. 1, 14) that the blessed evangelist John preached will always live in us through the help of his intercession. Through [...]

325 AT THE KISS OF PEACE. Grant us, O Lord, your peace from heaven and abide in us, so that the fraudulent kiss of the trai-

---

[a] On this Mass, see ROSE (ed.), *Missale Gothicum*, Introduction, p. 258–262 and Introduction, section The liturgical year. The character and sources of the Mass for John, next to the Mass for James and John in the Christmas Octave (see nos 37–45), remain enigmatic, as analysed in ROSE (ed.), *Missale Gothicum*, Introduction, p. 258–262. Given the fact that there is no reference whatsoever to John's death in the prayers of this Mass, it is probably best to characterise it as a Mass in commemoration of John's earthly birth, in line with the meaning of the word *natalicia*, translated as 'birth' in the *immolacio* (326). Even if liturgical commemorations of a saint's earthly birth are rare, they do appear in the Gothic Missal, e.g. John the Baptist (nos 368–373) and probably Agnes (see no. 106). On the complex case of Mary, see no. 98. On *natalicia*, see ROSE (ed.), *Missale Gothicum*, Introduction, p. 159 (ibid., p. 262, end of section b, erroneously mentions John the Baptist where John the Evangelist is meant).

[b] The phrase refers to the Apocalypse, meaning 'Revelation', rather than to the Gospel according to John. On the attribution of the Apocalypse to John the Evangelist, see ELS ROSE, 'John the Disciple, Christianity Medieval Times and Reformation Era', in HANS-JOSEF KLAUCK et al. (eds), *Encyclopedia of the Bible and its Reception* (Leiden: Brill, 2017), col. 486–487.

tor^a does not cling to our inner self,^b but that that peace which you left to your disciples^c remains undiminished in our hearts. Through.

326 PRAYER OF SACRIFICE. It is truly worthy and just, fair and salutary that we bring thanks to you, almighty God, while we celebrate the feast of the birth of your blessed apostle and evangelist John, who rejected his earthly father^d after having accepted the call of our Lord Jesus Christ your Son to be able to find the heavenly [Father.] He cast away the nets of the world, in which he was entangled,^e to pursue the gifts of eternity with a free spirit. He abandoned the ship floating on the waves to gain a firm foothold on the tranquillity of the ship of the Church. He stopped catching fish to pull along souls deeply immersed in the whirlpool of the world with the reed¹³⁰ of the doctrine of salvation. He stopped probing the depths of the sea^f and was made an investigator of divine mysteries.^g He made such progress that at the banquet of the holy and mystical supper he reclined on the breast of the Saviour himself,^h and such that the Lord, hanging on the cross, chose him as substitute for his Master as son of the Virgin,ⁱ and such that, more than all others, through preaching he revealed *the Word that in the beginning was God with God* (Ioh. 1, 1–2). Through Christ our Lord.

476

^a Cf. Matth. 26, 49.
^b *uisceribus*: interpreted spiritually in view of the prayer that peace may replace the treacherous kiss.
^c Cf. Ioh. 14, 27.
^d Cf. Matth. 4, 21–22.
^e Cf. Matth. 4, 21–22.
^f *pelagi profundi*: alliteration; see Introduction, section Style and figures.
^g *secretorum scrutator*: alliteration; see Introduction, section Style and figures.
^h Cf. Ioh. 13, 25. The reference to this scene might indicate that the feast originated in Jerusalem, where the Church of the Disciples on Mount Olivet is known as the place 'where John rested at Christ's bosom'; see ROSE (ed.), *Missale Gothicum*, Introduction, p. 261–262.
ⁱ Cf. Ioh. 19, 26–27.

XLV MASS FOR THE FIRST ROGATION DAY[a]

327 In this fasting, afflicted in body and contrite in heart, we repeat our prayers to you, most merciful God, that abstinence from sin is given to us through corporal abstinence, so that when the body is kept from food, you who are the true food that restores will be born in our hearts. Through [...]

328 COLLECT. We bring thanks to you, O Lord, holy Father, almighty and everlasting God, who, after the transgression of the fast by tasting of the forbidden,[b] has restored us to the temperance of salvation through Christ. We ask you in this fast, prostrate and in humility, to give us an upright heart, averse to sin, and to fortify us with a willing spirit devoted to mortification, so that after the fast you will lead us to the pasture of eternal refreshment.[c] Through [...]

477

329 AFTER THE NAMES. Yours, O Lord, is the food that through daily nourishment refreshes us to endurance, and yours is the fast through which, on your command, we restrain the flesh from dangerous delight. For our consolation you appointed the alternation of the times, so that the time to eat nourished our bodies through simple refreshment, and the time to fast[d] made them meagre to a righteousness pleasing to you. Accept this oblation kindly, which we offer because of the fasting of a three-day mortification, and sanctify it, and mercifully grant that our heart, preserved from bodily temptation, may likewise rest from sins. Through [...]

[a] On the early-fifth-century Gallic origin of the *Rogationes* – three days of fasting preceding Ascension – see Introduction, section The liturgical year.

[b] Cf. Gen. 3.

[c] Ps. 23, 2 (Vulgate 22, 2) brings together the words *pascua* and *refectio* in one verse, though not as closely as the present prayer.

[d] *tempus edendi ... ieiunandi tempus*: chiasmus; see Introduction, section Style and figures.

330 AT THE KISS OF PEACE. Your refreshment, O Lord, is tasted by our restrained bodies *with a broken spirit* (Ps. 51, 17ᵃ), and we therefore pray to you, prostrated by the penitence of fasting, while we only seek through your mercy what we do not merit through our deeds, that in the spirit we perceive the sweet sustenance of your love, which may ignite our hearts, free of food, to love our neighbour. Through [...]

331 PRAYER OF SACRIFICE. It is truly worthy and just that we seek you through observation of the fast, *you who are the true and living bread that descends from heaven* (Ioh. 6, 50–51). While we humble our bodies through fasting, by bringing this offering as your servants with a devoted heart we ask that you so mercifully look upon the humiliation of this fast, which we fulfil for our sins during this three-day observation, that you absolve those who fast from their sins, which immerse those who do not abstain from food[131] in the transgression of depravity. Through Christ the Lord.

XLVI LIKEWISE A MASS FOR THE SECOND ROGATION DAY

478

332 God, through whose example fasting is given[b] after tasting of the forbidden, which came in through the disobedience with regard to the tree,[c] bless our hearts, Lord, subjected to you by the mortification of fasting, through the illumination of your revelation,[132] and while from your heavenly seat you look down on us, lying in the mire of dregs and filthy garment of fasting,[d] raise us up through the progress of virtue. Through [...]

---

[a] Vulgate: Ps. 50, 19.
[b] Cf. Matth. 4, 2.
[c] IRENAEUS OF LYONS, *Aduersus haereses* 3.22.4; see also nos 316 and 98.
[d] A reference to the Old Testament practice of covering the head with ash and putting on a sackcloth when performing penance; see e.g. Ion. 3, 5–6; Dan. 9, 3 and esp. Is. 58, 5. The latter passage criticises this ritual of fasting, comparable to Matth. 6, 16–18.

333 COLLECT. Almighty and everlasting God, we ask that our bodies,[a] wearied by the mortification of fasting, be cleansed from all sins of the flesh, and that the weakness of the flesh is not able to rule over those who lie prostrate in the humiliation of this fast. For you, Founder of sobriety, *if you so desire you can* (Matth. 8, 2; Luc. 5, 12) quickly have mercy on us, so that we reflect on spiritual things and, with your help, conquer the desires of the flesh. Through [...]

334 AFTER THE NAMES. God, who approves the purity of heart that through fasting from food pursues not only human happiness: deign through this fast so to inwardly illuminate the eyes of our heart that, in these things that humankind does not know, we please you through abstinence from sin in secret.[b] Since this is a gift from you that we abstain from food, may it be a gift from you that through fasting we are also cleansed from sin. And pour out from the desirable fount of abundance the rain of the Holy Spirit over these offerings, so that, received by those who fast, they cleanse all sins and sow in them the strength of good conduct. Through [...]

479

335 AT THE KISS OF PEACE. Almighty and everlasting God, wipe away all stain of sin from those who lie down in the humility of fasting, so that when the secrets of our heart are cleansed by abstinence from food and the disturbances of quarrels are excluded, the love of you and of our neighbours[c] will grow in our hearts. Through [...]

---

[a] *uiscera*: a physical interpretation seems to be justified here because of the fatigue brought about by physical fasting.

[b] *in occulto*: cf. Matth. 6, 17–18, where the Vulgate gives *qui uidet in abscondito*; the commentary tradition, however, often gives *uidet in occulto* or *uidet occulta*; see Brepolis Vetus Latina database, fiches 27–30, 39, 41, 43, 44, 46 at http://apps.brepolis.net.proxy.library.uu.nl/vld/index.html (consulted 12 May 2015).

[c] Cf. Marc. 12, 30–31.

336 PRAYER OF SACRIFICE. It is truly worthy and just [that we seek[a]] you with the contrition of our whole heart[b] in the fast, almighty and everlasting God, through Christ our Lord. For he, instructing us in the secrets of your mysteries by revealing the branch of peace,[c] borne to Noah's eyes in the beak of a dove,[d] portrayed for us with that green tree the glorious sign of the cross, which the image of the dove decorated in honour of Christ, showing through the blessing of the [Holy] Spirit that it must be revered[e] by all. And we desire in innocence to be equal to this creature,[f] and we pray to be blessed by that same Spirit whose shape it has adopted. During this fast, instituted with three days of humiliation, while we carry this invincible sign in front in the

---

[a] This prayer lacks both the accusative and infinitive that normally follow *Vere dignum et iustum est.* I suggest to add *nos … quaerere*, in accordance with nos 331 and 341; see ROSE (ed.), *Missale Gothicum*, p. 479.

[b] Cf. Ps. 51, 17.

[c] *pacificum nemus*: in the Vulgate (Gen. 8, 11) as well as in exegetic texts, the olive leaf is usually indicated with the word *ramus*, while *surculus* also occurs, and *folia* is given as an explanatory synonym; see Brepolis Vetus Latina database at http://apps.brepolis.net.proxy.library.uu.nl/vld/index.html (consulted 23 September 2015). The word *nemus* ('a wood', 'grove') does occur in the Vulgate: a number of times in the Old Testament, besides its derivative *nemorosus* (woody), e.g. Num. 13, 21 and Num. 24, 6. To signify a single tree it occurs mainly in poetry, according to LEWIS and SHORT, *Latin Dictionary*, s.v. *nemus*. BLAISE, *Dictionnaire*, does not mention this meaning. It is therefore remarkable that the word is used in this poetic way in the Gothic Missal; see Introduction, section Style and figures. On the olive leaf as harbinger of peace (*pacificum*), see *Sacramentarium Gregorianum Hadrianum* 335a, ed. JEAN DESHUSSES, *Le sacramentaire Grégorien: ses principales formes d'après les plus anciens manuscrits*, Spicilegium Friburgense, vols 16, 18, 24 (Fribourg: Éditions universitaires, 1971–1982), vol. 16, p. 173–174, and AUGUSTINE, *De doctrina christiana* 2.16.24, ed. JOSEPH MARTIN, CCSL 32 (Turnhout: Brepols, 1962), p. 50.

[d] *ore columbae*: cf. Gen. 8, 10–11.

[e] It is not entirely clear to what *colendum* refers. Grammatically it is related to *arbore* (tree), but as far as content is concerned it more probably refers to *Christi*, certainly if one has Christ's Baptism in the Jordan in mind, where the dove appeared representing sanctification through the Holy Spirit: 'that Christ must be honoured by all' (cf. Matth. 3, 16; Luc. 3, 22).

[f] On the innocence and purity of the dove, see AMBROSE, *De Noe* 19.67, ed. KARL SCHENKL, CSEL 32.1 (Vienna: Tempsky, 1897), p. 462.

crowd of the faithful,[a] praising your majesty by singing psalms,[b] we ask, almighty God, that you accept all the prayers of the people and everything that is given to you in this same ritual by the people subjected to you, and that you will so bless them through this fast that they are considered worthy to be delivered from all sins. Through Christ the Lord.

480   ## XLVII MASS FOR THE THIRD ROGATION DAY

337 God, whom not one sense of mortals, burdened by the allure of the use[133] of the flesh, is able to know unless it is illuminated by you through the atonement of fasting, drive from our hearts through abstinence the multitude of sins born of the abundance of gluttony, so that the pure devotion of a new life, which you will mercifully give, also serves you after completion of the fast. Through [...]

338 COLLECT. Now at the end of the three-day fast, we pray that your purity comes into our bodies,[c] afflicted by the mortification of fasting, and we ask you that you from your holy dwelling[d] graciously hear the sinners who lie prostrate in the filth of their wretchedness, that you give us the fount of your grace and spread out a path along which, after fasting from fleshly foods, we go to the eternal refreshment of the pasture.[e] Through [...]

[a] A reference to the processions that took place during the three Rogation days, in Dutch referred to as 'Kruisdagen': Days of the Cross.

[b] The institutor of the feast, Mamertus of Vienne, placed special emphasis on the singing of psalms during the processions, see MEENS, *Penance*, p. 30 and footnote 76; cf. CAESARIUS OF ARLES, *Sermo* 208.3, ed. MORIN, CCSL 104, p. 834.

[c] *uisceribus*: here again, the prayer for purity could concern physical purity.

[d] The use of the plural *atria* is poetic; see Introduction, section Style and figures.

[e] Ez. 34, 11–16 describes the good life of the sheep pastured by the good shepherd; see also Ioh. 10, 9 and Ps. 23, 2.

339 AFTER THE NAMES. Look favourably, so we ask, O Lord, upon the offerings of humble fasters. And while you bless the gifts present here, since we receive them, let them lighten the innermost of our heart through the medicine of your love, so that fleshly and weak works do not keep in their grasp those whom Christ, as Founder of the fast, has redeemed as Saviour. Through [...]

340 AT THE KISS OF PEACE. God, you who have overcome   481
the indulgence of abundance through your dedication to abstinence and have given the purity of chastity so that you are
known, look willingly upon us with your countenance, and
grant to those who fast peace with their neighbour and with
you, which, when you ascended to the Father, you left for us to
follow.[a] Through [...]

341 PRAYER OF SACRIFICE. It is truly worthy and just, and it is most worthy that you alone are sought by those who fast, you who are the Teacher of abstinence and Giver of eternal chastity,[b] and who, while you only desire a faithful heart from those who fast, cleanse all stain caused by unbecoming abundance. For in the book of Leviticus you clearly made known these holy fasts through your servant Moses, through whom you commanded that we must humble our souls in order not to be banished, as the people given over to the gluttony of eating were driven out.[c] And by fulfilling this fast for us,[d] your Only-begotten sanctified it such that he not only opened the lost kingdom through fasting, but also granted forgiveness of sins. Therefore accept willingly the fasts that you instituted, while through them you absolve us from all sins. Through Christ our Lord.

[a] Cf. Ioh. 14, 27.
[b] Cf. Matth. 22, 30.
[c] Leu. 23, 26–32 describes the practice of fasting and abstinence from work related to the Day of Atonement; Leu. 23, 39 mentions the punishment of excommunication: 'For anyone who does not fast during that entire day shall be cut off from the people'.
[d] Cf. Matth. 4, 2.

After the Sanctus in all three Masses you say:

342ª O Lord, holy Father, almighty God, deign therefore in the days of these fasts to be mindful of this oblation of your faithful who serve you,ᵇ whose faith you are acquainted with and whose devotion you know, [this sacrifice] which they offer to you as an offering for their souls. And we pray for their desires that are pleasing to you, that you absolve them of all sin and that you deign to keep them for the rest of the time in which they are allowed to accept food, such that while they lead a modest life they do not become entangled in the snares of sin, provoked by sumptuous meals. Through Christ our Lord.

[Deign], O God, so we ask, [to make] this oblation in all respects blessed and accepted, etc.ᶜ

482

ª The present prayer *Hanc igitur oblacionem familiae tuae* echoes the *Hanc igitur* as part of the canon of Mass. This fixed set of prayers circulated in Merovingian Gaul, as the Bobbio Missal testifies, where the texts are included in the *Missa cotidiana Romensis* (f. 10r–16r; the *Hanc igitur oblacionem* is on f. 13r). The Gothic Missal probably contained the *canon missae* as part of the *Missa cotidiana 'Rominsis'* which begins at f. 261v, where the manuscript breaks off after the first prayer (no. 543). See also nos 365 and 527. On the transmission of the *canon missae* in early medieval Gaul, see SMYTH, *Liturgie oubliée*, p. 40–45; YITZHAK HEN, 'The Liturgy of the Bobbio Missal', in HEN and MEENS (eds), *The Bobbio Missal*, p. 150–152.

ᵇ *tibi adstantes* could mean 'who stand near you', but in liturgical texts it often has the more specific meaning of 'serving', or 'celebrating'. Here, it concerns the faithful rather than the clergy, so that the word refers to the participation of the faithful in the Eucharistic rites. See BLAISE, *Dictionnaire*, s.v. *adsto* and BLAISE, *Dictionnaire du Moyen-Âge*, s.v. *adsto* and *astans*; see also BLAISE, *Vocabulaire*, p. 504 (section 364); ROSE (ed.), *Missale Gothicum*, Introduction, p. 156 (*circum(ad)stantes*) and nos 94, 137 and 272 above. On the performance of Mass, see Introduction, section The performance of prayer.

ᶜ Apparently a new prayer starts here, though this is not made visible in the manuscript. The prayer *Quam oblacionem* is part of the fixed *canon missae* (see footnote a above). It is only indicated by the first words, after which the text was apparently assumed to be known (*et reliqua*).

XLVIII COLLECTS FOR THE ROGATION DAYS IN VARIOUS SAINTS' CHURCHES[a]

343 NOW IN SAINT PETER'S. God, Refuge of the poor, Hope of the humble and Salvation of the wretched, mercifully hear, through the intercession of the most blessed Peter, the blessed founder of your Church, the prayers of your supplicants on the day of this three-day fast. And grant to our times tranquillity from sin and likewise from [our] enemies, so that the abundance of your mercy comforts those who may rightly be afflicted through the justice of your scourges, because the blessed Peter obtains this [for us.] Through [...]

344 COLLECT. Almighty and everlasting God, who gave the office of bishop to the blessed apostle Peter, [by] giving him the keys of the heavenly kingdom to bind and loose souls,[b] mercifully hear our prayers on the day of this fast and [grant], so we ask, that through his intercession we are delivered from the bonds of our sins. Through.

345 COLLECT IN SAINT PAUL'S. Look, O Lord, so we ask, upon our infirmity, and come quickly to our help with your love in the days of this fast, which the threefold consecration has extended with the number three, through the intercession of your blessed apostle Paul, so that you console with your mercy those whom you correct through your righteousness. Through [...]

483

346 LIKEWISE A COLLECT. Hear our lament, so we ask, O Lord, in the days of fasting, through the threefold number consecrated to the Trinity, and we ask you through the intercession of the blessed Paul, our master and teacher, that for you the offence of

---

[a] On the celebration of the *Rogationes* as a 'stational liturgy', see Introduction, section The liturgical year.

[b] Cf. Matth. 16, 19; see also no. 150.

the sinner does not prevail over your mercy, which you always grant to your repentant supplicants.[a] Through [...]

347 PRAYER IN SAINT STEPHEN'S. Grant, so we ask, almighty and merciful God, that the great and blessed deacon Stephen gives the help of his intercession to our weakness, afflicted in the days of these fasts, who as imitator of the Passion and love of the Lord was the first to excel through the bloodshed of martyrdom, and that he always be a perfect mediator and, by your grace, a willing helper. Through [...]

348 LIKEWISE A COLLECT. May the prayer of your blessed deacon and martyr Stephen, so we ask, O Lord, accompany our supplications, extended in this fast, and may we be supported by his prayers so that your mercy protects us in our weakness. Through [...]

484

349 LIKEWISE A PRAYER IN SAINT MARTIN'S. Extend your right hand, so we ask, O Lord, to your people who on the day of their[134] fasts pray for your mercy, that through the intercession of the blessed Martin we avoid imminent terrors, receive the solace of everlasting life[135] and obtain eternal joy. Through [...]

350 LIKEWISE ANOTHER [PRAYER.] God, Author of the fasts, Institutor of abstinence, who by embracing the outer form of fasting expelled the gluttony of abundance, so that the soberness of chastity would rule in us, look mercifully on these your supplicants, O Lord, who dedicate themselves to the fasting of a three-day abstinence. And through the intercession of the most high and

---

[a] Literally 'to the tears of your supplicants'. On the importance of tears in the process of repentance and forgiveness, see BEVERLY M. KIENZLE, 'Penitents and Preachers: The Figure of Saint Peter and his Relationship to Saint Mary Magdalene', in LOREDANA LAZZARI and ANNA MARIA VALENTE BACCI (eds), *La figura di San Pietro nelle fonti del medioevo*, Atti del convegno tenutosi in occasione dello Studiorum universitatum docentium congressus (Viterbo e Roma 5–8 settembre 2000), Textes et études du moyen âge 17 (Louvain-la-neuve: FIDEM, 2001), p. 248–272, at p. 258–262.

blessed man Martin, [and] entreated through him, pour out upon us all the grace of your blessing, that as this fast, instituted to the fear of your cult, overcomes the gluttony of the appetite, so your illumination of our senses overcomes all conflagration of our sins. Through [...]

351 PRAYER IN SAINT GREGORY'S. Almighty and everlasting God, we humbly pray to your majesty, satisfied by your gifts of fasting and exhausted by all kinds of mortification, that when the darkness of sin is expelled from our hearts, you make that on this day of fasting, through the intercession of our most high bishop Gregory, who is receptive to divine mysteries, we come to the true light that is Christ.

352 COLLECT. Almighty and everlasting God, at whose command the flesh is restricted from pleasure through the mortification of fasting and our restricted flesh knows its Creator through mod-   485
eration, grant in this fast to all who believe in you, through the intercession of our most high apostolic father Gregory, that they exercise unblemished service, so that, even if sin approaches those who fast and strength deserts them, your protection, almighty Father, perseveres for them. Through [...]

XLVIIII MASS FOR THE ASCENSION
OF THE LORD[a]

353 God, who through the exhortation of the doctrine of the Gospel commands your Church *to set its mind on things that are above* (cf. Col. 3, 2) and to raise itself up to that height to which the Saviour of the world has ascended, grant to your supplicants that they pursue with [their] understanding what many have seen with their eyes, so that at the second coming of the Mediator those who have believed in your promises are enriched with gifts. Through [...]

[a] On this Mass, see Introduction, section The liturgical year.

354 [COLLECT.] Almighty and merciful God, grant to us that as we trust that the Saviour of humanity sits with you in your majesty, we experience that *he remains with us until the end of the age* (Matth. 28, 20), as he promised. Through [...]

486

355 AFTER THE NAMES. O Lord, we bring the offering today because of the ascension of your Son into heaven. Grant, so we ask, that through him, thanks to this venerable exchange of gifts,[a] we rise up to your glory. Through [...]

356 AT THE KISS OF PEACE. God, who, while you ascend to the divine throne,[b] do not cease to teach us with the authority of the Gospel to observe peace,[c] mercifully grant us your peace, so that while we flee from the abyss of discord, we may reach the heights of heaven. Through [...]

357 PRAYER OF SACRIFICE. It is truly worthy and just [that we bring thanks to you] through Christ our Lord, who died for our sins[d] *and was raised for our justification*[136] (Rom. 4, 25). *He ascended far above all the heavens* (cf. Ps. 68, 33,[e] Eph. 4, 10) and [is] elevated to the throne of your glory. And he is *seated at your right hand* (cf. Rom. 8, 34) and has poured out the promised Holy Spirit in *the children of adoption* (cf. Rom. 8, 15). While we rejoice at *your altars, O Lord of hosts* (Ps. 84, 3[f]), we therefore bring you *offerings of praise* (Hebr. 13, 15) with the angels and archangels. Through Christ the Lord.

[a] On the word *commercium*, see note 1.

[b] *subsellia* can refer to the judge's seat. It does not occur in the Vulgate. Blaise refers to the Gothic Missal for the use of the word: BLAISE, *Dictionnaire*, s.v. *subsellium*. Christ is here addressed as God (*Deus*), as is more often the case in the Gothic Missal.

[c] Cf. Ioh. 14, 27.

[d] *qui mortuus est propter peccata nostra*: the Vulgate gives *qui traditus est propter delicta nostra*, but the wording found here occurs in the commentary tradition; see Brepolis Vetus Latina database, e.g. fiche 15 at http://apps.brepolis.net.proxy.library.uu.nl/vld/index.html (consulted 24 September 2015).

[e] Vulgate: Ps. 67, 34. The translation in NRSV deviates from the Latin ('O rider in the heavens, the ancient heavens').

[f] Vulgate: Ps. 83, 4.

L MASS FOR THE HOLY DAY OF PENTECOST[a]

358 God, light and life of the faithful, the unutterable magnitude of whose gifts is venerated through the testimony of today's feast, grant to your people that they understand with the mind what they have learned through a miracle, so that *the adoption* (Rom. 8, 15) that the Holy Spirit has invoked in them has nothing tepid in love and nothing divergent in confession. Through [...]

487

359 COLLECT. May *the Spirit, the Comforter* (cf. Ioh. 14, 26; Ioh. 15, 26[b]), who proceeds from you,[c] so we ask, O Lord, illuminate our minds and guide us to all good work, as the Son of truth has promised us. Through [...]

360 AFTER THE NAMES. May our gifts, so we ask, O Lord, be blessed through the grace of your Holy Spirit, that through them we are reborn from all our sins as *children of your adoption* (Rom. 8, 15). Through [...]

361 AT THE KISS OF PEACE. O Lord, holy Father, almighty and everlasting God, through whose Spirit the entire body of the Church is multiplied and ruled, conserve in the new offspring of your people the grace of sanctification which you have given,[d] so that, renewed in body and mind, with the help of the security of peace they always present to you a pure soul and a pure heart. Through.

---

[a] On this Mass, see Introduction, section The liturgical year.

[b] NRSV gives 'advocate' or 'helper'; SOUTER, *Glossary*, s.v. *paracletus* gives 'consoler'; LEWIS and SHORT, *Latin Dictionary*, s.v. *paracletus* give 'comforter'.

[c] The Spirit proceeds from the Father rather than the Son, in contrast to the *filioque*, which was added to the creed in the early medieval West and later caused the schism between the Latin and Greek Churches; ROSAMOND MCKITTERICK, *Charlemagne: The Formation of a European Identity* (Cambridge: Cambridge University Press, 2008), p. 311–315; ANTHONY E. SIECIENSKI, *The filioque: History of a Doctrinal Controversy* (Oxford: Oxford University Press, 2010), 68–69.

[d] On Pentecost as a Baptism term in early Christianity, see EVERETT FERGUSON, *Baptism in the Early Church: History, Theology, and Liturgy in the First Five Centuries* (Grand Rapids, MI-Cambridge: William B. Eerdmans, 2009), p. 345.

488   362 PRAYER OF SACRIFICE. It is truly worthy and just that we here and everywhere bring you thanks and glory in your works, O Lord, holy Father, almighty and everlasting God. Especially on this day, on which the most holy Easter feast is concluded with the mysteries of fifty days, on which [the year] is brought to an end and new beginning[a] while the intervening spaces between the days rebound over their own steps, and on which the dispersion of languages, brought about to cause confusion, is united by the Holy Spirit.[b] For today the apostles, when they suddenly heard *a sound from the heavens* (Act. 2, 2), received the symbol of the one faith, and *in various languages* (Act. 2, 4[c]) they passed on the glory of your Gospel to the peoples. Through Christ our Lord.

LI MASS FOR SAINT FERREOLUS AND SAINT FERRUCIO[d]

363 [PREFACE.] Most beloved brothers, let us humbly pray to the Lord our God, who gave to his holy martyrs Ferreolus and Ferrucio certain rewards of future joys in the strife of the present life, while through the inextinguishable glow of their love they

---

[a] It is unclear what the subject of *colligerunt* should be. I chose to add *annus*, interpreting it as a reference to the idea that the closing year returns to its starting point. Another interpretation would be to add *omnes* or *omnia* as the subject of *colligerunt* (and thus to read, therefore, what is written and not *colligitur*). This would refer to Pentecost as the gathering of harvest, central to the celebration of Pentecost in the Jewish tradition; see ROSE (ed.), *Missale Gothicum*, p. 488. In the Christian tradition, and in this prayer too, the celebration of the first fruits is understood spiritually as the gathering of the newly converted. The parallel prayer in *Bobbio Missal* 311 (ed. LOWE, p. 93) gives *colligitur*. The version in *Sacramentarium Bergomense* 773, ed. ANGELO PAREDI, *Manoscritto del secolo IX della Biblioteca di S. Alessandro in Colonna in Bergamo. Trascritto da Angelo Paredi. Tavole comparative da Giusepe Fassi* (Bergamo: Monumenta Bergomensia, 1962), p. 205 refers directly to Act. 2, 1 with the variant *et mysticus numerus adimpletur*.

[b] Cf. Act. 2, 4–11.

[c] *aliis linguis* and *uariis linguis* both occur in the Vulgate and in the Vetus Latina (e.g. VLD, fiche 5–7: Itala); see Brepolis Vetus Latina database at http://apps.brepolis.net.proxy.library.uu.nl/vld/index.html (consulted 24 September 2015).

[d] On this Mass, see ROSE (ed.), *Missale Gothicum*, Introduction, p. 300–303.

understood that through loss they would acquire the sweetness of life and by dying they would trample upon death. And for them this fleeting day was concluded with the bitterness of urging pains [and] access to eternal light was opened up.[a] May he grant to us his servants that, as not a single kind of torment broke them even though their bodies deserted them,[b] so no burdens of this world through a pernicious certainty may deflect us from the intention to serve him, and that this divine [glow][c] of his love ignites the strength of our faith and consumes in us all seeds[137] of bodily vice. Through [...]

364 COLLECT. God, whose love your most pious confessors and martyrs Ferreolus and Ferrucio confessed[138] through their blood and confirmed through their death, who, while they so gladly spent for you the gift of life obtained from you, testified that all die in order to live:[139] grant that, through the merits of our life, we honour the faith that they left in our hearts, written with their own blood, and that what we admire in them we may imitate, what we venerate we may love, what we honour with praise we may pursue in our way of life. Through.

489

365 AFTER THE NAMES. Now that the names of our brothers and beloved have been enumerated,[140] let us pray for the mercy of the Lord, that he will bring about that in the middle of Jerusalem, in the congregation of the saints, these names will be enumerated to him by the angel of sanctification, to the beatitude of eternal joy, and that through his power he will sanctify this offering of ours after the prefiguration[141] of Melchisedek.[d] And that he will also

---

[a] *concluditur, aditus aeternae lucis aperitur*: asyndeton; see Introduction, section Style and figures.

[b] A reference to the *Passio Ferreoli et Ferrucionis*, AASS *Junii IV*, vol. 24, p. 5–15, esp. p. 7; cf. ROSE (ed.), *Missale Gothicum*, Introduction, p. 302.

[c] A noun related to *diuinus ille* is lacking; see ROSE (ed.), *Missale Gothicum*, p. 488.

[d] The prayer implicitly refers to three prayers in the *canon missae* (see no. 342): Melchisedek (*Supra quae*); the angel carrying the sacrifice (here: the names of those who bring the sacrifice) to heaven (*Supplices*); the names of the deceased (*Memento* of the deceased); cf. ROSE (ed.), *Missale Gothicum*, Introduction, p. 302–303.

mercifully grant the prayers of those who offer in this oblation, that through the commemoration of the blessed martyrs Ferreolus and Ferrucio and all the saints, and assisted by their prayers, they are deemed worthy to obtain not only protection for the living but also rest for our beloved deceased. Through.

366 PRAYER AT THE KISS OF PEACE. *Wondrous among your saints* (Ps. 68, 35[a]), O Lord of hosts, give to us sinners through the patronage[b] of your blessed martyrs Ferreolus and Ferrucio, [that as] they merited through their virtue the crowns of martyrdom, decorated with pearls [and] precious stones,[c] we by their help obtain forgiveness of sins through your grace. And grant us that the union of lips brings about the bond of souls and that the service of the kiss of peace contributes to perpetual love. Through.

490

367 PRAYER OF SACRIFICE. It is worthy and just, indeed truly worthy and just [that we praise you.] Whenever we commemorate the combat of the saints we praise you, and we ascribe to your virtues that through which we proclaim your martyrs Ferreolus and Ferrucio, for their crown is your glory. For through your only-begotten Son Jesus Christ our Lord and Saviour you taught that mortal bodies bear the palm of precious martyrdom. But we rightly proclaim your merits[142] when[143] we venerate the deeds of such very strong martyrs, you who through the love of your goodness ignite the hearts of the people to the combat of heavenly glory. For the reward is of your strength: the torments of the saints. For while their bodies were subjected to the cruel executioner the blood shed by the martyrs served you. The blooded hand of the

---

[a] Vulgate: Ps. 67, 36. The translation in NRSV deviates from the Latin ('Awesome is God in his sanctuary').

[b] *patrocinium* is the protection of a patron for his *clientes*. In a Christian context, it usually refers to the patronage of a saint; see BLAISE, *Dictionnaire*, s.v. *patrocinium*. In a liturgical source it might offer a clue as to its origins; see the discussion concerning the prayers for *Rogationes* in ROSE (ed.), *Missale Gothicum*, Introduction, p. 16–17, but also the emphasis on certain saints as patrons of the Gallic Church in general without a local patrocinium: ibid., p. 251.

[c] Cf. *Passio Ferreoli et Ferrucionis*, AASS vol. 24, p. 6; see also ROSE (ed.), *Missale Gothicum*, Introduction, p. 301–302.

magistrate's attendant[144] brings triumph to you, and whoever voluntarily[145] subjected the necks to the sword[146] triumphed for you, and whoever is subjected to the claws and flames has carried away the palm of your name. Therefore you, O Lord, have something to rejoice in whenever we honour the commemoration of such great strength. And rightly[a] you grant heavenly gifts to each individually, you who near and far acquire such great love through your saints. After such great generosity of your love, who would not prepare his soul for the desire of martyrdom? Or who would not be roused to combat when he sees the victory of the martyrs rewarded with the great fruit of their labour? We therefore ask, O Lord, that you admit us to share in the reward, we who celebrate the memory of their precious virtue in the commemoration of your saints Ferreolus and Ferrucio. May you grant this, so that your servants prepare to persevere in the course of the work begun, so that they who believe in you and serve you not only are deemed worthy to gain a place of righteousness with you, even if not in first or second place of the reward,[b] but also cry out with the angels and archangels, saying: [Holy, holy, holy...]

491

LII MASS FOR THE BIRTH[c] OF SAINT JOHN THE BAPTIST

368 God, who adorned blessed John the Baptist with the testimony of truth, grant, so we ask, that we listen to the example of his humility, so that we desire to understand what he accomplished and to comprehend with all love what he acquired. Through Jesus Christ.

---

[a] *Nec inmeritu*: litotes; see Introduction, section Style and figures.

[b] *remunerationis sortem*: cf. AMBROSE, *Expositio psalmi CXVIII* 17.3, ed. MARC PETSCHENIG, CSEL 62 (Vienna: Verlag der Österreichischen Akademie der Wissenschaften, 1913/1999 Michaela Zelzer), p. 378.

[c] The celebration of a saint's earthly birth (*nativitas*) in addition to his or her birth to eternal life (*natalis, natalicia*) is exceptional. Cf. the cases of Agnes and John the Evangelist and perhaps Mary above; see ROSE (ed.), *Missale Gothicum*, Introduction, p. 159, s.v. *natalicia*. On the Mass for the birth of John the Baptist, see ibid., p. 252–253 and 254–257.

369 COLLECT FOLLOWS. Almighty and everlasting God, who has commanded that your Forerunner John the Baptist was born *to prepare the ways for your Only-begotten* (cf. Luc. 1, 76; Matth. 11, 10), grant, so we ask, that you bestow the help of his intercession [and] prepare the will to fulfil [your] commands. Through our Lord.

492

370 AFTER THE NAMES. Almighty and everlasting God, who through the birth of blessed John the Baptist made this venerable day eminent for us, we ask you that your Forerunner, *who has arisen among the children of women as the greatest of all* (Matth. 11, 11),[147] entrusts our weakness to your love, and that he procures such consolation of love for our beloved whose names have been recited, that they may be received there, even if as the last, where the Baptist abides as highest:[a] in the kingdom of the heavens. May you [deign to grant...]

371 COLLECT AT THE KISS OF PEACE. God, who through the birth of blessed John the Baptist [made] this venerable day eminent for us,[148] give to your flock the grace of spiritual joys and *guide* the hearts of all the faithful *into the way of salvation and peace* (Luc. 1, 79). Through.

372 PRAYER OF SACRIFICE. It is truly worthy that we always bring thanks to you, here and everywhere, O Lord, holy Father, almighty and everlasting God. For you are wondrous in the splendour of all your saints, who through the birth of blessed John made the present day venerable for us,[149] since he, *greater than whom is no one*

493 *among the children of women* (Matth. 11, 11), was born through the working of the power of your grace.[150] Give to your faithful the learning of spiritual joys and *guide* the hearts of all the faithful *into the way of salvation and peace* (Luc. 1, 79), so that he who was revealed through the testimony of the messenger[b] fulfils [the testimony of] the messenger with his presence. Through Christ our Lord. Through whom your majesty.

[a] Matth. 11, 11 phrases the opposite, namely that those who appear in the kingdom of heaven even as the last are greater than John.

[b] Cf. Luc. 1, 11–17. On John the Baptist as *nuntius* of Christ, see ROSE (ed.), *Missale Gothicum*, Introduction, p. 140.

373 BLESSING OF THE PEOPLE.[151] God, who revealed the birth of
Saint John through the word of Zacharias.[a] AMEN.[152]
Grant, so we ask, that [we] who celebrate his day of birth devoutly
rejoice in his intercession. AMEN.
That your servants, who have gathered for the day of his birth, are
saved by [his] merits, [and] are helped through the intercession of
all the saints [and] through the merits of his prayer.[153] AMEN.
Grant, Lord, that the angel Gabriel, who put the speaking Zacharias to silence, assists them as intercessor, and that they are helped
through [his] merits and saintly example.
May he [bless] you.

LIII MASS FOR SAINT PETER AND SAINT PAUL[b]   494

374 Almighty and everlasting God, who has consecrated this day
with the martyrdom of the most blessed apostles Peter and Paul,
grant to your Church, spread throughout all the world,[c] that it is
always guided by the teaching of those through whom the beginning of faith came about. Through our Lord Jesus Christ your Son.

375 COLLECT FOLLOWS. Hear your people, so we ask, O Lord,
who pray to you under the protection[d] of your holy apostles Peter
and Paul, that, saved by your help, they can serve you with a secure
devotion.

376 COLLECT AFTER THE NAMES. We celebrate, O Lord, the
long awaited solemn feast of your blessed apostles Peter and Paul.

---

[a] This is an ironical comment on Luc. 1, 57–63, where Zacharias was made
mute so that he could not reveal the promised birth of his son, but could only comment on it after it had become manifest to 'all neighbours and relatives' through
Elizabeth's delivery.

[b] On this Mass, see ROSE (ed.), *Missale Gothicum*, Introduction, p. 244–251.

[c] *toto terrarum orbe*: see no. 3. The word is used here in its 'original' Roman
context; but compare nos 417 and 429 where it occurs in the context of more 'pe-
ripheral' saints.

[d] *patrocinio*: see no. 366.

Grant, so we ask, that the honourable glory of the passion, as it has given them perpetual splendour, may bestow on us the desired forgiveness, and that you consider the names of those that have been recited[154] worthy to be counted[155] in the Book of Life. Through him, who lives with you [...]

495

377 COLLECT AT THE KISS OF PEACE. God, Creator of peace, God, Giver of love,[156] mercifully grant us your peace, and grant that while we celebrate the feast of your blessed apostles Peter and Paul, through their intercession we are considered worthy to obtain the security of peace and forgiveness of sins. Through our Lord Jesus.

378 PRAYER OF SACRIFICE. It is truly worthy and just that we always and everywhere bring thanks to you, O Lord, holy Father, almighty and everlasting God, especially today in honour of your most blessed apostles and martyrs Peter and Paul, whom your election[157] has deigned to consecrate to you, such that blessed Peter's worldly art of fishing was converted into a divine doctrine, in order that you would free the human race from the depths of this world with the nets of your teaching.[a] For *you changed the heart and the name of* his fellow apostle *Paul* (cf. Act. 13, 9),[b] and the Church rejoices that *he who first was feared as a persecutor* (cf. I Tim. 1, 13) is now for her a teacher[c] of heavenly commands. Paul was made blind that he might see,[d] Peter denied that he might believe,[e] you handed over to the one the keys of the heavenly kingdom[f] and you gave to the other the knowledge of divine law in order to call the gentiles.[158] For the latter teaches, the former opens,[159] both have therefore received the reward of eternal

[a] On the content of the prayer and its connection to Roman prayers in honour of Peter (and Paul), see ROSE (ed.), *Missale Gothicum*, Introduction, p. 250.
[b] On the double conversion of Paul, see no. 245 and ROSE (ed.), *Missale Gothicum*, Introduction, p. 250.
[c] On Paul as a teacher, see ROSE (ed.), *Missale Gothicum*, Introduction, p. 250–251.
[d] Cf. Act. 9, 17–18.
[e] Cf. Matth. 26, 69–75; Ioh. 21, 15–19.
[f] Cf. Matth. 16, 19.

strength. Your right hand raised up the one when he walked on the water, lest he would drown,[a] while you helped the other, who was *shipwrecked three times* (II Cor. 11, 25), to withstand the dangers of the deep sea. The one vanquished *the gates of hell* (Matth. 16, 18), the other the *sting of death* (I Cor. 15, 56[b]). Paul was beheaded because he was established by the gentiles as head of the faith, and Peter followed Christ as head of us all while the steps to the cross were laid out beforehand.[c] To whom all [angels] rightly [sing: Holy, holy, holy...]

379 BLESSING OF THE PEOPLE ON THE FEAST OF THE APOS-   496
TLES PETER AND PAUL. God, who made the tears of Peter[d] and the letters of Paul shine as a twin-born light for the members of the Church, by which they are protected against darkness. AMEN. Look mercifully on this people, you who made that Peter with his key and Paul with his doctrine open the heavens. AMEN. So that while the leaders show the way,[160] the flock can approach where both equally, the shepherd through the crucifixion and the teacher through the sword,[e] have reached the gathering [of the saints.] Through our Lord.

---

[a] Cf. Matth. 14, 28–33.

[b] On the choice of words (*aculeum* for *stimulum*), see no. 52.

[c] Cf. Ioh. 21, 18–22: the end of the conversation between the risen Christ and Peter by the Sea of Tiberius. After Peter's threefold confession of his love for Christ, the words predict 'the kind of death by which he would glorify God': '... when you grow old, you will stretch out your hands, and someone else will fasten a belt around you and take you where you do not wish to go'. In the subsequent verses, Peter's imitation of Christ is again emphasised, when he asks about John's fate and receives the answer: 'If it is my will that he remain until I come, what is that to you? Follow me!' These verses in John 21 are generally interpreted as foretelling Peter's martyrdom, which is repeated in the *Quo vadis* legend included in the Acts of Peter, where the risen Christ meets Peter at Rome's gate to predict Peter's crucifixion; see *The Acts of Peter*, transl. James K. Elliott, *The Apocryphal New Testament. A Collection of Apocryphal Christian Literature in an English Translation Based on M.R. James* (Oxford: Clarendon Press, 1993), p. 424–425.

[d] Cf. Matth. 26, 75 and see no. 346.

[e] On the earliest tradition of the martyrdom of Peter and Paul, see RÉGIS BURNET, *Les douze apôtres. Histoire de la réception des figures apostoliques dans le christianisme ancien* (Turnhout: Brepols, 2014), p. 191–199.

LIIII MASS FOR THE FEAST OF ONE
APOSTLE AND MARTYR

380 Lord God, wondrous splendour of all the saints, who consecrated this day by the martyrdom of your blessed apostle *N,* grant
to your Church to rejoice worthily in such a great apostle, that
with your mercy we are helped by both his example and his merits.
Through our Lord your Son.

381 COLLECT FOLLOWS. We humbly pray to your majesty, O Lord,
that as this blessed apostle *N* was a preacher and teacher for your
Church, he is also an eternal mediator for us. Through our Lord
Jesus.

497

382 COLLECT AFTER THE NAMES. Let the offered gift gladden
us, so we ask, O Lord, that, as we praise you in your apostle as
wondrous, through him also we receive the abundance of forgiveness.[161] Grant us the exchange of gifts[a] which he[162] so desired, that
he, whose perpetual merit we celebrate on earth through the most
holy mystery, requests for us earthly and eternal help. Through
our Lord.

383 PRAYER OF SACRIFICE. It is truly worthy and just that [we]
praise you, almighty God, especially on the feast of this your blessed apostle *N,* on which his glorious blood was shed for Christ,
whose venerable and annually recurring solemn celebration is ever
perpetual and new. For *in the sight of your majesty the death of your
righteous remains precious* (Ps. 116, 15),[b] and the increase of joy is
restored when the beginning of eternal happiness is celebrated
anew. We humbly ask you, almighty God, that you deign to give
us your apostle *N* as intercessor for our sins and as patron [of] our
needs, that he who shed his holy blood on behalf of truth[163] himself receives our prayers in the sight of your majesty, and that we so
please him through the gift of our worship,[164] that when we plea to

---

[a] *conmercia:* see note 1.
[b] Vulgate: Ps. 115, 6, not 115, 15 as in ROSE (ed.), *Missale Gothicum,* p. 497.

him on earth he deigns to commend us in heaven to the Lord Jesus Christ. To whom all angels rightly sing [Holy...]

LV MASS FOR THE ANNIVERSARY OF THE PASSION OF SAINT JOHN THE BAPTIST, MARTYR[a]

498

384 [PREFACE.] Most beloved brothers, let us in unity, with humble confession and meek devotion, beseech God the Father and the Son and the Holy Spirit, that we who celebrate today the passion of the holy martyr John the Baptist,[b] the voice of prophecy, the Forerunner of the Word, the end of the [Old] Law,[c] a shining lamp, are illuminated, protected and sanctified[165] through his intercession, so that he who shed his holy blood on behalf of truth[166] deigns for us to pour out our prayers before God. Through our Lord.

385 COLLECT FOLLOWS. Almighty God, while we serve your majesty with these praises, we sing of the solemn feast in honour of your most blessed martyr John the Baptist, whose passion we celebrate today, and we humbly pray that, if you are willing to grant this in your mercy, we are helped through the prayers of him whose merits we honour. Through.

386 AFTER THE NAMES. Look mercifully upon the gifts of your people, so we ask [you], almighty God, which we offer you on this feast of your most blessed martyr John the Baptist, that we, cleansed of our sins through the sanctification of this perfect sacrifice, are deigned by you worthy to obtain forgiveness.[167] Through.

---

[a] On this Mass, see ROSE (ed.), *Missale Gothicum*, Introduction, p. 253–258.

[b] As described in Matth. 14, 1–12.

[c] This is a reference to John as the transition from the prophets of the Old Testament (the Old Law), and to Christ as the beginning of the New Law.

387 COLLECT AT THE KISS OF PEACE. Accept our supplications, so we ask, O Lord, and strengthen the prayers of your Church through the intercession of your martyr John the Baptist, whom we venerate in your honour, who was even found worthy that you offered yourself to be baptised [by him],[a] Saviour of the world. It is worthy that he merits this, that he unites us all, who have obtained the grace of your Baptism, through the intervention of his merits. Saviour of the world.

499

388 PRAYER OF SACRIFICE. It is worthy and just, fair and salutary that we always bring thanks to you, almighty and merciful God, [and] that the *head* of your martyr is mingled with this meal of your mysteries, mindful of the Gospel, and that it is sacrificed, as if *on a platter* (cf. Matth. 14, 8) of radiant metal, on the table of your mercy. Let there be for us, O Lord, a joyful praise, let there be in honour of the martyr a remembrance of the song of victory. And let the music of the faithful people mingle with these heavenly and lofty powers, which at your right hand sing with one voice under threefold repetition: HOLY, HOLY, HOLY.

LVI MASS FOR THE FEAST OF SAINT SIXTUS, BISHOP[168] OF THE CITY OF ROME[b]

389 Lord God, insuperable force of the faithful, who, amid the adversities of life on earth,[169] comforts us especially through the glorification of the saints, [and who] unceasingly urges [us to the greatest examples of patience through the victory of] your [holy Sixtus]:[c] arouse in your Church, O Lord, the Spirit that he served, that we strive to love what he loved and to practise the works that he taught. Through our Lord Jesus your Son.

---

[a] Cf. Matth. 3, 13–15.

[b] On this Mass, see ROSE (ed.), *Missale Gothicum*, Introduction, p. 282–285.

[c] The prayer is clearly incomplete. The addition in ROSE (ed.), *Missale Gothicum*, p. 499 follows the suggestion given by Bannister and Mohlberg with reference to the parallel prayer in the Mass for Lawrence in *Sacramentarium Veronense* 749, ed. MOHLBERG, p. 95.

390 COLLECT FOLLOWS. Almighty and merciful God, grant us 500 that the recurring feast of your blessed martyr Sixtus gives us perfect liberation and salvation. Through our Lord.

391 COLLECT AFTER THE NAMES. Hear our supplications,[170] O Lord, and favourably grant us perpetual mercy through the intercession of your martyr Sixtus, and may you command that the names of our beloved that are recited are announced in the heavenly Book. Through our Lord.

392 COLLECT AT THE KISS OF PEACE. Accept the worthily offered oblations, so we ask, O Lord, and grant that our salvation increases thanks to the merits of the blessed bishop and martyr Sixtus. And mercifully instil in us that vigorous love which burned in him. Through him whom [...][171]

393 PRAYER OF SACRIFICE. It is truly worthy and just, it is fair and salutary that we incessantly sing praise to you, O Lord, holy Father, almighty and everlasting God, through Christ our Lord, who through his coming[172] permitted the people who believe in him to pass over to the heavenly kingdom. For those who offer themselves as witnesses of your truth kill the enemy[a] while they are killed, to whom belongs the holy and venerable martyr Sixtus, whose feast is celebrated today. For having received the insignia of the apostolic seat, and perceiving that he was the most prominent of bishops,[173] on receiving the occasion of the salutary martyrdom 501 he not only freed himself from the sordid contagiousness of the world but also formed an example for others. For his excellent minister the venerable Lawrence, who followed him, also quickly received the palm of victory as a distinguishing mark that he had to endure as punishment, in order to be deemed worthy to obtain eternal glory. Through Christ.

[a] i.e. the devil; see no. 156.

LVII MASS FOR THE FEAST OF THE HOLY MARTYR LAWRENCE[a]

394 God, Saviour and Ruler of your faithful, almighty and everlasting God, hear the prayers of today's feast, and mercifully encourage the Church by receiving the joys through the glorious passion of your martyr the blessed Lawrence. Let the faith of all be increased by the birth of such great virtue, and let the hearts of us who rejoice in the sacrifice of the martyrs be ignited such that, with your mercy, we are helped by his good work, through whose example we rejoice. Through our Lord.

395 COLLECT FOLLOWS. God, Creator and Ruler of the world, who consecrated this day by the martyrdom of your deacon Lawrence, mercifully hear your supplicants and grant that [we] all, who venerate the merits of his martyrdom, are delivered through his intercession from the eternal flames of hell. Through the Lord.

502 396 COLLECT AFTER THE NAMES. Grant us, O Lord, such abundant grace through the feast of the blessed martyr Lawrence, that the Christian people[b] learns from the contest of such a great battle[174] both to strengthen steadfast patience and to rejoice at the righteous victory.

397 COLLECT AT THE KISS OF PEACE. Let *the righteous prayer* (cf. Iac. 5, 16) of Saint Lawrence protect us, so we ask, O Lord, and may that for which our conscience does not presume to hope be given to us through the prayer of him who pleased you. Through our Lord your Son.

---

[a] This Mass is discussed together with that for Sixtus in ROSE (ed.), *Missale Gothicum*, Introduction, p. 282–285.

[b] *populus christianus* can refer to the liturgical congregation, as in *Itinerarium Egeriae* 43, ed. PAUL GEYER et al., *Itineraria et alia geographica*, CCSL 175 (Turnhout: Brepols, 1965), p. 37–90, at p. 84–86, but also to Christianity as the elected people: AMBROSIASTER, *Commentarius in Pauli epistulas ad Galatas* 4.29, ed. VOGELS, p. 53.

398 PRAYER OF SACRIFICE. It is truly worthy and just, almighty and everlasting God, that [we] offer you *sacrifices of praise* (Hebr. 13, 15) on [the feast] of so great a martyr as Lawrence, you who today received the living sacrifice through the ministry[175] of this your deacon the blessed martyr Lawrence through the flower of a pure body. We have heard his voice through the song of the psalm that sings,[a] saying: '*You have tried my heart, God, and visited me by night* – that is, in the darkness of the world – *you have tested me with fire and no wickedness was found in me* (Ps. 17, 3)'. O glorious strength of combat! O unshakeable steadfastness of the confessor![b] Laid on the gridiron, the living limbs sizzle, and while the flames roar, fuming their burning smell, they spread a fragrance of incense before the nose of God.[c] For this martyr says with Paul: '*We are the good aroma of Christ to God* (II Cor. 2, 15)'. Indeed, living on earth, he did not consider how he could be delivered from the peril of suffering, but how he could be crowned amid the martyrs in heaven. Through Christ our Lord, through whom [...]

503

LVIII MASS FOR THE HOLY MARTYR HIPPOLYTUS[d]

399 Grant us, almighty and merciful God, that the venerable feast of your blessed martyr Hippolytus for us increases devotion and salvation. Through our Lord your Son.

[a] The phrasing of the prayer might indicate that Ps. 17 was sung during this Mass.

[b] The style of this prayer is typical of the Gallican tradition, given the characteristic O-exclamations which recall the prayers of sacrifice in the Masses for Agnes, Stephen, Leodegar, Symphorian and Martin, and the *Exultet*; see Introduction, section Style and figures.

[c] Reference to Lawrence's martyrdom in the *Passio sanctorum Xysti et Laurentii* 28 in *Passio Polochronii*, ed. HIPPOLYTE DELEHAYE, 'Recherches sur le légendier romain', *Analecta Bollandiana* 51 (1933), 72–98, at p. 92–93.

[d] On this Mass, see ROSE (ed.), *Missale Gothicum*, Introduction, p. 285–288.

400 COLLECT FOLLOWS. Grant us, almighty and merciful God, that the recurring feast of your blessed martyr Hippolytus gives us perfect liberation and salvation. Through our Lord.

401 COLLECT AFTER THE NAMES. God, glory of your people, grant us, so we ask, all prosperity because your martyr Hippolytus prays for us.[176] Through our Lord your Son.

504

402 COLLECT AT THE KISS OF PEACE. May the blessed martyr Hippolytus be heard when he copiously prays for us, so we ask, O Lord, so that your medicines give us salvation. Through our Lord.

403 PRAYER OF SACRIFICE. It is truly worthy and just, almighty and everlasting God, [that we praise you], who suddenly made the blessed Hippolytus, still occupied by his service to the tyrant, a companion of Lawrence. Consumed by spiritual ardour, while he truthfully confessed your only-begotten Son our Lord *in the presence of the powers* (cf. Ps. 119, 46), he was subjected to punishment, bound with fetters, pierced with thistles and torn apart by the ferocity of horses.[a] And after obtaining the palm of martyrdom, perpetual life,[b] he is crowned with his converter[177] and teacher Lawrence. Through Christ our Lord.

LVIIII MASS FOR THE FEAST OF THE HOLY MARTYRS CORNELIUS AND CYPRIAN[c]

404 Holy and almighty Lord, whom Cornelius and Cyprian have confessed with their victorious blood and thereby have become

[a] The details correspond with the *Passio Polochronii*, in which Hippolytus's martyrdom is connected to that of his teacher Lawrence; see ROSE (ed.), *Missale Gothicum*, Introduction, p. 287–288 and *Passio Polochronii* 31, ed. Delehaye, 'Recherches', p. 95.
[b] There is no conjunction in *palma martyrii uita perpetua*: an asyndetic connection representing the equality of martyrdom and eternal beatitude.
[c] On this Mass, see ROSE (ed.), *Missale Gothicum*, Introduction, p. 288–289.

venerable, grant, so we ask, that they both help us continually. Through.

405 COLLECT FOLLOWS. May the holy Cornelius and Cyprian bestow on us their customary help, O Lord, and support us with ever equal intercession. Through the Lord.

406 COLLECT AFTER THE NAMES. May the festivities of the 505 blessed martyrs and also bishops Cornelius and Cyprian protect us, so we ask, may their prayer commend us to you, O Lord, that you grant eternal consolation to our beloved who rest in Christ. Through.

407 COLLECT AT THE KISS OF PEACE. Extend to us your mercy and be the defender and custodian of your people, that they can celebrate the venerable feast of your saints Cornelius and Cyprian in the certain gathering of the assembly. Through.

408 PRAYER OF SACRIFICE. It is truly worthy and just that we always and everywhere bring thanks to you, almighty and everlasting God, and that we praise you in the virtue of your holy martyrs. For you have crowned those who feed the holy flock in different parts of the earth, on the grounds of one and the same faith, even if in different times, with the uniform and equal confession of your name. Through our Lord, through whom [...]

LX MASS FOR THE FEAST OF THE HOLY BROTHERS JOHN AND PAUL[a]

409 Almighty and merciful God, we ask that the double joy of today's feast sustains us, which proceeds from the glorification of your blessed martyrs John and Paul, who were made brothers by 506 the same faith and passion. Through.

[a] On this Mass, see ROSE (ed.), *Missale Gothicum*, Introduction, p. 289–290.

410 COLLECT FOLLOWS. Almighty and everlasting God, may we be helped by the support of the brother-martyrs, joined by one birth and the same palm of martyrdom, lest our sins burden us in the face of your righteousness. Through.

411 COLLECT AFTER THE NAMES. Mercifully receive, O Lord, our prayers and graciously make them acceptable to your love for the sake of the supplication of your righteous John and Paul, and let them, united in their blood relation and faith, grant us the protection of solace. Through.

412 COLLECT AT THE KISS OF PEACE. Look upon the gifts, so we ask, O Lord, which lie displayed on your altar for the commemoration of your blessed martyrs John and Paul, that as you brought them glory through these blessed mysteries, you mildly grant us forgiveness. Through the Lord.

413 PRAYER OF SACRIFICE. It is truly most worthy and just, almighty God, that we praise you on [the feast] of these martyrs John and Paul, companions through their brotherhood and equally through their blessedness, whom you made brothers through the circumstances of their birth and kindred through their splendid martyrdom, so that they became both the glory and flourishing offspring of the venerable Mother Church. Willingly accept the sacrifice offered in memory of their martyrdom, O Lord, and purify us through it, just as through the intercession of these martyrs, that we are deemed worthy to sing a hymn of praise to you with free voices and united hearts, when, with the angels and archangels, we cry out to you: HOLY.

507

LXI MASS FOR THE FEAST OF THE MOST
BLESSED MARTYR SYMPHORIAN[a]

414 [PREFACE.] Now that we have begun the service of our devotion to the solemn ceremony on the day sanctified by heavenly
mysteries, most beloved brothers, *let us praise the Lord in his sanctuary* (cf. Ps. 150, 1), while we also venerate him with the honour
of the most blessed martyr Symphorian, bringing thanks to him
for the victory and glory of him whom he strengthened against
the weakness of his body when the force of his spirit yielded, and
against the cruelty of the punishment through the vigour of hope,
and whom he surrounded as with a wall[b] of faith, and, through the
approach of victory, carried to the reward of immortality. Let us
also pray that the same strength will not abandon us in this world,
even if we do not fight in the same combat. And as the exhortation of his devout[178] mother raised him up to gain victory in this
battle, so let the faith of the catholic Church, guarded impeccably,   508
guide us to forgiveness and carry us to the crown. Through our
Lord Jesus Christ.

415 COLLECT FOLLOWS. God, glorious protection of all the saints,
who did not deny help to your blessed martyr Symphorian and
deigned to call him to this glory through the wicked mockery of
death, grant that a similar faith may join us to martyrdom, whom
the time of martyrdom did not allow to remain in the stride.[c] And
as the hard and dangerous path placed him in paradise through the
tribulation of martyrdom, so [let] the contempt for the pleasures of
this world [place] us [in paradise.] Through our Lord.

---

[a] On this Mass, see ROSE (ed.), *Missale Gothicum*, Introduction, p. 296–300.
[b] This is probably a reference to the city wall from which Symphorian's 'devout
mother' (*pia mater*) encouraged her son to perseverance: *Passio Symphoriani* 7, ed.
RUINART, p. 82; ROSE (ed.), *Missale Gothicum*, Introduction, p. 298.
[c] *in stadio*: refers both to the *stadium* where the early martyrs found their death
and to the (spiritual) combat as described by early Christian writers: BLAISE, *Dictionnaire*, s.v. *stadium*. The phrase as a whole refers to the notion that martyrdom is
a 'privilege' of the early Christians, no longer 'granted' to contemporary (seventh-
century) faithful, see no. 33.

416 COLLECT FOLLOWS.[a] Now that the names of those who offer have been recited, let us pray for the mercy of almighty God, most beloved brothers, that the desire for faith is poured into the people who *pay their vows* (Ps. 61, 8)[b] on the altar in honour of the blessed martyr Symphorian, so that those who are not bound to the merits of martyrdom[c] are strengthened by his guidance. And as he, after the imprisonment of the dungeon, after the bands of the punishments and after the hunger of fasting,[d] has full enjoyment of the endless joys of eternity, so also the souls of the deceased, after liberation from the oppressions of hell, rest *in the bosom of* father *Abraham* (Luc. 16, 23).[e] And may he deign to grant this, who [...]

417 COLLECT AT THE KISS OF PEACE. God, generous Giver of all good things, who amid the company of martyrs, resplendent in snow-white faith, spread throughout all the world,[f] gave us through your bright grace the precious and singular martyr Symphorian, generously grant to the daily prayers of your supplicants that in the life hereafter we are joined to the company of him over whose feast we exult with devoted joy, [and] that we are deemed worthy, through the bodily kisses of the people, to be bound to spiritual love. Through.

509   **418 PRAYER OF SACRIFICE.** It is worthy and just, fair and salutary that we offer you *sacrifices of praise* (Hebr. 13, 15) in honour of your blessed martyr Symphorian, O Lord, eternal God, through

---

[a] *Collectio sequitur*: despite the title, the prayer is clearly a Collect after the names (*collectio post nomina*).

[b] Vulgate: Ps. 60, 9.

[c] The notion of martyrdom as a privilege resounds once again (see above and no. 33).

[d] Cf. *Passio Symphoriani* 4, where the torments of imprisonment and hunger are narrated, ed. RUINART, *Acta primorum martyrum*, p. 81.

[e] *Abrahae patris gremio*: the Vulgate has *in sinu*; in the commentary tradition *in Abrahae gremio* also occurs, e.g. in AMBROSE, *Expositio euangelii secundum Lucam*, 8.13, ed. ADRIAEN, p. 302; AUGUSTINE, *Sermones* 14.3, ed. CYRIL LAMBOT, CCSL 41 (Turnhout: Brepols, 1966), p. 186; CAESARIUS OF ARLES, *Sermones* 31.4, ed. MORIN, CCSL 103, p. 137.

[f] *toto orbe terrarum*: see no. 3.

whose solemn ceremony both the manifested reason of things and the perfect wisdom of virtues fortify us, who has deserved to shine, not only through the splendour of his earthly birth[179] but also through the sublimity of his heavenly virtues. Resplendent through a favourable descent, he is raised up to the eminence of favourable martyrdom,[a] who followed the blessed fathers Andochius and Benignus,[b] elected to reach the palm through the glow of martyrdom. While he followed the torment of the present things, he completed instruction in future things, and, through the devout[180] conversation with his mother, he was transferred to the reward. For she impressed on him that he should not fear death, since for martyrs life is not taken away but changed.[c] O admirable grace of the faith! She exults with zeal in the life of her blessed and glorious son. She rejoices while it was thought that she mourned; certain as she was of the rewards of your kingdom, she urged her son with immense joy because she knew that those who die in Christ live, and that the life they have lost is given back to them because he restores it.[d] He is therefore rightly honoured in your name, who has honoured you with his blood, who was tormented for you in suffering, glorified through you in the grave, who has honoured you with the sword,[e] who reigns with you in heaven, who deserved to come through the anxiety of the present tribulation to the fullness of heavenly joys. Through Christ our Lord, through whom [...]

---

[a] The Latin for 'favourable' is *faustus*, which is also the name of Symphorian's father according to the *Passio Symphoriani* 1 (ed. RUINART, p. 79).

[b] The *Passio Symphoriani interpolata*, dated to the sixth century, links Symphorian to the cult of the martyrs Benignus (Dijon) and Andochius (Saulieu), who acted as Symphorian's godfathers; ROSE (ed.), *Missale Gothicum*, Introduction, p. 297 and 299. On the cult of Benignus in Dijon as central to the history of Christianity in Burgundy, see IAN WOOD, 'Topographies of Holy Power', p. 143–145.

[c] The final phrase directly quotes Symphorian's mother in the *Passio Symphoriani* 7, ed. RUINART, p. 82.

[d] Another reference to the words of Symphorian's mother: 'We may not fear the death that without doubt leads to life' (*Timere non possumus mortem, quae sine dubio perducit ad uitam, Passio Symphoriani* 7, ed. RUINART, p. 82).

[e] i.e. through dying by the sword, see *Passio Symphoriani* 6.

LXII MASS FOR THE HOLY AND MOST BLESSED MAURICE AND HIS COMPANIONS[a]

419 [PREFACE.] Most beloved brothers, let us pray for the mercy of the almighty Lord during the solemn ceremony of this day of the six thousand and six hundred martyrs,[b] that he who conferred on his people such great glory of martyrdom also gladdens this day for us with the immeasurable mildness of his mercy towards our sins. Through our Lord Jesus.

510

420 COLLECT FOLLOWS. God, who has given your holy men of Agaune intrepidity[181] against persecution to defend the name of Christ, and has urged their soul to acquire the resplendent grace of your dignity through martyrdom, hear your supplicants, and grant that, as they were deemed worthy through your gift to be crowned with beatitude, so we also be made guiltless without any stain of sin through their advocacy and with your help. Through the Lord.

421 PRAYER AFTER THE NAMES. Now that the names of our beloved have been heard, let us pray to the almighty Lord that, while he accepts the prayers of his people and his ministers,[182] he accepts our oblations, which we offer in commemoration of the saints of Agaune and for the souls of our beloved, to a good and sweet fragrance.[183] Let us therefore be supplicants, that we are helped by the devout prayers of the most blessed patriarchs, prophets, apostles and martyrs and all the saints. Through.

---

[a] On this Mass, see ROSE (ed.), *Missale Gothicum*, Introduction, p. 303–309.

[b] The number of martyrs, considered equal to the number of soldiers in Maurice's legion, is given in the *Passio Acaunensium martyrum* 3 (*sex milia ac sexcentos viros*), ed. KRUSCH, p. 33. The *Passio* is dated 450 and written by Eucherius of Lyons. The parallels between the prayers and the *Passio* are very close, which might imply that Eucherius compiled the Mass himself; see ROSE (ed.), *Missale Gothicum*, Introduction, p. 309. On the textual relationship between the texts, see ROSE (ed.), *Missale Gothicum*, Introduction, p. 71, footnote 15.

422 COLLECT AT THE KISS OF PEACE. God, for whom the faith and devotion[a] of your saints is the most agreeable and delightful sacrifice, support your people, who as a supplicant before you request your mercy through the mediation of your saints of Agaune, and grant that those who have offended you through the error of their sins are deemed worthy to please you through the intercession of your saints. Through.

511

423 PRAYER OF SACRIFICE. It is worthy and just, truly fair and just that we bring thanks to you, O Lord, holy Father, almighty and everlasting God. For you, O Lord, have called the army of the Thebans, destined to execute your people, so suddenly to you by the grace of your command that they preferred to be killed through their diligent devotion rather than to be saturated with the blood of Christians.[184] And while they did not hesitate, with your help, to take upon themselves the burden of persecution, they inclined the head for the persecutors,[b] and when the fury of the enemy, under the pressure of the number,[185] decided that the people of God must perish, that tenth part was put to death that became the first in the vanguard of martyrdom. A loud clamour arose in the camp, the strength to die was scorned, the hard struggle over the acceptance of martyrdom was provoked. The people of God was pierced by the sword, the blood of the innocent was shed, faith was preserved unimpaired. You protected your soldiers, O Lord, such that patience was not wanting in suffering, neither steadfastness in confession. Amid the beautiful and blessed combats of the saints, the glorious faith[c] was more fearful of being divided from the community of comrades in arms[d] than of being glorified through the hand of the executioner. For all the people of

512

---

[a] *fides atque deuocio*: as in *Passio Acaunensium* 3, ed. KRUSCH, p. 33; cf. ROSE (ed.), *Missale Gothicum*, Introduction, p. 306–307.

[b] *ceruices suas persequentibus inclinare*: cf. *Passio Acaunensium* 10, ed. KRUSCH, p. 37.

[c] *gloriosa confessio*: this personification to indicate the faith of the martyrs is a poetic element; see Introduction, section Style and figures.

[d] *cummiletonum*: cf. *Passio Acaunensium* 9, ed. KRUSCH, p. 36; ROSE (ed.), *Missale Gothicum*, Introduction, p. 308.

God burned with the eagerness of such ardent faith, that if perse-cution of the body was delayed, devotion to the passion was at the forefront. For such was the steadfastness of the people and of the enemy, that rage later found nothing to kill, and nothing glorious remained that could be killed. Through the prayers of the martyrs this holy city of the men of Agaune has become the salvation of the present [and] the aid of future times, for this [place] has been flooded by a wave of blood and consecrated by the community of precious bodies. We therefore rightly bring due praise to you, O Lord, amid the choirs of the martyrs and the voices of the angels, while we say with exultation: HOLY [...]

424 COLLECT AFTER THE SANCTUS. Let us pray, most beloved brothers, that, through the inspiration of heavenly grace, our Lord and God sanctifies this outer appearance to be consecrated to his service, and showers the blessing of humanity with the fullness of divine favour. Through our Lord Jesus.

LXIII MASS FOR THE HOLY MARTYR LEODEGAR[a]

425 Most high, almighty and everlasting God, who has com-manded that the life of your blessed bishop [and] martyr Leode-gar, whose annual feast we celebrate with devout hearts, would go through the afflictions of this world, we ask that you, through his intercession, serving the people of your grace, cherish the faith-ful in this time in order to lead them to the heavenly kingdom.[186] Through the Lord.

513   426 COLLECT FOLLOWS. God, you who have tested your blessed martyr Leodegar in combat, and have sustained the tested in an-guish while you deigned to take him up this day in the heavenly joys, grant to us your servants that we who do not deserve glory

---

[a] On this Mass, see ROSE (ed.), *Missale Gothicum*, Introduction, p. 312–316 and 15–16.

may through his intercession be deemed worthy to receive forgiveness of sins. Through.

427 COLLECT AFTER THE NAMES. Now that the names of those who offer have been recited, most beloved brothers, let us pray to the majesty of the Lord, that he who transferred the life of his most high bishop [and] martyr Leodegar to the crown deigns to grant through the intercession of the holy patriarchs, prophets, apostles and martyrs, hermits and virgins and all the saints that the oblation of this sacred [feast] which is offered obtains correction[a] for the living and remission of sins for the dead. And may their names, which are made public here through the recitation, be inscribed in the heavenly Book.[187] May he deign to grant this [...]

428 COLLECT AT THE KISS OF PEACE. Let your peace, O Lord, flow into our hearts, and [as][188] today the heavenly court has taken up your blessed martyr Leodegar because of his pursuit of peace when he abided in this world: let the bond of peace and the pursuit of love be also mildly given to us sinners in [this] time because his merits support us. Through the Lord.

429 PRAYER OF SACRIFICE. It is worthy and just, truly fair and beautiful, that we always bring praise and thanks to you and extol your praises here and everywhere, O Lord, holy Father, almighty and everlasting God, through Jesus Christ your Son our Lord, who was begotten from the foundation of the world. You have spread the revealed Word of the Father, established from the beginning of this world,[b] throughout all the earth,[c] where your blessed martyr bishop Leodegar, from the depths of this world, torn by various mutilations,[d] trod on the pomp and splendour of the world and its frailty. And you deigned, O Lord, to help him, so that he would despise the love for this world and deserved to acquire the

514

---

[a] *emendationem*: see no. 53.
[b] Cf. Ioh. 1, 1–3.
[c] *per totum orbem terrarum*: see no. 3.
[d] As described in *Passio Leudegarii I* 29, ed. KRUSCH and LEVISON, p. 310.

heavenly things. *Carrying his cross* (cf. Matth. 16, 24) and *following you as his shepherd* (Ier. 17, 16), however, he relinquished all present things to possess the delicacies of paradise. O blessed man,[a] bishop Leodegar, who, after his body was released from bonds through the designs of the godless, his countenance stripped of lips and deprived of eyes, when exile was brought to an end[b] and after he had left behind the inconstancies of the world and had suffered diverse torments, bequeathed an example for the bishops through his suffering and through his patience. Finally set free in life perpetual, having penetrated into the heavenly kingdom, he is united with the choir of angels[c] and rewarded with *the crown of flowers that never fade away* (I Petr. 5, 4),[d] from which many relics later flowered in Gaul.[e] We therefore pray to you, O Lord, that we your servants and all your people, who remember such a great shepherd,[f] will be deemed worthy to obtain forgiveness of sins because his merits support us. Through Christ our Lord, to whom all angels [...]

430 AFTER THE SANCTUS. *Hosanna [in] the highest. Blessed is he who comes in the name of the Lord* (Matth. 21, 9). O truly blessed voice, with which the powers of angels and archangels sing together, which today, at the passion of your blessed martyr Leodegar, prompts us to come out in one voice in praise. And you, God, Father of all, who gives us forgiveness of sins, we ask: grant the oblivion of past sins, you who have given the crown to the martyrs after their victory.[189] Through our Lord. Who on the day [...]

---

[a] On the O-exclamations in a number of saints' Masses in the Gothic Missal, see Introduction, section Style and figures.

[b] Cf. *Passio Leudegarii I* 29, ed. KRUSCH and LEVISON, p. 310.

[c] *angelorum choro*: cf. *Passio Leudegarii I* 35, ed. KRUSCH and LEVISON, p. 317.

[d] In I Petr. 5, 4 the crown of glory (*gloriae*) is imperishable, while here the adjective *inmarciscibilibus* is linked to the flowers (*floribus*).

[e] A first transfer of relics is dated 384, to Poitiers, a fact mentioned in the *Passio Leudegarii I*. Cf. ROSE (ed.), *Missale Gothicum*, Introduction, p. 15 and 314.

[f] *pastorem*: the repeated qualification of Leodegar as a 'shepherd' brought Mohlberg to the conviction that the Mass was written in Autun itself as an eyewitness account: MOHLBERG (ed.), *Missale Gothicum. Das gallikanische Sakramentar*, p. 103; see further ROSE (ed.), *Missale Gothicum*, Introduction, p. 316.

431 AFTER THE CONSECRATION. We do this, O Lord, to com-   515
memorate your Passion, we do this, Father of Jesus Christ, who
has given us a new law instead of the old one.[a] Grant us, through
the intercession of your blessed bishop [and] martyr Leodegar,
whose annual commemoration we celebrate today, that this your
blessing descends upon this bread and this cup through the transformation of your Holy Spirit, that you bless these things by blessing them and sanctify them by sanctifying, so that all we who will
have partaken of both these blessings are deemed worthy to acquire the reward of eternity and everlasting life. Through.[b]

LXIIII MASS FOR A SINGLE MARTYR [I]

432 May this holy prayer of your holy martyr *N*, so we ask, O
Lord, which venerably shines through holy virtues, reconcile us.

433 COLLECT FOLLOWS. May the blessed martyr *N* commend us
through his faithful intercession, so we ask, O Lord, so that we,
strengthened by support that pleases you, acquire the forgiveness
we do not deserve. Through our Lord.

434 COLLECT AFTER THE NAMES. Hear, O Lord, our supplica-
tions.[190] Mercifully grant us perpetual mercy through the interces-   516
sion of your most blessed martyr *N* and graciously accept the gathered gifts, that they contribute to the consolation of the deceased
and the salvation of the living. Through.

435 COLLECT AT THE KISS OF PEACE. God, Creator of peace,
God, Giver[191] of love, mercifully grant us your peace, and grant
that while we celebrate the passion of your martyr *N*, through his

---

[a] Cf. Rom. 7, 6.

[b] Although Leodegar is the most recent saint in the Gothic Missal, and the
immolatio seems to betray a close relation between the author (and users?) of the
text and this martyr, the remainder of the Mass, particularly this post communion prayer, contains remarkably few specific elements referring to Leodegar and his
martyrdom; ROSE (ed.), *Missale Gothicum*, Introduction, p. 316.

intercession we are considered worthy to obtain the security of peace and forgiveness of sins. Through.

436 PRAYER OF SACRIFICE. It is worthy and just, truly worthy and just that we bring thanks to you, O Lord, holy Father, almighty and everlasting God. For you [this] solemn feast is held, for you [this] holy day is celebrated, which the blood of your blessed martyr N, shed as a testimony to your truth, has marked with the magnificent honour of your name. Through Christ our Lord, through whom.

LXV LIKEWISE A MASS FOR A SINGLE MARTYR [II]

437 May the glorious intervention of your holy martyr commend us, so we ask, O Lord, so that what we cannot attain through our deeds we may obtain through his prayers. Through.

517

438 COLLECT FOLLOWS. May your holy martyr N gladden us everywhere, so we ask, O Lord, so that while we remember his merits at today's feast we experience his protection in the growth of virtue.[192] Through.

439 COLLECT AFTER THE NAMES. May your holy martyr N intercede for us, so we ask, O Lord, who shed his blood for your glorious name, and may you command that through his intercession the names of our beloved that have been recited are announced in the heavenly Book. Through.

440 COLLECT AT THE KISS OF PEACE. Let the holy prayer of your holy martyr N protect us, so we ask, O Lord, and may that for which our conscience does not presume to hope be given to us through the prayer of him who pleased you. And look with serene love upon the gifts present here, that they may be imbued with the blessing of the Holy Spirit, and pour into our hearts that strong

love through which the holy martyr *N* entirely overcame all bodily torments. Through.

441 PRAYER OF SACRIFICE. It is worthy and just, truly worthy and just, almighty and merciful God, that [we] always honour you through the praise of the martyrs and that [we] bring thanks on the present feast of your holy martyr who confessed you, to whom you have given the palm of heavenly victory. Grant also to us, through his help, the cleansing and forgiveness of sin, that we too through [your] mercy exult in you in whom he rejoices in glory. Through.

LXVI LIKEWISE A MASS FOR A SINGLE MARTYR [III]

518

442 Grant, O Lord, so we ask, that we are gladdened by the annual solemn ceremony of your holy martyr *N*, so[193] that we make progress through an example of such great faith. Through.

443 COLLECT FOLLOWS. Hear our prayers, O Lord, so we ask, and through the intercession of your blessed martyr *N* mercifully admit them before the countenance of your majesty. Through.

444 COLLECT FOLLOWS.[a] May *the righteous prayer* (cf. Iac. 5, 16) of your holy martyr *N* accomplish help for your faithful, so we ask, O Lord, so that we are partakers of the lot of him to whose feast we are devoted. Let what we offer benefit the welfare of the living and the repose of the deceased. Through.

445 COLLECT AT THE KISS OF PEACE. Mercifully receive, O Lord, our prayer with the gifts of sacrifice placed upon [your altar.] Graciously make them acceptable to your love for the sake of the supplication of your martyr *N*, and mercifully instil in us that steadfast love that burned in him. Through.

---

[a] This prayer, entitled *collectio sequitur*, entails the common themes of a collect *post nomina*: recommendation of the gifts and prayer for the living and the dead.

519   446 PRAYER OF SACRIFICE. It is truly worthy and just, almighty and everlasting God, that [we] praise you in the triumph of all the martyrs, for through your gifts and presents we venerate with today's solemn celebration the passion of your blessed martyr *N*, who for the sake of the confession of Jesus Christ your Son endured various torments, and since he decisively defeated them he deserved the crown of eternity. Through Christ our Lord, to whom rightly all [angels sing: Holy...]

LXVII MASS FOR SEVERAL MARTYRS [I]

447 God, who sanctified for us today's solemn ceremony in commemoration of your most blessed martyrs through the passion of *N* and *N*, hear the prayers of your people, and grant that we are helped through the merits and intercessions of those whose feast we celebrate today. Through the Lord.

448 COLLECT FOLLOWS. Grant, so we ask, O Lord, [through the intercession] of your holy martyrs *N* and *N*, that they devote the help of their prayers to us, and through their intercession we evade your anger, which we deserve by reason of our errors. Through.

520   449 AFTER THE NAMES. Kindly accept the gifts we offer, O Lord, that we who are impeded by our offences are helped through the prayers of your holy martyrs *NN*.

450 COLLECT AT THE KISS OF PEACE. Be favourable, O Lord, to our prayers, and illuminate these oblations of your people with the presence of your strength through the intercession of your martyrs *N* and *N*. And to those who celebrate the memory of your [martyrs], give that love through which they decisively defeated all torments inflicted on the body. Through him.

451 PRAYER OF SACRIFICE. It is worthy and just, almighty and everlasting God, that [we] praise you as victor over death and conqueror in martyrdom, also on today's feast, on which we celebrate the memory of your martyrs *N* and *N*, of whom we gladly commemorate their steadfastness in combat and consider the reward of victory. And we therefore ask you that you grant us to become followers of your blessed martyrs *N* and *N*, and that you, who gave them eternal beatitude for their steadfastness in combat, decide to allow even those far remote[a] to participate in their reward. Through Christ our Lord, to whom rightly all [angels sing: Holy...]

LXVIII LIKEWISE A MASS FOR SEVERAL MARTYRS [II]

452 Hear our prayers, O Lord, which we offer in commemoration of your holy martyrs *N* and *N*, that we who have no trust in our [own] righteousness are helped by the merits of those who have pleased you. Through our Lord your Son.

521

453 COLLECT FOLLOWS. Be favourable, O Lord, to our prayers, and through the example of your holy martyrs *N* and *N* let the flame of your love be kindled in us, that on your command we are partakers of those of whom you have made us followers. Through.

454 COLLECT AFTER THE NAMES. May we be helped through the prayers of your holy martyrs *N* and *N*, so we ask, O Lord, so that what our ability [can]not obtain is given through the prayer of those who are considered righteous before your countenance. And may eternal rest embrace those whose names have been recited before the holy altar. Through our Lord.

[a] The word *ultimos* probably refers to those converted at a late moment, peoples far removed from the Christian community, and perhaps also to the most humble among the Christian community.

455 COLLECT AT THE KISS OF PEACE. Almighty and everlasting God, who ignites the flame of your love in the hearts of the saints, grant to [our] hearts[194] that same faith and power of love, so that we may benefit from the examples of those in whose triumphs we rejoice. Through.

456 PRAYER OF SACRIFICE. It is truly worthy and just that we bring thanks to you, almighty and everlasting God, through Christ our Lord, you who are glorified *in the assembly of your holy martyrs, great and awe-inspiring above all that are around you* (cf. Ps. 89, 7[a]). Indeed all your creatures serve you, for they recognise only you as Author and Lord, and in all their work all your saints praise and bless you:[195] they who by confessing with a free voice the great name of your Only-begotten, *that is above every name* (Phil. 2, 9), *in the presence of the kings* (Ps. 119, 46) and powers of this world, triumphed over their persecutors and over the devil, and through a glorious death shed their precious blood for you. We therefore bless you, O Lord, in your works, and through the commemoration of your holy martyrs *N* and *N* we praise you with the angels and archangels, *thrones* and *dominions* (Col. 1, 16), and with cherubim and seraphim,[b] who unceasingly cry out your glory, saying: HOLY, HOLY, HOLY.

522

LXVIIII LIKEWISE A MASS FOR SEVERAL MARTYRS [III]

457 God, you who give that we rejoice in the temporary commemoration of your holy martyrs, grant, so we ask, that we are counted saved among that part in which they abide, glorious by reason of the confession of your name. Through.

[a] Vulgate: Ps. 88, 8.
[b] Cf. no. 110.

458 COLLECT FOLLOWS. God, *before whose countenance the death of your saints is precious* (Ps. 116, 15ª), grant that what gave them a devoted death brings life to us, the faithful.

459 COLLECT AFTER THE NAMES. Hear, O Lord, the prayers of those who offer, accept their gifts, forgive their sins. And through the intercession of your holy martyrs, grant to our beloved who rest in Christ consolation *in the land of the living* (Ps. 116, 9ᵇ). Through our Lord.

523

460 COLLECT AT THE KISS OF PEACE. Almighty and everlasting God, grant to us your servants that, as your martyrs strove *for the prize*[196] *of the heavenly calling* (cf. Phil. 3, 14), so we also gain the victory after the enemy has been conquered, and that we preserve with unstained hearts the peace which we pursue with the lips of the mouth.[197] Through the Lord.

461 PRAYER OF SACRIFICE. It is worthy and just, almighty and everlasting God, [that we bring thanks to you], for faith derives steadfastness from you, weakness derives strength, and all that is cruel in the persecutions, all that is terrible in death, you make to be conquered by the confession of your name. We therefore bless you, O Lord, in your works, and praise you through the glorification of your holy martyrs *N* and *N*, imploring that you command them to intercede for [the faithful] who venerate those whom you elevate through the perpetual reward. Through Christ our Lord, through whom [...]

ª Vulgate: Ps. 115, 6 (and not 115, 15 as in ROSE (ed.), *Missale Gothicum*, p. 522).
ᵇ Vulgate: Ps. 114, 9.

LXX MASS FOR ONE CONFESSOR

462 God, Rewarder of the souls of the faithful, grant that through today's celebration of your holy confessor and bishop *N* the solemn ceremony is honoured by us, and that we obtain forgiveness through the prayers of those who have pleased you. Through our Lord.

524

463 COLLECT FOLLOWS. Hear our prayers, O Lord, which we offer in commemoration of your holy confessor *N*, that before your countenance he who worthily deserved to serve you is ever resplendent, and that *the prayer of the righteous* (cf. Iac. 5, 16), pleasing to you, supports us. Through.

464 COLLECT AFTER THE NAMES. Let the annually recurring feast of your holy confessor and bishop *N* gladden us with devotion, so we ask, O Lord, that through this service of devout oblation blessed reward accompanies him, and the satisfaction of holy service is given to us. Through.

465 COLLECT AT THE KISS OF PEACE. Protect your servants, so we ask, O Lord, through the zeal of sincere[a] love and through the intercession of your most blessed confessor and bishop *N*, and instruct us in spiritual teaching through the bond of love. Through.

466 PRAYER OF SACRIFICE. It is truly worthy and just that we always and everywhere bring thanks to you, O Lord, holy Father, almighty and everlasting God, who is glorified by the confession of the saints. For you extol not only the glorious merits of your martyrs with distinguished rewards, but you also kindly grant that they who accomplish sacred service with suitable servility,

525

enter [into] the joy of their Lord, so that he who has appeared *trustworthy in little* – in the small occurrence, therefore, of the present life – is certainly appointed *over many* good *things*

---

[a] *non fictae*: 'not feigned', litotes; see Introduction, section Style and figures.

(cf. Matth. 25, 21) in the blessedness that remains eternally.[a] Through Christ our Lord.

LXXI MASS FOR SEVERAL CONFESSORS

467 Protect us through *the prayer of your righteous ones* (cf. Iac. 5, 16), so we ask, O Lord, that we are encouraged through the help of those by whose support we are surrounded. Through.

468 COLLECT. May the holy *prayer of the righteous* (cf. Iac. 5, 16) sustain us, so we ask, O Lord, so that it makes us, not encumbered by earthly influences, long unceasingly for the heavenly things. Through.

469 AFTER THE NAMES. We bring you, O Lord, a *sacrifice of thanksgiving* (Ps. 50, 14; Ps. 50, 23; Ps. 107, 22) in commemoration of your venerable saints. Grant, so we ask, O Lord, that what contributed to their glory serves towards our salvation.[198] Through.

470 AT THE KISS OF PEACE. May the blessed confession of your 526 most blessed saints make the offerings of your servants agreeable, so we ask, O Lord, and may those things that through our merits are less appropriate become pleasing to you through *the prayer of your righteous ones* (cf. Iac. 5, 16). Through.

[a] The phrase is a free quotation of Matth. 25, 21 (cf. Luc. 19, 17). Where the Vulgate has *super pauca*, the present prayer (*in modico*) matches an Itala manuscript of the Vetus Latina; see Brepolis Vetus Latina database, fiche 5 at http://apps.brepolis.net.proxy.library.uu.nl/vld/index.html (consulted 28 September 2015). The same wording is already found in the ancient Latin translation of IRENAEUS OF LYONS, *Aduersus haereses* 4.11.2, ed. ROUSSEAU, SChr 100.2, p. 502 (the Latin translation is difficult to date: MOHRMANN, 'Origines de la latinité', p. 112) and in AUGUSTINE, e.g. *Enarrationes in Psalmos*, 115.1, ed. ELIGIUS DEKKERS and JEAN FRAIPONT, CCSL 40 (Turnhout: Brepols, 1966), p. 1653. The addition that interrupts the quotation here (*in modico, hoc est in paruo uitae praesentes excurso*) is perhaps inspired by GREGORY THE GREAT, *Homiliae in euangelia* 40, 1.9.2, ed. RAYMON ÉTAIX, CCSL 141 (Turnhout: Brepols, 1999), p. 60.

471 PRAYER OF SACRIFICE. It is worthy and just, indeed it is truly worthy and just [that we bring thanks to you, O Lord, holy Father, almighty and everlasting God], who, not only through the strength of your martyrs but also through that of your confessors, are marvellous. For although they are famous through their martyrdom, who endured in public the bitter punishments [and] torments, likewise [famous are] those who in secret, afflicted by the prospect of punishment [and] spiritually tortured[a] by obedience to the doctrine, have followed in their footsteps. Through Christ the Lord.

LXXII MASS FOR THE HOLY BISHOP MARTIN[b]

472 O Lord, grant us, who on this day celebrate the burial[c] of your most high priest,[d] our father[e] bishop Martin, that as we most devotedly celebrate his commemoration, we likewise faithfully follow his work. Through.

---

[a] The notion of torture itself becomes spiritualised. See no. 33.

[b] Although the Mass of Martin is probably inserted as a separate *libellus*, it does not occur at a random position in the Gothic Missal but at the end of the Masses for confessors, for whom Martin was the model. See on this Mass, ROSE (ed.), *Missale Gothicum*, Introduction, p. 316–324, and on its position in the codex, p. 21–22.

[c] *deposicione*: Martin died in Candes, a village in the diocese of Tours, on 8 November. His body was taken to Tours, where his burial took place on 11 November, from then on commemorated as Martin's *natale*, see ROSE (ed.), *Missale Gothicum*, Introduction, p. 319–320 and 321, and Introduction, section The liturgical year.

[d] *sacerdos* signifies both 'priest' and 'bishop' (see no. 232). The combination with *summus*, echoing the biblical high priest, e.g. Marc. 14, 53; Marc. 15, 31; cf. BLAISE, *Dictionnaire*, s.v. *sacerdos* (4c), is equally ambivalent, because ever since Tertullian the term *summus sacerdos* has been used to distinguish a bishop from his *presbyteri*, i.e. rank and file priests: BLAISE, *Dictionnaire*, s.v. *sacerdos* (6) with reference to TERTULLIAN, *De baptismo* 17. Jacques Fontaine translates SULPICIUS SEVERUS, *Vita Martini* 26.5 in an abstract manner: 'ayant la plénitude du sacerdoce'; ed. FONTAINE, SChr 133, p. 314. I translate it here as 'priest' to avoid redoubling *episcopi*, also included in the enumeration.

[e] *patris nostri*: this address suggests a community with a specific veneration of Martin of Tours, perhaps Poitiers?

473 COLLECT. God, who has deigned to give us today's holy celebration by reason of the burial of your praiseworthy and venerable priest and bishop Martin, grant, so we ask, that what we cannot obtain through our prayers, we are deemed worthy to acquire through his intercession.[a] Through.

474 AFTER THE NAMES. Now that the names of those who offer have been heard, let us humbly pray to the ineffable mercy of almighty God, most beloved brothers, that he deigns to bless and sanctify the names of us, who on this celebrated day bring the offering in honour of his holy bishop Martin, because he helps us, and that what has been gathered today to [his] honour also serves to our salvation.[b] Through.

527

475 AT THE KISS OF PEACE. Incline, O Lord, your ear to the prayers of your people and give that peace which, according to your command, is enduring, [and] may you also deign to give this in particular, that we keep that same love[c] which, through your help, your bishop Martin deserved to obtain in this world. Through.

476 PRAYER OF SACRIFICE.[d] It is worthy and just, O Lord our God, that we honour you in hymns of praise for the holy Martin.

---

[a] Paraphrase of SULPICIUS SEVERUS, *Epistola* II.18, ed. FONTAINE, SChr 133, p. 332–334.

[b] See also no. 469 for a similar but subtly different closing sentence.

[c] Here the word *caritas* indicates, in a technical sense, the act of charity for which Martin became famous: he shared his cloak with the poor man. This is generally described in French as 'La charité de Saint Martin', a term also used to designate visual depictions of this scene from SULPICIUS SEVERUS, *Vita Martini*, 3.1–3, ed. FONTAINE, SChr 133, p. 256–258. The word *caritas* itself occurs only twice in Sulpicius's *Vita*: c. 2.7, to describe Martin's general attitude towards his fellow soldiers, and c. 26.5, to describe his love as a bishop towards his clergy.

[d] On the style and structure of this prayer in relation to similar prayers in the Gothic Missal, see Introduction, section Style and figures.

For already when he was a catechumen,[a] set on fire by the gift of your Holy Spirit, he was so perfect that he clothed Christ in the poor, and that the Lord of the world put on the garment that the poor man had received.[b] O blessed bounty with which God[c] was clothed. O glorious division of the cloak[199] that has clothed a soldier and a king. To clothe the God of the godhead[200] is an inestimable gift that he has deserved. Rightly have you entrusted him with the reward of the confession of your [name.][201] Rightly was he not subjected to the savagery of the Arians.[d] Rightly, confident through such great love, Martin did not fear the torments of the persecutor, for the glory of his martyrdom[e] was so great that, with the small size of his cloak, he merited not only to clothe God but also to behold [him.][f] O imitable generosity of spirit. O venerable strength of virtues. He so carried out the office of the episcopate which he had accepted,[g] that through the model of his commendable life he enforced obedience to doctrine. Through his apostolic strength[h] he has granted a medicine to those who believed, such that he saved some through his prayers and others through his ap-

528

---

[a] The word *tirocinium* has a military background and is particularly fitting for Martin, who converted to Christianity from a life as a soldier and was baptised while still in military service. It was already in use early on in Christian Latin to indicate the period of the catechumenate which preceded the Baptism of an adult, e.g. in TERTULLIAN, *De paenitentia*: BLAISE, *Dictionnaire*, s.v. *tirocinium*.

[b] Reference to SULPICIUS SEVERUS, *Vita Martini* 3.3, ed. FONTAINE, SChr 133, p. 258, where after the division of the cloak Christ appears in a dream vision to Martin clothed in the latter's mantle. The story echoes Matth. 25, 31–46, the Works of Mercy, of which vs. 40 is quoted in c. 3.4.

[c] The more abstract *diuinitas* is used here, which is characteristic of poetic language, see Introduction, section Style and figures.

[d] SULPICIUS SEVERUS, *Vita Martini* 6.4–7.

[e] Martin is the first saint-not-martyr to be honoured with a hagiographic narrative and a proper feast day. The prayer clearly addresses him as equal to the martyrs, even if martyrdom itself was not granted to him. On this topic see no. 33 and ROSE (ed.), *Missale Gothicum*, Introduction, p. 323.

[f] Another reference to Martin's dream vision according to SULPICIUS SEVERUS, *Vita Martini* 3.3, in which he 'saw Christ' (*uidit Christum*); ed. FONTAINE, SChr, p. 258.

[g] Sulpicius Severus describes Martin's episcopacy in *Vita Martini* 10, ed. FONTAINE, SChr 133, p. 272–274.

[h] Cf. SULPICIUS SEVERUS, *Vita Martini* 20.1, ed. FONTAINE, SChr 133, p. 294.

pearance.[a] May we be deemed worthy, O Lord, through this your venerable strength to which the tongue, with its merits, does not suffice to pray, to imitate with your help the works of the holy Martin. Through Christ our Lord.

LXXIII SUNDAY MASS [I]

477 God, who manifests your omnipotence to us particularly by sparing and pitying, multiply your grace over us, that you make [us], hastening to your promises, partakers of the heavenly things. Through.

478 COLLECT. Almighty and everlasting God, who has the power to be endlessly merciful, look graciously upon the meek servility of our humility, so that the perpetual help of your defence saves the souls subjected to you. Through.

479 AFTER THE NAMES. We pray, O Lord, that you grant a place of consolation, light and peace to these [names][b] and all who rest in Christ. And if some are bound by the burden of sins, the darkness and punishments of hell,[c] grant to [them] the grace of your mercy, so we ask. And may you command them to pass over to rest, and may you order them to be united *in the first resurrection* (Apoc. 20, 5–6) with your saints and the elect, *so that they are your portion in the land of the living* (cf. Ps. 142, 5[d]). Through.

529

---

[a] Sulpicius Severus describes Martin's healing powers in *Vita Martini* 16–19, ed. FONTAINE, SChr 133, p. 286–294 and in his *Dialogi* II.4 and III.6–9, ed. CHARLES HALM, CSEL 1, p. 185, p. 203–207. It is remarkable that the prayers do not refer to Martin's ability to bring the dead back to life, as described in SULPICIUS SEVERUS, *Vita Martini* 7–8, ed. FONTAINE, SChr 133, p. 266–270.

[b] On the ritual of the names, see Introduction, section The prayers of Mass.

[c] The 'burden of sin' is linked without conjunction to the 'darkness and punishments of hell': an asyndeton to make the effect even starker; see Introduction, section Style and figures.

[d] Vulgate: Ps. 141, 6.

480 AT THE KISS OF PEACE. God, for whom the greatest sacrifice is a concordant soul, for whom the most pleasing[a] burnt offering is a peaceful and pure conscience, grant us, so we ask, that the union of lips brings about the bond of souls, and that the service of the kiss of peace contributes to perpetual love.[202] Through.

481 PRAYER OF SACRIFICE. It is worthy and just that we bring thanks to you, O Lord, holy Father, almighty and everlasting God, that we bring due praise with devout honour to you, and celebrate the inexpressible exultation of your wondrous deeds with the veneration of a devoted heart. Therefore we praise, we bless, we worship you,[b] the ineffable Creator of all things. Through Christ our Lord.

482 AFTER THE SANCTUS. Truly holy, truly blessed [is] our Lord Jesus Christ your Son, who has come from heaven to dwell on earth, has become man to live among us, was made a sacrifice to make us priests. For he who on the day before [...]

530   483 AFTER THE CONSECRATION. Show [us] grace, almighty God, teach [us] your doctrine, [for] you are the sacred teaching[203] that brings us salvation, you are the ransom. Teach us perseverance where you have taught us doctrine, so that you deliver us through this oblation, you who also die for mortals. Through.

484 BEFORE THE LORD'S PRAYER. We cannot give sufficient thanks to you, O Lord, holy Father, almighty and everlasting God, for such great gifts of your mercy, through which you vivify us, sanctify us, prepare us for eternity.[c] Moreover you give us,

---

[a] On the word *pinguis* connected with offerings, see no. 291. Dan. 3, 40 (Vulgate division) and Am. 5, 22 use the word in combination with *holocaustum*. The entire prayer brings to mind Ps. 51 (50), which emphasises the preference for spiritual offerings over material oblations.

[b] *laudamus, benedicimus, adoramus*: asyndeton; see Introduction, section Style and figures.

[c] *nos uiuificas, sanctificas, aeternitates praeparas*: asyndeton; see Introduction, section Style and figures.

through the institutions of your only-begotten Jesus Christ our Lord and Saviour, the grace of your love to pray even for what we do not deserve. Therefore, mindful of his teachings, let us say: [Our] Father.

485 after the lord's prayer. Deliver us from all evil, almighty God, and since only you have the power to do this, grant that this solemn sacrifice sanctifies our hearts while in it we believe, [and] blots out our sins while of it we partake. Through.

486 after the eucharist. Fed by the bread of life and drenched by the cup of salvation, most beloved brothers, let us bring thanks to the almighty God our Father, while we implore his mercy, that he deigns to preserve in us for ever this holy gift of his blessing, unblemished and unviolated, which we have received in honour of his name. Through.

487 completion of mass. Refreshed by the body and blood of our Lord Jesus Christ [and] restored to eternal [life],[204] let us gladly pray for the mercy of the Lord. Through.

531

LXXIIII LIKEWISE A SUNDAY MASS [II]

488 Almighty God, lead us in the way of justice, that we do these things and consider those that we can justify before you on the day of judgement. Through.

489 collect. We humbly pray for the immeasurable and awe-inspiring grace of your love, almighty God, that through your help all temptations of earthly sins and worldly dangers depart from us, and that in your catholic Church the devotion to faith remains unimpaired. Through.

490 after the names. Now that we have heard the enumeration[205] of the names, most beloved brothers, let us pray to the God

of love and mercy, that he graciously receives what has been offered, [and that] he does not allow that one of those for whom the offerings are broken is ever excluded[a] from his gift, and that as he considers the merits as well as the sins of the living and the dead, he commands that the last pertain to grace, the first to forgiveness. Through.

532

491 AT THE KISS OF PEACE. Sink into our hearts, almighty and everlasting God, and enter into the temples that *this cornerstone* (cf. Ps. 118, 22) has built, that through him we can bring the offerings prepared for your majesty to you who has created the holy and has mercifully granted us peace. Through.

492 PRAYER OF SACRIFICE. It is worthy and just that [we] with devout honour bring praise to your majesty, holy Father, almighty and everlasting God, and that we celebrate the inexpressible exultation of your wondrous deeds with the veneration of a devoted heart. For you, the incomprehensible and ineffable Lord and Creator of all things, who is always to be feared, [you] we perceive, believe, follow and worship through Jesus Christ your Son, our God and Lord and Saviour. To you we offer this pure sacrifice of your glory while we honour you with our hymns of praise, together with the angels and archangels and the innumerable multitude of divine messengers,[b] who in the sight of your majesty praise you without ceasing, saying [Holy, holy, holy...][206]

493 AFTER THE SANCTUS. Truly holy, truly in the highest, our Lord God, your Son, the King of Israel. Who on the day before [...]

---

[a] The Latin word used (*exterus*) may signify 'outside the Church', thus in the work of CYPRIAN, *Epistula* 67.6.2, ed. GERARDUS F. DIERCKS, *Sancti Cypriani episcopi epistularium*, CCSL 3C (Turnhout: Brepols, 1996), p. 446–462, at p. 456–457; cf. BLAISE, *Dictionnaire*, s.v. *exterus*; SOUTER, *Glossary*, s.v. *exterus*.

[b] The word *nuntius* for angel is rare and occurs primarily in the work of Christian poets, e.g. Lactantius, Prudentius, as well as in the early Spanish liturgy, see BLAISE, *Dictionnaire*, s.v. *nuntius*; BLAISE, *Vocabulaire*, p. 235 (section 112); see also no. 205 and Introduction, section Style and figures.

494 AFTER THE CONSECRATION. Through this we pray to you, O God, almighty Father, that as we preserve obedience to the holy mystery, so heavenly strength serves[207] to our defence. Through.

495 BEFORE THE LORD'S PRAYER. Grant, O Lord, to your servants that when we pray we speak with confidence, as you deigned to command us to speak: [OUR] FATHER.

496 AFTER THE LORD'S PRAYER. Deliver us from evil, almighty God, and keep us in that which is good, you who lives and reigns.

533

497 AFTER THE EUCHARIST. Now that we have received the sacrament of the heavenly body and are revived by the cup of eternal salvation, let us bring thanks and sing our praises to God the almighty Father. Through.

498 COMPLETION OF MASS. We bring thanks to you, O God, through whom we celebrate the holy mysteries, from you we beseech gifts of sanctity and mercy.[208] Through the Lord.

LXXV LIKEWISE A SUNDAY MASS [III]

499 [PREFACE.] Let us pray, most beloved brothers, to the eternal majesty of God, that he protects the holy Church through the expanse of the entire world, that he grants priests[209] an upright walk of life, that he gives eternal life to the [Christian] people,[210] that he gives suitable protection to virgins, widows, orphans and penitents and to all who are in whatever needs, and that he hears prayers that are pleasing to him, that he gives reward to travellers,[a] relief in needs, help in troubles. Through our Lord Jesus Christ his Son, who always lives and reigns with him, God in the unity of the Holy Spirit, for ever and ever.

[a] *perigrinacionibus*: see no 238.

534   500 COLLECT. God, you who are *rich in forgiveness* (Is. 55, 7) and therefore have willed to assume the humility of the flesh in order to leave us examples of humility and make us steadfast in whatever suffering, grant that we always keep the good things that we have received from you, that whenever we fall into sin we are lifted up by penitence. Through our Lord Jesus Christ your Son, who always lives and reigns with you, God in the unity of the Holy Spirit for ever and ever.

501 AFTER THE NAMES. Now that the names of those who offer have been enumerated,[211] let us pray for the mercy of God, that he makes those who offer to be pleasing to him and that he receives the [oblations] that they offer, sweet-smelling in a fragrance of incense. May he give eternal beatitude to the deceased, for whom these [oblations] are offered, [and] the grace of his love to the living. And because he does not cease to give them freely what is necessary, although they do not deserve it, may the reward of beatitude also be given[a] to them for whom this oblation is not offered. Through our Lord.

502 AT THE KISS OF PEACE. God, almighty Father, even if we are not worthy we pray for the mercy of your love, that you make peace-loving all who you invite to pray to you in the holy Church. May they feed one another with the food of concord and may they cut off the growth of disputes, and may those who approach one another with kisses, embrace [one another] with an ever pure heart, and may even those of whom it is not seen that they kiss one another with the lips, strive to be peace-loving. Through.

535   503 PRAYER OF SACRIFICE. It is worthy and just, truly fair and just, ineffable, incomprehensible, eternal[b] God, that we always bring thanks to you who unceasingly cherishes us in your immeasurable mercy. For who can worthily praise your power,

---

[a] *non negetur*: litotes; see Introduction, section Style and figures.
[b] *ineffabilis, inconpraehensibilis, sempiterne*: asyndeton; see Introduction, section Style and figures.

whose divinity is not seen through a mortal gaze and whose greatness is not explained in words? It therefore suffices that we love you as Father, venerate you as Lord, recognise you as Creator, embrace you as Redeemer.[a] Grant, most merciful Ruler, that we can climb the way of the narrow path that you command,[b] so that we can reach everlasting beatitude, and that we are not restrained by any obstacles, but that to us the course of that path is salutary eternity. Through Christ our Lord, through whom [your] majesty [...]

504 AFTER THE SANCTUS. Truly holy, truly blessed in the highest, O Lord our God, Jesus Christ your Son, King of Israel, who, *led as a sheep to the slaughter and as a lamb silent before its shearer, so did not open his mouth* (Is. 53, 7; Act. 8, 32). For he who on the day before [...]

505 AFTER THE CONSECRATION. Great is this gift of mercy, which has taught us to celebrate the sacrifices of our redemption, as our Lord Jesus Christ offered [himself] on earth. And through him we pray to you, almighty Father, that you behold with gladness the gifts placed on your altar, and that you overshadow all this with the Spirit of your holy Son, so that what we have received from this your blessing, we may obtain in the glory of eternity. Through.

506 BEFORE THE LORD'S PRAYER. Mindful of your teaching, O Lord, we pray and say [Our Father...]

536

507 AFTER THE LORD'S PRAYER. Deliver us from evil, Author of all good things, God, deliver us from all temptation, from all offence, from all heresy, from all work of darkness, and establish us in all good work and grant peace in our days, Author of peace and God of truth. Through.

---

[a] *diligimus, ueneramur, suscipimus, amplectimur*: asyndeton; see Introduction, section Style and figures.

[b] *angusti callis ... semitam* echoes Matth. 7, 13–14.

508 AFTER THE EUCHARIST. Fed by the spiritual banquet, let us pray to the Father and the Son and the Holy Spirit that when the desires of the flesh have been mortified our way of life is in all things spiritual. Through.

509 COMPLETION OF MASS. Preserve among us, O Lord, the gift of your glory, that we are safeguarded against all stains of the present world through the powers of the Eucharist which we have received. And may you deign to grant this.

LXXVI LIKEWISE A SUNDAY MASS [IIII]

510 God, let the voice of our supplication rise up to the ears of your grace, and let your mercy come to us. Through.

537   511 COLLECT. May the offering of our devotion, O Lord, be acceptable to you, that it absolves us from our sins and rescues us from imminent evil. Through.

512 AFTER THE NAMES. The faithful offer gifts and prayers to you, O Lord of hosts. Accept the marks of homage indebted to your name for the peace of your Church, for the commemoration of all the saints, for the purity of priests[212] and servants, for peace[213] among kings, for the abundance of [good] things and for tranquil times, for the perseverance of virgins and the chastity of widows, for the protection of orphans and the alleviation of penitents, for the salvation of all the living and for the rest of the deceased. Through.

513 AT THE KISS OF PEACE. Tear us away from all iniquity, almighty God, and make us rejoice in your peace. Through.

514 PRAYER OF SACRIFICE. It is worthy and just [that we bring thanks to you], invisible, inestimable, immeasurable[a] God and Father of our Lord Jesus Christ, who, by taking on the form of an

---

[a] *inuisibilis, inaestimabilis, inmensae*: asyndeton.

enduring sacrifice, offered himself as the first to you as a sacrificial lamb and as the first taught to be sacrificed.[a] You indeed, almighty God, all the angels [praise...]

515 AFTER THE SANCTUS. Holy among holies, blessed on earth, our Lord Jesus Christ, who on the day before [...]

516 AFTER THE CONSECRATION. We believe, O Lord, we believe   538
to be redeemed in the breaking of this body and in the shedding of your blood. We also trust that we are deemed worthy to fully enjoy in eternity, through hope, what we hold here for the time being. Through.

517 BEFORE THE LORD'S PRAYER. Instructed in divine doctrine and taught through salutary admonishment, we dare to say: [Our] FATHER.

518 AFTER THE LORD'S PRAYER. Deliver us, almighty God, from evil and establish us in what is good, empty us of sins and fill us with your virtues. Through.

519 AFTER THE EUCHARIST. May your body, O Lord, which we have received, and your cup which we have drunk, adhere to our body,[b] [and] grant, almighty God, that no stain remains where pure and holy sacraments have entered. Through.

520 COMPLETION OF MASS. Hear the prayers of your servants, almighty God, and grant that by your grace we preserve unspoiled in us these holy gifts which we have received by your grace.

[a] *qui ... hostiam se tibi primum obtulit et primus docuit offerri*: on this formula and its relation to CYPRIAN, *Epistula* 63.14, see SMYTH, *Liturgie oubliée*, p. 402–406.

[b] *in uisceribus nostris*: here again the purity of the sacrament, which is *medicina mentis et corporis*, seems to concern the body.

539 ## LXXVII LIKEWISE A SUNDAY MASS [V]

521 God, you who keep us by ruling us, justify us by sparing us: rescue us from temporary tribulation and generously grant us eternal joys. Through.

522 COLLECT. God, merciful Teacher of those who seek refuge in you, release us from all fellowship of evil, and may you not allow that we are bound by any bond of iniquity, so that whence is full love for us, thence is also freedom without danger.[214] Through our Lord.

523 AFTER THE NAMES. Hear, O Lord, the prayers of those who offer, accept their gifts, forgive their sins. And through the intercession of your saints, grant also to our beloved who rest in Christ, consolation *in the land of the living* (Ps. 116, 9[a]). Through.

524 AT THE KISS OF PEACE. Almighty and everlasting God, benign Giver of peace and Creator of the human race, grant to your servants the true will to concord and pour [into them] the grace of your love. Through.

525 PRAYER OF SACRIFICE. It is worthy and just, fair and just that we here and everywhere always bring thanks to you, O Lord, holy Father, almighty and everlasting God. For through your love 540 you are a Father for us, while through your power you remain our Lord, for you deigned *to adopt as children* (Rom. 8, 15) those whom their origin had made slaves,[b] and heavenly rebirth raised up to life those whom their earthly birth had plunged into death. You indeed, almighty God, all angels [praise, singing: Holy...]

526 AFTER THE SANCTUS. Truly holy, truly blessed in the highest, O Lord our God, through whom we humbly pray that you look mercifully upon this oblation which we offer to you for the faith, stability and concord of your catholic Church, for the cleans-

[a] Vulgate: Ps. 114, 9.
[b] Cf. Rom. 8, 15; Rom. 8, 21; Gal. 5, 1.

ing of vices and remission of sins, for the glory of the martyrs and the rest of the deceased, that by looking upon it you sanctify it, by sanctifying it you bless it[a] through the holy and blessed Jesus Christ, your Son our Lord, who on the day before […]

527 AFTER THE CONSECRATION.[b] Mindful of the suffering of our most glorious Lord and of his resurrection from hell, we bring you, O Lord, this immaculate sacrifice, this rational sacrifice, this bloodless sacrifice, this holy bread and this cup of salvation, praying that you deign to pour out your Holy Spirit in us while we eat and drink in order to approach eternal life and the everlasting kingdom. Through.

528 BEFORE THE LORD'S PRAYER. Not by reason of our merits, almighty God, but obedient to the command of Jesus Christ your Son, we dare to say: [OUR] FATHER.

529 AFTER THE LORD'S PRAYER. Deliver us from present and future evil, almighty God, deliver us from perils, from infirmities, from the snares of sin, and prepare us for all that is good. Through our good and blessed Lord. 541

530 AFTER THE EUCHARIST. Let us entreat in harmonious prayer the mercy of God, that these salutary sacraments, received by our bodies,[c] purify our soul and sanctify our body, and confirm [our] body[d] and soul equally in the hope of heavenly things. Through.

---

[a] *uti hanc oblacionem […] aspicias, aspiciendo sanctifices, sanctificando benedicas*: asyndeton.

[b] The prayer is similar (with some minor changes) to AMBROSE, *De sacramentis* 4.6.27, ed. FALLER, p. 57; see SMYTH, *Liturgie oubliée*, p. 41 and 43. The idea of 'bloodless sacrifice' already appears in ORIGEN, *Contra Celsum* 1.15, 17, 13, ed. PAUL KOETSCHAU, GCS Origenes 1 (Leipzig, 1899), vol. 1, p. 144, 147, 142; cf. JOHN VAN ENGEN, 'Christening the Romans', *Traditio* 52 (1997), 1–45, at p. 9, footnote 35.

[c] *uisceribus*: interpreted physically as the receiver of the physical elements of the Eucharist.

[d] *uiscera*: interpreted physically in view of the all-embracing (body and soul) salvation of the Eucharist.

531 LIKEWISE A COLLECT. God of justice, God of mercy, God of immortality and life, God of splendour and glory, we ask you and we pray that, revived by divine gifts, we are preserved to this beatitude by you [and] for you. Through.

LXXVIII LIKEWISE A SUNDAY MASS [VI]

532 [PREFACE.] Most beloved brothers, entangled in numerous bonds of sins, let us take refuge in the singular remedy of divine absolution, and through [this] sacrifice let us humbly pray to the Lord, who we daily embitter through our bad deeds, that, rescued from all contagion by the protection of his right hand, he makes us heirs of the heavenly kingdom. Through.

533 COLLECT. Incline your ear, almighty God, and be for us the Ruler of the present life, so that you be the Giver of the future [life.] Through.

542

534 AFTER THE NAMES. Now that the names of those who offer have been enumerated,[215] let us pray to the Lord, most beloved brothers, that he accepts their offering among the gifts of the saints, whose commemoration must be held by us, so that they deign to be mindful also of us. Let us also pray for those who have gone before us in the peace of the Lord, that the Almighty deigns to raise them from the dead, separated from the horror of hell [and] placed *in the bosom of Abraham* (Luc. 16, 23), *to their first resurrection* (cf. Apoc. 20, 5–6), which he will bring about. Through.

535 AT THE KISS OF PEACE. God, through whose mouth was made known that you gave peace to all and *left* the statutes of *peace* (cf. Ioh. 14, 27),[a] pour into our hearts zeal for peace and goodwill,[216] so that we, purged of the blemish of all sin, may with unstained hearts preserve the peace which we pursue with lips and mouth. Through.

---

[a] *pacis statuta*: see no 295.

536 PRAYER OF SACRIFICE. It is worthy and just, fair and just that we here and everywhere always bring thanks to you, O Lord, holy Father, almighty and everlasting God, who delivered us from perpetual death and from the furthest seats of hell. Death had come indeed through a woman, but life has come through a virgin, downfall indeed through a tree, but salvation through the tree [of the Cross].ª In Jesus Christ, who restored the eternity of his life to the body, death was brought to an end. With multitudinous virtue all the militias of the heavens sing due hymns of praise to him, and they sing of your glory while they proclaim unceasingly, saying [Holy, holy, holy…]

537 AFTER THE SANCTUS. *Hosanna in the highest, blessed is he who has come* (Matth. 21, 9) from heaven to abide on earth, who has become flesh in order to give his life to the faithful through his Passion. For he who on the day before […] 543

538 AFTER THE CONSECRATION. Now that we fulfil with oblations the most holy solemnities of the solemn rites according to the order of the high priest Melchisedek, we pray with a devout heart to you, eternal majesty,[217] that through the working of your strength we collect in the cup the bread, changed into flesh, and the wine, changed into blood, that flowed from you on the cross, from your side. Saviour.

539 BEFORE THE LORD'S PRAYER. Acknowledge, O Lord, the words that you have instructed and forgive the presumption that you have commanded. For it is ignorance not to recognise fault and obstinacy not to obey the command, through which we are instructed to say [Our Father…]

ª *interitus per lignum, sed in ligno salus*: the first *lignum* refers to the 'tree' in paradise, while the second indicates the 'wood' of the cross, which is assumed to be made of the tree of paradise; see no. 317. Ambrose is more explicit: *mors per arborem, vita per crucem*; AMBROSE, *Expositio euangelii secundum Lucam* 4.7, ed. ADRIAEN, CCSL 14 (Turnhout: Brepols, 1957), p. 108. For the parallel between Eve and Mary in Irenaeus, see no. 98.

540 AFTER THE LORD'S PRAYER. Deliver us from evil, O Lord Christ Jesus. We eat your body which was crucified for us and we drink your holy blood which was shed for us. May your holy body be to our salvation and your holy blood to the remission of sins, here and for ever and ever in eternity.

544

541 AFTER THE EUCHARIST. Let us bring thanks to almighty God, for he has restored us with heavenly bread and spiritual drink, while on the grounds of his benign mercy we hope that, through the outpouring of his Holy Spirit, the grace of sincerity continues in those in whom the strength of heavenly food has entered. Through.

542 COMPLETION OF MASS. We bring thanks to you, O God, through whom we celebrate the holy mysteries, and we pray to you for gifts of sanctity and purity through the grace of your Holy Spirit. Through the Lord.

LXXVIIII ROMAN DAILY MASS

543. God, who is offended by sin and appeased by penitence, look upon the lament of the afflicted, and mercifully avert from us the evil which you rightly inflict on us. Through.[a]

---

[a] The first prayer of this incomplete Mass is also found in the *Missa cotidiana Romensis* in the Bobbio Missal, a Mass that also includes the *canon missae*. This confirms the assumption that the *canon missae* was also present in the Gothic Missal before it was mutilated; see no. 342.

NOTES TO THE TRANSLATION

1. The word *commercium*, often used in the plural, refers to the exchange of gifts in the ritual of the Eucharist. The faithful bring their offerings as the gifts of that which they have received from God, and offer them to be consecrated and given back to them as the body and blood of Christ. See ROSE (ed.), *Missale Gothicum*, Introduction, p. 156.

2. *nostra substantia*: the word *substantia* has a range of meanings in the prayers. It may usually be read as 'being, nature' (3, 162, 161, 307) but refers once to 'richness, property, wealth' (236). Its use in the *Exultet* (225) is multilayered and commented on there. Here, it refers to the mortal being (nature) of humankind, while their participation in the Eucharist allows them to share in the *forma* (body) of Christ. The translation is based on BLAISE, *Dictionnaire*, s.v *forma* (4): 'que nous nous trouvions à la ressemblance de celui en qui notre nature vous est unie'.

3. *spiritibus*: a variety of words refer to the (immortal) soul of humans; *spiritus*, but also *uiscera, mens, anima, animus*, while the latter terms refer in other contexts to 'heart' or 'mind'.

4. *litteris ... caelestibus*: The Book of Life, in which the names of the elect are inscribed, is denoted with a variety of terms in the Gothic Missal, of which *caelestis* or *aeternalis pagina* (both singular and plural) and *liber uitae* are the most frequent. The use of *litterae* in the sense of 'written document', 'record', or even 'account book' (LEWIS and SHORT, *Latin Dictionary*, s.v. *littera*, 2, 3 and 5) is unique to this sacramentary. See also nos 177, 182, 294, 391, 427, 439 and Introduction, section The prayers of Mass.

5. *collectio ad pacem*: *pax* becomes a technical reference to the kiss of peace (*osculum pacis*) and was already used as such – without *osculum* – in the third century; see BLAISE, *Dictionnaire*, s.v. *pax* (11).

6. *immolatio missae*: the title literally signifies 'sacrifice of Mass' but is translated throughout as 'prayer of sacrifice' and as a synonym for *contestatio*. For a discussion of this choice and the semantic distinction between *immolatio* and *contestatio*, see Introduction, section The prayers of Mass.

7. *pietas* has a variety of meanings, usually including goodness, piety and love, but often singling out one in particular. In some cases the word plays with the combination of love and piety (e.g. no. 414).

8. *familiam*: the assembly of faithful is referred to by words with a variety of backgrounds and political and social connotations: familial (*familia*), ethnic (*plebs, populus*), concerning citizenship (*ecclesia*). On *familia*, see ROSE (ed.), *Missale Gothicum*, Introduction, p. 135.

9. The collect following the Institution narrative is entitled either *Collectio post mysterium* or *post secreta*. Both titles are translated here as 'Collect after the Consecration'; see Introduction, section The prayers of Mass.

10. The sentence contains two subjects: 'this your people' with the accompanying participle (*hic populus ... ambulans*), and the subject (second person singular) of the verb 'pour over' (*infundas*); this example of a nominativus absolutus (or anacoluthon) is discussed in ROSE (ed.), *Missale Gothicum*, Introduction, p. 97.

11. *plebem*: the Latin synonyms *plebs* and *populus* are both translated as 'people'; see ROSE (ed.), *Missale Gothicum*, Introduction, p. 141.

12. *populum*, indicating the faithful, is singular, while the relative pronoun (*quorum*) is in the plural but *animus* is again in the singular. I chose to adapt this to more regular English usage.

13. *uotis*: the word can refer to prayers as well as vows (no. 41); ROSE (ed.), *Missale Gothicum*, Introduction, p. 148.

14. The manuscript gives *nter*, read here as *dignanter*, see ROSE (ed.), *Missale Gothicum*, p. 358.

15. Both the relative pronoun and the corresponding participle (*qui ... ingressus*) and 'the world' (*mundus*) are nominative (subject); see the proposed alteration *quem ... ingressum, mundus* in ROSE (ed.), *Missale Gothicum*, p. 358, following Mohlberg's edition.

16. *mentis*: see note 3.

17. On the word *indultor* in the context of this prayer (and similarly nos 377 and 435), see BLAISE, *Dictionnaire*, s.v. *indultor* (1) and (3) and ROSE (ed.), *Missale Gothicum*, Introduction, p. 109.

18. The word *munerator* occurs only in the Gothic Missal, see ROSE (ed.), *Missale Gothicum*, Introduction, p. 122.

19. On the word *contestatio*, see note 6 and Introduction, section The prayers of Mass.

20. For this specific meaning of *sollemnitas*, see SOUTER, s.v. *sollemnitas*, who refers to CYPRIAN, *Epistula* 56.3.

21. *sollemnia* (also in the singular) can, without the genitive *missarum*, also refer to the sacrifice of Mass. See BLAISE, *Dictionnaire*, s.v. *sollemne*.

22. The word *amator* means 'lover' or 'friend'.

23. *Accedat ad te uox illa intercedens pro populo, pro inimicis quae orabat in ipso martyrio*: the structure is not entirely clear. Two versions of this prayer occur throughout the Latin sacramentaries: one with the relative pronoun *quae*, referring to *vox* as here in the Gothic Missal, and one with a masculine relative pronoun: *Accedat ad te vox illa intercedens pro populo, qui pro inimicis orabat in ipso martyrio* (thus the sacramentaries of Gellone, 2064, and Angoulême, 1810). In the latter version, *intercedens pro populo*, if it refers to Stephen, seems to be a nominative cum participle construction. Perhaps what is meant is *Accedat ad te vox illa intercedentis pro populo, qui pro inimicis orabat in ipso martyrio*: 'May this voice of him, who in martyrdom itself prayed for his enemies, reach you'.

24. *uota*: see note 13.

25. *quoniam in te uiuimus omnia opera tua et in factura eorum te conlaudant et benedicunt omnes sancti tui*: see also no. 456, where the Latin is equally confusing. In the first place, the meaning of *factura* is unclear. It generally signifies '(act of) creation', 'creature' (BLAISE, *Dictionnaire*, s.v. *factura*), also 'work', 'handiwork' or 'deed' (STELTEN, *Dictionary*, s.v. *factura*), and usually refers to God's handiwork (SOUTER, s.v. *factura*). In the present context *factura* seems to refer to the creative work or (miraculous) deeds of the saints, which is uncommon. Secondly, the grammatical construction, with *eorum* used as a possessive pronoun referring to the subject (*omnes sancti tui*), is irregular, although the opposite – the use of a reflexive possessive pronoun when it does not refer to the subject – is a common trend in Vulgar Latin and the Gothic Missal: see ROSE (ed.), *Missale Gothicum*, Introduction, p. 88–89. Alternative readings in contemporary or slightly later sacramentaries may help to solve the problem. Thus the *Liber sacramentorum Engolismensis* 1694 gives *Qui gloriaris in concilio sanctorum, tibi enim seruiunt, teque solum auctorem et Dominum recognoscunt, et omnes factorem eorum te conlaudant, et benedicunt te sancti tui*: '...you who glory in the council of your saints, for they serve you, they acknowledge you alone as their Creator and Lord, and all your saints praise and bless you as their Creator' (Eng 1694). In modern prayer books a different version is found: *Tibi enim seruiunt creaturae tuae: quia te solum auctorem et Deum cognoscunt, et omnis factura tua te collaudat, et benedicunt te sancti tui* ('For Thy creatures serve Thee, because they acknowledge Thee as their only Creator and God; and Thy whole creation praiseth Thee, and Thy saints bless Thee'; *Eucharist Sacramentary. North American Old Catholic Church* (s.l., s.a.), p. 129).

26. The gerund *triumphando* is treated here as a participle.

27. For the similar yet slightly different syntactic situation in comparison to nos 46 and 48, see Translation principles.

28. The relative pronoun and the accompanying participle (*qui ... exorti*) are in the nominative while they have the function of object, the subject of the sentence being 'hoar frost of persecution' (*quaedam ... pruina persecutionis*). In my interpretation of the Latin I follow Caesarius of Arles: *quos ... exortos*; ROSE (ed.), *Missale Gothicum*, p. 369.

29. The reflexive pronoun *suo* is used while it refers not to the subject of the sentence (*grex*, the flock) but to the Holy Innocent. On this and similar occurrences, see ROSE (ed.), *Missale Gothicum*, Introduction, p. 88–89.

30. *hos populos tuos*: in order to distinguish *populos* from its more common singular use, I translate it here not with 'people', but with 'servants' in the sense of 'faithful'.

31. *in regnum hereditariae claritatis*: the word *claritas* often relates to the manifested glory of Christ: BLAISE, *Dictionnaire*, s.v. *claritas* (4); ROSE (ed.), *Missale Gothicum*, Introduction, p. 136, s.v. *gloria*; CHRISTINE MOHRMANN, 'Note sur doxa', in CHRISTINE MOHRMANN, *Études sur le latin des chrétiens*, vol. 1: *Le latin des chrétiens* (Rome: Edizioni di storia e letteratura, 1958), p. 277–286.

32. On the passive infinitive ending on -e, see ROSE (ed.), *Missale Gothicum*, Introduction, p. 89.

33. The repetition of *ut qui* ('that he') gives the prayer a colloquial character.

34. *Hunc superuenturae sollemnitatis diem*: literally 'this day of upcoming celebration'.

35. *terram promissionis*: literally 'land of promise': the adnominal genitive *promissionis* is used (instead of the adjective *promissam*). For similar Hebrew influence on the Latin of the first Bible translations, see ROSE (ed.), *Missale Gothicum*, Introduction, p. 104 (where this example is not mentioned) and CHRISTINE MOHRMANN, 'Quelques observations linguistiques à propos de la nouvelle version latine du psautier', in CHRISTINE MOHRMANN, *Études sur le latin des chrétiens*, vol. 3: *Latin chrétien et liturgique* (Rome: Edizioni di storia e letteratura, 1965), p. 197–225, at p. 218–219.

36. *hanc annuam sollemnitatis nostrae deuotionem*: previous editors have interfered with the Latin text in order to relate 'annual' to 'celebration' rather than to 'devotion'. See the notes in ROSE (ed.), *Missale Gothicum*, p. 378.

37. The position of *in tuis mirabilibus* is ambiguous. It is not explicitly linked to *adesse*, while on the other hand it is difficult to link it to *sacratas*, to which *tibi* is already connected.

38. In classical grammar the verb *adesse* would require the dative (*cordibus*) rather than the accusative *corda*. This example is not mentioned in ROSE (ed.), *Missale Gothicum*, Introduction, p. 80, though *captum ... adfuit* in no. 130 is.

39. *aquas regenerantibus*: the construction is a mix of accusativus and ablativus absolutus, see ROSE (ed.), *Missale Gothicum*, Introduction, p. 95.

40. Literally 'to the expectation of all [expecting] him'. I therefore revise my view on the spelling of *expectationi*, which represents a dative and does not need to be interpreted as an ablative; cf. ROSE (ed.), *Missale Gothicum*, p. 381. I interpret *se* as referring to Christ, used instead of *eum* in a reversal of the more frequent tendency to use the reflexive possessive pronoun in place of the demonstrative pronoun; see ROSE (ed.), *Missale Gothicum*, Introduction, p. 88.

41. On this sentence as an example of *attractio*, see ROSE (ed.), *Missale Gothicum*, Introduction, p. 103–104: the object of *iubeas adgregare* is included in the relative pronoun *quorum*. For a regular version of the same sentence, see no. 84.

42. Smyth's remark on a presupposed change to the second person plural is confusing (SMYTH, *Liturgie oubliée*, p. 359 footnote 3): the manuscript (as well as Mohlberg's edition, to which Smyth refers) gives *iubeat*.

43. For the use of *adgregare* instead of a passive infinitive, see no. 61 and note 32, as well as ROSE (ed.), *Missale Gothicum*, Introduction, p. 89.

44. Note the antecedent *eos*, omitted in the parallel sentence in no. 78.

45. The participles *praesumentes* and *oboedientes* in the first half of the text clash with the main clause with the predicates (*indigni*) *sumus [...], sed iubemur dicere* in the second half, see Translation principles and cf. no. 20.

46. Blaise gives 'mourir' for the passive form of *transferre*. BLAISE, *Dictionnaire*, s.v. *transfero* (2).

47. *quam ... tribuis proficere ..., absolue*: an instance of *attractio*: the relative pronoun *quam* takes the case of the object (accusative) that belongs to the verb in the main clause, *absolue*, while it relates directly to the verb in the relative clause, *tribue*, which would require an object in the dative. A regular sentence would be *et eam, cui tribuis proficere ..., absolue*. For a discussion of similar instances, see ROSE (ed.), *Missale Gothicum*, Introduction, p. 103–104.

48. The prayer, consisting of one long sentence, is complicated by the two relative clauses, of which only the first (*qui ... habitasti*) relates to the addressee (*Deus*) of the actual prayer (*praecamur*).

49. *uirgo faeta*: I follow the suggestion by Tomasi in his 1680 edition, reading *feta (foeta)* (pregnant, breeding, productive) for *faeta*. See notes in ROSE (ed.), *Missale Gothicum*, p. 390.

50. *Per quam nobis inspirata gaudia successerunt*: alternative translation: '...through whom unexpected joys have succeeded...' This solution (*insperata* for *inspirata*) is suggested by Bannister in his 1917–1919 edition and adopted by Mohlberg in his edition of 1961. See the notes in ROSE (ed.), *Missale Gothicum*, p. 390.

51. *adsumpsit*: the specifically Christian meaning with reference to the Incarnation is only given under the noun *adsumptio* by BLAISE, *Dictionnaire*, s.v. *adsumptio* (1). See also ibid., s.v. *adoptio* (4).

52. Perhaps the Latin should read *gratiam promerere*: 'to merit grace'.

53. The word *concordator* is very rare and does not occur in Antiquity; Blaise gives the *Gothic Missal* as the only source (BLAISE, *Dictionnaire*, s.v. *concordator*). Cf. ROSE (ed.), *Missale Gothicum*, Introduction, p. 110–111.

54. *inlegati fuerint* (for *inlegati sint*): the periphrastic form of the passive perfect is typical of Vulgar Latin; cf. ROSE (ed.), *Missale Gothicum*, Introduction, p. 92 and HERMAN, *Vulgar Latin*, p. 75–77.

55. *decator*: a hapax legomenon which is found only in the Gothic Missal. ROSE, *Missale Gothicum*, Introduction, p. 110–111.

56. Blaise indicates that in the patristic period the ablative *obtentu* has the meaning of 'thanks to, through': BLAISE, *Dictionnaire*, s.v. *obtentus* II. In his medieval dictionary he adds the meaning 'intervention (of a saint)': BLAISE, *Dictionnaire du Moyen-Âge*, s.v. *obtentus* I.

57. This spiritual meaning of *salubriter* is rare; Blaise gives Augustine, the Mone Masses and the Gothic Missal as examples: BLAISE, *Dictionnaire*, s.v. *salubriter*.

58. *plenum sollemnitatis effectum*: on the use and meaning of *effectus* in liturgical texts, see WALTER DIEZINGER, *Effectus in der römischen Liturgie. Eine kultsprachliche Untersuchung* (Bonn: Hanstein, 1961); BLAISE, *Vocabulaire*, p. 177 and 196; MARY PIERRE ELLEBRACHT, *Remarks on the Vocabulary of the Ancient Orations in the Missale Romanum* (Nijmegen: Dekker & Van de Vegt, 1963), p. 198–199; ROSE (ed.), *Missale Gothicum*, Introduction, p. 157; ROSE, '*Emendatio* and *Effectus*'.

59. The sentence *In quo proficiens fidei latitudo* contains a nominative cum infinitive construction, which is typical of Vulgar Latin: ROSE (ed.), *Missale Gothicum*, Introduction, p. 97.

60. The construction *uitae beatitudinem* can be interpreted as a genitivus pro adjectivo ('blessed life' instead of 'blessedness of life'); see ROSE (ed.), *Missale Gothicum*, Introduction, p. 104.

61. *causa amoris sui*: *causa* is generally used as a postposition, but here it is placed before the word to which it belongs.

62. In theory, *suae* could also refer to Andrew, since the choice for the indicative or reflexive pronoun is not always precise in Vulgar Latin in general or the Gothic Missal in particular; ROSE (ed.), *Missale Gothicum*, Introduction, p. 88.

63. I revise my interpretation in *Missale Gothicum*, p. 402 (triumpho] *intell.* triumphum), preferring to read *in triumpho* as an instrumental ablative (on which phenomenon, see ibid., Introduction, p. 68 and 172). For 'martyrdom' as a translation of *triumphus*, see ibid., Introduction, p. 146.

64. The adjective *caelestis*, used in the plural as a noun, may refer to celestial beings in general but also more specifically to God: BLAISE, *Dictionnaire*, s.v. *caelestis* (5).

65. The use of the word *affatus*, mainly occuring in (classical) poetry (LEWIS and SHORT, *Latin Dictionary*, s.v. *affatus*), is remarkable in a liturgical text, particularly with regard to the Lord's Prayer, usually indicated in the Gothic Missal as *oratio (dominica)*.

66. The Latin construction is incomplete. The main clause, linking line 1 (*Deum omnipotentem, fratres karissimi*) with line 7 (*supplici oratione poscamus*, line numbers according to ROSE (ed.), *Missale Gothicum*, p. 405–406) introduces a subordinate clause beginning with *ut* (line 7) and ruled by the verbs *exaudiat* and *eruamur* which comprise the actual prayer (lines 8–10). However, in line 3 a subordinate clause introduced by *ut* already occurs, followed by the elaborate relative clause introducing the parallels between Mary and Eulalia. This first *ut* has no proper sequel, and the relative clause *per quem* is not connected to the main verb *poscamus*. A simpler solution would be to assume that the second *ut* in line 7 is redundant, but this does not alter the lack of a main verb to which the first *ut*-clause in line 3 can be linked.

67. *simultatum discussor*: this prayer is given by Blaise as a *locus* for *discussor*. BLAISE, *Dictionnaire*, s.v. *discussor*.

68. *christiani nomini* can be interpreted in two ways. *Christiani* could be seen as an *adjectivum pro genitivo*, as discussed in ROSE (ed.), *Missale Gothicum*, Introduction, p. 98, were the similar example in no. 420 is referred to: 'the name of Christ'. In the present context, *christianum nomen* could also refer to the Christian community: 'all those that bear the name of Christ'.

69. *per hanc Petri petram*: *per* should be read as *super*.

70. The preceding sentence begins with *Hinc est quod* ('Hence it is that...'), followed by a miracle performed or experienced by Peter. The present sentence is followed by four sentences all beginning with *Hinc* ('Hence') and sharing similar content. It is possible that *Hic* ('He') at the beginning of the present sentence is written instead of *Hinc*. Note that in the parallel prayer in *Bobbio Missal* 121, only the first sentence of the sequence starts with *Hinc* (*est quod mare,* etc.), followed by four sentences introduced by *Hic*. The final sentence in the Gothic Missal, *Hinc tanta fidei dotem* ('Hence, he aspired to such a great gift of faith'), is lacking in the *Bobbio Missal*, ed. LOWE, p. 37.

71. *officium*: a reference to the duties performed by domestic servants as well as to the liturgical office of praise: BLAISE, *Dictionnaire*, s.v. *officium*.

72. *servitus*: a reference to the servitude of slaves but also, particularly in a liturgical context, to the duties of those involved in the ritual of Mass: BLAISE, *Dictionnaire*, s.v. *servitus*.

73. Blaise gives the Gothic Missal as one of few *loci* of the word *agmen* meaning 'multitude' ('foule'): BLAISE, *Dictionnaire*, s.v. *agmen*.

74. On the meaning of *pugillus* in this context ('hand', 'fist'), see BLAISE, *Dictionnaire*, s.v *pugillus*, who gives a similar example in VENANTIUS FORTUNATUS, *Carmina* 3.9.69.

75. *recensitis*: the word echoes the 'censor's register' of the Roman imperial period: LEWIS and SHORT, *Latin Dictionary*, s.v. *recensio*, with two references to Cicero. The absence of the word in Blaise's Dictionaries, both patristic and medieval, as well as in his *Vocabulaire latin des principaux thèmes liturgiques*, is remarkable.

76. *substantia aeternitatis* is an example of the adjectivum pro genitivo construction ('eternal being' instead of 'being of eternity').

77. I deviate from the punctuation proposed in ROSE (ed.), *Missale Gothicum*, p. 418 and read instead: *Proficiat fidei uigilanti amoris tui perseuerantia, morum temperantia, misericordiae prouidentia, actuum disciplina*, in accordance with *Corpus benedictionum pontificalium*, ed. EUGÈNE MOELLER, CCSL 162 ('Turnhout: Brepols, 1971), no. 9, p. 4.

78. For a more fluent version of the same prayer, see *Sacramentarium Gellonense* 318, ed. DUMAS and DESHUSSES, p. 40: *semine posuisti nostrorum remedia peccatorum concede nos opere mentis*, etc.; see also the notes in ROSE (ed.), *Missale Gothicum*, p. 418.

79. This prayer is an addition in Merovingian cursive to the main text. It stands out because of its highly irregular orthography, see ROSE (ed.), *Missale Gothicum*, Introduction, chapter II.B (p. 37–66 passim) and MOHLBERG (ed.), *Missale Gothicum. Das gallikanische Sakramentar*, p. 14. See also Translation principles.

80. *consono modolamenum* is interpreted here as *consonum modulamen*, in contrast with the note in ROSE (ed.), *Missale Gothicum*, p. 422.

81. The phrase is difficult to interpret because of the sequence, particularly the placing of *deuotae intenti*. The conjunction *et* between *conuenienter* and *deuotae* makes it tempting to follow Tomasi in his reading *deuote* (adverb) for *deuotae*. Nevertheless I draw *deuotae* to *mentis*, bearing in mind that the word order is very fluent in this prayer. Whichever reading is best, the phrase in all its complexity includes a chiasmus: *ieiuniis – orationibus // mentis – corporis*. See also Introduction, section Style and figures.

82. For *pura tuae dilectione* Bannister and Mohlberg read *puram tuae dilectionis*, which creates a pleonasm: pure purity. I prefer to read *pura tui dilectionem et proximi puritatem*, linking *pura* to the brotherly kisses (*fraterna oscula*). For the writing of *ae* for *i* see ROSE (ed.), *Missale Gothicum*, Introduction, p. 51 (where this example is not discussed).

83. *quatriduanus* (Ioh. 11, 39) is a biblical neologism and refers to the four days Lazarus spent in his tomb before Jesus passed by; cf. ROSE (ed.), *Missale Gothicum*, Introduction, p. 115.

84. The original accusative of *tuam* is corrected in the manuscript to *tua*, though *in pacem tuam ... translati* would be more regular.

85. Once again the auxiliary verb *iobeas* (for *iubeas*) is combined with an infinitive ending on -e, while a passive form would be expected. See ROSE (ed.), *Missale Gothicum*, Introduction, p. 89.

86. *dicere laudem*: I interpret this as *dici laudem*; cf. ROSE (ed.), *Missale Gothicum*, Introduction, p. 90.

87. *laudes*: interpreted as *laudis*; this example of i-e exchange is not mentioned in ROSE (ed.), *Missale Gothicum*, Introduction, p. 38–40.

88. *odor suauitatis*: on the use of a genitive instead of an adjective, see ROSE (ed.), *Missale Gothicum*, Introduction, p. 104, where this prayer is given as an example.

89. *defendo* is usually constructed with an accusative alone or, in poetry, with a dative (LEWIS and SHORT, *Latin Dictionary*, s.v. *defendo*). Here and in no. 221 the combination *morte defende/defendat* is found, which suggests either an orthographic variant (*morte* for *morti*) or the loss of word final -m (*morte* for *mortem*). In addition, it is likely that sentence contamination diffuses the structure of the prayer, for *morte ea* probably also belongs to *diabulo* as part of the explication of *a fortissimis aduersariis*: 'deliver us from the strongest adversaries: from the devil and from that death that is stronger than all things'.

90. *creaturam regenerationis* can also be read as a genitivus pro adjectivo: 'creature of rebirth = reborn creature'; see ROSE (ed.), *Missale Gothicum*, Introduction, p. 104.

91. *concide nobis pie petitionis effectum*: on *effectus* in liturgical prayers, see note 58.

92. The manuscript gives *suspendia*, but I would propose to amend this to *stipendia* on the basis of parallel prayers in the sacramentaries of Bergamo (483) and Skt Gallen (514), as indicated in the editions by Bannister and Mohlberg; see ROSE (ed.), *Missale Gothicum*, p. 434.

93. *ad sextam*: the manuscript gives *ad se*; I follow Mohlberg and Bannister in line with *Missale Gallicanum Vetus* 123, ed. MOHLBERG, p. 33.

94. *mysteria*: interpreted here as *ministeria*, in accordance with CHRISTINE MOHRMANN, 'Exultent divina mysteria', *Ephemerides liturgicae* 66 (1952), 274–281; cf. FUCHS and WEIKMANN, *Das Exsultet*, p. 38–39 and see ROSE (ed.), *Missale Gothicum*, p. 437.

95. It has been suggested that the beginning of the phrase is lacking here: [*Haec est nox*], *in qua...* FUCHS and WEIKMANN, *Das Exsultet*, endnote 32 on p. 134. The modern version (*Missale Romanum* 1970) has a fourfold structure of *Haec est nox*-sentences; see also KELLY, *Exsultet*, p. 36.

96. *incensi*: the word could also be an adjective referring to a suppressed noun *caerae*, as FUCHS and WEIKMANN, *Das Exsultet*, p. 81 suggest (without explaining the incongruence between the female [*caerae*] and the male form of *incensi*).

97. *ministrorum*: the Latin equivalent for the Greek διάκονος is *minister*; ROSE (ed.), *Missale Gothicum*, Introduction, p. 139; see also FUCHS and WEIKMANN, *Das Exsultet*, p. 82.

98. *accendit*: FUCHS and WEIKMANN, *Das Exsultet*, p. 88 interpret this as a perfect tense.

99. *famulis et famulabus*: the creation of the plural form *famulabus* to make an explicit distinction between the sexes is biblical, and similar to *filiabus*; see ROSE (ed.) *Missale Gothicum*, Introduction, p. 179.

100. On the meaning of [*gratiarum*] *actio* in a Eucharistic context, see ROSE (ed.), *Missale Gothicum*, Introduction, p. 148.

101. *sacerdotibus*: often used for 'bishop', it is translated here as 'priest' in the sense of the celebrant who presides over the Eucharist; cf. BLAISE, *Dictionnaire*, s.v. *sacerdos*; SOUTER, *Latin Glossary*, s.v. *sacerdos*.

102. *misericordiae spiritus* can also be translated as 'merciful Spirit' when read as a genitivus pro adjectivo: ROSE (ed.), *Missale Gothicum*, Introduction, p. 104.

103. On the word *sator*, used here in a poetic sense, see ROSE (ed.), *Missale Gothicum*, Introduction, p. 123.

104. *pausancium* ('those who rest [in the grave]'): the euphemism first developed in later Latin but not necessarily only in the work of Christian authors: LEWIS and SHORT, *Latin Dictionary*, s.v. *pauso*.

105. In the Latin text, the word *spiritus* is inserted before the verb *prosequatur*. It is unclear whether this word is in place; in the parallel prayer in *Bobbio Missal* 225, ed. LOWE, p. 69, it is omitted, and most modern editors of the Gothic Missal suggest likewise to leave it out.

106. *huius infancia famulo tuo illo*: the Latin is difficult to interpret. The simplest solution is to read *infanciam* for *infancia*, as indicated in ROSE (ed.), *Missale Gothicum*, p. 446, following MOHLBERG (ed.), *Missale Gothicum*, p. 65. However, Mohlberg's alternative suggestion, reading *huic infanti* for *huius infancia/m*, makes more sense, creating a dative that serves as the object of *benedicere*: *huic infanti famulo tuo illo*, and thus indicating that the name of the infant to be baptised is to be called where the rubric *illo* requires it.

107. *quae indiget dietatem*: I interpret the sentence as *qui indigent deitatis*: ROSE (ed.), *Missale Gothicum*, p. 447; Mohlberg and Bannister read *pietate* or *aetate* for *dietatem*.

108. *litori*: read *litore*.

109. *ut sanctificet hunc fontem, ut omnes, qui discenderint in hanc fontem*: the syntax is colloquial. Instead of *ut omnibus, qui discenderint in hanc fontem, faciat lauacrum beatissimi regeneracionis*, etc., the case of *omnibus* is adapted to the relative clause (*omnes qui discenderint*), after which *eis* fulfils the function of dative required by *faciat*. Note also that the noun *fons* is treated first as masculine, then as feminine in the same phrase.

110. *in remissione omnium peccatorum*: can also be translated as 'for the remission of the sins of all'.

111. *uere* can be read as an adjective (*ueri / uerae*) belonging to *baptismatis*, as I did in ROSE (ed.), *Missale Gothicum*, p. 448, but it could also be interpreted as an adverb belonging to *reparetur*.

112. See also no. 255 with almost the same construction. Perhaps *omnis*, written for *omnibus*, is intended as a dative, similar in form to *eis*. On the transfer of forms from one declension to another, see ROSE (ed.), *Missale Gothicum*, Introduction, p. 68–69 (neuter plurals with a singular meaning are treated as first declension forms and declined accordingly: *membra, uiscera, crisma*) and 83–85.

113. *in remissione omnium peccatorum*: can also be translated as 'for the remission of the sins of all'.

114. The word *aufetis* is difficult to interpret. Bannister and Mohlberg read *neophytis* in its place and I follow them: ROSE (ed.), *Missale Gothicum*, p. 450. Vanhengel also follows this suggestion, see M.P. VANHENGEL, 'Le rite et la formule de la chrismation postbaptismale en Gaule et en Haute Italie du IVᵉ au VIIIᵉ siècle

d'après les sacramentaires gallicans. Aux origines du rituel primitif', *Sacris erudiri* 21 (1972–1973), 161–222, at p. 166.

115. *Baptizatis et in Christo coronatis, quos dominus noster a crisma petentibus regeneracione donare dignatus est*: I follow Bannister and Mohlberg, who interpret *petentibus* as part of the ablativus absolutus construction: *baptizatis chrisma petentibus et in Christo coronatis quos dominus noster regeneracione donare dignatus est*, cf. ROSE (ed.), *Missale Gothicum*, p. 451.

116. The faithful offer their gifts and take back the consecrated oblations from the altar: see note 1.

117. Easter Day is the central moment of the liturgical year, as is made clear by the decoration of the opening page of this Mass in the manuscript (f. 169v); for a colour reproduction, see ROSE (ed.), *Missale Gothicum*, Introduction, chapter 1, and see the digitized manuscript at http://digi.vatlib.it/view/MSS_Reg.lat.317 (last consulted 12 April 2017). On the grammar of the Mass's title, see ibid., p. 454.

118. *exaudi me, rogo ... clamantem*: the ending of the participle is congruent to the antecedent *me*, while it is situated more closely to the first person singular *rogo*.

119. *aeternalibus ... pagines*: literally plural, as is common when it signifies 'book in which the elect are inscribed' according to BLAISE, *Dictionnaire*, s.v. *pagina*.

120. *prosequor* in the context of the Eucharist signifies, according to Blaise, 'poursuivre, continuer l'effet de'. BLAISE, *Dictionnaire*, s.v. *prosequor* (3).

121. *aeternitatis dominum* can also signify 'the eternal Lord' when read as a genitivus pro adjectivo; ROSE (ed.), *Missale Gothicum*, Introduction, p. 104.

122. *die sabbato*: on the designation *sabbatum* for Saturday, see ROSE (ed.), *Missale Gothicum*, Introduction, p. 172.

123. In the Vulgate text the possessive pronoun is *eius*, in accordance with regular grammar. On the use of *suus* instead of the indicative *eius*, see ROSE (ed.), *Missale Gothicum*, Introduction, p. 88–89 (where this example is not included).

124. *deuorator*: the word is a neologism in this text, see ROSE (ed.), *Missale Gothicum*, Introduction, p. 109, as well as in the works of Augustine and Gregory the Great: BARTELINK, 'Denominations of the Devil and Demons', p. 201–203.

125. *quem*: read as *quam*.

126. The sentence includes some remarkable participle constructions. Thus, *emittens spiritum* occurs next to the subject *terra tremuit*, so that it appears to be an anacoluthon. Moreover, *abscondentes radios suos* is linked to *astra migrauerunt*, so that the neuter plural *astra* is linked to the participle *abscondentes* (instead of *abscondentia*), which might be an accusative absolute. On absolute constructions in the Gothic Missal, see ROSE (ed.), *Missale Gothicum*, Introduction, p. 94–98.

127. *comiacio*: for *comitatio*; the compound would be a hapax legomenon.

128. *adsumptam ... formam*: accusative absolute; see ROSE (ed.), *Missale Gothicum*, Introduction, p. 96.

129. *aeterne*: interpreted here as an adverb belonging to *gaudentes*, while it could also be read as *aeternae*, an adjective to *eclesiae*.

130. The word *calamus* refers to a pen as well as a fishing rod, since both are made of reed: LEWIS and SHORT, *Latin Dictionary*, s.v. *calamus*.

131. For *uorarum* I read *ciborum*, as in the *Sacramentary of Bergamo* 706, ed. PAREDI, p. 196; see ROSE (ed.), *Missale Gothicum*, p. 477.

132. *inspiracionis* could be translated more literally: 'through your act of breathing into us your Spirit'.

133. *usus* in the phrase *Deum, quem nullus mortalium sensus usus carnis inlecebra praegrauatus ... agnuscit* is difficult to interpret. Mohlberg suggests to read *esus*: 'eating' or 'food', MOHLBERG (ed.), *Missale Gothicum*, p. 85; cf. ROSE (ed.), *Missale Gothicum*, p. 480.

134. I revise my suggestion to amend the reflexive pronoun *suorum* to *tuorum* in ROSE (ed.), *Missale Gothicum*, p. 484.

135. Literally *life of immortality* (*vitae inmortalitatis*); this could well be a case of genitivus pro adjectivo: see ROSE (ed.), *Missale Gothicum*, Introduction, p. 104.

136. On *iustificatio* as a lexicological neologism, see ROSE (ed.), *Missale Gothicum*, Introduction, p. 112.

137. SOUTER, Glossary, s.v. *fundamentum*.

138. The verb *assero* has a rich variety of meanings, including 'to set free a slave', 'to appropriate', 'to declare it one's own possession'. See LEWIS and SHORT, *Latin Dictionary*, s.v. *assero*. Blaise also translates the word as 'to affirm (one's religion), to confess': BLAISE, *Dictionnaire*, s.v. *assero*.

139. The Latin entails a double negation: *neminem non pro uitae mori testantur* ('they proclaimed that no one does not die on behalf of life').

140. *recensitis*: see note 75.

141. *praeformatio*: a rare word not found in the classical dictionaries. Blaise translates it as a synonym for *prefiguratio*: 'prefiguration, symbol, type' and situates the word in an allegorical context: BLAISE, *Dictionnaire*, s.v. *praeformatio*.

142. *tuis meritis*: interpreted as the object of *exhibemus* and read as *tua merita*.

143. The relative pronoun *quo* seems to indicate a temporality rather than refer to an antecedent in the preceding phrase.

144. *Lector* signifies an attendant to a magistrate, assigned a.o. with the task to execute judgements and death penalties: LEWIS and SHORT, *Latin Dictionary*, s.v. *lector*. In the post-classical period the term briefly became a synonym for *carnifex*: 'executer', see BLAISE, *Dictionnaire des auteurs du Moyen Âge*, s.v. *lector*.

145. *uoluntaria colla*: 'their willing necks'.

146. *gaudio*: read as *gladio*; ROSE (ed.), *Missale Gothicum*, p. 490.

147. *qui inter natos mulierum omnibus maior surrexit*: a later corrector amended the construction by adding the negation *non* after *maior*. To complete this correction the nominative *qui* should have been changed into an ablative of comparison, *quo*, as Mohlberg and Bannister suggest; see ROSE (ed.), *Missale Gothicum*, p. 492. In this sense the phrase is found in no. 372, similar to Matth. 11, 11: ... *non surrexit inter natos mulierum maior Iohanne Baptista...*

148. The sentence, which is in principle identical to the beginning of no. 370, is incomplete here. I suggested to add the finite form *fecisti*: ROSE (ed.), *Missale Gothicum*, p. 492, following Bannister and Mohlberg. It might be even more plausible to add *fecisti insignem*, so that the parallelism between both prayers is complete.

149. Or, as in nos 370 and 371: 'who through the birth of blessed John the Baptist made this venerable day eminent for us', see previous note.

150. A comma could be added after *maior*, ROSE (ed.), *Missale Gothicum*, p. 493 line 1. The reference to Matth. 11, 11 given ibid., p. 492, should be 372, 5/6 ille – maior] cf. Matth. 11, 11.

151. The present prayer is a later addition in an uncial letter and is marked by many vulgar traits, as becomes clear in ROSE (ed.), *Missale Gothicum*, Introduction, ch. II.B (p. 37–66), at p. 40, 48 and passim.

152. At three points where an *Amen* would be expected here, a sign in the form of the Chi-Rho monogram is drawn.

153. The sentence lacks conjunctions.

154. The sentence seems to be incomplete, since *eorum* ('of those') has nothing it refers to. The variant in no. 391 is more comprehensible: *nomina quae recitata sunt nostrorum carorum* (likewise 439). For other inconsistencies in the formula, see no. 78 and ROSE (ed.), *Missale Gothicum*, Introduction, p. 103–104.

155. *censeas*: 'to assess, tax, esteem'. The word resounds the task of the *censor* and the relevance of the *census* as the person who keeps record of the 'registering and rating of Roman citizens, property, etc.': LEWIS and SHORT, *Latin Dictionary*, s.v. *censeo* I.A.1 and 2. *census*.

156. *indultor*: see note 17.

157. *electio*: it is possible to interpret this as a personification of God and to translate the sentence as 'whom you in your election have deigned to consecrate to you'.

158. *gentes*: the word has a neutral meaning here, not necessarily the gentiles as opposed to the elect but rather the peoples who have *not yet* come to conversion, see ROSE (ed.), *Missale Gothicum*, Introduction, p. 136; BLAISE, *Vocabulaire*, p. 290 (section 160). Likewise, the *gentibus* mentioned below (line 17 Latin edition) also have a positive connotation, as they acknowledged and established (*conprobatur*) Paul as the head of the Christian faith. The translation 'gentiles' is chosen with reference to NRSV, e.g. I Tim. 2, 7 (*doctor gentium*).

159. *ille* (*introducit*) clearly refers to the latter (Paul) who is the teacher, while *hic* (*aperit*) refers to the former (Peter) who, as the key holder, opens the kingdom of heaven.

160. *praeuiare*: a Christian neologism, signalled by Blaise in the works of Jerome, Ambrose and Pauline of Nola, see BLAISE, *Dictionnaire*, s.v. *praeuio*; SOUTER, *Glossary*, s.v. *praeuio*.

161. Mohlberg suggests that a new prayer, the *collectio ad pacem*, begins here, though the manuscript gives no cause to assume that this is a different collect; see MOHLBERG (ed.), *Missale Gothicum*, p. 94 and ROSE (ed.), *Missale Gothicum*, p. 497.

162. *eius*: refers to the apostle celebrated in this Mass; see the parallel prayer *Liber sacramentorum Gellonensis* 1205 (*Liber sacramentorum Engolismensis* 1075, *Sacramentarium Gelasianum Vetus* 929): *Praebeant nobis Domine quesumus apostoli tui desiderata conmercia.*

163. The phrase *ut qui pro ueritate sacrum sanguinem fudit* recurs in no. 384.

164. On this particular meaning of *obsequium/obsequia*, see ROSE (ed.), *Missale Gothicum*, Introduction, p. 159, s.v. *obsequium*.

165. The passive voice in the translation conceals the fact that God the Father, Son and Holy Spirit (*Deum patrem et filium et spiritum sanctum*) is the implicit

subject of the verbs illuminate, protect and sanctify (*inluminet, defendat et sanctificat*).

166. The phrase *ut qui pro ueritate sacrum sanguinem fudit* also occurs in no. 383.

167. *ut perfecti ... peccatorum*: an alternative translation would be: 'that we, cleansed through the sanctification of this perfect sacrifice, are deigned by you worthy to obtain forgiveness of our sins'.

168. *papa*: the word could initially refer to any bishop, but occurs from the sixth century more exclusively to indicate the bishop of Rome. SOUTER, *Glossary*, s.v. *papa*; BLAISE, *Dictionnaire*, s.v. *papa*. To talk about the third-century martyr Sixtus as 'the pope' would be an anachronism, although late seventh-century users of the Gothic Missal may well have seen him as such; cf. the prayer in the Good Friday intercessions *pro beatissimo papa nostro*, *Missale Gallicanum Vetus* 96, ed. MOHLBERG, p. 28.

169. *mundana*: the word is corrected into *mundanae*, which brings the prayer in line with *Sacramentarium Veronense* 749, ed. MOHLBERG, p. 95: *inter mundanae conuersationis aduersa*.

170. *Adesto supplicationibus nostris*: a standard expression, translated by Blaise as 'écoutez nos supplications': BLAISE, *Vocabulaire*, p. 172 (section 61).

171. It is not clear how the prayer would end. This is the only collect that concludes with *per eum quem*. More regular is *Per eum / Per Iesum Christum, per quem maiestatem tuam laudant angeli* (e.g. 55, 86).

172. *aduentus*: the word also refers to the liturgical period that commemorates Christ's Incarnation (as well as the eschatological second coming) in anticipation of Christmas; see ROSE (ed.), *Missale Gothicum*, Introduction, p. 155.

173. *primum ... sacerdotum*: expresses the awareness of Roman primacy; see note 168.

174. The combination *agonem certaminis* is pleonastic, as Blaise indicates. He translates it as 'de l'engagement d'une telle bataille', referring to the same prayer in the Mass for Lawrence in *Sacramentarium Veronense* 743: BLAISE, *Vocabulaire*, p. 232 (section 110).

175. Each saint offers his or her service to God, but the deacons in particular, whose office is indicated as *ministerium* (synonym for *diaconatus*); ROSE (ed.), *Missale Gothicum*, Introduction, p. 139.

176. The Latin text is confusing because of the probably superfluous *ut* in the middle of an ablative absolute construction that is already split by the insertion of *quaesomus*; ROSE (ed.), *Missale Gothicum*, p. 503.

177. The word *lucrator* is a Christian neologism indicating someone who wins another (for the faith), often applied to the apostles. BLAISE, *Dictionnaire*, s.v. *lucrator*; ROSE (ed.), *Missale Gothicum*, Introduction, p. 109.

178. *pie* refers both to the mother's faith as exemplary for Symphorian and to her love towards her son.

179. The plural (*natalium*) is uncommon.

180. *pietate*, as *pie* in no. 414, signifies both the mother's piety and her motherly love for Symphorian (see note 178).

181. *audaciam*: forms of the verb *audeo* occur frequently in the *Passio Acaunensium*, e.g. c. 2 and 4; see further ROSE (ed.), *Missale Gothicum*, Introduction, p. 306.

182. The text distinguishes between the faithful laity (*plebis*) and the clergy: priests and bishops (*ministrorum*).

183. On the construction *odor suauitatis* as a genitivus pro adjectivo, see note 88.

184. The Latin is complex and problematic. In addition to the suggestions in ROSE (ed.), *Missale Gothicum*, p. 511, *ut* in line 6 (Latin edition) seems to be superfluous, and after *excepere* in line 7 a comma could be added.

185. *denummerationis instantia*: several alternatives are given in ROSE (ed.), *Missale Gothicum*, p. 511. I chose to translate *de numerationis instantia* ('under the pressure of the number'), but one could also read *denuntiatione iterata*: 'with repeated summons', referring to the repeated order of emperor Maximian to have the Christians killed in *Passio Acaunensium 6*: *denuntiatione iterata*, ed. Krusch, p. 35; ROSE (ed.), *Missale Gothicum*, Introduction, p. 307.

186. The construction is complex. I suggested to read *plebem* for *plebi* in line 4 (Latin edition), following Bannister and Mohlberg, ROSE (ed.), *Missale Gothicum*, p. 512. *plebi* could also be read as a dative dependent on *famulantem*, in which case *plebem* should be added as the object of *foueas* and *perducas*.

187. *in caelestibus paginis*: the form is plural; see note 119.

188. The Latin text is complex, since the relative *qui* in line 2 (Latin edition) seems to imply the presence of two subjects in the relative clause (*qui* and *caelestis aula* at the end of line 3). I follow Bannister and Mohlberg in their suggestion to read *et quia* for *qui*, ROSE (ed.), *Missale Gothicum*, p. 513.

189. *qui nobis ueniam tribuas de peccatis*: I suggested to omit *qui* in line 5, ROSE (ed.), *Missale Gothicum*, p. 514, but one could also read *et* for *ut* in line 4 and interpret *tribuas* as a subjunctive in the relative clause, as I do in the present translation.

190. *Adesto supplicationibus nostris*: see note 170.

191. *indultor*: see note 17.

192. *in augmentum uirtutum*: 'to the growth of virtue', possibly to be read as *augmento uirtutum*, 'through the growth of virtue'.

193. The suggestion to read *et* for the second *ut*, following parallel prayers (e.g. *Sacramentarium Veronense* 1181), is not strictly necessary; cf. ROSE (ed.), *Missale Gothicum*, p. 518.

194. An example of the many synonyms for 'heart' in this type of Latin: here both *cordibus* and *mentibus* are translated as 'heart'; see Translation Principles.

195. *in omni factura eorum te conlaudant et benedicunt omnes sancti tui*: see note 25.

196. *brauium* written for *bradium*, see ROSE (ed.), *Missale Gothicum*, p. 523.

197. *in labiis oris*; cf. no. 295 *labiis ore*: 'with lips [and] mouth'.

198. Although the closing phrase in no. 474 seems similar, the passive voice of *conlatum* in 474 and the temporal indication *hodie* make no. 474 a more direct reference to the ritual of the Eucharist than no. 469.

199. The word *chlamys* is of Greek origin and is used in a military context according to LEWIS and SHORT, *Latin Dictionary*, s.v. *chlamys*. In SULPICIUS

SEVERUS, *Vita Martini, uestis* (3.1, 3.3) alternates with the more technical *chlamys* (3.2, 3.3); ed. FONTAINE, SChr. 134, p. 482–484.

200. *deum deitatis* probably means 'the highest God', in a similar sense as *dominus dominorum*: the Lord of lords = the highest Lord.

201. *confessionis tuae*: literally 'of the confession of you'.

202. *concede nobis – proficiat caritati*: this part of the prayer (l. 3–5 Latin edition) is similar to no. 366.

203. *mysterium*: on this word and its range of meanings, see ROSE (ed.), *Missale Gothicum*, Introduction, p. 168. In the context of this prayer, where the importance of teaching is emphasised, I followed BLAISE, *Dictionnaire*, s.v. *mysterium* (5): 'sacred teaching; revelation of knowledge'.

204. *in aeternum restituti*: it is unclear whether *aeternum* is used as a substantiated adjective ('restored to eternity'), or written for *aeternam [uitam]*, which cannot be ruled out in the context of this prayer with its many orthographic variants.

205. *recensitis*: see note 75.

206. The prayer stands out for its poetic quality, firstly in view of the climax *sentimus, credimus, sequimur et oramus*, and also through the word *nuntius* (see the footnote to 'messengers'). The reference to no. 481 as a parallel in ROSE, *Missale Gothicum*, p. 532 should be 492, 2/4 laudes – celebrare (Go 481).

207. The verb *operor* is used to indicate how the sacraments, or God through the sacraments, establish salvation in the faithful: BLAISE, *Dictionnaire*, s.v. *operor* refers to AUGUSTINE, *De doctrina christiana* 4.16.33, ed. JOSEPH MARTIN, *De doctrina christiana libri IV*, CCSL 32 (Turnhout: Brepols, 1962), p. 1–167, at p. 140.

208. More common would have been *a quo sanctitatis et misericordiae dona deposcimus*.

209. *sacerdotibus*: refers to those who preside over Mass, priests and bishops alike; see note 101 and footnote d on p. 290.

210. The Latin text gives *populis*, without further qualification and in the plural: the community of the faithful, also as opposed to the clergy, here specified as *sacerdotibus*. On the words *populus, plebs, gens* in the Gothic Missal, see ROSE (ed.), *Missale Gothicum*, Introduction, p. 136 (*gens*) and 141 (*plebs, populus*).

211. *recensitis*: see note 75.

212. *sacerdotum*: see note 101 and 209, and no. 472.

213. *pacabilitas*: the word occurs only in the Gothic Missal: BLAISE, *Dictionnaire*, s.v. *pacabilitas*; BLAISE, *Dictionnaire du Moyen Âge*, s.v. *pacabilitas*; CHARLES DU FRESNE SIEUR DU CANGE, *Glossarium mediae et infimae latinitatis* (repr. Graz: Akademische Druck- und Verlagsanstalt, 1954), s.v. *pacabilitas*.

214. *tuta libertas*: the suggested amendment *tota libertas* in ROSE (ed.), *Missale Gothicum*, p. 539 is not necessary.

215. *recensitis*: see note 75.

216. The parallel prayer no. 295 inserts *affectum* after *uoluntatis*: 'and the desire for goodwill'.

217. The last folio of the manuscript has suffered damage; concerning the problematic passages, see ROSE (ed.), *Missale Gothicum*, p. 543–544.

INDEXES

BIBLICAL QUOTATIONS

RELEVANT BIBLICAL PASSAGES

NON-BIBLICAL QUOTATIONS AND REFERENCES

SUBJECTS

NAMES